ON AN EMPTY STOMACH

ON AN EMPTY STOMACH

Two Hundred Years of Hunger Relief

Tom Scott-Smith

CORNELL UNIVERSITY PRESS   ITHACA AND LONDON

First published 2020 by Cornell University Press
Printed in the United States of America

Library of Congress Cataloging-in-Publication Data

Names: Scott-Smith, Tom, 1980– author.
Title: On an empty stomach : two hundred years of hunger relief / Tom Scott-Smith.
Description: Ithaca : Cornell University Press, 2020. | Includes bibliographical references and index.
Identifiers: LCCN 2019032685 (print) | LCCN 2019032686 (ebook) | ISBN 9781501748653 (cloth) | ISBN 9781501748677 (pdf) | ISBN 9781501748660 (ebook)
Subjects: LCSH: Food relief—History. | Humanitarian assistance—History. | Starvation—History. | Emergency mass feeding—History. | Nutrition—Research—History.
Classification: LCC HV696.F6 S39 2020 (print) | LCC HV696.F6 (ebook) | DDC 363.8/83—dc23
LC record available at https://lccn.loc.gov/2019032685
LC ebook record available at https://lccn.loc.gov/2019032686

For Sue and Ali

Contents

Illustrations

Preface

I began this book in 2012 while observing a large feeding operation in South Sudan. I had been studying the daily lives of aid workers and had become particularly interested in how humanitarians deal with large numbers of hungry people. With so much scholarly work on the international politics of relief, my aim was to focus on the microlevel practices, and in the refugee camps of South Sudan I found a fascinating world of objects and activities, rituals and regulations. Every morning, just as the sun came up, I accompanied an army of aid workers as they dispersed across the landscape, measuring people's bodies with a brightly colored strip of plastic tape. I watched as they sorted refugees into categories, determining their eligibility for food. I took part in enormous food distributions, in which mixtures of soya, corn, oil, and vitamins were handed out in plastic bags. I then began to trace the food that had been manufactured for this purpose, examining how it was stored, packed, mixed into a precise nutritional balance, and then reconstituted over cooking fires.

This book emerged from a question that kept returning to me during those long summer months in 2012. After observing the feeding schemes and reading the humanitarian handbooks, I began to wonder why aid agencies managed hunger in such standardized and specific ways. I knew that relations between people, society, and food were extraordinarily complex; I knew that hunger was tied into what Audrey Richards long ago called a "nutritional system": an intricate web that extended from cultural beliefs to agricultural practices, mealtime rituals to the division of labor.[1] In South Sudan, however, aid workers were using procedures that focused very narrowly on nutrients and the body. They concentrated the human need for food into a table of nutritional requirements that largely abstracted the complex role of politics, culture, and society, and presented hunger as a technical issue.

In the anthropological spirit of questioning the taken for granted, I began asking aid workers why they followed these standardized procedures. Many of their responses surprised me. My interlocutors knew very well that food systems are socially embedded and that diet is culturally formed, but they argued that such concerns were often irrelevant in emergencies. If people were starving, they said, then aid agencies had to get nutrients into bodies as quickly and efficiently as possible and to do this they followed procedures that emerged from decades of nutritional discovery, transforming hunger into a biological problem. Such an approach, I was told, was more rational and efficient. It had been tested over time, proved through experience, and could alleviate suffering more effectively.

After leaving South Sudan I began exploring these nutritional practices in greater detail, and it soon became clear that the narrative of progress was, at best, simplistic. Many of these systems had been widely contested, based on ideas of the empty stomach that were themselves culturally embedded and historically contingent. Beneath the science, in other words, there was a shifting debate, a range of disputes concerning the right procedures for feeding people and the correct foods for disasters. By the time I sat down to write this book, therefore, my anthropological study had become more historical. It still emerged from an anthropological starting point—questioning why people did things in certain ways—but it proceeded through historical methods. The resulting book is a "history of the present": an exploration of how humanitarian strategies for managing hunger have changed profoundly over the last two hundred years.[2]

My central argument can be expressed relatively simply: that humanitarian practices, even at the most technical level, reflect the social and political conditions of the age. The way humanitarians feed hungry people, in other words, is influenced by prevailing patterns of power, systems of thought, and approaches to governance. Foucault's work has certainly been useful in this analysis, helping make greater theoretical sense of the way that starvation and its management have changed, but I have also drawn inspiration from the more sprightly and lightly theorized combinations of history and anthropology that may be known to more general readers. Sidney Mintz's magnificent study of sugar, *Sweetness and Power*, is one prominent example, but James Vernon's more traditional historical work on hunger has also been an important reference point.[3] Such books form a model for how history and anthropology can be combined: two disciplines that illuminate how humans live in such different ways, surrounded by different material conditions, driven by different ideas about basic needs. Historians show us these worlds in the past (which, as the saying goes, is another country), and anthropologists illustrate differences across the globe, but both disciplines force us to reconsider the things we take for granted. They help to build what is best described as an "inventory of possibilities," reminding us that other eras and societies have done things very differently.[4]

A Note on Terminology

Perhaps the biggest challenge in writing this book has been coming up with a definition of humanitarianism. This, after all, is a notoriously capacious term, which has been used to describe activities as diverse as peacekeeping, state building, medical assistance, and bombing campaigns. Over the past two hundred years it has also shifted in meaning, beginning as theological position—a belief in Christ's humanity rather than his divinity—and then, in the 1840s and 1850s, coming to describe sentimentality in excess, a perverse preoccupation with the lives of distant and deviant people. It was only in the twentieth century that the word took on an unambiguously positive meaning, and not until the 1990s that it replaced "disaster relief" to describe a growing international industry rather than a broad concern for human welfare.[5]

Without wanting to delve into definitional debates in too much depth, this book has been guided by the idea that humanitarianism is first and foremost a set of *practices*. It should not be defined by its intentions and ethical motivations, which are inevitably compromised and complex; nor can it be defined by its concrete outcomes, since "relieved suffering" is so often ambiguous and contested. Humanitarianism, to put it simply, is characterized by what people do in its name. It is a set of standardized activities, which can be relatively stable at any particular historical moment, while shifting a great deal over time.

Rather than applying contemporary standards to the past, therefore, this book traces techniques that were promoted as humanitarian in each period. This avoids anachronism while allowing the connection of disparate events into a longer-term narrative. Colonial interventions and civilizational improvements were, in the 1920s, widely considered humanitarian. Thirty years before that even animal rights and vegetarianism were "humanitarian" concerns. After World War II the word *humanitarianism* described large-scale transformations as well as emergency relief. It is only relatively recently, therefore, that the term has been distinguished from development to describe the short-term relief of basic needs.

Ideas of hunger and its treatment have also changed profoundly over the last two hundred years, as will become clear in this book. In the 1920s the idea of ending starvation was connected with attempts to transform the "savage" diet. Fifty years before that the treatment of hunger was directed at the industrial urban underclass, including the establishment of semipermanent soup kitchens in the slums. After World War II humanitarianism embraced large-scale schemes of modernist improvement, bringing a whole new set of technological ideas to bear on the problem of hunger. In light of these changes, one cannot apply a narrow and contemporary standard of what counts as "humanitarianism" to a lengthy historical story.

In addition to humanitarianism, there are some other terms that require explanation. In particular, readers will notice that I often reach for the term *hunger* when perhaps a more precise term is more appropriate. Hunger generally refers to a variety of situations that are caused by insufficient food: it is an expansive word that can indicate many situations and conditions. *Malnutrition*, meanwhile, is a more precise technical term, which refers to a biochemical condition: it is often treated as synonymous with undernutrition, but it also embraces overnutrition and is intrinsically linked with the rise of nutritional standards. *Starvation* is another term entirely, which refers to a situation where hunger begins to threaten life and the lack of food causes physical breakdown. I use all of these terms in this book, but I most often reach for "hunger" because it is the most inclusive way to describe both social and physical processes. Unlike many other terms—for example, "malnutrition"—it has not yet been fully colonized by medical discourse and practice.

One final clarification is in order before proceeding: that this is deliberately a study of Western humanitarianism. There are, of course, many other manifestations of care and compassion around the world, and a burgeoning literature on humanitarianism in the global South.[6] My focus in this book, however, is on the contexts, circumstances, and cultures of the Western institutions that have dominated the relief industry up to the twenty-first century. This, in other words, is an instance of "studying up," examining the worlds and worldviews of institutions that have wielded particular power and influence over the contemporary landscape of relief.[7] My decision to focus on Western institutions, therefore, should not be interpreted as an instance of ignoring or writing out other humanitarian histories. It is a decision based on a belief that my own society requires particular scrutiny due to its colonial interventions around the world.

A Note on Sources

This history has been written from a variety of sources, gleaned from aid agency archives as well as published materials and interviews. The list of archives can be found at the start of the bibliography, and the documents I used in these collections included newspapers, organizational reports, correspondence, memoirs, and other written accounts. Correspondence, mostly from the archives of aid agencies, offered a vivid narrative of practice in the field, often meticulous in its detail, yet subjective and incomplete. Meeting minutes were more formal in tone, lacking colorful descriptions but explaining how decisions were made. Memoirs provided eyewitness accounts, although they were often dubious as factual accounts and very much driven by sensationalism. Historical journal articles provided something else entirely: details about the objects and technologies that were used in the planning of a nutritional intervention, and a summary of settled knowledge.

None of these other sources, however, captured my imagination quite like a handbook. In many ways this whole project began with humanitarian handbooks, which I first studied in that Sudanese refugee camp. As I delved into the archives, moreover, handbooks always struck me as a particularly fascinating genre of document, which revealed best practice in each era as well as acting as a repository for the humanitarian imagination. These are not documents that accurately reflect what was actually done on the ground—as this was inevitably disrupted by chaos and disorganization—but they do reflect how humanitarians would *like* the world to be organized. Norbert Elias has shown what can be drawn from the study of handbooks in his magisterial work on the evolution of manners, which compared handbooks of etiquette over six centuries and traced changing norms of behavior.[8] Similarly, I have used handbooks to show how aid workers organized the world, how they made sense of the world, how they sought to act on the world around them. These did not just inform others or publicize opinion, but instructed aid workers how to act. Most important, they encapsulated a particular *concept* of the empty stomach and the ways in which it should be filled.

Early on in this research, while sitting in the Bodleian Library, I came across a handbook by the International Refugee Organization (IRO): a short-lived, postwar institution for assisting the displaced. Embedded within their procedural guidelines was a document for IRO administrators to reproduce and complete when ending someone's assistance. I imagined the administrators, their pens hovering over this form, ready to categorize recipients into one of the following fourteen options: (1) Acquired new citizenship, (2) Well-adjusted in new community, (3) Does not accept plan of repatriation or resettlement, (4) No effort to be self-supporting, (5) War criminal, (6) Voluntarily helped the enemy, (7) Extraditable criminal, (8) German ethnic origin as defined by constitution, (9) Support from own government, (10) Participated in organization for overthrow by armed force of own government, (11) Leader of movement discouraging repatriation, (12) Military or civil service employee at time of applying, (13) Died, (14) Whereabouts unknown.[9] I was immediately struck by this document's similarity to the opening lines of Foucault's *Order of Things,* which quotes Borges's fictional encyclopedia dividing animals into the following fourteen categories: (1) Belonging to the emperor, (2) Embalmed, (3) Tame, (4) Suckling pigs, (5) Sirens, (6) Fabulous, (7) Stray dogs, (8) Included in the present classification, (9) Frenzied, (10) Innumerable, (11) Drawn with a very fine camelhair brush, (12) Et cetera, (13) Having just broken the water pitcher, (14) That from a long way off look like flies.[10] Foucault used Borges's encyclopedia to look askance at systems for organizing the world, to produce a sense of disorientation and to force his readers to ask themselves: Why categorize animals in such bizarre ways? Why choose such seemingly unrelated categories? My aim in this book is the same. I start by looking skeptically at our systems for managing hunger, asking: Why categorize starving people in these particular ways? Why place foods into these particular classifications? Why measure hunger on the body and judge meals by their nutrient contents? Such questions allow us to unravel our particular historical moment and the path of recent history.

Acknowledgments

This book would have been impossible without the support, advice, and guidance from a large number of people. There are too many to name, and my reluctance to provide an exhaustive list derives as much from a fear of whom I might include as from a fear of whom I might leave out. For me, reading acknowledgments has never been quite the same since one of my tutors, a big beast in the world of sociology, described them as a performance, a self-interested construction of scholarly alliances. This has long filled me with dread. Who knows what kind of academic persona I might unwittingly present? Such anxiety permeates many acknowledgments sections, with the possible exception of one recent example that read, simply, "I blame all of you. Writing this book has been an exercise in sustained suffering. The casual reader may, perhaps, exempt herself from excessive guilt, but for those of you who have played the larger role in prolonging my agonies with your encouragement and support, well . . . you know who you are, and you owe me."[11]

I cannot in good faith adopt this blitzkrieg approach, not least because I have been lucky enough to draw on so many circles of help and support in the long process of writing this book. Three communities, in particular, deserve particular thanks. First of all, to my colleagues at Queen Elizabeth House and the Refugee Studies Centre at the University of Oxford, where I have found my intellectual home among a critical and kindly community of scholars. Particular thanks must go to Matthew Gibney, for his advice on political theory, book titles, and puns, and to Georgia Cole, Myfanwy James, and Faith Cowling for reading sections of the manuscript so carefully. I am also very grateful to Dawn Chatty and Jocelyn Alexander for their wise guidance in the early stages, and to Cathryn Costello for her perspicacious commentary on so many issues. There are many others I am indebted to as well, but I hope my colleagues and friends will forgive me if I extend my thanks to them privately and individually, resisting the public display for a more meaningful private one.

Second, there are those who assisted me in many practical ways during the course of my research, from archivists preparing documents, librarians ordering books, friends offering beds, and those involved in reading, commenting, and editing this text. Again, there are too many to name, but I am particularly grateful to Roger Haydon at Cornell University Press, who gave this project so much support and encouragement from the very beginning, as well as to the whole production team at Cornell. Thanks also to the staff at the Bodleian Library in Oxford and the library of the United Nations Office at Geneva, who were always so willing to assist, and particularly to Christopher Hilton at the Wellcome Library, Sarah Rhodes at the Social Sciences Library in Oxford, and Fabio Ciccarello at the David Lubin Memorial Library in Rome. I am also grateful to Emily Baughan and Rebecca Gill for helping me access parts of the Save the Children archives when they were not easily accessible, and to Rosie Dodd for helping access the Oxfam archives before they had been transferred to the Bodleian Library. Neil Lee and Emma Drever provided regular and gracious hospitality when I was working in London at the start of this project, and the initial period of fieldwork that launched this study was very much helped by Geofrey Otim, Monica Emiru, John Fenning, and Sarah Hayward.

The third circle of support has been by far the most important: my family, who have provided a loving home and unstinting encouragement throughout the whole process. My wife, Morag, and two wonderful daughters, Rosa and Thea, have been constantly supportive, inspirational, and most important, enormously fun. Without them this project would have been impossible, and I am so grateful for their patience and encouragement throughout. My parents, as well, have helped me for decades, bringing me up in a spirit of optimism and inquisitiveness and more recently providing coffee, conversations, childcare, and so much practical help with the intricacies of everyday life. They have helped me in more ways than I can mention, and so it is to them, with so much love and thanks, that I dedicate this book.

ON AN EMPTY STOMACH

INTRODUCTION
Humanitarian Approaches to Hunger

When Alexis Soyer was appointed head chef at the Reform Club in London, his first task was to construct new kitchens. The club had been created in 1836 for supporters of the Great Reform Act, and the new premises soon rose up over Pall Mall in a distinctive, Palazzo style. Soyer's kitchens extended cavernously underground, a haven of culinary sophistication containing new technologies such as gas cookers, large refrigerators, and steam-powered contraptions that could warm plates, turn spits, and draw water. When the building finally opened its doors in 1841, therefore, the British public flocked for guided tours.[1] Soyer had cooked at Queen Victoria's coronation a few years earlier and had already become a celebrity—arguably the world's first celebrity chef—but he now settled into his new life of expensive ingredients, elite clients, and complex culinary contraptions.[2] By 1848, however, he was looking for a change, and he began to shift his attention from the gentlemen's clubs of London to the worst of the nation's slums, making a surprising announcement in the newspapers that year. Soyer declared that he would do for the poor what he had done for the rich and transform the organization of kitchens.

Soyer began by accusing existing soup kitchens of serving food that was inadequate and unpleasant, usually burned or underdone, and he published a range of new recipes that were later collected in a book entitled *Soyer's Charitable Cookery*.[3] The aim, he explained, was to "take every possible advantage of every kind of nutritious substance" and "convert them, by study and judgment, into a wholesome and cheap aliment for the millions."[4] Soyer's recipes were based

1

on dripping, vegetable peelings, meat scraps, flour, barley, and large quantities of water; they were to be cooked in huge vessels of over a hundred gallons and stirred with "a piece of board the shape of a cricket bat."[5] His plans were received enthusiastically in the press, not least because the great chef made extravagant claims to expertise. Soyer claimed he had balanced economy and nourishment to make the perfect soup, using ingredients that were "not sufficiently appreciated or used to the greatest advantage by the industrious classes."[6] This narrative was credulously accepted by the media, and *The Times*, for example, soon reported that "a bellyful of Soyer's soup, once a day" would be "more than sufficient to sustain the strength of a strong and healthy man."[7]

Philanthropists lined up to adopt Soyer's new proposals, and soup kitchens cooking his recipes soon appeared across London. His proposals generated political interest largely because British government was keen for a quick fix in Ireland, which was going through "Black 47," its most terrible year of famine.[8] Soyer's plans seemed an attractive, even magical, proposition for the government: by converting cheap ingredients into a treatment for bodily ills he offered economy, efficiency, and a seal of celebrity approval. Within a few weeks of his first proposal Soyer had been recruited as a government advisor and dispatched to Dublin to build "model soup kitchen" next to the Royal Barracks by the sea. He worked fast and hard, and by April 5, 1847, the soup kitchen was ready for a grand opening, with many dignitaries assembling for the launch.[9]

The preparation, distribution, and consumption of Soyer's soup took place inside a wooden building, with kitchen and dining room all housed under a single roof. The scale was vast, and Soyer's structure was described in a number of laudatory newspaper reports as well as immortalized by an engraving in the *Illustrated London News*.[10] Correspondents described with great enthusiasm the "excellent" taste of the food, the efficiency with which the kitchen was run, and the enormous boiler that produced the soup in such huge quantities.[11] Once it opened the whole institution was run with militarylike efficiency, and the historian Christine Kinealy provides a particularly vivid sense of the scene.

> The process of receiving the soup was strictly regimented. Entry to the tent was through a narrow zigzag passage; a bell signaled that the paupers could enter the main tent; [and] while they ate, the next group waited in the passage. Within the eating area, there were long tables, which were set with bowls and spoons, attached to chains. A prayer was said before eating commenced. A quart of soup was provided per person, and a further quarter pound of bread was to be handed out and consumed outside. The whole process was estimated to take no longer than six minutes.[12]

At the center of Soyer's soup kitchen was a huge, thirteen-foot boiler, which became the subject of some fascination in the press. A correspondent at the *Times* described how its network of pipes, pots, and steamers emerged from "metallic box-shaped vessels" where the "materials for the soup are placed." The ingredients, he wrote, were "heated by steam, conveyed by means of iron pipes from the central boiler, and by a slow digestive process the entire of the nutriment contained in the materials is extracted without having its properties deteriorated."[13] Reports like this portrayed an almost alchemical quality to Soyer's method. It seemed that his elaborate contraptions and technological wizardry enabled him to feed more people on fewer supplies than had ever been attempted before.[14] Another reporter attributed the same feat to Soyer's special "dripping," which formed the basis of every recipe. This was "so savoury ... so nourishing, that with a trifling sum Paddy could be fed, and fed too so that he could dig drains, cut turf and spade gardens on an advanced strength."[15] Soyer fueled these ideas, claiming he could distill the essence of measly vegetable peelings and convert them into a nourishing soup, and he later described with great pride how his kitchen managed to reach over five thousand people a day, matching even the messiah in his drive to feed the poor.[16]

FIGURE 1.   Soyer's Irish soup kitchen. *Illustrated London News,* April 17, 1847, 256. © Illustrated London News Ltd/Mary Evans.

The Birth of Humanitarianism

According to most narratives, international humanitarianism was born in the middle of the nineteenth century, with the Crimean relief of Florence Nightingale, the memoirs of Henri Dunant after the Battle of Solferino, and the foundation of the Red Cross in 1863.[17] There were, of course, many previous manifestations of philanthropy in the West, but they had been more amateur, smaller-scale, more localized pursuits. It is generally recognized that something changed in the mid-nineteenth century, however: something that gave humanitarianism a more organized, international, and professional form. This came accompanied by a revolution in moral sentiments, a rising culture of altruism, a range of transnational connections that linked distant strangers, and a set of distinctly modern technologies that facilitated international action such as the telegraph, the steamship, and the growing circulation of newspapers.[18]

Alexis Soyer emerged from this context. His public expressions of altruism, his interest in new technologies, and his attempt to help people in distant lands were wider features of the age. He moved in the same circles as Florence Nightingale and later helped her establish kitchens at Scutari during the Crimean war.[19] His model soup kitchen in Ireland, therefore, demonstrates how hunger was being tackled in the middle of the nineteenth century, at the very birth of modern humanitarianism. As I explain in the next chapter, the soup kitchen had already been around for half a century when Soyer turned his attention to philanthropy and was firmly rooted in the classical period, soaked in the legacies of the Elizabethan Poor Laws. A man named Count Rumford standardized the soup kitchen model in the 1790s, but this was just one step on the road to its modernization. Soyer scaled up the soup kitchen to match a new industrial age. He expanded the vision, turning this much older technology of relief into something described by one contemporary as the "soup-shop of soup-shops . . . the boiler of boilers, the one that sung the requiem to all that had gone before."[20]

Before Soyer arrived on the scene the soup kitchen, or "soup-shop," had long been arranged around five central features. First, the relief was organized on a small and local scale, usually with the involvement of the neighborhood elites. Second, admission to the feeding scheme was regulated by patronage: it was distributed to "deserving cases" that were known to the benefactors directly or through some trusted intermediary. Third, the relief was distributed communally, with recipients eating in a large hall and food combined in a single, enormous pot. Fourth, the food was vernacular in the sense that it was made from local ingredients and was recognizable to the poor as the kind of meal they would usually consume at home. Finally, the soup kitchen was based on a very moralizing attitude to hunger: a belief that it was not simply bad luck that led to starvation, but a moral failing. This made the soup kitchen far more than a mechanism for delivering food. It was also, in many respects, a way to transform behavior.

Over the course of the next ten chapters I will show how the classical soup kitchen ended up being replaced by a very different approach. Contemporary techniques for managing extreme hunger look very different, with each of these five features turned on their head in the century and a half since Soyer's death in 1858. First of all, large aid agencies now work with an international rather than local reach. Instead of rooting relief in the local context and neighborhood, humanitarians espouse universal principles, aiming to reach everyone in the world by virtue of their common humanity. Second, admission to aid programs now tends to be based on physical measurements rather than personal relationships. Instead of letters of recommendation from "respectable people," it is now anthropometric indicators that determine access to feeding schemes. Third, food is usually distributed in individual portions rather than communal kitchens. Instead of feeding everyone from the same pot, nutritionists provide carefully balanced rations targeted at specific kinds of people. Fourth, the food provided is technical rather than vernacular. Instead of being based on local ingredients and staple foods, these rations are often constructed with additives, preservatives, stabilizers, emulsifiers, and imported, processed commodities. Finally, the attempts to change behavior in humanitarian feeding regimes are far less explicit. There may be some emphasis on "nutritional education," but the central idea today is that assistance should be given in proportion to need rather than on other considerations such as reputability or moral character.

These five transformations give shape to the book as a whole, forming a key part of my central argument. Some readers will already have exceptions in mind; indeed, there are many nuances in the world of humanitarian assistance, and food relief comes in many forms. Sometimes it is still provided by local agencies and is not always international in scope; it can be distributed on the basis of socioeconomic status rather than body shape, and other measures often supplement anthropometric techniques; soup kitchens have certainly not gone away, and hot food is still a component of "supplementary feeding" schemes around the world. Despite these nuances, however, the overall trend remains. A century and a half ago, the dominant response to starvation was to set up a soup kitchen rooted in local patronage. Today, however, we are more likely to see a medicalized, individualized, and rationalized procedure, with anthropometry as the basis of admission.

Contemporary Relief

It is hard to choose a modern-day moment that illustrates contemporary human-itarianism as clearly as Soyer's Irish soup kitchen does for the world of 1847, but a good place to start is to look at the handbooks that govern relief. The *Sphere Handbook* is perhaps the most famous example.[21] This set of minimum stan-dards, which was first published in the year 2000 after consultation with more than four hundred humanitarian agencies, shapes the approach of relief workers in many contexts and contains hundreds of rules and indicators over five spe-cialized areas with around a hundred pages devoted to the management of food and nutrition alone. The guidance set out for emergency feeding, for example, contains a breakdown of the biochemical content of foods, nutritional require-ments disaggregated by age and sex, and a list of deficiency diseases. It contains the combined wisdom of nutritional experts and policy committees that have been built up over the last century or more, and its detail and reach is, to say the least, a long way from the simple pamphlet of eccentric recipes penned by Soyer, the Victorian celebrity chef.

Over the past thirty years, humanitarian handbooks like *Sphere* have prolifer-ated in number, expanded in form, and become ever more intricate.[22] The aid agency Oxfam, for example, has gradually accumulated guidelines and speci-fications for emergency feeding. In 1971 Oxfam relied on just a short, stapled booklet of thirty pages to direct all humanitarian activities, but their collection of handbooks now extends to a whole library of lengthy documents, including an equipment catalogue that runs more than five hundred pages alone.[23] Since the 1980s these handbooks have established a process for managing malnutri-tion that begins with the measurement of the upper arm.[24] This is known as the MUAC, or mid-upper arm circumference: an anthropometric indicator that mea-sures malnutrition through the wastage of subcutaneous fat in the limb. This form of anthropometry is based on a powerful basic principle—the thinner the arm, the greater the need—and it has led to many visually arresting images, including the well-known campaign that described the MUAC as the "bracelet of life."[25] To operate the MUAC band, aid workers take a bright strip of tape, wrap it around the arm of a malnourished child, and read a color-coded scale. A red measurement indicates the most serious malnourishment, which leads to priority treatment.

The MUAC process seems simple, but it is just one part of a much larger system that includes a complex body of reference data, a range of assessment cri-teria, and the prescription of different food types. This system is best illustrated by recounting a visit I took to South Sudan in the summer of 2012, where the mid-upper arm circumference lay at the heart of humanitarian relief.[26] Malnutri-tion in the South Sudan refugee camps that year was a serious problem, especially

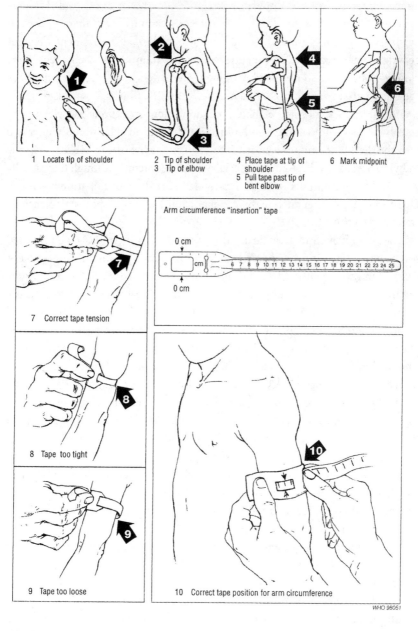

1 Locate tip of shoulder	2 Tip of shoulder
	3 Tip of elbow
		4 Place tape at tip of
		   shoulder
		5 Pull tape past tip of
		   bent elbow
			6 Mark midpoint

Arm circumference "insertion" tape

0 cm

cm   6 7 8 9 10 11 12 13 14 15 16 17 18 19 20 21 22 23 24 25

0 cm

7 Correct tape tension

8 Tape too tight

9 Tape too loose

10 Correct tape position for arm circumference

WHO 98051

FIGURE 2. Instructions for measuring the mid-upper arm circumference. *Management of Nutrition in Major Emergencies* (Geneva: World Health Organization, 2000), 176. Courtesy of the World Health Organization.

among children. The mid-upper arm circumference, however, allowed aid workers to divide everyone into three main categories and to direct them to the relevant assistance programs. If the upper arm yielded a red measurement, the refugee was given access to a "therapeutic feeding programme," where patients were
closely monitored and provided with high-energy foods designed to build back
their strength and body mass. If the upper arm yielded a yellow measurement,
the individual was deemed eligible for "supplementary rations": a selection of
cereals fortified with vitamins and minerals to be cooked at home and integrated
into the diet. If the upper arm fell into the green zone of the MUAC strip the
individual was not admitted to a specialist feeding scheme, although they usually
received "general rations" that were provided regardless of nutritional status.[27]
Other sources of sustenance, in this corner of South Sudan at this particular time,
were hard to come by.

The red, yellow, and green arm measurements on the MUAC tape indicated
severe, moderate, and negligible malnutrition. Small groups of aid workers,
called "community outreach teams," implemented this process of triage by working through the refugee camps every day, setting off each morning to measure
the upper arms of every child under five. I often joined the teams as they traveled
through the refugee camps, observing how their days began by gathering people
at convenient locations, lining them up, and taking the MUAC of everyone they
found. They first measured height with a rough stick—a thin branch taken from a
local tree with notches carved into the bark—and after excluding everyone over a
certain height, deemed too old for targeted nutritional assistance, the team would
measure the arm circumference of the remaining children.[28] The refugees moved
through this process relatively silently, and it was refined and practiced to such
an extent that more than two hundred people could be examined in just over an
hour. In some ways, this was similar to Soyer's arrangement of the soup kitchen,
which had also ordered people and space.[29] Yet here it was all about assessment.
In South Sudan that summer I found silent measurement of the body, efficiency
in the line, and rapid administrative referral.

After the initial assessment, refugee children and their families were directed
to one of several camp feeding centers, which each had their own procedures.
Children with a yellow mid-upper arm circumference, for example, were sent to
the supplementary feeding center, where refugees filed through various stages of
registration and instruction before being given a bag of protein fortified maize
meal known as Corn-Soy Blend. To get the food they first had to sit in a large
open area for hygiene training, where they were taught the correct use of water
and utensils. Next, they were led to a small gazebo in front of a wood fire, where
they were given a cooking demonstration and told how to make fortified cereal
into porridge. After a long wait they were led to the distribution hut, where the

children in each household were counted, registered and measured again. Finally, the mother or carer was sent away with packets of the Corn-Soy Blend, or CSB, which was designed to offer a nutritionally balanced everyday staple.[30]

Children with a *red* mid-upper arm circumference, meanwhile, went through a rather different procedure. Having been classed as severely malnourished, they were admitted as outpatients at a medical facility and received a food called Plumpy'nut. This was a thick, peanut paste, which came in small silver sachets adorned with red and white text; it was made from vegetable fat, sugar, peanuts, and skimmed milk powder. In South Sudan, Plumpy'nut was distributed after close anthropometric monitoring, with aid workers keeping detailed measurements of weight, height, and mid-upper arm circumference. Three sachets of Plumpy'nut were prescribed each day—and "prescribed" is the correct term, since this was very much a personal, medical dosage—and the sachets bore the instruction "only be used under medical supervision." Malnourished children were expected to return regularly to the clinics and each time they were measured again, before receiving a further supply of the peanut paste. This process continued until their body was back within the bounds of what was normal.

From Soyer to South Sudan

Unlike the Victorian soup kitchen, the procedure in South Sudan was governed by dispassionate physical measurements and consumption took place *away* from the distribution center. The advantage of CSB and Plumpy'nut, at least for the aid workers, was that they did not need to be consumed on site, making distribution cheaper and easier. These technical, specialist foods contained all the body's essential nutrients in a compact form. CSB, for example, contained cornmeal for carbohydrates, soy flour for protein, sugar for extra calories, and a number of vitamins and minerals to prevent micronutrient deficiencies. To prepare it, refugees were told to reconstitute the flour in boiling water and cook it for around ten minutes, which resulted in a thick, sweet, warm porridge, a little like a sweet corn tortilla mashed up in a bowl. It was not the kind of food the refugees usually ate—their staple food was sorghum, which was ground and made into bread called *kisra* and eaten with okra, goat meat, or lentils—but it provided a one-stop solution. It was a rationalized, efficient solution to hunger, offering what pulses provide, what greens provide, what meat provides. All the nutritionally important parts of a varied diet were packed into this pale grey powder, which provided nutrients without the foodstuffs that usually carried them.

The nutritionists in South Sudan, as a result, tended not to speak of foods at all. They spoke, instead, of nutrients. Their concern was not with the foods people usually ate, or with the ways these foods could be grown or purchased, but with ways of getting nutrients into the bodies of refugees as quickly and efficiently as possible. Humanitarian handbooks echoed these calculations, describing foods by their nutritional content, humans by their daily nutritional requirements, and the act of feeding people as a statistical exercise that calculated calories and cost. This was one of the most stark and visible differences between Soyer's Irish soup kitchen and the procedures used in contemporary South Sudan. The former distributed foods with tangible material qualities, whereas the latter focused on the invisible nutrients that food contained, which could not be sensed directly.

From Soyer to South Sudan: these vastly different moments mark the beginning and end of this book. My aim is to connect them, to show how over the last two hundred years approaches to the empty stomach have changed profoundly. This produces partly a history of humanitarianism, and partly a history of ideas; indeed, it is not just practices for feeding the starving that have changed over the decades, but our understandings of hunger and food. Approaches to the empty stomach, ideas of what constitutes food, and notions of why it matters to human functioning are all essential for making sense of why and how humanitarians act as they do. The overall path of this book, therefore, may be driven by the contrast between the two emergency feeding regimes—between Soyer and South Sudan—but much of the material I discuss along the way is more varied, and among other things, I will examine the feeding of workers in industrial canteens, the role of government in shaping basic diets, the influence of medicine and the military, and the integration of high modernist technology.

My central argument in this book can be articulated relatively simply: that the way one *conceives* of the empty stomach is a crucial determinant of how one actually treats it. The most mundane humanitarian techniques are built on the edifices of thought—about food, about starvation—that have changed a great deal since Soyer's Irish soup kitchen was first opened on the Dublin seafront. To take the most visible changes first of all, the past two centuries has seen a rationalization, individualization, and medicalization of the feeding process. Whereas Soyer's soup kitchen drew on personal knowledge of a pauper's situation to determine who would be fed, contemporary emergency nutrition relies on impersonal bodily measurements. Whereas Soyer's soup kitchen offered communal nourishment from massive cauldrons, emergency nutrition today is based on individualized, foil-wrapped rations. Whereas Soyer's soup kitchen distributed vernacular foods made with recognizable ingredients, emergency nutrition now provides specialist foods manufactured to technical specifications. These changes, in turn, reflect some more fundamental historical transitions. In the early nineteenth century any kind of philanthropist could make a subjective judgment of taste, devising "economical" recipes for the poor. Nowadays, however, a particular kind of expert—the nutritionist—determines if a package of food contains the correct specifications for success. In the Victorian soup kitchen it was whole communities who were judged and fed, while an individual's eligibility was always linked to their background. Nowadays, however, access to aid is based on body shape and personalized rations are distributed with warnings *against* sharing—either on medical or nutritional grounds.[31]

Perhaps most significantly, however, changes to humanitarian nutrition have been shaped by the rise of nutritional science. In 1847 scientists understood relatively little about nutrients or the physiological process of starvation. Hunger tended to be measured in relation to socioeconomic conditions, and humanitarians were more concerned with people than with the cells within bodies. Starvation, as a consequence, was tackled in the community—through soup kitchens or food-for-work schemes—and hunger was seen as a shared experience, affecting whole classes of people. In addition, there was a highly moralistic approach in this earlier period. As James Vernon has pointed out, it was not until the middle of twentieth century that starvation was seen as the result of bad luck or poor government rather than a moral failing on the part of the poor.[32] This allowed a crucial shift to take place around the Second World War, when an explicitly medicalized paradigm started to take root. From the 1940s onwards, starvation began to be widely understood as a biochemical state: a physical problem rather than a moral one. Hunger, therefore, was recast as a biological rather than a social deficiency, and feeding programs began to resemble those I observed in South Sudan: concerned with the much narrower task of getting the right nutrients into the right bodies, at the right time.

How Aid Reflects the Age

This book is the story of that humanitarian transformation: the story of how Soyer's model soup kitchen, with its steam-punk boilers and chained-down spoons, gave way to the fortified flours and regimented measurements of South Sudan's feeding schemes. It is a story that can be framed with reference to the transitions sketched in this introduction—from collective to individual feeding, from vernacular to technical foods, and from local to international pursuits—each of which will be described and explained in the chapters to follow. Yet this book also contains a more fundamental argument: *that aid reflects the age.* Humanitarianism, in other words, does not follow a simple, linear path of improvement and refinement, but is profoundly shaped by the conditions in which it takes place.[33]

This argument is already well accepted when it comes to humanitarian agencies and their history, but it has rarely been applied to the technical practices that prevail in the field. Indeed, studies of institutional politics, donor priorities, and policy development have always linked humanitarianism to the wider geopolitical environment, and it is generally accepted that the choppy waters of global politics shape humanitarian institutions and interventions, directing attention to certain kinds of crisis, urging a certain kind of response, and framing aid to reflect wider strategic priorities.[34] These sociopolitical waves, however, are usually presented on the surface of a deeper, calmer sea. The day-to-day activities of relief, which go on beneath the surface, are generally presented as more settled, shaped not by politics and power, but through the purity of reason and science. The idea that aid reflects the age, in other words, may be regularly applied to institutions and their policies, but is not commonly extended to the technical activities of relief.

My task in this book is to look at the turbulence under the water: to show how, at least in the case of emergency feeding, the technical humanitarian practice as well as the wider institutional environment emerges from a sociopolitical context. Generally, this task is far easier for the past than for the present. We would say without hesitation that the soup kitchen reflected important facets of Victorian society—the rigid hierarchy, the distinctive morality, the paternalism, the nature of community and class, and so on—but we may be more reluctant to draw similar conclusions about the contemporary world. The way starvation is managed today seems more logical, more rational, our use of anthropometric measurements seems more objective, our distribution of fortified foods seems more effective, and our whole humanitarian system seems, at first glance, to be as *un*contaminated by political and social systems as the Victorians' soup kitchen was so terribly tainted by theirs.

Things, of course, are not that simple. Science and technology studies (STS) has long shown how society and politics influence *all* forms of knowledge, and one of its early slogans was the need for symmetry: the idea that we should apply the same analytical standards to good and bad science, that we should not assume social and political influences only intrude when science goes wrong.[35] The point was to reject Mertonian sociology, which held that good science manages to isolate itself entirely from the wider sociopolitical world, and that only bad science—such as phrenology—was corrupted.[36] The early writers in STS reminded us that science *always* involves a social process, a form of negotiation involving the human as well as the physical world.[37] This lesson can be applied elsewhere, since it is important to remember that Soyer *also* believed he was rational, modern, and efficient; he *also* set out to be rigorous by offering food only to "deserving cases" that could be verified by personal knowledge.[38] To our contemporary eyes this rigor is a sham, and Soyer's beliefs are clearly a product of his historical period. Yet contemporary practices are equally rooted in their sociopolitical contexts, and as in Soyer's time, we can say that aid reflects the age.

What historical trends, precisely, have shaped our contemporary regimes of emergency feeding? In this book I identify four underlying shifts that have had a profound impact on the character of contemporary relief. The first is bureaucracy and rationalization. As should be obvious from this introduction, contemporary emergency nutrition is a highly bureaucratic activity: it is based on social distance rather than proximity, managed through the accumulation of statistics, and it always has an eye on speed and efficiency. Compared with the nineteenth-century soup kitchen, it can feed more people than Soyer, more than the messiah, reaching millions of people around the world. Like all forms of bureaucracy, however, it comes at the expense of personal connection. It counts and acts on people dispassionately, offering fewer opportunities to engage with the *person* surrounding the empty stomach. It is very efficient, but it too often ignores people's culture, their background, and their biography.

The second shift has been toward greater equality and universalism. It should be equally clear from this introduction that, at least in theory, emergency nutrition today is a highly egalitarian pursuit. It treats all people equally, it applies the same standards to everyone, and it compares all bodies to the same set of growth statistics. Regardless of culture, background, or circumstance, every person is treated in the same way, and if they fall below an internationally recognized baseline there are common procedures to admit them to a feeding scheme. In contrast to the nineteenth-century soup kitchen, the most important principle today is impartiality: providing assistance according to need. But like other forms of universalism, this can come at the expense of the group. As the individual becomes the unit of analysis, culture and community begin to recede.

The third shift has been the growing influence of commerce and capitalism. Contemporary emergency nutrition has become tied to the political economy of food, balancing cost and calories, while importing foods rather than purchasing them locally. Emergency nutrition usually relies on fortified cereal blends made from the largest agricultural surpluses in the American period of postwar abundance (Corn-Soy Blend is an excellent example). This system has produced fantastic quantities of food, as well as unprecedented opportunities to tackle the empty stomach. Yet efficiency has not necessarily meant fairness. The poor often end up receiving foods they have little desire to eat, and starvation becomes a market opportunity: a fresh domain for the restless mobility of capital to find openings for profit.

The fourth and final shift has been the rise of science and technology. Modern emergency feeding is based on the idea that science can improve on nature and that technology can produce a more rational type of food. Assessments have been based on surveys of body shapes, and humanitarian responses have become organized around a modernist style of management. This approach has improved the effectiveness of aid and our knowledge of starvation, but the flip side is a new form of elitism.[39] The treatment of starvation has turned into an expert domain, and hunger is now often tackled without political engagement. Many of the new technical foods, moreover, are disgusting.

As should be apparent, each of these transformations offers limitations as well as opportunities, and in the conclusion to this book I frame this in terms of a Faustian bargain of modernity, analyzing each of the trade-offs in depth.

Two Hundred Years of Hunger Relief

The structure of this book is broadly chronological, starting with a detailed examination of the soup kitchen, moving through the first stirrings of hunger's medicalization, and ending with the rise of fortified foods and anthropometric instruments. Indeed, the first two chapters concern the period from around 1790 to the middle of the Victorian era, examining the soup kitchen and the rise of early nutritional science. Chapter 1 describes how the soup kitchen, based on an Elizabethan model but subsequently scaled up to meet the vast needs of a new urban underclass, became a standardized technology of relief by the middle of the nineteenth century. It returns to Alexis Soyer as well as a man called Count Rumford, who brought the soup kitchen into the modern age. This transition is explored further in chapter 2, which compares a substance named osmazome and a product called Extract of Meat. The former epitomized a premodern approach to nutrition and came shrouded in alchemical mystique, whereas the latter claimed to embody rational nutritional science and was circulated in an increasingly global economy. Taken together, these two chapters illustrate the way that ideas of food and hunger were changing on the cusp of the modern world.

In chapters 3, 4, and 5, I examine the implications of this transition. Chapter 3 shows how modern nutritional science was put to the service of government and used to shape human conduct in institutions such as workhouses, schools, and industrial canteens. In this period the calorie became a widely used unit of energy, and the human body was conceived as a working machine. Chapter 4 turns to examine how this affected communal relations, explaining how, by the start of the twentieth century, the diet was seen to shape not just individual strength but the fate of entire communities. The success and failure of nations was attributed to food in an approach known as dietary determinism. Chapter 5 then explains how this expansive vision was taken to the League of Nations, producing a golden age in the history of humanitarian nutrition. It was golden not so much in results as in its ambition and scope, bringing nutrition to the center of international policy.

Chapters 6 and 7 concern an important turning point in the history of humanitarian nutrition: the impact of the Second World War. They describe how new forms of emergency feeding emerged from the ruins of global conflict and how the ambition of humanitarian nutrition became more restricted as a result. Chapter 6 examines the foods pushed by military planners, which were long lasting, nutritionally balanced, and easy to transport. Chapter 7 then turns to look at the experiments carried out on starving people in the 1940s, when hunger was medicalized and intricate examination regimes rolled out in emergency conditions. In this period the expansive visions of the interwar period contracted and hunger, accordingly, became more narrowly conceived as a biochemical and medical problem.

The final three chapters turn to the postwar era, when humanitarian nutrition began to resemble the system we have to this day. Chapter 8 concerns the period of high modernism, when expansive ambitions of scientific progress promised new foods from a variety of fantastical sources, including algae grown on sewage, fungi grown on oil, and inedible leaves that could be boiled into protein curd. These projects encapsulated the vision of a cheap, efficient, mass-produced famine treatment that could finally end starvation. Chapters 9 and 10 then develop the main theoretical contribution in this book: the idea of "low modernism." Chapter 9 shows how expansive modernist dreams came to be realized through more commercially viable interventions, including the manufacture of profitable commodities such as Corn-Soy Blend. Chapter 10 then examines how low modernism did not just involve a commercial mentality, but also took a highly practical turn with the development of small-scale devices such as the MUAC band. Taking the story into the 1980s and 1990s, this chapter shows how a new generation of compact solutions began to act on the problem of measurement and micronutrient deficiencies: objects that worked on a smaller scale, such as Sprinkles and Plumpy'nut, indicating both the hopes and the limitations of new technology.

Before ending this introduction, a few words are in order regarding the theoretical apparatus underpinning this book, which tends to be collected toward the end of each chapter and has been more or less contained so it can be skipped without great harm to the historical story. Each of these sections ties into a wider argument that has been influenced by Foucault's historical work, focusing on the longer-term transition to modernity. Foucault may have not published anything explicitly about humanitarianism in his lifetime, but the subject nevertheless permeates his writings and many of his best works touch on humanitarian themes in some way. He is well known for examining the penitentiary, the clinic, and the asylum, but his treatment of these topics is usually framed in terms of a humanitarian reform that aimed at minimizing suffering. After outlining the reform of punishment, for example, or healthcare, or the treatment of the mentally ill, Foucault has pointed out that these reforms were not, as usually understood, examples of progress, but just different technologies of power. "Did you *really* think that the prison was a humanitarian improvement on the stocks and the gallows?" he seems to ask us in *Discipline and Punish*. Well, it wasn't; it was just a technology of power that targeted the soul rather than the body, administered punishment in private rather than public, and sought control over life and not death. "Did you *really* think that modern mental healthcare was a humanitarian improvement on confinement in asylums?" he asks us in *Madness and Civilization*. Well it wasn't; it was just a technology of power that tried to cure people rather than understand them, ignored their ravings rather than taking them seriously, and forced them to conform rather than allowing difference to flourish.

My aim in this book is to leave the reader with a similar question. Did you *really* think that modern techniques of emergency feeding were an improvement on the Soyerian soup kitchen? The answer gets more ambivalent as I move through the book, but the Foucauldian provocation is certainly a useful start. In the end, contemporary emergency nutrition can be read as a technology of power that is shaped by the assessment of bodies rather than communities, the provision of nutrients rather than foods, while seeing hunger as biological rather than a social problem. Is this an unqualified improvement? I am not as skeptical and pessimistic as Foucault when it comes to my final analysis; indeed, my conclusion develops the idea of a Faustian bargain to describe the complexities of this shift to modernity. Some things are better, others are worse; some provide opportunities, others close them off, but the important thing is that we do not treat the history of humanitarianism as a simple history of progress. It is, in reality, far more complex, both in its large-scale patterns of operation, and in its microlevel techniques.

FROM THE CLASSICAL SOUP KITCHEN TO THE IRISH FAMINE

The attraction of Soyer's soup kitchen was precision, not originality. It had an aura of efficiency, with a meticulous arrangement of working parts. From the shiny soup boiler to the chained-down spoons, from the queues of paupers to the six-minute bell, every inch of space, every moment of time, was carefully accounted for. But the *idea* wasn't new. In 1840s Britain, soup was already a well-established part of poor relief, and pottage had been a humble staple for centuries.[1] The basic model of the Tudor alms house involved bread and broth served in a public kitchen: an approach that had been extended under the Elizabethan Poor Laws and existed far beyond Europe as well.[2] Imarets could be found across the Ottoman Empire, and "soup shops" existed in China during the Qing dynasty.[3] The soup kitchen, therefore, did not begin with Soyer. In fact, if there was a key figure in the development of the soup kitchen it was an American natural scientist named Benjamin Thompson, who was born at Woburn, Massachusetts, in 1753.

Combining diverse interests in physics, philosophy, and social engineering, Benjamin Thompson very much fitted the mold of eighteenth-century upper class intellectuals. He is best known for his contribution to thermodynamics, undertaking some groundbreaking experiments concerning convection, insulation, and friction. After moving to Bavaria in 1785, Thompson entered government service under Elector Karl Theodore, and he was later given the title of Count Rumford—the name by which he is commonly known. He soon became famous for his practical inventions, eventually transforming the soup kitchen into an industrialized and standardized model of relief. Rumford used his discoveries on heat to develop a range of fuel-efficient stoves and kettles. He applied his knowledge of insulation to develop warmer clothing for the Bavarian army. He explored methods for heating and ventilating homes. His most durable material legacy was the Rumford fireplace: an invention to save coal and reduce smoke that can still be found in many European and American houses.[4]

Count Rumford's commitment to everyday reform generated a new word, "rumfordizing," which meant improving and refining something in accordance with natural laws. In the 1790s he started to rumfordize the soup kitchen.[5] He introduced a new, fuel-efficient hearth and advocated economies of scale that would come from catering masses of people in one place. He promoted a recipe that made the most of cheap and filling ingredients such as barley, potatoes, and peas. He argued that the poor should *always* eat in a public kitchen, receiving food in return for work, and he tested these ideas in Bavaria, establishing a new model soup kitchen with characteristic arrogance and authoritarianism.[6] It was opened on January 1, 1790, a traditional day in Munich for almsgiving, and it involved the cooperation of local police, who were instructed to arrest any beggar they found and bring them to the new institution. Rumford later boasted of how quickly he cleared the town of those "detestable vermin" who "infested the streets."[7] The vagrants were initiated into the basic principles of Rumfordian relief: regular hot meals in return for labor and good behavior.

Rumford's model received an enthusiastic reception amongst reformers and politicians in the 1790s. Amplified by the unstable backdrop of poor harvests, high grain prices, and revolutionary upheaval, Rumford was able to tap into a growing discontent with existing charitable systems throughout Europe. In Britain, for example, Rumfordian relief was vigorously promoted in pamphlets and through the missionary zeal of organizations like the Society for Bettering the Condition and Increasing the Comforts of the Poor.[8] By the start of the nineteenth century, such soup kitchens had become "all but universal" in the major British population centers, a "more or less permanent feature of life" in the slums.[9] Rumford's reforms spread further across Europe as well: Napoleon set up model soup kitchens across France, and they could also be found in Belgium, Italy, and Switzerland. In some places, meal tickets were illustrated with Rumford's name and image.[10]

The attraction of Rumford's soup kitchen was simple: he promised it would reduce scarcity and unrest. He used his status as a famous scientist to harness "natural laws" about "human nature," claiming that he could make the poor more industrious and reduce widespread hunger. This chapter examines Rumford's concern for order and control, which extended to the food he served and the behavior he expected of his beneficiaries. Indeed, Rumford saw his role as calibrating a machine, guiding soups and the starving alike in order to produce a more balanced society. These features began to change as the soup kitchen developed to meet the scale of need in urban areas, culminating in Alexis Soyer's "soup-shop of soup-shops" in Dublin. Rumford's vision of the soup kitchen, however, acted as a pivot between the classical and modern periods, before nutritional science emerged onto the scene.

Rumfordizing Relief

Rumford claimed that his soup kitchens were able to get the best from people. He sought to shape and improve poor communities, and he drew on the analogy of a machine to explain his intentions. The soup kitchen, he believed, was a machine that could maximize human industry, with the soup acting as a reward for good conduct and an encouragement to persevere in good habits.[11] His hearths and recipes were meant to be a model of efficiency, inspiring frugality on the part of the poor. Rumford claimed that he had discovered how humans responded to stimuli and incentives: "How necessary it is to be acquainted with the secret springs of action in the human heart," he wrote in one pamphlet, "to direct even the lowest and unfeeling class of mankind! The machine is intrinsically the same in all situations. The greatest secret is *first to put it in tune* before an attempt is made to play upon it. The jarring sounds of former vibrations must be stilled, otherwise no harmony can be produced; but when the instrument is in order, the notes *cannot fail* to answer to the touch of a skillful master."[12]

Rumford saw himself as the skilled master of the soup kitchen machine, manipulating its inputs and outputs. Just as his fuel-efficient stove drew on natural laws to maximize the use of heat, the soup kitchen would make the most of human nature. Rumford treated all aspects of the kitchen in a similar way: spaces, structures, even the starving themselves were there to be rumfordized, and his reforms began with the soup. Rumford's first innovation was to argue that water made soup particularly nourishing. "What surprised me," he wrote, was the "very small quantity of *solid food* which, when properly prepared, will suffice to satisfy hunger."[13] Diluting soup aided taste and digestion, he argued, as well as making it more nourishing. Rumford drew on a strange analogy to prove his point. Just as plants could be fed by water, he believed, so could the poor.[14] This was a convenient belief, since it allowed Rumford to cut costs and increase efficiency, reporting with pride about the "trifling expense at which the stoutest and most labourious man may be fed."[15]

Rumford's "science" of food was more about giving the *impression* of satiation than it was about biochemical nourishment. His concern was to promote a certain *experience* of eating, providing something that *appeared* to satisfy hunger. In the spirit of "directing the lowest class of mankind" he added stale bread as a topping on the soup before serving. This, he explained, promoted mastication and "prolong[ed] the duration of the enjoyment of eating."[16] Stale bread was cheap, he argued, and difficult to chew, making poor people *think* they had eaten more while delivering the experience of satiation at very little cost. Rumford developed his recipes with a similar concern for economics. He based his soup on potatoes, which were cheap but unpopular at the end of the eighteenth century. If they were boiled enough, however, Rumford realized that they would combine with the other ingredients to form a heavy mash of miserly but uncertain provenance.[17] To prolong the eating of this soup still further, Rumford instructed that soup should be consumed from the edge of the bowl to the middle, eaten slowly to prolong the experience of eating. His descriptions concerning the correct way to eat a cheap "pudding" made of cornmeal took such detail to an absurd new level, beginning with the instruction that such a pudding should be sliced "about half an inch, or three quarters of an inch, in thickness" before "being laid hot upon a plate."

> An excavation [should then be] made in the middle . . . with the point of a knife, into which a small piece of butter, as large perhaps as nutmeg, is put, and where it soon melts. To expedite the melting of the butter, the small piece of pudding, which is cut out of the middle of the slice to form the excavation for receiving the butter, is frequently laid over the butter for a few moments, and is taken away (and eaten) as soon as the butter is melted. . . . The pudding is to be eaten with a knife and a fork, beginning at the circumference of the slice, and approaching regularly towards the centre, each piece of pudding being taken up with the fork, and dipped into the butter, or dipped into it in part only, as is commonly the case, before it is carried into the mouth.[18]

Rumford sometimes apologized for his ponderous detail. "If I am prolix in these descriptions," he wrote, "my reader must excuse me . . . persuaded as I am that the action of food upon the palate, and consequently the pleasure of eating, depends very much upon the *manner* in which the food is applied to the organs of taste."[19] The idea, once again, was to manipulate the feelings of the eater, creating a more efficient soup kitchen in the process.

The rumfordization of the soup kitchen also extended to admission. To receive a meal, each person was required to work and their output was closely monitored. Standardized forms were used to record attendance and labor rates, with meal tickets distributed to those deserving of support. Everything was made clearly visible in ledgers, tables, and charts; indeed, the measurement of costs and the quantification of inputs and outputs dominated management of the institution. If anyone was in doubt about his intentions, Rumford emblazoned the legend "No Alms Received Here" in gold above the soup kitchen door.[20] Often known as a "House of Industry," the idea was that food would only be provided if work had been expended, making Rumford's soup kitchen essentially self-financing. All that was needed was to put it in tune, he thought; then the machine would run itself.

Rumford made particular use of the "natural habits" of children to develop his idea that the soup kitchen could be self-sustaining. "Nothing is so tedious to a child as being obliged to sit still in the same place for a considerable time," he wrote in one essay, describing how he made newly arrived children sit silently and watch others work, so as to "inspire them with the desire to do that which [the] other children, apparently more favoured, more caressed, and more praised than themselves, were permitted to do."[21] He summed up the idea by with the following phrase: "To reform their minds it is necessary to know their habits." To manipulate the "secret springs of action in the human heart," in other words, children were initially forced to sit still and "obliged to be spectators of this busy and entertaining scene." This meant that they would soon become "so uneasy in their situations, and so jealous of those who were permitted to be more active, that they frequently solicited with the greatest importunity to be permitted to work, and often cried most heartily if this favour was not instantly granted them."[22]

The End of the Classical Soup Kitchen

To understand the significance of the Rumfordian soup kitchen, it is important to appreciate that Rumford was transforming a smaller, more local affair: an institution that was specific to a town or area. In Britain, these had been financed through "charitable subscriptions" in which four to five hundred of the "most respectable local inhabitants" came together to pay for premises and food.[23] Local elites then ran these soup kitchens with a committee of management chosen from the subscribers and a team appointed to run the day-to-day operations. Traditionally, the whole process occurred at the local level, making soup kitchens very much grounded in communal politics. These small-scale soup kitchens were built on the moral economy—the ancient obligation of the wealthy to the worst off—and were oriented around a "politics of provisions." This was a negotiated exchange in which the aim of the soup kitchen was not just to feed the hungry, but to quell unrest and mitigate rebellion.[24] The earlier soup kitchens, therefore, were an insurance against disturbance, an investment in stability.

A second, and related, feature of the earlier soup kitchen was its foundation in patronage. In return for their financial contribution, subscribers would receive six meal tickets for people "deserving of assistance." These tickets were inscribed with a written recommendation, and were "to be disposed of to such distressed families as are known or recommended as proper objects" for the soup kitchen's beneficence.[25] If the wealthy subscriber did not know any needy families they could return the tickets to the committee, who would dispose of them in other ways. Often this meant asking "reputable housekeepers" to recommend a "sober and industrious individual or poor local family."[26] Admission, therefore, relied on direct knowledge of people's character. The "reputable householder" had to declare in writing that the ticket holder "really wanted relief" as well as confirming that they "will feel thankful and desirous of the benefits arising from the tickets that are to be distributed by the committee."[27]

As the nineteenth century proceeded and Rumford's ideas began to spread, the soup kitchen lost this mooring in the local context. It became larger, more ambitious, and more industrial in its scope. Soup kitchens began to serve ever-larger areas, promoted not just as a solution for pauperism and unrest, but also to improve much wider economic conditions. Part of the rationale for early nineteenth-century soup kitchens was that they would reduce the consumption of corn and lower the price of bread. As one pamphlet put it, "The food they receive is but a part of the benefit . . . they are [also] taught, from a knowledge of the nature and quality of this food, and the price at which it can be prepared, to feed themselves in a more frugal manner."[28] When they saw the value of potatoes, the theory went, the poor would stop buying bread. As a result scarcity would end, prices would fall, and order would return. It was a strange logic that assumed demand rather than supply was the problem, while uniting behavior and relief into a much larger technology of power.

As the newer soup kitchens spread, their foundation in local patronage began to erode. In London, for example, the Spitalfields soup kitchen began its life on a small-scale subscription model, organized by a Quaker grain merchant and a metropolitan police magistrate—local figures who had a clear interest in preventing unrest.[29] Over time, however, this soup kitchen began to assist an ever-larger industrial underclass, serving hundreds of thousands of gallons of broth every year. It became widely known, and its mealtimes were flooded with hungry people.[30] Faced with a new, industrial era, such institutions had to operate on a new, industrial scale. They invested in "great, gleaming steel soup digesters," which could "reduce an entire cow to enough stock for hundreds of quarts of soup and only a few pounds of waste."[31] They became preoccupied with order and layout. They planned the layout of space very carefully and gradually shortened the amount of time people could eat inside them. This Rumfordian model of efficiency gradually developed into to Soyer's huge tables and chained-down spoons, as the scale of relief shot ever upwards.

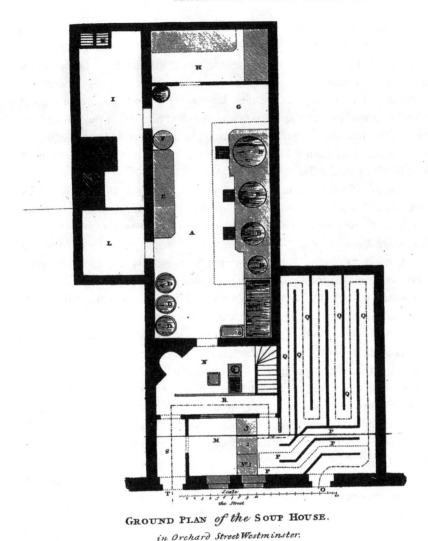

GROUND PLAN *of the* SOUP HOUSE.

in Orchard Street Westminster.

FIGURE 3. Ground plan of the soup house in Orchard Street, Westminster. Patrick Colquhoun, *Suggestions Offered to the Consideration of the Public* (London, 1799), 15. Reproduced with the permission of Senate House Library, University of London, GL Kress 18081.7.

As soup kitchens were scaled up, it became impossible to regulate attendance purely through personal recommendation. The size of the urban poor and its lack of connection with traditional elites meant that many people could not get hold of meal tickets, as there were not enough patron-client relationships to go around. "If relief was to be effective in alleviating hunger and preventing unrest," wrote John Bohstedt, "it had to be applied massively and impersonally."[32] This meant offering meal tickets for purchase: you no longer needed a patron; you simply needed cash. The new regime was meant to teach poor people about economics and value. As one pamphlet put it, "The poor are apt to undervalue everything they receive," but the soup kitchen sold it to them at a subsidized price.[33] Rumford praised the outcome. It embodied his ideal of the self-sustaining machine that could cover its own costs. The idea was that the original contributors would sell meal tickets, get a return for their "investment," and the need for subscribers would disappear.[34]

By the time Soyer proposed his vast Irish soup kitchen in 1847, admission by patronage had largely disappeared. As Bohstedt put it, the politics of provisions had been "gutted" and the soup kitchens in Ireland had been left without "resources of local wealth and leadership."[35] Soyer's institution, for example, had been imported from London, its funding and staff arriving from overseas, and its fundamental disconnect from the local population was epitomized by its geographical situation: located at the Royal Barracks, a powerbase of foreign rule. This soup kitchen, therefore, had become less about the local politics of provisions and more about cross-border colonial control. Removed from its earlier, communal moorings it was, at least in Ireland, barely rooted in the local political environment at all.[36]

This led to another big change in this model of relief: the decline in communal eating. Soup kitchens had previously been communal spaces. They served cooked meals from one large pot, and people would generally eat in the same large hall. The industrialization of the soup kitchen, however, made this less and less common, offering fewer opportunities to share food in a common space. The poor might still be fed from a giant vat, but they were discouraged from socializing, and efficiency and scale had become the watchword. Indeed, the whole institution was now designed for rapid consumption, ensuring that time was not taken away from productive labor. One pamphlet boasted that the whole process of feeding each individual would take "half an hour at most" and that many people could be "dispatched within a period of from one to fifteen minutes."[37] Queuing systems helped promote speed, with one philanthropist recommending that the poor be enclosed within a "maze of railings" to "promote facility and regularity in the delivery of the soup."[38] In other systems hungry people would bring a vessel to the open window of the soup house, after which they would leave from a different doorway in silence. "Everyone follows another," explained the author of this particular scheme, and "there is no necessity for uttering a word."[39]

By the time of the Irish famine nearly fifty years later, any sense of community had been made impossible. Soyer's soup kitchen ushered people through the eating area so quickly that they had little more than six minutes to eat. They were not allowed to eat bread with their soup, as it would take too long, so this was distributed at the exit of the kitchen as an incentive to eat more quickly. Soyer pioneered other innovations, such as immovable bowls sunk into tabletops and chained-down spoons for a hundred people.[40] Soyer's was not even the most unsociable soup kitchen in Ireland: the *London Evening News* reported from a horrific establishment in Cork that was "walled in and surrounded with sheds," in which the soup was passed down to hungry people, who were held in pens like cattle. "On entering, they are classified and stationed in the order in which it is intended to serve them, in a row of pens or enclosed places," read a newspaper report from the time. "There is then a communication from the kitchen in the rear, through which the homminy is handed in tins, containing a quart each. . . . The whole 800 are served in about three hours, and are then let out by the lower gate. . . . A fresh batch of 5–600 [are then] admitted as before, and fed in the same way."[41]

Soup, Satire, and Resistance

As the soup kitchen was scaled up in Ireland and the London slums, the food itself became more degraded. In theory, the soup kitchen was meant to distribute something familiar, something the recipients might eat at home. As one pamphlet put it, the kitchens should provide "food to which the laboring people have been accustomed" so that "there will be no prejudices to combat, and no complaints on account of introducing a new article of food."[42] The reality was rather different. The quality of food was cruel and unusual, and became an easy target for critics. The radical William Cobbett, for example, railed against the "Subscription Tribe" that organized these institutions, declaring that poor people "want not Soup and Old Bones and Bullock's Liver; but they want their rights."[43] The soup served up in soup kitchens, Cobbett colorfully claimed in another pamphlet, constituted little more than "an insipid and flatulent compound" made from "dirt and bones."[44] Even members of the establishment agreed, albeit in more genteel tones. Lord Wycombe, for example, wrote that "Count Rumford has his merits, but I do not think the invention of bad soup by the union of Ox Heads with Potatoes the noblest flight of human genius."[45]

Ox heads were, indeed, *la saveur du mois* in the soup kitchen. Recipes described how to turn them into broth, a lengthy process that took over seventeen hours. The following instructions, for example, come from a prominent pamphlet that informed aspiring philanthropists how to make soup from old bones and bullock's heads.

> The water in the cauldron must be in a boiling state at six o'clock in the evening. . . . After the meat is weighed and adjusted, it is cut up, and the

bones are split longitudinally, broken into small pieces, and put into the boiler. . . . Soon after this, and before the fat melts, the bloody and foul particles float up and are skimmed off. Then the boiler is closed up and continues boiling or simmering for twelve hours until six o'clock the next morning. . . . [At this point,] the pease and barley are put in and the boilers are filled up with water . . . the labourers continue to stir the soup frequently to prevent the vegetables from burning, always covering it at the intervals. At eight o'clock the pepper and salt are put in, and the onions at nine; when the boilers are again filled up with water, and at eleven the delivery of the soup commences. At this period, the meat, which has then been seventeen hours in the boilers, is nearly dissolved, and only appears as particles or threads floating in the soup. . . . The strength of the soup depends much on the quality of the meat. Bullocks heads, well cleaned, may be used with advantage along with the other meat.[46]

Critics like Lord Wycombe may have scoffed at Rumford's suggestion that this combination of ox heads and potatoes was in any way remarkable, but the recipes remained more or less the same forty years later. Indeed, little had changed by the time Alexis Soyer was promoting his own thin and watery soup, which inspired a similar reaction and some delightful satire. A writer in *Punch* penned mocking praise: "The soup is delicious," he declared; "the more I take of it, the more it brings water into my mouth."[47] A letter to the *Times* dismissed it contemptuously as "not so much soup for the poor, but poor soup."[48] The *Nation*, a republican newspaper in Ireland, called it "dysentery-juice" and published a delightfully satirical poem imagining the soup being cooked by three witches from Macbeth.[49]

> Double double, toil and trouble
> Fire burn, and boiler bubble
> Scale of codfish, spider's tongues
> Tomtit's gizzards, head and lungs
> Of a famished French-fed frog
> Root of phaytee digged in bog
> Of D'Israeli's heart a slice
> Roebucks gall, a grain of rice
> Celery heads paired to the tips
> Broughams nose, and Soyer's lips
> Sweetened by the Ponsonbys's
> Fastidious taste—it sure must please
> Such rude, ill-mannered folk as these.[50]

Sardonic poems were composed about Rumford as well. Charles Lamb, for example, made this concise offering, imagining a declaration by the great national scientist in front of his peers:

> I deal in aliments fictitious
> And teaze the Poor with soups nutritious
> Of bones and flint I make dilution
> And belong to the National Institution.[51]

The satirist Peter Pindar (a pseudonym for John Wolcot) composed a much longer poem, describing the "experimental dinners promised by the Count":

> Bones, oyster-shells, and hair and hoofs and claws,
> Shall too form jellies for the nicest jaws. . .
> By which slow movement in the mastication,
> Millions may soon be saved to this poor Nation!
> What gratitude, what thanks, to thee are due,
> Instructing a great Empire how to *chew*!
> In Workhouses, where ignorance abounds,
> And all the Poor, voracious, feed like Hounds,
> Sharp Overseers shall at the table stand,
> And *give the word*, with sarjeant-like command;
> Thus will their crackling Jaws in concert chime,
> And, like a Fiddler's Elbow, move *in time*.
> Oh! If I too might cater for the belly,
> Old fiddle-strings should make us vermicelli;
> Cockchaffers, with a very trifling art,
> Compose a Pie, at least a pretty Tart
> Soap-suds to Syllabubs and Trifles change,
> And Bullock's Lights and Livers to Blancmange;
> And Sheep's-dung, without quantities of studying,
> Glean'd from the fields, produce a fine plum pudding.[52]

Romantics like William Wordsworth went further than simply satire, earnestly blaming soup kitchens for degrading communal obligations and "destroy[ing] the bonds of domestic feeling among the poor." His poem "The Old Cumberland Beggar," for example, lamented how the new institutions of poor relief had alienated poverty-stricken classes from living and dying in the "frosty air," criticizing such "houses of industry" for forcing an exchange of demeaning work for measly gruel:

> May never HOUSE, misnamed of INDUSTRY
> Make him a captive! For that pent-up din

Those life-consuming sounds that clog the air
Be his the natural silence of old age!
Let him be free of mountain solitudes
And have around him, whether heard or not
The pleasant melody of woodland birds.[53]

From Classical to Modern Relief

Despite this resistance, the soup kitchen expanded in scale and scope throughout the first half of the nineteenth century, becoming distinctly modern in the
process. As Foucault has pointed out, the classical age was preoccupied with
identifying laws of nature, making them visible and putting them to use—an
approach that is very much visible in Rumford's work. The icon of the classical age, Foucault wrote, was the table: a space on which everything could be
laid out and seen in relation to everything else.[54] Natural specimens could be
laid out examined on tables. Information could be collected and classified on
tables. Scholars used tables to make order in the world, and the central aim of
knowledge in this period was to classify, to systematize. Rumford's meticulous
use of tables and ledgers to record every detail of the soup shop was a little like
Linnaeus's botany: Foucault's archetypal example of the classical age, which
ordered objects in an elegant system of classification. His belief in natural law
also fitted the way that divine rules were seen in this period to shape not just
biology but language and behavior as well. Foucault, in fact, presented "universal grammar" as an example of the belief in natural law: a language that
perfectly mirrored the world. This, like other natural laws, demonstrated how
God had devised a system of order, a "great chain of being," which it was the
task of scholars to uncover and understand.[55]

Human nature, natural law, and the table were typical Rumfordian concerns.
Like many other eighteenth-century natural scientists, he sought to establish his
"credentials as a reliable spokesman for Nature while simultaneously representing Nature as speaking for herself."[56] Rumford, indeed, imagined that he was a
"mouthpiece of nature," articulating natural laws and channeling them to productive ends.[57] His kitchens used classical forms of ordering: with their tables and
charts, they sought to identify the "secret springs" of human action, the essence of
objects and ingredients. Indeed, Rumford's whole approach centered on the metaphor of the machine, the ultimate system of order, which simply needed to be
tuned and put into action.[58] Rumford did not claim to be creating anything new;
his role was simply to uncover a preexisting order and set it in motion. This cor-
responded with the way many other natural scientists in this era saw themselves

in the world: "There was a world created by God, existing by itself, [and] the role of man was to clarify the order of the world."[59]

Rumford, therefore, was a creature of the classical age, but he had set about reforming a much older system, a model of relief that went back to Elizabethan times. Foucault made the comparison between classical thought and its predecessor particularly clear: classical scholarship, he argued, found order in the world by examining the difference between things, but earlier scholarship found order through similarities. The classical age was all about representation; the Renaissance was all about resemblance. Foucault cited wolf's bane as an illustration of the earlier system of order: a plant that was used in the Renaissance to treat the eye because it *resembled* the eye; it had seeds that appeared to be "tiny dark globes seated in white skinlike coverings," which looked like "eyelids covering the eye."[60] In this way, resemblance defined the object and its place in the world. This system of order, however, changed with classical botany and Linnaeus's systems of order, which relied not on similarities, but on *difference*. As the Renaissance faded away, knowledge became more systematic, and resemblance and its interpretation gave way to representation and its analysis. Only madmen or poets looked for resonances in radically different areas of life.[61]

After the classical came the modern, when the quest for knowledge sought not just to represent the world accurately but to uncover hidden structures as well. In Foucault's terms, the principles of knowledge in the modern era were no longer captured by the metaphor of the table, on which scientists would arrange things based on their visible properties, but by the metaphor of the microscope, where scientists identified complex internal configurations. As we will see in the next chapter, this is where Soyer was leading relief. The order of the world became founded not on differences that were visible to the naked eye, but on inner essences. Systems became based not on surface properties, but on functions. The structures of the world were no longer God given, unchanging, waiting for humans to piece it all together; they were, instead, identifiable only by looking carefully inside things and revealing the relationship between environment and anatomy. Foucault cited Cuvier, who had declared organic structure as prior to taxonomy, as the key transitional figure in biology. Modern classifications, in other words, now focused on the *function* of things rather than their preexisting nature.[62]

As we will see in the coming chapters, this shift had profound political implications for relief. Classical utopias involved "a fantasy of origins": they focused on the beginning of the world and its underlying order, which God had arranged at the moment of creation. The utopias of the modern period, however, were very different. They became a fantasy of endings. Scientists now wanted to remake the world, to improve it, to travel to a future destination where the world was a better place. They were "concerned with the final decline of time rather than with its morning" so their claims to knowledge were increasingly oriented around development and progress. "The great dream of an end to History was the utopia of [modern] systems of thought," Foucault perceptively put it, just as a dream of the world's beginnings drove the classical systems before it.[63]

This shift from classical to modern placed humans in a new role. They were no longer passive negotiators within a divinely sanctioned order; they became subjects within a world of objects.[64] They were able to take control of their environment and make it subservient to their ends. Classical scholarship—from which Rumford had emerged—uncovered order in the world but remained relatively uninterested in changing it. Modernity, in contrast, placed humans in the driving seat. Scholars began to adopt a more transformational role in relation to the empty stomach, taming and exploiting nature to drive society forward. "Once the order of the world was no longer God-given and representable in a table," wrote Dreyfus and Rabinow, "the continuous relation which had placed man with the other beings of the world was broken."[65] Classical attempts to *understand* habit and tradition, in other words, were replaced by the modern preoccupation with *transforming* habit and tradition. This began with the nineteenth-century soup kitchen reforms, which were accompanied by a sense that humans were no longer passive objects of a divine plan, but agents of their own destiny.

Count Rumford's Soup Improved

The fulcrum between the classical and modern periods marks the start of our narrative, with Soyer and Rumford at the center of the scales. As we shall see in the next chapter, modern nutritional science soon emerged, and, by the middle of the nineteenth century, humanitarian attention started to focus on deeper anatomical structures rather than surface systems of order. The empty stomach was soon presented as a deficiency in nutrients rather than a collective moral failing, and food became judged on its organic structure rather than the tangible qualities of taste and texture. Crucially, this cleared the path for an idea of human progress, and an attitude to filling the empty stomach that did not simply identify the laws of human behavior but sought to change them. Rumford, of course, did not share these modern preoccupations; he could not see nutrients, cells, or biochemical interactions. He focused on whole ingredients, visible and tangible properties, and he wrote about soups and stoves, potatoes and puddings. His system was justified by the feeling of soup in the stomach, the speed with which it could be crunched in the mouth. His science meant "portion control, the arrangement of food on a plate, the manner of food's preparation," and other discrete and visible things.[66]

Over the next century, all this would change, and by June 1863 the Victorian periodical, *All the Year Round*, was reporting on a new approach to the soup kitchen. The weekly magazine, which was founded and owned by Charles Dickens, had been sent "a small packet of greasy powder, labeled 'Count Rumford's Soup improved,'" offering a dried version of the broth that had been served in charitable kitchens for over half a century.[67] As the author of the article explained, "the benevolent idea was that in all impoverished districts there should be sold such packets professing to give the substance of a pint of good soup for a halfpenny." It was a dehydrated solution, relief reduced to a packet, which foreshadowed a future approach to humanitarianism. This replaced large, complex institutions with a small sachet; Rumford's revolutionary combination of fuel-efficient stoves, new recipes, and exchanges of work for sustenance had now been dried into a powder.

The correspondent, perhaps it was Dickens himself, tried making the soup. He "conscientiously followed the directions, which were simply to boil for three minutes in a pint of water over a moderate fire."

> The result was a thin brown liquid, by no means palatable. We boiled on for twenty minutes, stirring most assiduously, for the powder had a suspicious resemblance to a halfpenny-worth of groats seasoned with a dash of meat grease and a sprinkling of caraway-seeds. But the soup, though improved by more boiling, did not thicken, and although one might conceive it welcome to one perishing from hunger, starvation must, we thought, have set in very decidedly before anyone could be persuaded to gulp down a pint of it.[68]

The powder failed because of its taste, proving that this particular new technology was not yet ready to produce a sealed ration for the starving. Yet the authors of the article made some suggestions. "The dry groats of which gruel is made," they proposed, "[might be] cunningly mixed with pea-powder, burnt onion, dried celery, a pinch of dried and pounded herring, or other cheap flavourings. . . . The honest manufacture and sale of such soup-powders would, as our correspondent rightly feels, be of unquestionable advantage to the very poor."[69]

The dream had begun: nutrition in a compact form. Scientists and relief workers in the second half of the nineteenth century sought to find the essence of food, offering this in packets and tins, which did not become a significant part of relief work until the middle of the twentieth century. These soup sachets, however, were a premonition. The extensive network of working parts, the gleaming broth boilers, and the accumulated "knowledge" of human nature were now under threat from a newer approach, and Soyer, once again, was involved.

JUSTUS LIEBIG AND THE RISE OF NUTRITIONAL SCIENCE

The word *osmazome* was created in 1806, from the Greek *osme* (odor) and *zomos* (soup). It defined the savory essence of meat, the pungent scent of beef. It referred to the stock that was created from repeated reduction, becoming the basis of good bouillon or soup.[1] The French gourmand Jean Brillat-Savarin described osmazome as a "mysterious substance." "It is osmazome that gives merit to good soup," he wrote. "When caramelized, it forms the brown sauce of meats; by it is formed the brown crusts of roasts."[2] Brillat-Savarin viewed this "eminently savoury part of meat" to be the very essence of food—a belief that was entirely consistent with his almost mystical worldview. This was a man who had famously declared that "the discovery of a new dish does more for human happiness than the discovery of a star."[3] Osmazome was the essence of this star. It lay at the spiritual heart of food and was perceived as an almost indefinable flavor that uncovered the transcendental power of the palate.[4]

Osmazome first emerged from of a dispute in Paris, which had been provoked by the Rumfordian revolution. After soup kitchens had been established throughout the French capital in the early 1800s, physicians were still unsure why some soups were more nourishing than others. A prominent theory centered on gelatin, suggesting that this was the essence of meat. By boiling bones and isolating this clear jellylike substance, an aspiring philanthropist could get the core of meat's nutritive value at a fraction of the cost. The idea was an old one, but it had been promoted in Paris particularly vigorously in the wake of the French revolution.[5] Here, a new generation of politicians were acutely aware that food shortage was a threat to power, so they began looking for ways to feed more people from cheaper ingredients. Soup made from bones, it was claimed, could be just as nourishing as soup made from meat.[6] Various machines were developed to produce gelatin, not least Papin's Digester, an early pressure cooker that could crumble bones and cook them into gelatin cheaply and in large quantities.[7]

Osmazome was the elixir promoted to counter the arguments for gelatin. It served as the battle cry for authors who cared about the enjoyment of food.[8] If gelatin, that transparent, relatively tasteless, quivering substance, *was* what made meat nourishing, then it meant that *taste* did not matter to well-being. This seemed a depressing conclusion. Opponents of gelatin began drawing on studies that took place in 1820s and 1830s, which seemed to show that gelatin bouillon had failed to nourish people properly. In one study, a group of clinicians fed themselves almost exclusively on a gelatin diet for three months, reporting weakness, headaches, and digestive disorders.[9]

A group of scientists began to argue as a result that osmazome was the real source of good nutrition: a substance that could be made by soaking meat in cold water, bringing it to the boil, skimming off the albumen, cooling the liquid, removing the fat, and then reboiling it repeatedly. This left a sticky brown liquid, which became more and more like a paste the longer it was boiled.[10] The substance was rich in flavor, and as Brillat-Savarin had argued, was responsible for making "the reputation of the richest consommés" and causing "the dismissal of so many cooks."[11] It was, in essence, a stock that had been thickened and reduced repeatedly, characterized by a flavor we now call umami, yet osmazome became more than just a flavor. It was treated as a substance, an element, and the source of nutritive value.

The dispute between the proponents of osmazome and the advocates for gelatin rumbled on for years. The two sides agreed that meat contained a number of constituent substances and that both gelatin and osmazome were present in meat. They disagreed, however, about which substance produced the most nourishing soup. The dispute went so far as to generate a Gelatin Commission in the 1830s, established by the French Academy of Sciences, to determine whether or not animal gelatin was genuinely nutritious and acceptable for use in soup kitchens.[12] The commission took nearly a decade to report but it failed to reach any substantive conclusions; meanwhile, the remarkable rise of biochemistry soon rendered it irrelevant.[13] This chapter explains how these theories of gelatin and osmazome were eventually replaced by a more modern approach to the diet, illustrating this change by comparing two very similar products that emerged over the space of just a decade: a substance called Osmazome Food, which was promoted by Alexis Soyer, and one known as Extractum Carnis, or "extract of meat," which was promoted by the founder of modern biochemistry, Justus Liebig. These two products were essentially the same, but were marketed in radically different ways: the former framed by classical dietetics; the latter by modern nutritional science.

Modern Nutritional Science

It is hard to imagine a world without nutrients, without the idea that food is made up of invisible components that have different purposes in the body. Today, nutrients are everywhere: they are on the labels of the food we eat, in the advice section of newspapers, and they take a central part in our children's education as well as our dietary advice.[14] Nutrients, however, only emerged relatively recently, bursting onto the gastronomic scene just as Alexis Soyer's fame was at its peak. Indeed, 1847 is once again a key moment, as this was the year Justus Liebig published his popular book, *Researches on the Chemistry of Food*, which promoted a new and more systematic way of analyzing the diet.[15] Before Liebig it was alchemy rather than biochemistry that produced authoritative knowledge about foods, with alchemists using age-old techniques to break food into constituent properties.[16] This meant that food tended to be judged by its texture, flavor, and other tangible qualities. After Liebig, however, food was judged by its invisible nutrient content. This shift, from classical to modern, had big implications for hunger relief.

Both gelatin and osmazome emerged from the alchemical rather than modern tradition: they were the result of research into what made gravy wobbly, what made the crust of browned beef so savory, and what made soup so nourishing. Alchemists often used distillation to examine the essence of food in this way, heating a liquid and capturing the vapor that rose as part of the "spirit" of the original substance. This allowed alcohol to be identified and was the origin of the word for spirits. Brillat-Savarin saw the discovery of osmazome as a similar achievement, part of a search for the essence of food. Like alcohol, it was a project of purification that came from distilling a substance until it had been reduced to a kernel of basic matter—in this case, reducing a stock again and again until one was left with a sticky and flavorful paste. The result, Brillat-Savarin concluded, was that osmazome was the essence of meat, just as alcohol is the essence of wine. Osmazome, he believed, was why humans love food, just as alcohol is why we love wine.[17]

Like osmazome, the arguments for gelatin also emerged from the search for basic essences. One of the product's most enthusiastic advocates, Antoine-Alexis Cadet de Vaux, saw each piece of bone as "a bouillon tablet formed by nature," a distillation of nutrients that could be reused. He believed that "one pound of bones can yield as much broth as six pounds of meat," and argued that any other use of bone was a criminal waste. "One small box, one knife handle, or a dozen buttons made of bone: all of them correspond to a broth that has been robbed from the poor."[18] Early tests seemed to support this view. In one hospital, three-quarters of the meat that had previously been provided in soups was replaced by gelatin, and by 1828 several hospitals in Paris were installing equipment that could supply gelatin bouillon to their patients.[19] The Royal Medallion Mint in France distributed free gelatin soup to its workers, suggesting the recipe for armies in the field as well.[20] These developments, based on alchemical ideas, arrived in an increasingly modern context. Gelatin soup was soon saturated by the ideals of the French revolution, whose enthusiastic radicals sought an efficient way to feed state-supported populations.[21] The bones, moreover, could only be made edible through a complicated industrial technique of crushing, steaming, and rinsing under pressure.[22] Perhaps most significantly, gelatin was bland, its texture unpleasant, and so relied on the endorsement of experts: without them, it was hard to accept that it could be the essence of meat.

When Justus Liebig published *Researches on the Chemistry of Food* in 1847, however, he undermined many of the arguments for gelatin and osmazome and promoted the techniques of modern chemistry instead. For some years these new processes had been bubbling away, slowly undermining existing beliefs. Evidence had been accumulating that gelatin, in particular, contained little of nutritional value, and Liebig interpreted these studies in light of modern chemistry. One medical student, for example, tried to subsist for four days on gelatin and bread reporting weakness and digestive disorders, and a well-known pharmacist had fed himself and his family gelatin for several weeks before suffering sickness and violent headaches.[23] The French physiologist Francois Magendie, moreover, undertook large-scale feeding experiments with dogs, giving them gelatin diets and measuring how much weight they lost as a result.[24] This was enough for the French Academy of Sciences to establish a commission of enquiry, which cast doubt on the value of gelatin while failing to endorse osmazome as an alternative.[25] Ideas of diet were taking a new turn, which Liebig brought together in his influential new book.

One of Liebig's achievements was to popularize the three main macronutrients—carbohydrates, fats, and proteins—which came to structure modern nutritional science. The term *carbohydrates* came from William Prout, who examined "hydrates of carbon" in 1831—the single word appearing a little later via the German tendency toward compound nouns.[26] "Protein," meanwhile, came from Jöns Jacob Berzelius, a Swedish chemist who created it from the Greek word *proteios*, meaning of "primary importance," implying its centrality to human growth.[27] Fats were a common term, but Prout had added them as another main category, describing foods as saccharinous (carbohydrate), oleaginous (fat), or albuminous (protein).[28] Liebig later brought these terms together in his "giant intellectual synthesis" of recent advances, creating a structure that identified the central components of food.[29]

Liebig's other achievement was to refine biochemical methods. These had been based on the same system for years. Foods were placed in a flask and burned in controlled conditions, which caused the carbon in the organic matter to be converted into carbon dioxide and left a series of products—in ash and gas— that could be weighed or measured. Liebig made this process simpler by inventing a laboratory device known as the kaliapparat—a five-bulb apparatus that allowed chemists to conduct many more experiments far more quickly—and then linked the study of food with the study of animal physiology, comparing the makeup of the food consumed with the makeup of the substances excreted.[30] Using this method, a cow's diet of potatoes and grass, for example, could be broken down into its carbon, hydrogen, oxygen, and nitrogen content and then compared them with the chemical content of the cow's excretions. Such an input/ output comparison allowed Liebig to draw conclusions about bodily processes. It allowed him to look at what was eaten and then compare this with what was left in the form of milk, urine, and manure.

Liebig was soon applying this method to human diets. He focused on people living in controlled environments, particularly soldiers, whose food and excreta could be monitored closely. In one study Liebig examined the food consumed by German infantrymen in local barracks, measuring, "with the utmost exactness, every day during a month," what they ate right down to the "pepper, salt and butter." Each article of food was separately subjected to analysis alongside the soldier's feces and urine, which revealed a lot of dry numerical data interspersed with some surprisingly vivid social snapshots. The average weight of a soldier's feces, Liebig found, was 5.5 ounces "in the fresh state." The percentage of carbon in the feces was 11.31 percent, which was "very nearly the same proportion as in fresh meat." Liebig's experiments were sometimes compromised by soldiers sneaking away from the barracks and consuming an unknown amount of "sausages, brandy, beer and butter" in a nearby alehouse, but he only discovered this later by reading their sergeant-major's report.[31] By taking a painstaking and carefully documented approach to the analysis of diet, Liebig burned and measured, weighed and analyzed, then read and reported the soup and stool of soldiers to build a picture of human nutrition.

From Osmazome to Extract of Meat

"Osmazome" was still a common word in the middle of the nineteenth century, appearing in a variety of settings. Mrs. Beeton, for example, used it in her *Book of*

Household Management, describing osmazome as essential for lending flavor and perfume to food.[32] Marie Antonin Carême, chef to George IV and the Rothschilds, declared it to be the most savory part of meat.[33] Alexis Soyer even tried to bottle the substance, identifying commercial possibilities and filing a patent for "Osmazome Food."[34] Liebig's new science, however, gradually grew in popularity and osmazome soon sank into historical obscurity. This sticky, savory substance was revealed not to be a basic nutrient at all, but a combination of various elements, and by the end of the nineteenth century the word had disappeared almost entirely.[35]

The transition toward modern nutritional science can be illustrated by comparing Soyer's Osmazome Food with a very similar but far more commercially successful product: "Extractum Carnis," or "extract of meat." Soyer's patent had been filed in 1853 under the heading "improvements in preparing and preserving soups," describing a thick paste made from the "caramelized juices that are left in the saucepan after meat has been roasted."[36] Soyer's instructions explained how to take minced meat, boil it in a Florence oil-flask, and then reduce the resulting liquor until it had a "consistency like treacle."[37] The resulting Osmazome Food, Soyer claimed, could cure illnesses and "create a more lively circulation of the blood when it becomes sluggish and dull in old age."[38] This drew on the Galenic vocabulary of humors, blood, and vigor: language that was increasingly out of touch with the emerging nutritional science.[39] A number of commentators mocked Soyer, drawing not so much on the language of disgust and double standards, but rather emphasizing how modern biochemistry was showing Osmazome Food to be seriously insufficient.

The Lancet led the charge, railing against "soup quackery" in an editorial that explained how "no culinary digestion, or stewing, or boiling can convert four ounces into twelve, unless the laws of animal physiology can be unwritten and some magical power be made to reside in the cap and apron of the cook."[40] A medical correspondent to the *Times* agreed, declaring that it was "preposterous" to claim that Soyer's soup might feed a working man, when "every physician and physiologist knows that the digestive organs are incapable of assimilating sufficient nutriment from a liquid diet."[41] Criticism came from all parts of the country and every level of the medical profession. James Simpson, a well-known Edinburgh physician, advised Soyer to read more science before promoting his soups, and even Queen Victoria's doctor, Henry Marsh, took the time to write a book pointing to the inadequacies of such diet for laborers.[42] In reference to Soyer's defense that he had tested his soup on noblemen, the *Lancet* offered perhaps the best response: "Marquises, lords and ladies may taste the meagre liquid and pronounce it agreeable to their gustative inclinations. But something more than an agreeable titillation of the palate is required to keep up that manufactory of blood, bone and muscle, which constitutes the strong healthy man."[43]

Soyer's attempt to market his Osmazome Food, therefore, never got off the ground, but a far more successful product soon emerged under the supervision of none other than Justus Liebig. This was a remarkably similar substance to osmazome, but it relied not on the old fashioned language of humors and vigor, but on the modern vocabulary of nutritional science. Responding to the success of his book *Researches on the Chemistry of Food*, Liebig penned a recipe for something he called "extract of meat, or *genuine* portable soup," which had a very similar production process to Soyer's. It involved boiling beef in water until it acquired "a brownish color and the delicate flavor of roast meat," then evaporating this water until "we obtain a dark brown, soft mass" of paste that was portable and long lasting.[44] As Liebig explained, "half an ounce [of this paste] suffices to convert 1lb of water, with the addition of a little salt, into a strong, well-flavoured soup." Liebig described it as an alternative to "the tablets of so-called portable soup prepared in England and France," which were dominated by gelatin and had become early versions of the stock cube.[45] Harking back the earlier debate surrounding osmazome, he explained how "it has long been customary to ascribe the gelatinous matter" as the essence of good soup, but "there cannot be a greater mistake."[46] Liebig was discrediting gelatin in the same way that other critics had discredited osmazome: its failings were seen as chemical rather than aesthetic. Liebig could make this point with the authority of a nutritional scientist, recommending his own product for invalids, garrisons, explorers, wounded soldiers, and of course, for the weak and malnourished as well.

Industrial Production

Liebig's Extract of Meat (the name of a product he marketed rather than the concept) began life as just a recipe, but within two decades it had become one of the most widely recognized commodities of the Victorian era—giving rise to Bovril, the Oxo tower, and huge advertising campaigns featuring cards and recognizable motifs. Beef tea had long been used informally as a reassuring curative, but Liebig gave it a new scientific acceptability. He mobilized the powers of modern marketing, and the *Lancet* helped things along when it endorsed his recipe, with chemists soon producing it for sale under the Latin name Extractum Carnis. Beef tea, in this way, was given an increasingly medical justification and was even admitted as a legal drug in some jurisdictions.[47] By the 1850s, Liebig suggested making use of the plentiful beef stocks in Latin America to manufacture Extract of Meat in bulk, and although he lacked the entrepreneurial acumen to start such a process immediately, a railway engineer, George Christian Giebert, soon wrote to him with a proposal to get the idea off the ground.[48]

Giebert knew South America well, and after reading Liebig's works had decided that Uruguay would make a particularly good spot for a meat extract factory. Land was cheap, the ports were good, and there was a thriving leather industry with cattle carcasses available at a cheap price. Canning the meat or transporting it frozen was not technologically possible at the time, so carcasses were often left to rot and waste after the cattle had been skinned. Liebig's method of reducing the flesh to a flavorful paste seemed a good way to solve this problem.[49] The timing of Giebert's proposal was also fortuitous because meat consumption in Europe had begun to outstrip supply in the 1850s: prices were rising, and there was widespread concern about how best to feed the growing population. Nutritional science had already generated the idea that meat was the best way to rebuild tissue and muscle, and social commentators in the early 1860s were lamenting the lack of "nitrogenous food" available—in other words, a lack of protein and meat for workers.

The shortage of meat was seen to be of particular concern for the poor, because they lived "by the wear and tear of their muscles" and were "condemned by the present high price of meat to subsist upon food that cannot restore the power that is expended."[50] The idea, therefore, was that the poor were living off corporeal assets that they could not replace. It was the kind of calculation that would later become very familiar once nutrients entered into the world of statecraft. Given "the income and expenditure of the human body," the argument went, "the poor are living upon their capital, and of course sooner or later they must use themselves up."[51] Liebig saw an opportunity to create a partnership with Giebert that would not only profit from discarded carcasses of Uruguayan cattle but also help nourish the bodies of the poor potato eaters of Europe.[52] With much fanfare, Liebig's Extract of Meat was launched in 1865. This was a thick, dark brown, highly viscous liquid in glass bottles, which was marketed as uniquely nourishing. It was manufactured by pulping the discarded carcasses of cattle using vast iron rollers, soaking the pressed flesh in water, bringing this to the boil, skimming off the fat and then removing the residue of minced and boiled flesh. By repeatedly heating the resulting soup under pressure the cow liquor could be reduced to the consistency of molasses.

Liebig's Extract was received very positively, perhaps because it had been packaged like a medicine, adorned with the signature of a famous chemist, and surrounded by fantastical claims. A writer in the *Pharmaceutical Journal* argued that no other food was as effective at restoring the tissues of the body, and Liebig's promotional literature claimed that "thirty-four pounds of finest beef have been used in the production of a single pound of meat extract."[53] The implication, of course, was that all the goodness of the former could be found in the latter, and these claims were accepted in the *British Medical Journal*, which declared that physicians owed Liebig a "deep debt of gratitude" for his innovation.[54] Full-page advertisements were soon taken out to build on this early success. Everyone could now "have in [their] kitchens and hospitals the juice and essence of strong oxen now feeding on the Pampas," one claimed.[55] Samples were sent out to public figures and Florence Nightingale declared it "excellent."[56] By the end of the 1860s St. Thomas Hospital in London was reputedly ordering twelve thousand pots each year, and advertisements were declaring the product to be "indispensible in the sick room," the product of a new "age of humanity, science and invention."[57]

Liebig, therefore, succeeded where Soyer had failed. The French chef's attempt to market Osmazome Food in the 1850s had come to nothing, but the German chemist's very similar product flourished into one of the most successful food-stuffs of the era. Today, few people have heard of osmazome, but many know of Oxo, Fray Bentos, or Bovril—the legacy of Liebig's Extract. Perhaps most significantly, Liebig's success was built on the back of the new nutritional science. His product was revolutionary in its ingenious advertising campaigns, its transnational network of production, and in the way it fused science and entrepreneurship. It demonstrated, quite simply, that modernity had arrived in nutrition.

FIGURE 4. Advertisement for Liebig's Extract of Meat. *Ladies' Home Journal*, March, 1907, 60. Reproduced with the permission of the Bodleian Libraries, University of Oxford. Shelfmark Per. 2414 b. 3.

Classical Dietetics

As modern nutritional science grew in significance, a much older system fell away: classical dietetics. This had originated in ancient Greece and was quite unlike dietetics as we understand it today. In the original Greek, diet meant a "way of life" or "mode of being," and dietetics was a branch of medicine that was designed to maintain one's life and preserve one's health.[58] It was about far more than the diet, and was above all concerned with *maintaining* good health in all its forms: just one element of a medical system that also included diagnosis (identifying ill health) and therapeutics (treating ill health). Dietetics was all about preserving one's good health through an ordered system of living. Indeed, the word *diet* was linguistically connected with other routinized worlds, sharing the same term in ancient Greek with assembly, parliament, regimen, or routine.[59]

In the *Use of Pleasure*, Foucault devoted nearly fifty pages—the whole of part II—to the study of dietetics, exploring how the ancients made life a "work of art."[60] Classical dietetics, he argued, brought food into a much wider system of living, which was oriented around the central principle of balance. The distinctive purpose of dietetics, Foucault emphasized, was to prevent excess. The aim was to adjust one's life to changing circumstances in order to produce some kind of equilibrium in all areas: leisure, exercise, food, drink, sleep, cleanliness, sex, and so on. This was not just about self-improvement, but moderation. "The purpose of diet," Foucault wrote, "was not to extend life as far as possible in time, nor as high as possible in performance, but rather to make life happy and useful within the limits that had been set for it."[61]

Classical dietetics was influenced by Galen's idea of balance between the humors: blood, yellow bile, black bile, and phlegm. These were the four basic substances that, it was believed, made up the body. Each of the humors had a particular quality and was associated with one of the classical elements. Phlegm was cold, moist, and associated with water. Black bile was cold, dry, and associated with earth. Yellow bile was warm, dry, and associated with fire. Blood was warm, moist, and associated with air. Healthy people had all four humors in balance, but an excess of one or another had a negative impact on body and soul. Indeed, each humor was associated with a particular kind of temperament or behavior: an excess of cold, watery phlegm led to a phlegmatic, unruffled temperament; an excess of dry, earthy black bile led to a melancholic, analytical temperament; an excess of dry, firelike yellow bile led to a choleric, irritable temperament; and an excess of warm, moist blood led to a sanguine, sociable temperament.

Food was crucial to balancing the humors and adjusting one's temperament. Indeed, eating was an activity through which people could abide by the pair of ancient injunctions that so fascinated Foucault in his later life: the need to know oneself and care for oneself.[62] This was not just a matter of eating the correct food when one was ill. It was about knowing one's body, one's temperament, and one's circumstances. Care of the self involved making decisions that would correct an imbalance in the humors that might be caused by anything: changes in living arrangements, fluctuations in the climate, the passing of the seasons, variations in one's mood, or just the passage of time. Health, life, and diet were connected, and food had a corrective role. Crucially, the qualities and function of foods were obvious to the layman, so each person could have a role in deciding their correct diet. Ginger and onion were hot; cucumber and mint were cool; prunes and cheese were dry; yogurt and milk were wet. Such foods could intensify or counteract the presence of humors in the body, so that cool and wet foods, for example, could counteract an excess of yellow bile, which was associated with fire, or hot and dry foods could counteract an excess of phlegm.[63]

In this way of thinking about food, what you ate had to suit your circumstances. The aim was to correct the imbalance that was inevitable at certain times. Each person learned about the system and used it to adjust their diet, prevent illnesses, and correct their temperament. Through the consumption of cucumber and yogurt, for example, one could minimize conditions associated with yellow bile, such as a fast pulse, dry tongue, and rashes on the skin. This involved a degree self-knowledge. Everyone was considered the best judge of their situation; indeed, the ancient injunctions prescribed self-knowledge as a prerequisite for self-care. The temple of Apollo at Delphi was carved with a pair of maxims: "know thyself" and "nothing in excess," which captured both the starting point and the aim of the dietetic tradition. To care for oneself, one first had to know oneself. If one had a temperament that was naturally choleric (fiery and temperamental) or phlegmatic (cool and detached), one's dietary regimen had to take this into account. Foucault argued that this was not just a practical concern; it was a central part of moral culture. The daily care of the self was not just considered to be good for you, but also to be good in itself.[64] In this fusion of ethics and medicine, people's everyday decisions were pursued for moral reasons as much as for personal well-being, and questions such as where to situate one's house, what to do for one's employment, and of course, what one ate or drank, all had a deeply moral character.[65]

From Classical Dietetics to Modern Nutritional Science

The classical dietetic tradition, which had spread throughout Europe in the Renaissance, died away with modern biochemistry, and Liebig's science shifted attention inside the body. This had four main implications. First, it involved a profound change in judgments about food. Before the arrival of nutritional science, foods were judged by their visible qualities: they were seen as hot and dry or cool and wet. Diets were judged by the qualities everyone could see and understand, and to know a food, all you needed was to grasp how it appeared to the eyes, how it tasted in the mouth, where it came from, and how it felt in the belly. Liebig's discovery of nutrients, however, changed all that. From the 1840s the value of foods lay not in their tangible qualities, but in their deep, inner essence. Diets were judged not by what could be seen directly, but by what was invisible to the naked eye.[66] This affected dietary authority—a second implication of the shift. Whereas the main principles of classical dietetics were available to everyone, the principles of modern nutritional science narrowed the range of people who could speak with authority about food. Judging diet, in short, became an expert domain.

This second implication changed the nature of critique. Although Rumford had used scientific pretentions to make his system appear superior, the opposite could be claimed by anyone who looked. The contents and qualities of Rumford's recipes were perfectly clear to his opponents, who dismissed his soup as dirt, bones, and bullock's liver—or identified it as mostly water, which of course it was. Criticism of this type was democratically available, but the arrival of nutritional revolution gave scientists much more authority. William Cobbett's pamphlets condemning the "insolent societies of the soup kettle" were joined by critiques concerned with "soup quackery," and the scientists now claimed to see further than political radicals like Cobbett had ever done. Soup and other foods were now judged by something invisible—their biochemical composition—which led to a change in the balance of power.[67]

The third big change was the erasure of social context. In classical dietetics, food was embedded in politics, culture, and society. The food you ate was shaped by your place in the world: your culture, geographical origins, social standing, and demeanor. Steven Shapin has illustrated this with the well-known phrase "you are what you eat," which originated in the words of Brillat-Savarin, the proponent of osmazome. Brillat-Savarin's version of the saying was "tell me what you eat, and I will tell you who you are."[68] This matched a classical view of the world, reflecting the idea that a person's food should match their nature and position. Food, in other words, followed natural laws, and everyone ate the food appropriate to his or her situation and status. The diet and the self blended seamlessly into one another, with the environment shaping the individual and the individual shaping their environment. As Shapin explained, "The nature that you consumed and your nature molded themselves over time to each other's contours."[69] Englishmen of a certain standing, for example, ate beef because it agreed with their natures as well as shaping their natures. The poor, similarly, were destined to eat poor food.[70] In classical terms, "you are what you eat" meant that your diet reflected your personality, your nature, and your place in the world.[71]

After the modern nutritional revolution, however, decisions about food became dictated by rationality, not custom. Calculations became oriented around the *biological* utility of foods. This was a great culinary leveler: foods could now be equated with one another, and tradition was torn away. Some people were shocked to learn that "poor" foods, such as pease pudding, and "rich" foods, such as roast beef, could be nutritionally equivalent. The maxim "you are what you eat," therefore, was turned on its head. It no longer applied in a social context, but a biological context. It no longer indicated that your diet reflected your place in the world; it indicated that *your diet made your body what it is.* The phrase was now forward looking rather than backward looking: the saying emphasized what you might become if only you ate the right foods. The implication was that you should be careful what you eat, because this will have an effect on your body. It was a very different message from the earlier implication, which was, in essence, that your diet should reflect who you were, which could never truly change because you were trapped by your nature and place in the world.

The fourth implication of the nutritional revolution was political, and it proved to be the most profound and long lasting. In classical dietetics, food had been part of a holistic ancient philosophy, in which one's short-term aim was to eat the right kind of food, at the right times, and in the right environment; one's long-term aim, meanwhile, was to live in reflection, moderation, and equilibrium. The basic principle was temperance: "nothing in excess," to use the phrase inscribed on the Delphic oracle.[72] In Foucault's reading of the situation, such "care of the self" was directed at something modest—making life happy within a set of existing limits—and ethics was all about maintaining cosmic balance rather than transforming the world in accordance with expansive human desires.[73]

After the rise of nutritional science, however, this changed profoundly. The classical system of morality and politics was replaced by something new. Food became a way to *improve* humankind. It was no longer about cosmic balance or living in modest equilibrium, it became a tool of progress. By changing what you ate, you could change your constitution, your strength, and the power of your body. You could change the path of nations and cultures. You could allow human beings to gain more strength, live more efficiently, and achieve greater things. This moment was pregnant with modernist possibility, as the diet would no longer be simply a matter of caring for the self; it could be used to transform the world.

GOVERNING THE DIET IN VICTORIAN INSTITUTIONS

The Victorian jail was an ideal place to study the empty stomach. Hunger was widespread, prisons were closed, and surveillance could be taken for granted. Liebig had studied German soldiers because their living environment could be closely monitored—with the exception of the odd trip to the alehouse, the chemist could establish with considerable precision the food that had been eaten in the barracks—but the possibilities were even greater in prisons. Food for prisoners was always consumed at regular times, the same ingredients were provided for months at a time, and there was no possibility of surreptitious consumption. As a result, prisons offered "confined, controlled, almost laboratory-like" conditions for studying human nutrition.[1] Perhaps most important, hard labor meant that scholars could measure the energy expended as well as the nutrients consumed.

Hard labor had, for a long time, meant outdoor work—chain gangs, road building, and rock breaking—but punishment in the Victorian period was retreating behind walls. Prisoners were becoming more isolated from society, incarcerated and invisible, so fulfilling a hard labor sentence involved new systems and devices. The crank wheel was one example. This involved a handle, installed in each cell, which was placed at chest height and attached to a sand-filled drum: a set of paddles moved the sand around the drum and a meter recorded rotations. The treadmill was another example. This was a long cylinder with steps protruding from its circumference, on which prisoners would stand and climb as the drum rotated beneath. Both of these devices allowed a hard labor sentence to be met without leaving the walls of the prison. The treadmill, in particular, proved to be very popular. Designed in 1818 by William Cubitt, this machine, sometimes known as the "everlasting staircase," could accommodate dozens of prisoners side by side, stepping up from one paddle to the next, with thousands of steps required to fulfill the requirements of a sentence.[2]

The treadmill, at first, had a productive purpose—attached to a mill for grinding corn, or a pump to propel water—but as prisons expanded in the 1820s and 1830s it became more difficult to attach the mechanism to rural forms of infrastructure. Prisons were becoming industrialized, filled with ever-larger numbers of people and moved into large urban centers that were a long way from farms and agriculture.[3] The treadmill, therefore, became purely disciplinary. It offered only resistance to the effort of the prisoner, attached to a drum filled with sand or a large sail on the roof of the prison, which rotated and pushed against the breeze. This gave rise to the prisoners' phrase, "grinding the wind," to refer to hard labor.[4] Such pointless tasks were devised to keep prisoners busy with the minimum of organization and the widest possible scale. At Coldbath Prison in London, for example, William Cubitt installed eight treadmills that could occupy 362 men at any one time. Soon, however, the treadmill provided another purpose: as a way to study food and energy.[5]

In 1856, a physiologist named Edward Smith decided to use the treadmill at Coldbath to discover more about nutritional requirements: his aim was to find out exactly how much food prisoners needed. Smith was not the first scholar to pursue these interests. Gradations had been introduced to prison diets back in 1843, structured according to the length of imprisonment and the type of labor. The basic idea was that the food be "sufficient, but no more than sufficient, to maintain health and strength at the least possible cost."[6] More food, in other words, would be provided for prisoners doing harder labor, and better food for longer sentences. In some ways this seemed counterintuitive, because more food was given to people who had committed more serious crimes, but it was considered to be part of a rational penal regime that ensured the authorities could punish people without having to deal with serious health problems on their release. For the first two weeks of a sentence, for example, prisoners were given only bread and gruel because their bodies could take it. For the next six weeks, they received meat and potatoes twice a week, because otherwise they would waste away. After being in prison for more than two months they would receive meat and potatoes four times a week, with better quality soup on the remaining days.[7]

The idea behind this system was deterrence, ensuring that prisoners with shorter sentences would suffer the worst diets, and so would not reoffend. All the same, politicians and the press argued that the scales were too lenient. Carlyle and Dickens, in particular, called for a more severe regime to punish members of the "criminal class," whom they described as "miserable distorted blockheads" with "ape-faces, imp-faces, angry dogfaces, heavy sullen ox-faces."[8] William Guy, the government advisor on health in prisons, believed that diet was already excessive in prisons; as he put it, "The prisoner spends more time in bed than the working man does; he is warmly clad, lives and sleeps in a warm atmosphere, and is protected from the weather." The prison diet, Guy argued as a consequence, should be more punitive, more "unattractive and monotonous."[9] Edward Smith questioned the scales from the other direction. Prison diets, he argued, left inmates physically weak and vulnerable to unemployment on their release. This, he believed, benefited no one: if prisoners did not receive enough nutrition they would be unproductive both inside the institution and after their sentence.[10] The existing scales, he pointed out, were only estimates: they had not been not based on hard science. As a result, Smith set out to examine with ever-greater precision how much food the inmates consumed, and how much they needed to sustain their working bodies.

Like Liebig, Smith began by weighing prisoners before and after exercise, analyzing food and bodily waste, but he soon realized that the treadmill offered fascinating possibilities for the study of energy and nutrition.[11] He developed a new piece of equipment, "a rubber facemask covering nose and mouth," which could be attached to prisoners as they worked on the Coldbath treadmill. This contraption involved "a gasometer attached to the inspiratory part of the mask, a dehumidifier chamber, [and] a carbon dioxide absorption chamber containing caustic potash," enabling Smith to measure exhalation from the lungs as well as excreta from the bladder and bowels.[12] Using this device, Smith went far beyond Liebig, and after he was appointed chief medical inspector to the Poor Law Board in 1865, his study of the diet extended from prisons to workhouses. This was another set of government institutions where food was used for deterrence; indeed, workhouses were run on the principle of "less eligibility"—the idea that living conditions inside the workhouse should be lower than those of the lowest paid worker nearby.[13] The government was explicit about how food could help in this aim: "On no account must the dietary of the workhouse be superior or equal to the ordinary mode of subsistence of the laboring class of the neighborhood," read the foundational legislation.[14] This was initially achieved through appalling levels of neglect, but it later took on a more scientific character with the help of Edward Smith.[15]

Liebig had made the diet measurable; Smith now made it governable. His use of nutritional science was just the start of a late-nineteenth-century drive to "render food into hard figures": to calculate, plan, and govern. The calorie, as a measure of food, soon became central to this change. Popularized by Wilbur Atwater, it reduced food to a single number, a single unit of energy, and it had considerable implications for hunger relief. After the work of Edward Smith in

prisons came the "labor science" of the 1880s, and an extension of dietary measurement to national productivity in general. New concerns with energy and efficiency then seeped into older models of relief, illustrated through a generation of
soup kitchens that updated Rumford's legacy. The high point of this movement
came in the Edwardian period, when a colonial crisis attributed military failure
to the meals of the British working class.

Rendering Food into Figures

Nick Cullather famously argued that "the work of rendering food into hard figures
began just after breakfast on Monday, March 23, 1896, when Wilbur O. Atwater
sealed a graduate student into an airtight chamber in the basement of Judd Hall
on the Wesleyan University campus."[16] This was the day he began his experiments
with the calorimeter: a vast device in which the intake and expenditure of human
energy was measured and linked to the consumption of food. Atwater recruited
student volunteers and enclosed them in a large glass box, instructing them to do
specific tasks at various levels of exertion, such as clerical work, weight lifting, or
riding a stationary bicycle. He measured the subject's meals, which were passed
through an airlock, and made them breathe through a tube. Everything coming
in and out of the chamber was carefully measured, from food to excreta, and the
system was regulated through "a complicated arrangement of pumps, motors,
fans, and freezers."[17] Atwater used the calorimeter to see how many calories his
volunteers were ingesting as well as how much energy they were expending. It
was a far more advanced version of Smith's experiments, taking place over forty
years later. Most important, it made the energy content of food more clearly legible than ever before.

　　Cullather presented Atwater's experiment as the start of a long and deep connection between diet and statecraft, and it is easy to see why. Atwater's experiment was widely publicized, and compared to Edward Smith's study of the Coldbath treadmill, it was more thorough, advanced, and optimistic. Whereas Smith
worked narrowly in disciplinary institutions, Atwater studied individuals from
all walks of life. Whereas Smith conducted studies in the dark and backward
world of Victorian prisons, Atwater conducted his experiments in the bright
light of publicity. Whereas Smith's rubber facemask could only be worn for short
periods, the calorimeter could enclose people for days at a time, fitting furniture
such as beds, tables, and exercise bikes within its walls. It was perhaps no sur-
prise, therefore, when Atwater's "Wesleyan glass cage" appeared across the international media, with many reports written like a Jules Verne novel. His volunteer captives were presented as "prisoners of science," surrounded by a romantic

narrative of sacrifice and human advancement.[18] The possibilities of quantifying human energy, meanwhile, meant that the human body could be presented as an efficient machine working toward national productivity. As a result, Atwater's experiment seemed far more palatable than Smith's studies of real prisoners, those imp faces and miserable blockheads of Britain.

Atwater's fame seems a little out of proportion given than Smith had led the way, but he made a significant contribution to science: the calorie. Although it was not his creation, Atwater popularized this form of measurement, which had an enormous influence in the coming decades. Edward Smith had been considerably disadvantaged by the early language of nutritional science, which used an array of different measures to quantify the carbohydrate, fat, and protein content of foods—as well as a variety of different methods to quantify respiration, excretion, and consumption. The calorie, in contrast, was powerfully simple. It reduced food to a single number: to use the terms of Gyorgy Scrinis, it served as a "master nutrient," or "meta-nutrient," a single, standardized unit according to which all foods could be measured and compared.[19]

Although the word *calorie* had first appeared in an English textbook back in 1863, it was not until 1887, when Atwater began to publish a series of popular articles in the American press, that this term fully took root in the English-speaking world.[20] The calorie was significant because it linked food and labor directly. It compared the energy contained in food with the energy that was spent in human effort. Early experiments in Germany had produced charts of calorific requirements organized by profession and nationality, which meant that national authorities were soon able to compare the inputs and outputs of whole populations.[21] The calorie allowed governments to plan food production, compare the efficiency of different industries, and make detailed plans. The power of the new science was revealed with quite startling clarity once the calorie came onto the scene, since it allowed not just a calculation of efficiency, but also a comparison of national needs. By the time the "Wesleyan glass cage" was up and running in America, therefore, German scholars had already developed the tools that allowed all the complexities of food to be boiled down to their energy efficiency. The primary role of foodstuffs was to supply energy, and complex dietary needs of the population had been reduced to an aggregate energy input.

Anton Rabinbach has shown how this work was underpinned by a central, recurring metaphor: the idea of the human motor.[22] The human motor suggested that bodies were like working machines, turning energy into labor. The metaphor was crucial to everything from science to politics, saturating ideologies as diverse as Marxism and Liberalism. It was bolstered everywhere by the science of nutrition. The calorie converted food into energy, which could then be seen just like any other fuel: something that powered productive purposes. Just as

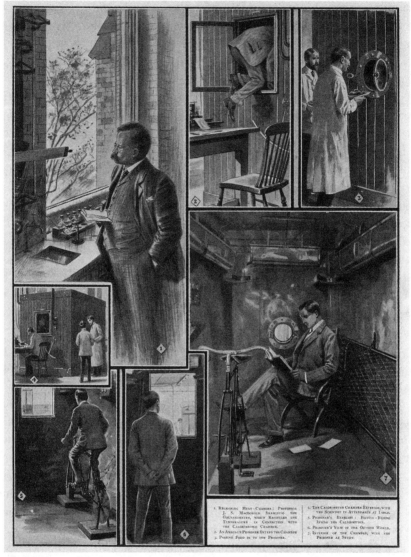

FIGURE 5. Inside a calorimeter. Samuel Begg, "Man as Machine: Registering the Heat-Energy of the Body," *Illustrated London News*, July 4, 1908, 13. © Illustrated London News Ltd/Mary Evans.

steam engines were powered by coal, and cars were powered by petrol, the human motor could be powered by food. The ultimate aim was to boost efficiency and improve the human body, just as the steam engine had been gradually refined and perfected. Many scholars in this era were excited by the possibility of a "vaccination" against fatigue, a magic bullet that would allow people to work longer hours without rest.[23] The utopia of superproductivity never arrived, but the idea of a human motor had a more prosaic and practical effect: pushing workers to eat the cheapest sources of energy that could power their bodily machines.

Taylorism, an industrial movement launched by Frederick Winslow Taylor to help managers examine and improve efficiency, underpinned a lot of this thinking. It advocated "time and motion" studies, which broke down the tasks of manual workers into their smallest possible components.[24] It treated workers as machines that could be adjusted and refined, identifying inefficiencies in every factory procedure while drawing on the new dietary science. The calorie, for example, helped factory managers look in even more detail at the inputs and outputs of production: if the energy value of workers' food was seen as part of the costs of production, then this could be factored into the precise price of inputs. Wages, meanwhile, could be set at a rate that maximized profits and were justified by the energy put in; employees were then offered just enough money for sustenance.

The Science of Labor

Atwater had already created a close relationship between nutrition and industry through a subject known as "the science of labor," which had particular influence in America after the great railroad strike of 1877. Its central idea was to appease workers and maintain profits without generating unrest, taking a less brutal line than Taylorism.[25] Adherents of the science of labor saw this approach as fundamentally conciliatory: the 1870s and 1880s had been marked by extensive industrial action in America, and the aim of the "labor scientists" was to place wages on a more rational footing. Believing that wages could be set objectively, they argued that rates of pay could be discovered by scientists just like any other fact. There was no reason, they argued, for class antagonism. Instead of determining wages through strikes and negotiation, the labor scientists argued that their neutral and dispassionate expertise could work out exactly how much workers should be paid.

The labor scientists achieved this by measuring the energy involved in different tasks and studying the supply and demand for various skills. Knowledge of nutrition played its part by collecting data on the cost of living. The key, Wilbur Atwater believed, was to gather information about nutritional requirements and to teach workers to eat more cheaply.[26] This required a great deal of data. Contraptions like the calorimeter were good for understanding how much energy was used in different forms of labor, but they did not provide information about food habits or the cost of commodities. Dietary surveys were therefore devised to supplement existing laboratory studies: rather than determining what people theoretically required, these measured what people actually consumed. Whereas laboratory studies explored the energy content of foods, dietary surveys examined what people actually ate.

The aim of dietary surveys was to count and weigh the food purchased in households, quantifying what was eaten and thrown out. Such surveys required a great deal of cooperation from participants, which was not always easy due to the (justified) suspicion that surveys might be used as grounds for reducing wages. As Neswald and Smith explain, "To conduct a survey, an investigator had to establish contact with and gain the trust of a family"; they then needed to "enlist cooperation for weeks or even months and make sensible enquiries into income, purchasing habits, and the contents of pantries and waste buckets." The extent of this interference was remarkable: "Surveyors took inventory of stocks, weighed all purchased food, tracked expenditures, [and] deducted food waste."[27] This was repeated regularly until the end of the study, when another full inventory was taken.

Atwater combined such data with his knowledge of energy values and, along with others involved in the new "labor science," he began to present his findings in the popular press. In a series of articles that appeared in *The Century* magazine, for example, Atwater concluded that hunger and poverty were caused not by low wages but by poor dietary choices, suggesting that "ignorant buying," "bad cooking" and "waste" were the central issues.[28] According to Atwater, the lessons of nutritional science were clear: adequate nutrition could be cheap, but it required that the working class ate beans, grain, and tougher cuts of meat. In other words, by eating cheaply they could effectively increase their wages, leaving more money for heating, clothing, and other necessities. Resistance to Atwater's dietary advice was often attributed to irrationality, ignorance, bloody-mindedness, or some other failing of character. If workers insisted on eating meat rather than legumes, he suggested, this was a result of their "pride." If they insisted on eating fruits and vegetables, this was a mere "conceit."[29] The working classes did not need fripperies and luxury foods, Atwater believed, which were just evidence of their misplaced aspirations. Poorer communities, Atwater concluded, were "beset with false pride and the petty ambition to go ahead of their neighbors"—and *this* should be the target of reform, not the wage rate or structure of capitalism.[30]

Like Don Quixote tilting at windmills, Atwater argued that strikes would achieve nothing: if workers stopped laboring in the hope for higher pay, he surmised, factory managers would simply find a cheaper way to power the task at hand. He described a strike in the late 1880s when a foreman simply sacked his workers because he could purchase a steam engine to replace them. "The work which had been done through the consumption of meat and potatoes," he explained, "was accomplished by the combustion of coal" instead.[31] Eating cheaply and accepting lower wages, therefore, seemed to be the only way for workers to keep their jobs. This, in turn, meant energy-dense foods with no vegetables, no color, and no texture. As late as 1915 scientists were claiming that "a can of tomatoes is little else than flavored water." Just as "a painter wishing to sell a landscape puts a figure with a red cloak in the center . . . in like manner, a restaurant puts a few lettuce leaves on a plate with a red tomato in the middle." The conclusion was inescapable: vegetables were merely adornments for the rich, "the work of an artist for a connoisseur."[32] The discovery of vitamins later complicated this argument, but the central idea of the human motor had become unshakable.

This idea remained influential right through to the Second World War, when prominent humanitarian handbooks were still declaring that "the human body is a working machine." As one put it, "you can no more get work out of the human machine if you have not provided the necessary food than you can run an engine without petrol and fuel oil."[33] Many politicians, in the interim, had fought against this view of food, but it proved surprisingly durable. Atwater had described his work in terms of a negotiation between "a Scylla of labor agitation and a Charybdis of physiological considerations," while swatting away a generation of left wing activism. Karl Marx had channeled the spirit of William Cobbett when deriding Rumford's soup as "pretty pigswill."[34] Rosa Luxemburg later took up the charge, condemning industrial canteens as part of the "crusade by capital against any trace of luxury, comfort and convenience in the life of the worker."[35] Nutritional advice from elites was an easy target for radicals and socialists because good quality food was a source of great comfort. Americans, in particular, had begun to see good food as part of the national dream, and, as Levenstein put it, "Eating better food, usually more meat and particularly more beefsteak, was one of the major rewards of hard work and a respectable job."[36]

Nutritionists, however, kept on presenting vegetables as artistic additions and steaks as a matter of pride. This exhibited not just a scientific mistake but a cultural one as well. Food, after all, was not reducible to fuel in the eyes of most people. It remained a marker of social distinction, a source of familial harmony, and an aesthetic joy to be celebrated.

Rumford Returns

In January 1890 a new soup kitchen opened in central Boston. It was a hundred years since Rumford had opened his classical version in Munich, and there had been some radical changes in ideas of food and hunger in the intervening years. Yet most philanthropists were still using the same basic tools to tackle starvation: huge saucepans, hot broth, and hunks of bread. There were good reasons for this. Relief was driven by practical concerns, and soup was a highly convenient form of food. All you really needed were a few basic ingredients and a source of heat. The resulting soup had the advantage of being quick to divide, easy to distribute, and could be made in large quantities from any ingredients available. The basic form of the soup kitchen, therefore, stood relatively unchanged after a century of scientific change. By the end of the nineteenth century, such institutions remained widespread.

This particular Bostonian soup kitchen, however, had a rather different character, bringing the teachings of Count Rumford together with the research of Wilbur Atwater. It was an intellectual alliance that had been catalyzed by a woman called Ellen Swallow Richards: a chemist, founder of home economics, and the first female professor at MIT.[37] Richards knew Atwater well, and was a fan of the Bavarian count. Like Rumford, she had been born in Massachusetts, and her praise for the count extended to his forcing of Bavarian beggars into work: "At that time," she explained, beggars were "an intolerable nuisance."[38] On the face of it, Richards's soup kitchen was like many others, serving basic broth and bread, but behind the scenes it was more modern and ambitious. Richards conceived of her new institution not just as a kitchen, but as an "experiment station" for food.[39] Her aim was to see it as a "laboratory," which tested new menus and tried them out on working-class families. Indeed, Richards had wanted to call her institution the "Rumford Food Laboratory," a name that captured both her inspiration and the scientific pretensions, but her colleagues convinced her that this would "puzzle and repel" the people she was trying to help.[40] It opened, therefore, with the rather more prosaic name of the New England Soup Kitchen.

The New England Soup Kitchen was created in an old wooden house on the corner of a downtown Boston street, and in addition to serving experimental soups, it also had a longer-term educational aim. Richards wanted to use the most recent scientific discoveries to teach the poor how to cook the most calorific food at the lowest possible price, and as a result she publicized cheap, energy-dense recipes. Many of the dishes served at the New England Soup Kitchen were completely devoid of color, made from cheap cuts of meat dunked in condensed milk and white flour, packed with energy but little joy. This theme continued in her system of distribution. The kitchen had only a takeaway counter, so that people would bring in their quart jars or pails to be filled, receiving pamphlets and other propaganda alongside the food they took away.[41] Leaflets contained the kitchen's recipes, accompanied by the latest nutritional advice and instructions explaining how to replicate economical menus in the home.

The educational aims of this institution extended to technology as well. Indeed, one of the kitchen's financial backers, an industrialist called Edward Atkinson, used the kitchen to promote a device called the "Aladdin Oven": a small, dark cave of a cooker, powered by a kerosene lamp, which could make cheap and bony cuts of meat far more digestible. According to one source, the Aladdin Oven "took five hours to reach boiling point" and could conjure up food with very little effort—hence the mystical name.[42] Atkinson had invented this contraption to wean his factory workers off expensive steaks, those dangerous sources of "pride" and "conceit," but "it had an alarming tendency, if left unattended, to burn through the table on which it stood."[43] Atkinson believed passionately in labor science and was undaunted by its drawbacks: he saw his oven as a material manifestation of that wonderful drive for efficiency. He loved the "natural workings" of the market, and when faced with labor agitation in his factories, he had refused to raise wages, responding instead by lecturing his workers on food preparation and inventing this bizarre wooden box filled with asbestos and kerosene.[44]

In many ways the Aladdin Oven was a natural extension of Rumford's gleaming soup digesters: an efficient machine to feed the masses by converting cheap parts of cattle into a nourishing broth. Unlike Rumford's contraption, however, this was designed for individual use, making it more suitable for the modern age. Its core purpose was as a time-saving device: laborers could put some cheap cuts of meat in the oven first thing in the morning, leave it there as they went to work, and have a meal ready at the end of the day—if their house had not burned down in the meantime. Ellen Richards installed the oven in her New England Kitchen as part of her educational demonstrations, but it was not very good for cooking at scale. Like the New England Kitchen in general, it was far more successful for propaganda than it was for the production of decent meals.

By 1893, the New England Kitchen had come to the attention of the Massachusetts delegation to the latest world fair in Chicago. This large-scale, glittering event, known as the World's Columbian Exposition, was being held to commemorate four hundred years since Columbus's arrival in the New World. Like many other world fairs of the period, it was designed as an optimistic symbol of modernity and industrial might, so was an ideal opportunity for Richards to popularize her kitchen and the new domestic science. After being asked to establish a version of her New England Kitchen for the Massachusetts pavilion she built a replica of white clapboard house and was finally able to use the name of her inspiration, Count Rumford. As Richards explained in one of her pamphlets, the aim of the "Rumford Kitchen" exhibit was twofold. "First, to commemorate the services to the cause of domestic science rendered by Count Rumford 100 years ago"; and "second, to serve as an incentive to further work in the same direction."[45]

The exhibit at the world fair was a clear manifestation of Richards's vision: it contained an Aladdin Oven, a few tables serving cheap lunches, and walls adorned with menus, charts, diagrams, and a series of inspirational mottos. These included "The Fate of Nations Depends on How They Are Fed"; "Wherefore Do You Spend Money for That Which Is Not Bread?"; and "A Man Too Busy to Take Care of His Health Is Like a Mechanic Too Busy to Take Care of His Tools."[46] It was clear that the driving force behind this institution was the metaphor of the human motor: consumers were mechanics caring for their bodily engines, buying food parsimoniously with a view to energy and efficiency, which would contribute to improving the nation as a whole. Staff at the world fair distributed tens of thousands of leaflets to spread the "genius" of Count Rumford.[47] "The Rumford Kitchen has chosen wisely its Patron Saint," declared one of the pamphlets, adding that his writings "are as practical and appropriate as if they had been written today instead of a century ago."[48]

Perhaps predictably, this lionization of Rumford did not go down very well with representatives of the labor movement. Eugene Debs, a socialist organizer at the time, mocked the whole idea, directing his ire especially at the Aladdin Oven, and accusing Atkinson of the age-old do-gooding sin of boiling bones into terrible soup. Calling him "Shinbone Atkinson," Debs pointed out that Atkinson had failed to grasp the most crucial purpose of a stove in the working-class home: providing heat. Stoves did more than just cook food, Debs pointed out; they served as a hearth, a centerpiece for social life, a method for heating the house. The Aladdin Oven did none of those things. The communal humiliation of Rumford's soup kitchens, as a result, was simply being replaced by a more individual humiliation. The Aladdin Oven denied its owners warmth while dispersing portions of bony stew. It was a criticism that nicely anticipated the way relief was heading: the problem, for Debs, was not just that the system was measly, but that it affected the strength of American workers. "[All] you have succeeded in demonstrating," Debs wrote to Atkinson, is "that an American laborer, by scientific methods, can feed himself at a cost as low as Chinamen."[49] Amid fears that Asian workers could underbid all white labor by subsisting on cheap rice, Debs was beginning to position food and nutrition not just as a family matter, but as a communal matter as well.[50]

Governing the Diet

On February 1, 1978, Foucault gave a lecture at the Collège de France with title "Governmentality": a semantic linking of governing (*gouverner*) with modes of thought (*mentalité*). It concerned the way that Western states changed profoundly in the nineteenth century, acting less in a simply coercive manner and more through a range of new techniques that counted, nurtured, and developed the population. The argument, very simply, was as follows. Government had previously been exercised on territory, but now it focused on the population. Government had previously been about controlling land, but it was now about controlling people. Government had previously aimed at extending the reach of the principality, but it now focused on extending the health and productivity of the population. This meant a shift in the nature of political power, which had previously been repressive and negative, but was now more productive and positive.

In his lectures around this time Foucault repeatedly emphasized how premodern state authority had been concentrated on spectacular acts of death, torture, and destruction. Power, in other words, had been about letting live or making die. In the modern era, however, power became focused on the opposite: not on death but on life itself, not destroying but nurturing the population. He called this biopower, and it is an important part of humanitarian nutrition. What we see in the hands of Edward Smith, Wilbur Atwater, and Ellen Richards is a process through which the management of food became part of government calculations. Liebig had made food measurable, Edward Smith made it governable, and from the 1850s a new range of strategies, technologies, and systems put these ideas into practice.

As Bryan Turner has pointed out, the diet began to enter governmental calculations when it "became important in the economic management of prisons." It later spread more widely in the "political management of society," and was then used to develop an "effective, healthy working class, supported on a minimum but adequate calorie intake."[51] Edward Smith had worked in a context where diet was designed to be minimalist and punitive, using food in a largely negative way to enforce discipline in institutions; Wilbur Atwater later developed a more expansive vision of diets, which could be used to increase productivity and maximize profits. Later still, the management of diet was used to improve communal strength, and the walls of Rumford Kitchen were adorned with the prescient words: "The Fate of Nations Depends on How They Are Fed." This was an idea that would become even more important in the years to come.

Foucault's lecture was never elaborated into a book, but it was quickly singled out for publication in English, appearing in the journal *Ideology and Conscious-*

ness in 1979 and later republished in *The Foucault Effect*.[52] It generated a whole body of mostly Anglo-Saxon scholarship on the nature of modern governance and became a significant subliterature in its own right. The central message seemed to be that we are being governed more and more, but this missed an important nuance: that the concept had been designed to explain a specific historical transition. Like many of Foucault's theories, it was a way to understand the changing role of the nineteenth-century state, not an attempt to produce a universal theory of politics.[53] Governmentality was about a particular expansion of state power, not a model for analyzing the state in all times and places.

Part of the problem was the word itself: the "governmentality" literature was hampered by a dreadful neologism, which was not just "ugly," as Foucault himself acknowledged in the lecture, but horrifically unwieldy and imprecise.[54] Foucault had given the term three different meanings in his lecture, defining governmentality as a set of techniques, a distinctive historical process, and a rationality of rule.[55] This was unclear enough, but when other scholars got their teeth into the notion, meanings and connotations proliferated. Some authors tried to transform governmentality into a coherent methodology, but this often missed what was most valuable about Foucault's original essay, which was an invitation to shift our focus.[56] Rather than focusing on the "structure and function of the state," Foucault was inviting us to examine the *practice* of governing. Rather than examining who holds the power, the idea was to explore *how* government works.[57] It was not, as Clifford Geertz memorably put it, an example of "Whig history in reverse," but a way to show how modern government was complex and multifaceted.[58]

The incorporation of the diet into governmental calculations was part of this growing complexity in statecraft. It continued until the end of the nineteenth century, as nutritional science became increasingly concerned with national and racial strength. There was a particular interest in this topic within Britain, which suddenly faced a seeming crisis in its productivity and power after the incredible growth of its empire in the second half of the nineteenth century. In particular, Britain faced a real blow to imperial prestige in the Boer War of 1899–1902, which demanded some kind of explanation. Within a few months of the war's beginning Boer forces had besieged the vital garrison towns of Ladysmith and Mafeking, leaving Britain with an expensive and lengthy conflict that dragged on for three years. It was only after the deployment of nearly half a million troops and expenditure of over £222 million that the British Army finally prevailed against a small force of only 35,000 Boers. By the end of the war a widespread sense of shame and disbelief had settled over the nation.[59] How could this possibly have happened? The answer, it seemed, lay in the health and strength of the British fighters. This, in turn, was attributable to their diet.

In January 1902, Major-General Sir John Frederick Maurice wrote a widely circulated article entitled "Where to Get Men."[60] This confirmed the worst fears of many commentators, revealing that nearly three-quarters of the men offering themselves up for service were too weak to fight. The army recruitment inspector confirmed this a year later, reporting that the physical strength of new recruits had been in decline for some years, and an "Interdepartmental Committee on Physical Deterioration" soon followed. The recruitment crisis gradually morphed into a wider domestic crisis.[61] The poor health of army recruits became nothing less than a "national danger," and their weakness seemed powerfully illustrated by those defeats against the hardy frontiersmen of South Africa.[62] Rudyard Kipling later captured this contrast in a series of mediocre verses, warning a new generation of youngsters that Britannia might fall because of the slum-reared men that were too feeble to defend it.

Nations have passed away and left no traces
And History gives the naked cause of it
One single, simple reason in all cases
They fell because their peoples were not fit.[63]

In the subsequent debate, diet became an important theme, and when the committee on "physical deterioration" finally published its report, it concluded that British soldiers were unfit because they ate such bad food.[64] Many workers were living on a diet of tea, bread, and margarine with little variation, which had produced a group of people with no strength or resilience to disease. Working-class diets had already been the topic of much hand wringing over the years, but the physical deterioration report demanded more concerted government action. Regular medical inspections were established in British schools, home economics was introduced into the girls curriculum to improve knowledge of nutrition, and physical exercise was introduced for young boys, with regular military-style drills. Perhaps the most significant change was the introduction of free school meals, which was passed into law with the Education (Provision of Meals) Act of 1906.[65]

The result of this crisis was an ever-greater interest by the British state in the diets of ordinary people, with government taking a more active role in nurturing the fragile bodies of the British working class. With pervasive militarism hanging heavily in the air, new nutritional policies were devised to improve the "national stock," to enhance the strength and vitality of the nation. British workers were fearfully compared with the German population, mighty beasts fed on sausages and sauerkraut, and such thinking became increasingly important as the First World War approached.[66] Military rations were examined according to their nutritional value, their longevity, the energy they could provide.[67] The size and strength of the working classes were studied to predict victory in future conflicts. There were echoes of the human motor, but the emphasis was subtly changing. This was not just about one body, or one factory, or one meal. It was a crisis of "national efficiency." Nutritional science was no longer simply about improving certain people. It was now about improving the fate of whole nations.

The approach would soon have a new name: dietary determinism.

COLONIALISM AND COMMUNAL STRENGTH

In 1906, David McCay began a series of investigations into the physique of Bengalis in Calcutta. He was interested in why there was a "lack of energy and vigour" in the Bengali race, why Bengalis were so weak and feeble. It was a common view at the time, and McCay merely had to cite a few anecdotes in support of his theory, which he said could "speak for themselves." "The ordinary shovel or spade used by the European workman," he claimed, "requires two Bengalis to work it: one makes use of it in the same manner as the European, the other by means of a rope tied above the iron part to assist in lifting." "Five or six times as many hands are needed in Indian spinning mills," he went on, "and three times as many in weaving sheds to produce the same result as in England." Higher wages in England, McCay claimed, simply reflected this difference in productivity, and McCay even used data on insurance premiums to prove his point. He concluded that even "from an insurance point of view, the life of the Bengali is very inferior to the European." This all seemed to prove his central point: that Bengalis were weaker, sicker, and less productive than Europeans.[1]

McCay was professor of physiology at Calcutta's Medical School at the time, and he soon formulated a hypothesis to explain these perceived differences in race and physical strength. His idea was that Bengali weakness was down to the diet, and he devised a series of experiments to test this notion. Drawing on data from two Calcutta colleges, one with a population of Bengali students and the other made up of Eurasian and Anglo-Indians, he compared the height, weight, and chest circumference of pupils. His study revealed that the Bengali students had very different physical characteristics, and McCay concluded that "the influence of diet is abundantly obvious." As he put it, "The two classes enter college about the same age, live in the same climate and under very similar conditions, but the results at the end of their college career are very different. The Anglo-Indian and Eurasian boys develop into strong, healthy men . . . while the Bengali students almost remain stationary as regards development." He added that this was evident in sporting performance: the Eurasian College cricket team, unlike the Bengali one, could "more than hold their own against the various [adult] clubs in Calcutta."[2]

McCay became preoccupied with this topic over the next few years, beginning new experiments on diet and strength, and he soon turned his attention to jails rather than schools, echoing the work of Edward Smith from half a century earlier.[3] This time he compared Bengali prisoners with other Indians further north—the Sikh and Pathan "races" that were known for their "manly physique and fighting spirit"—and once again McCay came to a bold and striking conclusion. "As we pass from the North-West region of the Punjab down the Gangetic plain to the coast of Bengal," he wrote, "there is a fall in stature, bodyweight, stamina and efficiency of the people." The races of northwest India "are on a distinctly higher plane of physical development," he claimed. "Their general muscularity of the body is decidedly better, their capabilities of labour are greater. They are smarter on their feet, more brisk and more alive to the incidents of every-day life, and they do not present such slackness and tonelessness as one is accustomed to observe in the people of Lower Bengal."[4]

According to McCay, the reason for this was again down to the diet. In the north of India people ate wheat chapatti, meat, and dairy products; in the south of India they mainly ate rice, which was considered by colonial administrators to be a particularly poor staple, responsible for many physical and moral shortcomings.[5] McCay presented his readers with a litany of complaints about the rice-eating Bengalis, including "want of vigour, tonelessness, general slowness of reaction . . . self-absorption, introspection . . . little power of attention, observation, or concentration of thought."[6] This was not an unusual perspective: Rice diets had long been considered a problem by colonial authorities, causing not just beriberi (a Vitamin A or thiamine deficiency) but perceived to cause weakness in general. Indeed, McCay was building on the much earlier work of physician Norman Chevers, who believed that the only way to rescue Bengalis from their "physical incapacity" was to make them take up a "higher" food staple.[7]

McCay and Chevers were promoting a somewhat optimistic view of development, as their notion was that this "physical incapacity" could be transformed by improving the diet. Weakness was not "*inherent* in the Bengali as a race," they stressed; it was a result of the diet, which could be changed.[8] As McCay put it, the diet could have dramatic effects on both physique and overall character, flowing from the "close relationship between the physical and moral development of men."[9] The implications of this idea were far-reaching, because there had been a long-standing belief amongst colonialists in India that some tribes were "more manly" and "warlike" than others.[10] This was known as the "martial races theory," and it went back to the British attempt to build an Indian Army after the 1857 rebellion. A series of anecdotal observations had gradually accumulated and become an accepted truth: that some "races and tribes" were better at fighting than others. The belief became entrenched through texts such as Bonarjee's *Handbook of the Fighting Races of India* and MacMunn's *Martial Races of India*, before gradually feeding into a wider strategy of governance.[11] Various "tribes" and "races" were soon governed in different ways, given different tasks by their British rulers, and even approached differently depending on their "essential attributes." Certain people were natural fighters, it was thought; others were natural agriculturalists. McCay's work was part of this context, as he argued that there would be greater military power and faster economic development if imperial governance could be informed by dietary science. By drawing soldiers and workers from groups with a "low standard of physical development," he warned, the British Empire was "apt to get recruits [that are] not only small but [also] unsteady, wanting in mental ballast as well as in physical strength."[12] Improving the diet of all races, however, could ensure that "lesser races" became as reliable as the stronger ones, improving the whole empire in the process.

McCay's research is a good example of the way that nutritional science moved out of Europe and into the colonial world in the first three decades of the twentieth century. Soon it was not just the strength of individual Western workers that became a governmental concern, but the strength of whole communities instead. The colonial world in this period was often treated as a vast nutritional laboratory, with scholars in the British Empire looking at the diverse people they governed and testing their different theories.[13] In this chapter I examine how David McCay along with Robert McCarrison, John Gilks, and John Boyd Orr examined diet and human difference in Africa as well as India, reflecting wider debates around racism and eugenics. Nutritional science was heading in an expansive new direction, and food was no longer just an input to the working body or a way to manage closed institutions; it was increasingly seen as responsible for the fate of whole communities, even the fate of the whole world.

Dietary Determinism in India

Diet was only one part of the "martial races" theory. When trying to explain what generated physical differences in human groups, colonial scientists also looked at the environment, genetics, and everything in between. Some suggested that cooler climates produced better soldiers than hot, steamy ones. Some argued that Aryan people were racially superior and had a better physique those of non-Aryan stock. Other explanations focused on a variety of seemingly spiritual themes, such as "early marriages, actinic rays of the sun, [and] sexual excesses."[14] Some focused on more concrete historical conditions, such as the idea that Bengalis had grown "soft" from long years of British rule while Punjabis had retained their "fighting spirit."[15] David McCay, however, rejected all these ideas. His contribution was to focus on the explanatory power of food, a view known as dietary determinism. This came in stronger and weaker forms: its weaker form suggested that the diet simply had an effect on the physique, but its stronger form suggested that diet also affected morals, mental ability, and "the position of a tribe or race in the scale of mankind."[16] In all forms, however, dietary determinism suggested that diet was the overriding factor that shaped health and human form.

A decade or so after David McCay published his research on this topic, another officer in the Indian Medical Service, Robert McCarrison, took up the idea of dietary determinism.[17] McCarrison had a similar background to McCay and took a similar approach to nutritional research in the colonial world, considering India to be the perfect place to study the effect of different diets. "Nowhere in the world is the profound effect of food on physical efficiency more strikingly exemplified than in India," he claimed; a country that "has some 350 million inhabitants made up of many races presenting great diversity in their characteristics, manner of life, customs, religion, food and food-habits." McCarrison went on to claim that "the tribes of the Indian Frontier, and of Himalayan regions, the Peoples of the Plains—Sikhs, Rajputs, Mahrattas, Bengalis, Ooriyas, Madrassis, Kanarese and many others—exhibit, in general, the greatest diversity of physique." As he put it, "each race is wedded to its own manner of living, to its own national diet," so "comparison between them is easy."[18]

In 1919, McCarrison began work at the Pasteur Institute in Coonoor and led the nutrition research unit for sixteen years. Rather than studying the Sikhs, Rajputs, Mahrattas, Bengalis, Ooriyas, and Madrassis directly, however, he retreated into the laboratory and experimented on rats. As his successor in Coonoor put it, much of his research was "simple in conception": rats were fed on "good" and "bad" diets, based on staple foods eaten by different groups in India. After being killed, these rats were weighed, measured, and photographed to show changes in the physique. Their "good" diets were replicas of the wheat and meat eaten by the martial races in the north; their "bad" diets were replicas of the rice diets consumed in the South and East. McCarrison's conclusions were powerfully reported in photographs of deteriorating vermin, illustrating how "on the good diets they thrived; on the bad, they failed to grow."[19] This directly echoed the work of McCay. McCarrison similarly concluded that "the level of physical efficiency of Indian races is, above all else, a matter of food. No other single factor—race, climate, endemic disease, etc.—has so profound an influence on their physique, and on their capacity to sustain arduous labour and prolonged muscular exertion."[20]

In many ways, McCarrison was simply supplementing McCay's work through laboratory study, but his conclusions went much further, as many practical implications flowed from the idea of dietary determinism. Perhaps the most significant was the idea that everyone should emulate the food of stronger human groups. McCay had believed that Bengalis could take a "great step forward" and become a "more virile and energetic people" if only they would change their diet.[21] McCarrison, however, was more explicit about who Bengalis—and everyone else—should emulate. He romanticized hill tribes in India, and reported on a lengthy visit to the Hunza Valley, whose inhabitants he described as "a race, unsurpassed in perfection of physique and in freedom from disease," whose diet consisted of "grains, vegetables and fruits, with a certain amount of milk and butter, and goat's meat on feast days." They enjoyed an "abundant crop of apricots," which they "dry in the sun and use very largely in their food"; their "span of life is extraordinarily long," he wrote, and they have hardly any call for medical care. "When the severe nature of the winter in that part of the Himalayas is considered," McCarrison concluded, "it becomes obvious that the enforced restriction to the unsophisticated foodstuffs of nature is compatible with long life, continued vigour, and perfect physique."[22]

In promoting the lifestyle of isolated societies, McCarrison was adding something new to the doctrine of dietary determinism: a romantic longing for some earthly paradise, sequestered from the outside world, uncorrupted by industrial civilization. There were many cultural resonances here, particularly of James Hilton's fictional account of Shangri-La and Guy Wrench's laudatory account of Himalayan health, which were both published around this time.[23] McCarrison's romanticism, therefore, demonstrated a rather different side to nutritional science: one that, after examining the iron engines and machinelike bodies of industrial workers in the metaphor of the human motor, had now taken a turn to examine the simple lives and unsophisticated foodstuffs of a premodern idyll. The implication was that Western diets were as inferior as Bengali ones; that the colonial center had become corrupted by modernity. Indeed, McCarrison was one of many nutritionists in this period who started to write about dietary decline in the West, comparing Hunza goats and grain with the processed foods and white bread of industrialized societies and condemning adulterated diets that, for some years, had been creating scandal after scandal at home.[24]

To illustrate the inferiority of industrialized Western diets, McCarrison took to splitting his rats into two groups, with "one group fed on a diet similar to that

DIET AND PHYSIQUE OF INDIAN RACES.

Hunza Hillman: Diet: whole cereal grains (mainly wheat), milk, vegetables and abundant fruits – apricots, etc; meat occasionally.

Average representatives showing weight in grams of 7 groups of rats fed from the same early age on certain national diets of India. The best of these diets (Sikh) was composed of whole wheat, butter, milk legumes, vegetables with meat occasionally. The worst (Bengalis and Madrassis) is one composed mainly of rice.

Tibetan Hillman : representative of dandy carriers, rickshaw-men, etc. Very hard worked. Average protein intake 175 grams daily, of which over 60% is derived from animal sources. The heat value of their diet may be as much as 6,000 calories daily (McCay).

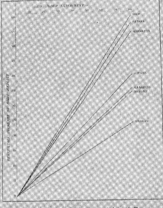

East coast cultivator: Diet: rice with dhal and vegetables and a small amount of fish, milk, and butter. Protein from 50 to 70 grams daily; calories 2,400 to 2,750 (McCay).

Percentage increase in body-weight of 7 groups of young rats, of the same initial aggregate weight fed on certain national diets of India. (vide photograph above).

Nepalese Hillman (Goorkha). Protein 120 to 130 grams, of which less than one third is derived from animal sources. Calories 3,000 to 3,200. Such people eat largely of the better class cereals – wheat, maize and good millets (McCay).

Bengali: Diet: rice, dhal, vegetables, oil with a little fish and perhaps a little milk. Protein, 50 grams daily; Calories 2,300 to 2,500 (McCay)

Mahratta

Sikh (McCay)

Pathan

Typical of rice-eating Madrassi. Diet contains little or no animal protein. Calories low. (McCay)

FIGURE 6. Diet and physique of Indian races. Robert McCarrison. *Nutrition and National Health* (London: Faber and Faber Limited, 1936), 18. Reproduced with the permission of the Bodleian Libraries, University of Oxford. Shelfmark 193522 e.20.

used by the Sikhs; the other on a diet such as is commonly used by the poorer classes in England." The foods eaten by the "Sikh" rats included milk, butter, meat, and wheat chapatti; the foods eaten by the "poor English" rats, meanwhile, consisted of white bread, margarine, boiled cabbage, tinned meat, and "over-sweetened tea with a little milk." McCarrison then presented photographs of the rats after eating these diets, and as he explained in the accompanying text, his "Sikh" rats "lived happily together" but the "English" vermin behaved very badly. "[They] did not increase in weight; their growth was stunted; they were badly proportioned; their coats were staring and lacking in gloss; they were nervous and apt to bite the attendants . . . and by the sixtieth day of the experiment they began to kill and eat the weaker ones amongst them."[25]

It is hard to find a more vivid description of dietary determinism than the work of Robert McCarrison, who encouraged his audience to read the fate of whole societies in the fate of his laboratory rats. The happy and stable traditional society of the Sikhs was contrasted with the tense maelstrom of hyper-competitive modernity amongst the industrial working class; diet was central to communal success, and it needed to be improved and controlled. It is also hard to imagine a better illustration of how, despite McCarrison's romanticism of the Hunza, dietary determinism could become a great leveler. It judged all diets with the same dispassionate eye, and it was revolutionary in moving away from the idea that India and Africa were dark, untamed, and fundamentally different places. This had been at the heart of medical thinking for years, and was the pervasive idea behind tropical medicine: the notion that colonies were savage, exotic environments, fundamentally different to our own.[26] McCarrison and his confreres developed a more universal and even egalitarian approach. They had backgrounds in physiology and nutrition rather than tropical medicine, and had been brought up with the notion that all bodies reacted the same way to environmental circumstances. The dietary determinists, therefore, applied the same standards to British and Bengali foods, to British and Bengali bodies. They judged them by the same physiological criteria, and found both of them wanting.

Dietary Determinism in Kenya

The tenets of dietary determinism soon found their way to Kenya, appearing in another study led by two very different men, John Gilks and John Boyd Orr. Their divergent backgrounds illustrated the intellectual origins of this new approach, as well as showing how nutrition was beginning to unite people across vast ideological divides. John Boyd Orr was a measured and reserved man who had been born in Scotland to a modest Presbyterian family. Highly educated, he possessed degrees in medicine, biological science, and had trained as both a teacher and a doctor in the Glaswegian slums. Orr had witnessed widespread poverty and malnutrition during this period, giving him a deep-seated and acute sense of injustice; later in life, he would become the first director of the Food and Agricultural Organization and would retire as a member of the liberal establishment, with a knighthood, peerage, and the Nobel peace prize.[27] John Gilks, however, was cut from a very different cloth. He was the same age as Boyd Orr, but had a more flamboyant character. He had long lived in Kenya and went around with a tame leopard called Starpit—coined, as one white settler recalled, by "the natives" who heard him repeatedly entreating the leopard to "stop it" when leaping onto patients' beds.[28] He was an active supporter of eugenics—a member of the council of the British Eugenics Society as well as the Kenya Society for the Study of Race Improvement (KSSRI)—and this meant that he combined his interest in diet with studies comparing the size of the Kenyan and European brain.[29] Like many other colonials he had ideas of racial hierarchy and particularly romanticized "warrior tribes": in this case the Masai in Kenya, who for him constituted the ideal of the noble savage.

When they met, John Boyd Orr had been in Kenya on a short trip to investigate a cattle disease, but he was persuaded by John Gilks to take a "medical safari" of the country's tribal reserves.[30] According to Gilks, by examining humans rather than cattle they could draw attention to the big contrast between two particular "native" groups: the Masai, who were tall and strong, and the Kikuyu, who were short and weak.[31] The problem was that the "weak" Kikuyu were the main source of the colony's labor—and this, once again, had military implications. During the First World War the British Army had found that 65 percent of Kikuyu recruits to the Carrier Corps were unfit for service, and Gilks and Orr set out to explain this difference in "physical efficiency," concluding that it was down to the diet.[32] As Orr later explained it, the Kikuyu were agriculturalists "who fed mainly on maize and other carbohydrate-rich foods"; the Masai, however, were pastoralists, "who owned big herds of cattle, sheep and goats, and whose diet consisted mainly of meat, milk, and blood drawn from living animals." The "physical characteristics and the incidence of the various diseases in the two tribes seemed very different," he concluded, "evidently due to the different nature of their diets."[33]

The two men set out to find out what, precisely, *was* that difference in these diets, and Orr initially wondered whether minerals were the issue. He had traveled to Kenya to examine a cattle disease called Nakuruitis, which, he found, could be cured by salt licks, and he reflected on whether the Kikuyu might be suffering from a similar deficiency. "We were doing feeding experiments with different groups of animals to find out the effect of their diet," he later explained, and "here were two tribes living under the same conditions." After observing that there was a "disease in cattle evidently due to the lack of some salts," Orr suggested that salts might benefit the Kikuyu as well.[34] His great hope was that an easily treatable mineral deficiency would solve the Kikuyu's small stature and "physical inefficiency"; in other words, he hoped that situation might respond to a technical fix. This was a dream that echoed throughout the ages. If the colonial scientists could identify what was missing in the local diet and replace it, then conditions could be easily improved. This belief was also promoted by one of Orr's backers in the British government, who claimed that the whole of Kenya's history could be explained and corrected by the absence of crucial minerals:

> The Masai found out long ago what was the matter with the country. It is short of phosphate, famine-short. It is short of salt and of all the sea elements. Millions of years—hundreds of millions of years—have passed since the African plateau was last under the sea. For sea beasts like ourselves, it is a constant strain. . . . So the Masai turned herdsmen, set the cows to concentrate the grass for them and took to milk diet— milk, meat, and blood. They lorded it amongst the starch-eating Kikuyu like wolves among sheep, fifty thousand of them amongst some two and a half millions. Tall, lean fellows. Their youths are 5 inches taller and 25 pounds heavier than their Kikuyu neighbours, and they kill a fighting lion in the open with their spears. Man is what he eats.[35]

This idea, that "man is what he eats," stands as a startlingly clear example of dietary determinism and also demonstrates how a new dream was taking root: the notion that humans could correct poor human development by making a few well-directed changes in diet. There was, of course, another big theme in these writings: race and eugenics, which had quickly become a central part of nutrition in the 1920s and 1930s. This was a complicated entanglement, which on the surface seemed contradictory. After all, dietary determinism had always stressed the significance of *environmental* conditions in explaining physical differences between human groups, whereas eugenics had stressed *biological* differences. Many of the dietary determinists, moreover, had been quite explicit in rejecting social Darwinism, arguing that weakness was not inherent to any race: Bengalis, for example, were not destined to be weak, but could change what they ate and become like the Sikhs: one of "the finest races in India" and "amongst the finest races of mankind."[36]

The possibility for improvement distinguished the dietary determinists from many hardline eugenicists, but it did not mean there was always a contradiction between the two. John Gilks, for example, argued that poor nutrition and poor intelligence could both be identified and corrected, and that coordinating these efforts was perfectly possible. He was part of a whole movement in the 1920s and 1930s known as "reform eugenics," which considered biology and the environment to work *together* in shaping human futures.[37] Perhaps the most famous proponent of belief was Julian Huxley, who headed a number of different organizations: UNESCO, the British Humanist Association, the World Wildlife Fund, as well as the British Eugenics Society.[38] This combination of progressive and racist causes illustrates not just how respectable eugenics had become, but also how it could comfortably coexist with agendas that seem now to be mutually exclusive. Huxley believed that eugenics could be a reputable form of science if only it were purged of unscientific prejudices; it could even become a progressive movement if it was applied consistently. As one of Huxley's colleagues put it, "It is not true that boiler washers, engine hostlers, miners, janitors, and garbage men . . . are necessarily idiots and morons"; and "it is not true that college graduates [and] people in 'Who's Who'. . . are physically, mentally and morally superior."[39] The ruling classes had been using eugenics to justify and entrench their position of power, but intelligence and strength, Huxley and others argued, had no relationship to class. "Suboptimal" individuals existed in all races and social groups, so eugenics could become part of a much wider scheme oriented toward reform and human improvement.

The idea of reform eugenics resonated with the racist but egalitarian application of dietary determinism, whose adherents applied similar lessons to the stunted working classes of England and the weak and feeble races of India. Gilks, for example, could combine his eugenicist beliefs with his interest in nutrition because the whole idea of reform eugenics was to present improvements to the diet as a first step in wider improvements to the community.[40] The movement was predicated on the idea that environmental circumstances had to be leveled before biological impediments could be identified. As they put it, "suboptimal" individuals existed across all social groups, so the only way to identify these individuals was to level out the influence of upbringing and environment. Reform eugenicists, moreover, believed that it was impossible to say with any confidence that someone's success in life was a result of biology until the result of nurture had been eliminated, which meant that improving environmental conditions had to come before improvements in biological reproduction. Both, in the end, were seen as essential to improve the strength of the population. Reform eugenicists argued that improvements in diet, healthcare, housing, and education made it easier to identify specifically *genetic* problems and eradicate them.[41]

The subtleties of dietary determinism have become difficult to appreciate because eugenics has become so rightly abhorred. The individuals involved were so obviously racist, and many of them promoted policies that are despicable today—even if these were often on a softer end of a very wide spectrum.[42] They may have tried to support and improve certain people, but they subscribed to the idea that humanity can be divided simplistically into races with shared attributes, which could be clearly identified on the body. McCarrison's work is a particularly good example. By displaying photographs of Punjabi and Bengali men, he compared "martial groups" with steely stares and "supine" southerners with bowed legs. Adjacent to these objectifying images were those of rats hanging down from their tails, in varying degrees of size.[43] The laboratory of the colonial world was made explicit here, implying not just that human groups could be studied like vermin, but also that they could be placed on a scale.[44] It is hard to see the subtlety and radicalism in images like this, yet the dietary determinists nevertheless had a humanitarian vision, wanting to transform the future of peoples while flattening the hierarchy of men. They may have reduced people to their racial characteristics, but they were developing a very different *explanation* of racial characteristics, which they believed could be changed.

Care and Colonial Ambition

Race was central to governmental strategies in the Victorian era, although Michel Foucault had surprisingly little to say about the topic. Of all the other "taken for granted" categories that he picked apart, race is now widely accepted as a social construction, but it barely appeared in his books, except for a few pages toward the end of the slim first volume of the *History of Sexuality*.[45] This seeming absence was filled for many readers in the 1990s, when the Collège de France lectures were made widely available and revealed a little more detail on Foucault's thinking about race.[46] The lecture series of 1976, in particular, had a great deal of material about race and biopower, and in the final lecture of that series Foucault identified what he believed to be a paradox. Biopower, Foucault reminded his listeners, involved the state taking on a nurturing role, yet it did not stop states from fighting wars, confining people, and administering widespread violence overseas. How, Foucault asked, could this be justified? How could a power oriented around fostering life be so violent? How could it kill "if its basic function is to improve life, to prolong its duration?"[47]

Foucault's answer was that race had a crucial role. Racism, he argued, divided the world into those to be nurtured and those to be killed. In many ways, this account was surprisingly unsubtle, seeing racism as just a negative and repressive phenomenon.[48] Imagining the imperatives of the racist state, he expressed how race justifies the elimination of "inferior species" so that the central population can become more vigorous.[49] He argued that the calculations of the modern state involved the death of the other, the death of the "bad race, the inferior race," which makes life "healthier and purer."[50] This suggested that there was a zero sum game involved in racism, and that all biopolitical divisions were made on racial grounds rather than more complex layers of identity. More important for the story of dietary determinism, he seemed to ignore the many more subtle ways that racism and governance come together to nurture as well as dominate.

When Laura Ann Stoler examined Foucault's lectures in the 1990s, she unpacked these relationships with a good deal more subtlety.[51] She showed how racism was central to facilitating colonial rule, how it designated gradations between citizens, subjects, and outsiders.[52] This was, however, still a rather orthodox application of Foucault's lectures, since Stoler focused on racism as a primarily exclusionary force in modern government. Like Foucault, she described racism as an ideology that divided those that could be nurtured from those that could be neglected. The dietary determinists, however, complicate this picture considerably. McCarrison, McCay, Gilks, and Boyd Orr were certainly involved in dividing people into groups, but they used racism primarily as an *inclusionary* rather than an exclusionary force. Racism was part of an ideology that fostered life rather than simply destroying it. Groups were essentialized in order to *incorporate* them into biopolitical projects. The identification of Bengalis as weak and Kikuyu as stunted, for example, was all about justifying processes of development.

To be clear, this "productive" use of racism could be just as insidious as the exclusionary move, and in some ways it was worse. It allowed fewer opportunities for differences and it stifled self-determination.[53] Yet it is important to realize that racism cannot simply be seen as facilitating governmental strategies that divided, killed, and let die. It also stood at the service of projects that sought to support, improve, and cure. Racism permeated biopower itself, becoming central to the evolution of humanitarian nutrition, as new people were included in an ever-widening sphere of humanitarian government. This happened, moreover, at the level of the group, in a process that Megan Vaughan later described as *unitization*. The diets and strength of colonial subjects were judged not on individuals, but on broader communal units.[54] Race had become not just a "precondition for exercising the right to kill," as Foucault put it, but also a precondition for exercising the right to improve whole communities.[55] Solutions to the empty stomach began to proliferate in this period, as communal diets, beliefs, and ways of life were placed under more detailed scrutiny.

Rising Aims

Perhaps the most ambitious study linking nutrition and ethnic groups was Audrey Richards's book, *Hunger and Work in a Savage Tribe*, which was published in

1932. Behind this seemingly racist title hid a remarkably subtle and ambitious attempt to place empty stomachs in context. It described itself as a "functional study of nutrition," and Richards was a committed functionalist: she subscribed to the idea that all rituals, beliefs, and customs had a fundamental social purpose. Her central argument in this book, therefore, was that the diet stood at the very center of community life.[56] In a powerful first line, she claimed that "nutrition as a biological process is more fundamental than sex": an opening that distinguished Richards from her academic supervisor, Bronislaw Malinowski, who had published a Freudian text in 1927 called *Sex and Repression in Savage Society*.[57] Richards was arguing that sociologists had neglected nutrition even though it was absolutely central to the organization of human life. In her words, it "determines, more largely than any other physiological function, the nature of social groupings, and the form their activities take."[58] Sex generated conflict, but food necessitated cooperation. By coming together to provide sustenance, she argued, food formed the basic structure of society.

This ambitious form of dietary determinism saw the empty stomach as responsible for social structure. Food, Richards argued, became a chief determinant of all human relationships. She used the diet to explain far more than the physiques of Kikuyu and Masai men, devoting her book to detailed descriptions of how food permeates social worlds. The first relationship of all, Richards clarified, was a nutritional one: it was the bond of mother and infant during breastfeeding. Weaning then became a process of learning wider social rules, including how to share, how to be hospitable, and how to behave when eating. The preparation of food later reflected and reinforced gender roles in the family, with women controlling the hearth and men producing food at a wider scale. Food then played an important part in initiation rituals, as adolescent men had to learn self-reliance and existing hierarchies, teaching everyone their place and position.[59]

Every element of life, Richards argued, is determined by the search for food, including religion, culture, and symbolism. Focusing on Bantu societies, she argued that a pregnant woman would not eat an ugly animal because she believed that she would give birth to an ugly child; a warrior would not eat a timid animal in case it passes this quality onto him; a betrothed man would avoid honey, because it meant his bride may slip away from him. Richards then described how the sensation of eating certain foods—like peppermint and mustard—led to certain taboos: hot foods, for example, were forbidden after battle, as men needed instead to cool their temperaments. In this way, food extended from the practical to the divine, playing a role in communicating with the ancestors. "The ritual meal binds the living and the dead," she wrote, "in this complex scheme of family obligations."[60] It also bound people to the environment around them, as humans developed a relationship with the cows and cattle they watched over for years, as "clan is linked to clan, and subject to chief, by a common system of obligations in the food producing scheme."[61] Sharing from the same pot became part of a marriage contract, an act of reconciliation. In multiple ways, food created bonds between different groups of people.[62]

In contrast to McCay and McCarrison, this was a more comprehensive view of dietary determinism, which demonstrated how the diet shaped far more than the physique. The earlier dietary determinists had been physiologists, still preoccupied with the metaphor of the human motor. As a result, they had a rather reductive view of the diet. Some diets, they argued, were more conducive to physical development than others, but the diet was primarily about weakness and strength. Audrey Richards went further. She introduced the idea of a "nutritional system," in which each society was deeply shaped by the need to alleviate hunger.[63] "Food must be eaten, prepared and cooked and won from the natural environment by a series of complicated economic tasks," she pointed out. Everything from the making of utensils to the construction of household dwellings was determined by the nutritional system.[64] Political structures, cultural beliefs, and economic organizations all went back to food. These "nutritive ties" bound people together, such that nutrition could never be simply about biological needs. It was about everything: power, control, agriculture, rituals, beliefs, routines, and the whole organization of the social world.

This marked the start of a golden age in the history of humanitarian nutrition, which extended throughout the 1930s. After Richards published her book in 1932, she was drawn into ever more ambitious development projects across the colonial territories. Within a few years there were a series of surveys and initiatives to tackle global hunger, such as new subcommittee of the Committee on Civil Research, Hailey's African Survey, and later the Colonial Development and Welfare Act in the UK, which focused on diet and development.[65] A cabinet Committee on Nutrition in the Colonial Empire (CNCE) was launched to "promote the discovery and application of knowledge in this field," and like many other of these initiatives, Audrey Richards was involved.[66] Following her lead, international conferences began to push past the view that nutrition was a narrow, technical problem, with a narrow, technical solution. They began communicating its social purposes and political implications. Such expansive visions flourished particularly in the 1930s League of Nations, which forged even more connections with human nutrition. Humanitarian approaches to hunger, therefore, began to grow and gain traction across the globe.

SOCIAL NUTRITION AT THE LEAGUE OF NATIONS

The basic problem faced by policymakers in the early 1930s can be summed up in six words: hunger in the midst of plenty.[1] It was a time of great contradictions: there was vast wealth in the world, but also great poverty; there were low prices, but mounds of produce; there was an abundance of food, but starving people. Grain was accumulating in warehouses, yet the unemployed were unable to purchase it. Lakes of milk and oil haunted Western politicians, who at the same time seemed unable to address malnutrition—a problem that had intensified even in the richest of nations. Against this background, humanitarian nutrition burst onto the international stage in an expansive and optimistic manner, with the League of Nations at the center of the action.[2]

The League had been involved in nutrition work since the middle of the 1920s as a clearinghouse for data. Countries would submit statistics about food supply, and the League collected such information without really developing any coherent international policy.[3] The Great Depression changed all that. Under new leadership, nutritionists in the League began to challenge the economic narrative surrounding the depression, which was, at least initially, an economic one.[4] At the London Economic Conference, convened by the League in 1933, conversations were dominated by economists who appeared to develop only one concrete proposal: "Restrict production drastically, create scarcity, and wait for prices to rise."[5] In the memorable phrase of Richard Hofstader, this involved solving hunger in the midst of plenty by doing away with the plenty, not the hunger.[6]

Nutritionists developed a different approach, arguing that it was ludicrous to reduce production when people were still starving. It made no humanitarian sense, they argued, to try and raise food prices when people could not even afford the food that was stockpiled. The key issue, they continued, was people, not the market. International efforts so far had focused on the overproduction of food rather than its underconsumption by individuals, and in 1934, the League published a lengthy report that developed this idea, known as the Burnet-Aykroyd report, after its authors.[7] It argued that malnutrition in the depression was caused by inadequate purchasing power rather than inadequate supply. This was nearly fifty years before Amartya Sen wrote his famous account of famine, and the League of Nations was making a similar point.[8] Rather than focusing on the supply of food, it argued that humanitarians should examine people's *access* to food. The problem was not insufficient supply; it was a lack of entitlement to the food that existed.

The Burnet-Aykroyd report had an immediate impact: discussion at the League had been scheduled for one afternoon, but it went on for three days and launched a holistic wave of thinking about nutrition.[9] A committee was established the following year, tasked with finding practical answers to the problems of malnourishment, which soon became an expansive, multidisciplinary body drawing on the expertise of a number of different agencies such as the International Labor Office, the International Institute of Agriculture, and the Child Welfare Committee. Their involvement reinforced the idea that this was an issue with many facets. Nutrition was connected to wages, to agriculture, as well as to child welfare and school feeding. The "Mixed Committee," as it was known, considered all these links, and the Committee on Intellectual Cooperation was also embraced, since any solution needed to involve education and research. The nutritionists in the League were reaching outward to other specialisms.[10]

The Mixed Committee was a multidisciplinary body that first met in 1936, chaired by the newspaper magnate Viscount Waldorf Astor.[11] Astor's opening address captured the spirit of the time, with its manifold relationships, its grand vision, and its expansive remit. Standing in front of an audience of economists, agriculturalists, politicians, and experts in public health, he linked their disciplines all back to food. "The problem we have to consider is highly complex and its scope is very wide," he began. "We are faced with a many sided problem, the solution of which must be beneficial to the Health, Economic, Agricultural and Social Life of the nations." He set out a web of connections that began with the individual's consumption of food and ended with the fate of the world. Unlike the earlier version of dietary determinism, this expansive idea embraced the globe rather than just the community: "If we are successful in our report," Astor claimed, "we can stimulate countries to cooperate on improving nourishment. This will raise public health and general welfare. It will improve standards of living [and] lead to increasing demand for agricultural produce. It will then give an impetus to world trade and lead to a period of prosperity." He concluded with a flourish: "This would turn our minds from thoughts of war to thoughts of peace."[12]

It was the middle of the 1930s and war was certainly in the air, but Astor's address represented the start of a golden age in humanitarian nutrition. It was golden not so much in its immediate results but rather in its influence, its ambition, and its willingness to forge links with other sectors. Also known as "social nutrition," the movement was defined by four main characteristics. First, it shifted attention from minimal to optimal nutritional standards. Second, it linked the solution of hunger to a range of progressive social causes. Third, it empowered the state to find a range of new solutions. Finally, it embraced the expansive ideas of dietary determinism that had been promoted by Audrey Richards, arguing that the diet was connected to cultural and social life.[13] Rather than trying to find the least a man could live on, the League of Nations now sought to identify which diets would be best for everyone's health. Rather than simply blaming the poor for their ignorance, the League saw poverty as a cause of hunger. Rather than simply collecting data on food consumption, the League recommended using all the levers of government to pursue a range of interconnected policies. Rather than viewing food only as nutrients, they stressed how food was central to social life.[14]

The golden age of social nutrition was incubated within the grand corridors of the newly constructed Palais des Nations. Its aspirations became extensive, and its findings rose up the international agenda. A chain of positive reactions, its adherents claimed, would follow from better nutrition for all: improvements in health, which would lead to greater productivity, which would generate higher wages and stimulate demand for goods. This, in turn, would lead to economic growth and more trade across the globe. It was a vision that appealed to politicians from all parts of the political spectrum, who promoted new work on the management of malnutrition as well as examining the possibilities of social change. By the late 1930s nutrients stood at the center of a vast network, with expanding connections around the world, but the imperatives of the coming war soon restricted these visions. The management of hunger after World War II eventually narrowed to a more technocratic concern, which focused on getting nutrients into bodies as quickly and efficiently as possible, and the nutritional golden age came to an end.

The Golden Age

The high point of social nutrition came with the opening statements of the Mixed Committee, when Lord Astor articulated the hopes and aims of the movement.

Although he was speaking on the eve of Germany's occupation of the Rhineland, Astor delivered his message with optimism and panache, placing faith in the power of nutrition and promoting it as a cure for the coming conflict. His narrative stressed how better nutrition could help produce stability, suppress "hyper excitability," and calm "political discontent." He called for positivity in place of "excessive pessimism" and argued that action on nutrition could improve relations between states. It could, he argued, stand as an antidote to those who were insistently dwelling on "the darker features of the situation."[15]

It was easy for Astor to be optimistic as his correspondence was forwarded from one large cosseted residence to another, and his words have an even more worrying ring when we consider that he was in favor of appeasement. One of his many homes was Cliveden, which was an enormous country house in Buckinghamshire that had become home to the "Cliveden Set," a purported conspiracy of aristocratic appeasers and expatriate Americans seen as friends of the Reich and disloyal to Britain.[16] If Astor was interested in nutrition, therefore, it may also have been because it served his interest in stability and détente. One of the remarkable things about the Mixed Committee, however, was that it did not just appeal to people with Astor's views but reached across the political spectrum. Those on the right were attracted by the idea that good nutrition would promote vitality, stability, and community well-being; to use Astor's words, nutrition could allow "robustness to replace weakness" and prevent "disharmony and discontent."[17] But those on the left liked the idea that good nutrition would improve worker's rights, leveraging higher wages and giving substance to the idea that all humans were of equal worth. The Mixed Committee, therefore, appealed to fascists as well as communists, liberals as well as radicals, and Astor had to work alongside men with radically different politics such as Dr. Ludwik Rajchman, the socialist director of the League's health secretariat.[18] In the words of Josep Barona, "No specific political ideology monopolised" this process, which was rather driven by "the general value of progress and modernity" that extended across the political spectrum.[19]

The inclusive reach of the Mixed Committee was particularly remarkable because nutrition had long been the site of a battleground between left and right. Industrialists had, for decades, used nutritional science to calculate the cheapest source of energy, using this to justify a squeeze on wages and suggesting that hunger was caused by the ignorance and conceit of the Western working classes. Against this view stood a left wing narrative, which argued that hunger was the result of poverty rather than behavior or ignorance. The problem, from this perspective, was a lack of purchasing power, which had been caused by low wages and a destructive change in structural conditions. Each narrative led to a different set of prescriptions. The right wing narrative suggested that the solution was education, not state intervention in the laws of supply and demand. The left believed that welfare, subsidies, and equality would tackle malnutrition. In relation to the colonial world, Michael Worboys has described these opposing views of hunger as the "endemic" and "epidemic" perspectives on hunger. The endemic view suggested that hunger was a persistent and intractable problem, caused by ignorance and laziness. The epidemic view suggested that hunger was a sudden outbreak, which could be caused by the shock of new structural conditions, the rise of unchecked capitalism, and the erosion of traditional life.[20]

The real skill of the Mixed Committee was to represent both of these perspectives simultaneously, to reach out across the divide. This ambitious and comprehensive spirit was reflected in the Final Report of the Mixed Committee, which stressed that *both* poverty and ignorance were to blame.[21] On the one hand, it stated, nutrition could be improved by public education and the promotion of basic nutritional principles. On the other hand, higher wages, free school meals, and the subsidization of "protective" (i.e., vitamin-rich) foods would help considerably. There was also a recommendation that concerned agricultural credits to boost food production and a trade policy geared to affordability. The overwhelming message was one of public responsibility. This was an early version of the domestic public policy consensus that emerged after the Second World War, uniting left and right through a commitment to the mixed economy, interventionist state, and a substantive vision of welfare.[22]

The reception of the Mixed Committee's report was remarkable, and, unusually for a League publication, it sold extremely well and was reviewed in major newspapers across the world.[23] The *Spectator* found its findings "little short of revolutionary."[24] An editorial in the *New York Times* declared that it was "the most important book of the year," musing that "if some extra planetary commission could take note of the snarl into which this planet has worked itself, the members would be filled with amazement and perhaps with Olympian compassion that it has taken us so long to get down to fundamentals."[25] The Mixed Committee report, many claimed, had finally got to the bottom of this most intractable challenge, tackling the issues underpinning international conflict. According to the *Washington Post*, the thrust of the new approach was that nutrition will "no longer be confined to the four walls of each household, but will become a national and international problem of paramount importance."[26]

The most radical part of this message was that the state had big responsibilities. "The conclusions of the whole matter are plain and inescapable," wrote George Newman in the *Observer*, as "the state has a direct responsibility both to educate its people and to facilitate their obtaining a sufficiency of the right foods."[27] Such interventionism was particularly significant, as the *Washington Post* reminded its readers, because it came not from "politicians of the left, but a committee of independent scientists, high government officials, representatives of big landlords, mostly conservative," which were presided over by "a man as little revolutionary as Lord Astor."[28] Some newspapers argued that it did not go far enough. The *Manchester Guardian,* for example, accused the Mixed Committee of "shirking" the economic question and avoiding any real structural change. The whole process, the newspaper argued, was an elaborate piece of "window dressing."[29] It was, nevertheless, window dressing that illustrated ambition and cross-party support, and it constituted a high point of social nutrition at the time.

Technical Accumulation

The expansive character of the nutritional golden age did not just lie in the broad political appeal, which united left and right. Nor was it simply a matter of an extensive connection between disciplines, from agriculture to economics, to public health. The golden age was broad and ambitious in a technical sense as well, because it established new and more precise methods for tackling the empty stomach. In the League of Nations this was led by a Technical Committee, also established in 1935, which was tasked with investigating a much narrower and more procedural set of questions about basic needs. At the time there was still no internationally recognized standard for the nutritional requirements of the body, despite the work of Voit and Atwater, and no universal recommendations for dietary intake. There had been some limited work on basic anthropometric data and clinical examinations, but there was still no agreed procedure for measuring malnutrition.

This was, however, the era when "sentiment" turned to "science"; when the relatively informal attempt to do good was transformed into a more ordered and bureaucratic system.[30] The trend had begun with the response to the 1921–22 Russian famine several years earlier, which was led by the American Relief Administration (ARA) under Herbert Hoover: an enormous organization, with a budget of hundreds of millions of dollars, that transformed the soup kitchen into a "model of efficiency and zeal."[31] The ARA kitchens had made many technical innovations: enrolling the assistance of local physicians to inspect the conditions of the starving, prioritizing those in the most need, and issuing strict instructions to control the distribution of food. The tone was set from the very top, as Herbert Hoover declared that he did not like anyone taking away food from the kitchens because he wanted to see the food go "down the children's throats."[32] The scale of relief was immense, and menus were "scientifically prescribed," with the ARA employing the biologist Vernon Kellogg to oversee emergency feeding. Meals were designed to provide "exactly the proper number of calories to maintain one child."[33]

FIGURE 7. This age of plenty. Cartoon by Sidney Strube. *Daily Express,* May 18, 1934, 10. © Strube/Daily Express/Express Syndication. Image supplied by the British Cartoon Archive, University of Kent.

The bureaucratization of relief was developed in a number of other agencies over the next few years. The newly formed agency Save the Children, for example, established soup kitchens throughout Russia and Eastern Europe in a similarly precise and ordered manner.[34] Like the ARA, Save the Children used doctors to conduct a physical examination and verify that people were truly malnourished. They issued "meal tickets" to the most needy individuals, which were made from a square piece of card with basic details printed in the middle and the days of the month around the edge. On arrival at the soup kitchen, the relevant date was cut off and a soup or stew was provided in return. Communal feeding took place in school halls, municipal buildings, or hospitals, and their performance was monitored by organizational representatives, who would close a kitchen if it was "badly run."[35] The menus were designed to meet nutritional requirements at the lowest cost, and were usually made from whatever commodities could be transported to the area (either savory soups made from beans, flour, lard and salt, or sweet ones made from rice, milk, flour, cocoa, and sugar).[36] The meals had an average cost that was carefully calculated and regulated, with pamphlets claiming an average of "1½d per head for a meal of 600 calories . . . administrative expenses included."[37]

It was this rational system of benevolence that ended up embraced by the League of Nations. A prescient article from 1923 praised the arrival of "Machine Age Humanitarianism," describing how "organizations as powerful as the governments of many European states" had been operating throughout Eastern Europe. Agencies like the ARA, this article argued, were bringing modern ideas from "the youngest of the nations" to "the oldest countries of the old world," delivering not just food, but "the shock of the machine age, the age of organization." Using biblical tales to illustrate the passing of ideas from West to East, the article continued by declaring that in "the land where the travelling Samaritan got down from his horse to bind the wounds of a single man dying by the roadside, America has sent fleets of freighters, thousands of tons of corn."[38]

This was just the beginning of a more rationalized form of relief, which combined Taylorist efficiency with the teachings of nutritional science—and particularly the "newer knowledge" of nutrition.[39] This involved knowledge of vitamins, whose discovery had complicated humanitarian work considerably. Before the arrival of vitamins, humanitarian feeding had involved a far simpler set of calculations: it was just about getting energy to the people who needed it. If the body was receiving the right number of calories, in other words, then its nutritional needs were being met. By the First World War, however, fruit and vegetables were beginning to be recognized as important "accessory factors" in the diet, which could no longer be dismissed as unimportant.[40] Their discovery can be traced back to 1911, when Casimir Funk came up with a collective name for these "accessory factors": vitamins. Believing them to be amines (a particular type of chemical compound), he proclaimed them "vital amines," and then contracted the term to "vitamines." It was later discovered they were not amines at all, so the final "e" was dropped, but the terminology remained.[41]

The work of Funk—alongside other biochemists like Frederick Hopkins and Christiaan Eijkman—implied that nutrition was a matter of quality, not just quantity, and they confirmed what many people had long suspected: that the nature of food was important, not just its energy content. Union leaders were soon mobilizing the new discoveries to demonstrate that the cheapest forms of energy were not enough for workers. Higher wages, they argued, were required to purchase "protective foods," and the League, in turn, embraced the new discoveries and began feeling its way between the political disputes. Focusing initially on procedures that standardized the manufacture of vitamins, the League of Nations later developed charts of minimal nutritional requirements that every human had to ingest. This was never a simple matter because such requirements had to be negotiated, and the meeting minutes from this period reveal some quite fascinating disputes, based around the idea that different people had different requirements, and that calorie consumption varied on exertion, body size, and climatic conditions. The Russian representative quibbled over whether the climate in his country was "cold" or "very cold," and discussions soon acknowledged that there was a significant variation "from country to country and from class to class, of such factors as height, weight, age of maturity, amount of work performed by women and children, etc." All this influenced how much food people would need and had to be ironed out in the new requirements.[42]

Such complexity made it "impossible that one particular scale should everywhere correspond with real values," the experts concluded, and that "no pretense of absolute accuracy could be made."[43] As one speaker argued, "It would be a mistake to establish a definite list" of human nutritional requirements because "science had not yet reached the point where all the necessary parts of a component diet were known."[44] Each year new vitamin or mineral seemed to be added to the lists, which became increasingly complicated over time. This led some representatives to toy with the idea of a simpler approach: just recommending a balanced diet, on the grounds that variety made for safety. The bureaucratic imperatives of the expert committee, however, demanded a more precise response, and the Technical Committee eventually provided a list of nutritional inputs, despite their own disagreements.

The second main task for the League was to standardize the measurement of malnutrition, a process that was similarly beset with complexities. One of the most common methods for measuring nourishment in the 1930s was the dietary survey: a process that involved examining what people consumed, usually by distributing "household account books" and requesting that housewives record all the food they had purchased. The main problem with this method was that it involved a high degree of trust and fastidiousness on the part of the housewife, but, as one report bemoaned, "in practice, household account books completed with care and conscientiousness are difficult to obtain, even when cash premiums or such rewards as free seats at the cinema are offered as an incentive."[45] Only a fraction of the household account books were returned, so researchers would resort to visiting the families directly to asking questions and take notes.[46] This was more reliable, but it was very expensive, since it required a great deal of academic labor. Moreover, it only worked for research subjects willing to permit the presence of strangers poking their nose into their lives.[47] Surveyors sometimes asked schoolteachers to quiz their (presumably honest) pupils about what kind of foods they had eaten for breakfast that morning, distributing forms that detailed everything right down to whether they had lemon, milk, fruit syrup or rum with their morning tea.[48] These techniques, however, only recorded the approximate "inputs" to the body: the type of diet that people claimed to consume.[49]

The contrasting set of methods became known as "outcome" approaches, which looked at the effect of diet on the body. These included clinical examinations, anthropometric measures, and biochemical testing, defining the problem not as an inadequate intake of nutrients but as the result on hunger on the physique. Such techniques became far more prominent in later years, but their nascent forms were summarized very neatly in a 1939 League of Nations publications authored by E. J. Bigwood.[50] Of the three "outcome" approaches that Bigwood recorded, clinical examinations were probably the most common. The ARA, for example, had used clinical examinations during the Russian famine, asking local doctors to give their opinion of an individual's state of nutrition: a process that would usually begin with a visual impression of the fat content of the skin, "often achieved simply by counting the number of visible ribs combined with a sense of 'healthy looks.'"[51] Later, more standardized techniques included the Dunfermline scale, which was designed to make clinical information comparable, but as one expert at the League explained, the challenge with clinical examinations was always that the circumstances were so different. It was hard to compare "like with like" when it came to different doctors and different bodies, and in any case "a slender individual must be judged quite differently than a more stoutly built person."[52] Even then it was hard to define what it meant to be "slender" or "stout," so clinical methods failed by being subjective.

The alternative was to use anthropometric (or somatic) methods, which rose to prominence after the Second World War. These were more objective and regularized, based on the idea that the body couldn't lie. Anthropometry was used in three main ways to measure malnutrition. First, it could be applied longitudinally: the same person could be measured at regular intervals to trace their growth and development.[53] Second, anthropometry could be applied cross-sectionally: a sample of people in a population could be measured to see how weights and sizes were distributed. Finally, anthropometry could be applied for nutritional screening, to see who was eligible for food. This final use for anthropometry was, in the 1920s and 1930s, by far the least developed, although Dr. Clemens von Pirquet had devised an early version of the technique after the First World War.[54] There were many problems, however, with these early attempts—not least because the measuring tools were rarely available, the methods were not yet standardized, and, most important, they were based on poor statistical data. Judging someone's level of malnutrition on the basis of a single measurement, to put it simply, required an idea of what would be "normal" in the first place, which was not accurately defined until the second half of the 1960s.

In addition to clinical and anthropometric methods, there was a third "outcome" approach: the biochemical method. This involved looking at bloods and bodily fluids, examining the presence of nutrients and biochemical makeup. The advantage of this approach, at least in theory, was that it was highly sensitive. Eating an inadequate diet took some time to become clinically visible, and it might be months before it led to significant changes in body shape. Deficiencies in vitamins and proteins, however, could be made visible in the blood straight away. Within a few decades these techniques would become the great hope of the high modernist era, with the idea that they could make the nutritional state of the body perfectly legible. Yet the testing equipment was always too expensive and cumbersome to used effectively in emergencies, so anthropometry would eventually come to dominate, on the grounds of its speed and simplicity.

Nutritional Expansion

Expansion was the core feature of the nutritional golden age, and a relatively marginal branch of science soon became an international cause célèbre. The reports of the Mixed Committee were debated widely in the press, while the Technical Committee transformed state-of-the-art science into practical guidance for humanitarians. Nutrients, in other words, were rising in prominence. They were emerging from relative obscurity to become a defining feature of the age. They had been invisible in Rumford's time, unspoken and unrecognized, but were now influencing world events as never before.

How did the nutrient gain power and influence? This is the kind of question that long interested Bruno Latour, who described power as a consequence of action rather than its cause. In one of his first books, the *Pasteurization of France*, Latour traced how a seemingly small and invisible object—the microbe—grew in influence after it was first identified in the nineteenth century.[55] The microbe, he argued, was always there, creating problems for human health, but Pasteur made it visible. The existence of microbes soon emerged into public consciousness and became connected to illness and disease. Once the idea spread, microbes became a standard feature of normal life, with whole institutions devoted to the management of hygiene. Germs then had an impact on politics, social relationships, and the organization of public space, becoming more important and influential as a result.

Nutrients had a similar trajectory. They always existed, providing sustenance to the human organism, but Liebig made them visible and their influence subsequently grew. They affected politics and social relationships, appearing in the management of institutions and the negotiation of wages. They became part of everyday conversation, shaping the decisions of housewives and the provision of relief to the poor. The identification of nutrients did not change the basic dynamics of life—people still thrived when they had food, and starved if they didn't—but knowledge of this new object transformed the *management* of hunger in new and important ways.

Latour has long criticized the assumption that power is a force one can possess. We say of a president, he has pointed out, that they "hold power," but simply "having" power achieves nothing on its own. To actually *exert* power we need other people and things, which perform the actions, obey the orders, and communicate the messages. This includes things as well as people, small objects as well as large. Latour's central insight was that the importance of an object is not related to its size, but its influence. Scale is an achievement, not a property. Scale is the *effect* of alliances and networks, not a quality that some things have and other things do not. We cannot assume any structural difference, he argued, between a "macro" actor, such as capitalism or bureaucracy, and a "micro actor," such as a door, a microbe, or a vitamin. The distinction between "micro" and "macro" is not natural and permanent, but created and open to negotiation.[56]

Nutrients, like microbes, gradually became "macro" actors in the 1930s, wielding power on the international stage. The activities in the League of Nations were a turning point, since by that time nutrients had already replaced older ideas about food, such as the theory of classical dietetics, and had become part of governmental calculations, influencing the management of workhouses and the politics of the school meal. In the 1930s, however, the influence of the nutrient extended even further, shaping the arrangement of factories and the nature of foreign policy.[57] They had become part of discussions in agriculture, economics, wages, health, and the body. In the golden age, nutrients were connected to a range of social issues and were valued right across the political spectrum.

These connections can be seen in the archives of the League, and particularly in the correspondence between health workers, nutritional scientists, physiologists, economists, statesmen, biochemists, farmers, and politicians. In such letters it was not just the bureaucrats making connections; the nutrients themselves were forming ever-wider alliances with different areas of life. The nutrients in meat had already been linked with the productivity of Kikuyu laborers; the nutrients in wheat had already been connected to the martial spirit of the "chapatti-fed races."[58] Now, similar connections were everywhere. The nutrients in milk were connected to the education of children in Britain.[59] The nutrients in vegetables were linked to the industrial future of Americans.[60] The nutrients in apples were linked to the tariffs and trade of oranges.[61] The simple nutrient, in this way, became relevant to a range of policy positions. It catapulted "from a tangible but somewhat amorphous presence" on the health scene to become center of the international stage.[62]

The End of Social Nutrition

By the late 1930s, events in the world disrupted the expansive aims of the League's social nutrition efforts, and social nutrition came under threat. Lord Astor wanted the Mixed Committee to move people's minds from "thoughts of war to thoughts of peace," but the opposite took place: thoughts of war drove the Mixed Committee into obscurity. The final report had sold well, but all efforts to get its recommendations implemented through new national "nutrition committees" fell flat, and the political situation was rapidly changing. The Spanish civil war, and particularly the bombing of Guernica in 1937, had foreshadowed the coming conflict, and a new humanitarian crisis began to develop in France. Here, refugee camps began filling up with starving, homeless people from Spain, and nutrients were needed to sustain starving bodies rather than more ambitious social visions. The optimistic ideas of the League were soon replaced by a series of narrower, technical questions that became increasingly important for the coming war: How to feed starving refugees? How to get the cheapest foods to the people that needed it? How to find calories that were light and transportable?

It was these questions that preoccupied humanitarians in the later part of the 1930s. The Quakers, for example, wrote to experts in the League for advice on relief diets that would be scientific and economical. "The funds of the society are limited," they explained, so it is "important to obtain the maximum food value for the money spent."[63] The experts, in turn, were initially reluctant to respond with anything concrete, since they were still preoccupied with the expansive hopes of social nutrition and concerned about promoting a standardized, technocratic response. "Approach[es] to the problem of famine relief must largely depend on local circumstances," they replied; stressing that "the relation between the available funds and the numbers to be fed, the facilities for the transport and storage of food, the supply of fuel, and many other factors, must influence the measures to be taken." Eventually, however, they suggested a number of possible diets "of extreme simplicity and cheapness," which were "not grossly inadequate from a physiological point of view." The cautious language surrounded a rather simple menu of skim milk powder, wholewheat flour, cod liver oil and salt, cooked into gruel and served with a daily ration of "anti-scorbutic material" (vitamin C). This advice was taken to the refugee camps of Spain, where Quakers and other humanitarians were learning how to deal with new and pressing circumstances of crisis.

The same pair of problems—limited money and massive need—recurred again and again in the Spanish civil war. Given the scale of the need, relief workers had no option but to become highly efficient, delivering not just food but "the shock of the machine age" all over again. One aid worker, Francesca Wilson, later described how she dealt with eleven thousand displaced people arriving in the camps every week: a situation that called for detailed surveys, comprehensive reports, and an efficient organization of space. She explained how relief workers sought to "break the camp into small units, each with elected representatives on a governing committee," how they ensured that the camps had "no more than 5000 occupants," and how they split the camps into "self-governing sections of 1000 each." "I have never known a transit camp where people looked so tidy, orderly and calm," Wilson concluded. "Loud-speakers kept the refugees informed of the plans made for them, and information bureaux answered their enquiries and found out their special needs and desires."[64] This efficiency was carried over to the organization of canteens and soup kitchens, where the meals were "planned scientifically to give the necessary calories and vitamins." Local doctors, meanwhile, helped to identify the most needy through techniques of nutritional assessment.[65]

This second wave of "machine age humanitarianism," therefore, was in some ways similar to the first. It was, however, more technical. After giving advice to charitable organizations in the Spanish civil war, the League of Nations began planning large programs of relief across Europe, predicting that a wider war would soon arrive. It came as expected, and by 1942, experts in the now diminished League were working on three central questions: "1. Which nutritive elements would be required [in wartime relief]? 2. How great would the quantities to be considered [sic], and 3. How can storage and transport of such quantities be most rationally effected?"[66] This generated an overwhelming concern with logistics. "It should be our object to send across the 'protective foods' in a compact, non-perishable form," stressed one expert; "a large quota of fish liver oils should be sent to those countries which are liable to rickets or vitamin A deficiency. Anti-scorbutic foods should be sent to those countries liable to scurvy ... [and] protein containing foods to those countries where famine oedema is a common feature."[67] Humanitarianism was becoming more and more a matter of narrow nutritional expertise, concerned with getting nutrients to the right place, in the right format, at the right time.

Gradually, visions of social nutrition became restricted in light of these new concerns. Rather than developing the connections between nutrients, agriculture, and health, the League of Nations developed connections between nutrients, logistics, and the body. Correspondence focused more on biological issues, and food was broken down into its component parts for relief. Sugar was stockpiled as "the most concentrated form of carbohydrate foodstuff" that "can be stored in a relatively small space."[68] Vitamins were manufactured as pills that were compact, lightweight, and cheap. Cod liver oil was distributed as a source of vitamin A and D, and Marmite as a source of vitamin B.[69] Iron was offered by providing "dried liver and cattle stomach" and vitamin C was generated by the "old trick" of allowing "cereal and legume grains to germinate before they are eaten."[70] The best supplies, one expert concluded, were "1. non-perishable, so we may start building up stocks now ... 2. compact and weigh as little as possible ... [and] 3. foods of the highest nutritional value." If the problem is tackled in this way, the memo concluded, "there will be a saving in money. Or, to put it the other way, a million pounds spent in this way will save more lives than a million pounds spent less scientifically."[71]

Nutrients were replacing foods as the central unit of delivery, and biological lives were replacing social well-being as the key criterion of success. This situation generated a profound shift in policy, which was encapsulated in a short recipe for homemade "anti-scorbutic material" distributed to relief workers in China. The recipe created a medicine by cutting oranges into fine shreds, macerating these shreds in alcohol for 24 hours, straining the liquid through cotton cheesecloth and then covering the pulp in boiling water.[72] By mixing the resulting liquids relief workers had a vitamin-rich medicine that was also analogous to the changing approach. Whole foods were being mashed into completely new forms. Citrus was cut back and turned into nutrients. Foods were made portable and governable. It was no longer the whole foods that mattered so much as the chemicals such commodities contained. In a similar way, the holistic ideals of social nutrition were being squeezed, reduced, and beaten to a pulp against the background of the Second World War.

MILITARY FEEDING DURING WORLD WAR II

Kathryn Hulme is best known as author of *The Nun's Story,* a novel about a Belgian nun who is torn between her religious duties and her personal aspirations. The story ends during the Second World War, when the novel's protagonist, Sister Luke, leaves her convent, choosing loyalty to the resistance over loyalty to the Church. In 1959 *The Nun's Story* was turned into a successful film starring Audrey Hepburn and was nominated for eight Academy Awards, establishing Hulme as a celebrated author in the United States and a prominent Catholic commentator. But there was a lesser-known element of Hulme's biography, without which the book, and the film, would not have existed: after the Second World War, Hulme worked for the United Nations Relief and Rehabilitation Agency (UNRRA) as a relief worker, managing a displaced persons (DP) camp in Wildflecken, Germany. She met a nun in the camp, whose life became the basis for the fictional character, and she wrote these wartime experiences into a memoir, *The Wild Place,* which won the *Atlantic* nonfiction award in 1953.[1]

Hulme's memoir was filled with vibrant characters and vivid descriptions, and it began with her arrival at Wildflecken, where people had been "rounded up under whatever roofs had been left intact, usually the roofs of the great Wehrmacht army barracks."[2] It depicted displaced people standing in carriages, their "haggard faces shawled, bonneted, turbaned, or simply wrapped around with shreds of old blanket wool."[3] It described the process of registration on arrival, when the refugees were given identification cards, rations, and dusted by DDT squads in what became known as the "human laundry."[4] Hulme's memoir also contained a particularly lovely account of food. After struggling to requisition food from the German authorities, she received a visit from an American sergeant with a trainload of surplus army rations. Each neat, wooden box contained an array of canned and branded goods, which were received by the relief workers with anticipation and delight:

> We slit the gummed tape sealing the carton . . . [and] our eyes popped as we lifted out a pound package of cube sugar, tins of cheddar cheese, of sardines, Nescafe, corned beef, tuna, Spam, dried milk, Crisco, a half pound chocolate bar, and seven packs of American cigarettes. "That's to help out the DP food ration," said the sergeant. "There's about fourteen thousand calories in that box . . . I've got four boxcars of this stuff down on the tracks, fifteen thousand food parcels. Got orders to stick around with my guard until you've unloaded. Then it's your baby."[5]

Hulme set about transferring the rations to a warehouse, but the task became difficult as crowds gathered around:

> It was as if the whole population had smelled that food right through the heavy cartons that packaged it, right through the tin that sealed in each wondrous unheard-of item. Before the first trucks had discharged their loads in the warehouse . . . the woods bordering the main road were alive with scurrying forms. Camp streets thronged with DPs chattering a language that did not even sound like Polish. Actually, it was the language of hysteria.[6]

The DPs assembled, demanding their ration packs with what, in Hulme's narrative, is an increasingly sinister chant, a frenzy of "Spam-maddened adults": "*pakiety . . . pakiety . . . pakiety.*" Meanwhile, the relief workers retreated inside the warehouse to decide what to do, convinced that if they distributed the packets directly the DPs would waste the rations and consume them all in "a single night of magnificent celebration." In the interests of order the relief workers broke up the wooden ration boxes, stacking the tins of different commodities into "ancient step pyramids" that soon stood "looming in the warehouse gloom." They decided that the supplies should not be released except in carefully planned meals, since "one fatty pink slice of Spam would be enough to throw our camp into a maddened uproar." The relief workers made an inventory, counting the rations and planning to combine the commodities into communal meals. They devised a special kitchen to cook milk and chocolate for supplementary feeding, and kept the revered commodities under close surveillance while releasing them little by little for feeding programs.[7]

This was all about control. Hulme was paternalistically claiming to act in the best interests of the DPs, and the DPs were expressing their agency, trying to govern what they ate. It was a struggle repeated in many camps and documented in many memoirs. Marcus Smith, for example, received a large number of American parcels in Dachau and split them up to use the chocolate for hospital patients, canned beef for evening meals, and cigarettes as payment for labor.[8] Alex Bryan received a consignment of British Army Pacific Packs in Solingen and started a child-feeding scheme with soup made from processed cheese.[9] Margaret McNeill converted army rations into communal meals, recounting the tensions this created.[10] The use of surplus army rations soon became a key part of humanitarian policy by the nascent United Nations, and relief workers often came into conflict with DPs when they controlled the valuable packages in the camps. In McNeill's narrative, for example, the DPs could not understand why the relief workers spent all their time breaking up the ration packs into individual commodities and then cooking special meals, rather than just giving them out directly. The relief workers, for their part, bemoaned the DPs' "incorrigible habit of taking all the tastiest ingredients out of the week's supply of food and making one delicious meal; after which followed a dreary period of nothing but watery pea soup."[11] In this battle for control the relief workers wanted to plan everything and control the intake of food. The DPs, however, wanted to use the ration packs as they wished. Even comparatively simple schemes caused dispute: when distributing chocolate to schoolchildren, for example, McNeill allocated it piece-by-piece, but the DPs said it should be given in whole bars, so the children could choose when to eat.[12]

Control and power, which is now so central to relief work, became crucial to humanitarian action in the Second World War. Compared to the expansive visions of "social nutrition" that had proliferated in the interwar period, relief in the 1940s was characterized by technical foods, precise nutritional needs, and calorie counting. The use of surplus rations was a good illustration of the era, as it combined technologies of preservation, nutrition, and ordered portability. Other forms of relief, however, took on a militaristic hue as well. In this chapter I examine how training programs for relief workers taught new military methods for feeding large numbers of people, how nutrients replaced foods in humanitarian efforts, and how this change in thinking generated a range of new and unusual technical foods. Perhaps the most vivid and disturbing example of these new technical foodstuffs appeared in Belsen, where military doctors experimented with new methods of emergency relief for concentration camp survivors. Whereas social nutritionists had linked nutrients to enormous global processes, these postwar relief workers were concerned with controlling far smaller interactions: the crowd of Spam-maddened adults chanting at the warehouse door, the dormitories of starving concentration camp survivors, and getting nutrients directly into bodies without any intervening distractions.

FIGURE 8.   Surplus stocks of US Army K rations. *Life Magazine*, October 8, 1945, 82. © Ralph Morse/LIFE Picture Collection/Getty Images.

Soldiers and Humanitarians

In many ways, the association between soldiers and humanitarians was quite natural. Both had a similar logistical task: they had to sustain large numbers of people, often in distant and remote locations, with cheap, lightweight, and energy-dense food. The similarity between military and humanitarian camps grew from a direct historical relationship, as the allied armies managed relief work across Europe in the immediate postwar period, only later passing this task onto civilian agencies that continued with the same techniques.[13] Liisa Malkki is one of many scholars who has traced the links between humanitarianism and postwar army methods, noting how military "technologies of power" that were "associated with the care and control of refugees" transferred directly to a new generation of aid workers.[14] The memoirs written by relief workers in this period show how this worked in practice. Refugee camps were superimposed on army barracks, their inhabitants registered and numbered; the displaced were fed in communal kitchens, their nutritional needs calculated with calorific precision.[15] Each new arrival was dusted with DDT powder in a process Primo Levi has described as a "purification and exorcism." Cleansed of their former lives, the displaced emerged with new humanitarian identities.[16]

All the major aid agencies embraced military practices. Even the Quakers, perhaps the most pacific of relief organizations, sent their recruits to Europe in grey uniforms after providing them with an intensive training course that, in the words of one participant, resembled "army manoeuvres."[17] Recruits received a lecture from Arthur Koestler, who told them how to manage vast camps of former concentration camp inmates who would act "like a dog on a chain." "It is no use expecting anything like a normal reaction to any remark or action," he warned them, telling the new aid workers to use a firm paternalistic hand.[18] Camps needed to be closely controlled, the trainees were told, and "any sentimentality would be most unwise." Recruits were advised to maintain "quite a large degree of externally applied discipline"—a point that was emphasized in one case with the very understated and rather tortured phrase: "the minimum possible amount of discipline is not necessarily the optimum amount."[19]

Francesca Wilson was one of the relief workers trained in this way, and she later published a handbook that echoed much of this advice. Relief workers, she said, needed managerial skills, particularly the ability to delegate, monitor, and order people around. Women, she thought, were particularly well suited to these tasks, as a powerful matriarch had the "sort of aura . . . that made simple peasant people fear her a little, but trust and obey her too." There was, however, a danger that such women would become "quickly intoxicated by power." "I have seen some who have begun well, turn over-night into dictators. In a trice they are surrounded by sycophants. They appear in the press as Mothers of Starving Millions. Their tours become royal processions. No flattery is too gross for them." Ordering people was a fine skill, it seemed, requiring humility as well as strength.[20]

This paternalistic or maternalistic approach seeped into the provision of food as well. Quaker trainees were instructed on nutrient categories and

economical menus; they learned the calorie value of foods and practiced recipes for mass feeding. Much of this material was based on army handbooks,
and new recruits were taught to build a "field kitchen" according to military
designs including the famous Aldershot Oven, conceived at the British Army
school of cookery.[21] Relief workers were also taught to closely supervise cooks
from other cultures, who, they assumed, had doubtful understanding of basic
nutritional science. It was important not to "cook cabbage for ten hours, until
all the vitamins were lost," one training manual specified—something that was
never learned in British institutions. Other parts of the manual, which advised
against "boiling cod liver oil in cocoa," revealed how odd some nutritional
practices had become.[22]

As nutritional training became influenced by militaristic approaches, army
rations were an essential tool for relief. These conveniently compact and long-
lasting packages were particularly valuable for meeting the immense challenges
of postwar Europe. As Tony Judt put it, the continent was "a picture of utter mis-
ery and desolation," with "pitiful streams of helpless civilians trekking through a
blasted landscape of broken cities and barren fields."[23] The army rations offered a
glimpse of a more plentiful world as well as having the advantage being portable,
energy-dense, nutritionally balanced, and long lasting. The US Army had ended
the war with nearly 1 billion pounds of surplus combat rations, and around
125 million of these, including around 550 million pounds of ration components, were purchased by UNRRA for around $100 million.[24] This was less than
their true value, but represented a mutually convenient arrangement: the rations
were costing a great deal for the US Army to store but could be used immediately
by UNRRA since they were "excellent for keeping people alive."[25]

Many of the rations sold by the US Army had been designed by Ancel Keys,
a physiologist from the University of Minnesota. He had personally developed
the most well-known and technological advanced version of these foods, known
as the "K-ration" after his surname. The K-ration provided particularly high-
calorie, low-weight food for mobile combat troops and came divided into breakfast, lunch, and supper units, small enough to be carried in the pocket. Other
rations, such as the C-ration, were devised along similar lines, made up of tinned
meals such as beef stew or sausage and beans, packaged along with spreads, jams,
crackers, and extras such as instant coffee, chewing gum, and chocolate. Bigger cartons, such as the "10-in-1 ration," had been devised for teams of soldiers,
offering ten meals in one packet. They had been stockpiled for an anticipated
ground invasion of Japan, which never took place, and at the end of the war the
army had to get rid of what was left. In addition to selling hundreds of millions of
ration packs to UNRRA, many were transferred to the nascent aid organization,
CARE, becoming aid packages for families in Europe.[26]

Once UNRRA had purchased the rations, a "technical bulletin" was issued to tell relief workers how to use them. The pamphlet suggested innovative recipes, for example taking ten biscuits, a day's cocoa allowance, and a sachet of lemonade crystals from the C-ration to create a diet for small infants. This intriguing meal involved mixing the cocoa into a paste with a little water, pouring more boiling water over the biscuits, and then mashing these ingredients with the lemonade into a "gruel consistency." To use the K rations, the technical bulletin suggested melting a can of cheese "in a pan over hot water," before "adding a few mess kit spoonfuls of boiling water and stirring until a smooth mixture is obtained." To finish the meal it instructed relief workers to add some soaked biscuits.[27] Kathryn Hulme adopted similar techniques as she sheltered in the warehouse gloom, planning diets that controlled the intake of nutrients. As she saw it, this approach ensured that scarce resources were used as effectively as possible.

Counting Calories

As the last DPs were resettled in the 1950s, Jacques Vernant concluded that the great majority of them had been living in camps "where a paternal administration drew up the menu, fix[ing] meals and curfew times . . . according to carefully worked out scales."[28] These scales were part of a wider paternalistic ethos, and when it came to food they were based on nutritional requirements established at the League of Nations ten years previously.[29] Such standards had made food governable, and the calorie, in particular, allowed food to be turned into a quantifiable unit.[30] Relief handbooks persistently framed food in terms of nutritional inputs, and it almost seemed as though humanitarians had forgotten about the foods actually eaten in their transformation of meals into nutrients. As one handbook put it in 1945, "Enough to eat, in the final analysis, does not mean enough bread, or enough soup, or enough potato; it means enough of each of the *nutrients* of which food is composed."[31]

This was by no means an obvious way of seeing food, and its novelty can be illustrated by comparing it with some popular cartoons from the same period. These suggested that enough to eat meant *precisely* enough bread, enough soup, or enough potato. To think in terms of nutrients or calories was alien, even mean. One cartoon from *Die Zeit*, for example, represented calories as bubbles, ephemeral and fantastical, floating up from the hungry masses trying to catch them on their plates.[32] Another, in a Berlin women's magazine, showed a child asking his mother "Do we always have to eat calories? Couldn't we occasionally eat a nice piece of cake?"[33] Even the protective qualities of fresh foods like oranges and apples had been reduced and delivered as a pill. An Indian cartoon during the

Bengal famine, for example, satirized the use of vitamins by showing emaciated figures transforming into corpulent masses of flesh on ingesting a tiny tablet.[34]

Vitamin pills, however, represented a great hope for humanitarian workers. John Maynard Keynes may have mocked this nutritional obsession, suggesting how ridiculous it was that something as miniscule as a vitamin should become the priority for postwar Europe, but UNRRA distributed millions of pills in the first years of its existence, and many aid workers saw vitamins as the perfect combination of scientific advancement, logistical power, and military efficiency.[35] All the goodness of fresh fruit and vegetables could now be reduced to a tablet, macerated into a medicine, and such methods of delivering nutrition were attractive because they could be controlled, producing order in chaotic conditions. Francesca Wilson, for example, extolled the virtues of the vitamin pill when recounting her conversation with a fellow relief worker about the differences between the two world wars. Utilizing a particularly relevant military metaphor, she recounted her friend exclaiming "What child's play it will be this time! We were groping in the dark then [but] now we know what vitamins are needed for every type of malnutrition. A bomber load of vitamins will be enough to cure a whole population."[36] Such motifs of militarism and mobility demonstrated an intense desire to control the messy realities of postwar Europe. As formidable airplanes were imaged dropping tiny curing tablets, a number of other new products were developed with similarly compact qualities.

Many of the new foods were existing products given a specifically humanitarian purpose. Cod liver oil, for example, which had been an ancient remedy for the infirm, was now endorsed as a source of vitamin A and D. Marmite, a salty yeast extract, was found to be rich in vitamins. Bemax, a wheat germ–based "tonic food," was repurposed to feed the hungry.[37] The idea in all cases was to isolate essential nutrients and recombine them in the field, finding a precise formula that built strength and avoided "refeeding syndrome": too much solid food that caused starving people to die prematurely. In the Bengal famine of 1943, for example, the British Army experimented with various ingredients to produce the "Bengal famine gruel."[38] This was a "mixture of powdered milk dissolved in boiling water, laced with enormous quantities of white sugar and flour," which "resembled a thick, white soup, its taste, excessively sweet."[39] It was a treatment based on a Victorian culture of feeding the sick with high-protein fluids—mixtures of milk, sugar and water "to be administered until the digestive strength returns"—but placed on a more scientific footing.[40] The aim was to get the right nutrients directly into the body without the dangers of too much solid food. Many experiments, however, led to failure.

Some doctors injected starving bodies with nicotinic acid, believing niacin deficiency to be a cause of their swelling bellies.[41] Others experimented with

THE ILLUSION OF THE GERMAN CALORIES

A cartoon by Szewczuk in "Die Zeit," Hamburg.

FIGURE 9. The illusion of the German calories. Cartoon by Mirko Szewczuk. *Manchester Guardian*, December 13, 1946, 8. Originally published in *Die Zeit*, 42/1946. © Szewczuk/Die Zeit. Reproduced with the permission of the Bodleian Libraries, University of Oxford. Shelfmark N. 22891.

Ventriculin: a proprietary extract of desiccated hog's stomach, which was thought to help the intestine absorb nutrients. The foul smell of this powder had to be disguised by adding it to a glass of very cold water, but the Ventriculin never fully dissolved, leaving the tongue coated with coagulated duodenum.[42] Just like breaking down the components of a production line through time and motion studies, or breaking down the nutritional needs of the human with calorific precision, the aim in all these experiments was to disassemble meals into their component parts. Physicians knew milk worked, so they broke this into Casilan: a powder made from casein—the protein found in milk.[43] They knew vitamins were important, so they manufactured pills or injected them directly. They knew absorption was important, so they administered "desiccated, defatted duodenal powder."[44] This, in effect, was the deconstruction of diet. It was concerned with efficiency, but it achieved this not just by consolidating the diet into a single set of numerical measures, but by disaggregating it, fragmenting it, breaking it down into ever more precise components.

Meals for Millions

In 1944, a new humanitarian food was invented in Rome, devised by a chemist at the Peroni brewery. He took some powdered malt, soaked it with oats in hot water, and strained the wort through a linen cloth.[45] This left a pale yellow liquid, sweet to the taste, which was used as a milk substitute for young children. It was known as Maltavena, an idea that came from a British aid worker called Bernard Ward Perkins, who was trying to recreate a soya milk mixture he had used during famine conditions in China.[46] Perkins was one of those fascinating characters that punctuate the history of relief: bursting with enthusiasm and liberal with his ideas as well as his letter writing. A correspondent at the British Ministry of Food described him as "an extraordinary old boy, [who] first popped up with his Maltavena when he was working in Rome on an honourary basis for the British Red Cross. . . . He is an enthusiast who knows little about nutrition and much of his knowledge is wrong anyway. Through sheer force of character he has introduced certain notable people in Maltavena."[47]

His force of character certainly worked. Perkins's letters punctuate the postwar files of several prominent aid agencies, and his correspondence reached individuals as diverse as Bernard Montgomery, Charles de Gaulle, and Victor Gollancz.[48] His basic idea was to produce a substitute for milk, which could be produced cheaply across a continent in which the dairy industry had been decimated, with manufacture taking place in breweries that were still operational after the war. The use of malted grains and the process of mashing and filtering would be familiar to any brewer, producing a vitamin-rich milk substitute. Perkins believed his man-made replacement for milk might even be an improvement on milk: young children, he argued, would find his milk substitute even easier to digest and absorb, because the starch in the cereal had been broken down during the malting and soaking process very much as it would do in the digestive tract.[49] There had long been a vibrant commercial market for milk substitutes in the West, associated with a narrative of improvement and civilization, but this was being explicitly brought into the field of emergency relief alongside an emerging high modernist mentality.

In 1945 the Maltavena recipe was passed onto the British Ministry of Food, who gave the formula to the Guinness brewery in Park Royal for testing.[50] The brewers there adjusted it, adding wheat flour and skimmed milk, and developed guidelines for its manufacture. UNRRA expressed an interest, requesting that the formula be tested on rats, and by 1946, it was being used in Dortmund, manufactured in the Union Brewery and distributed by the Friends Relief Services.[51] In 1948 it was used on an even bigger scale, when the British Medical Research Council began working with a German company in Hamburg to produce a version of the product called Lactavena.[52] At this point there were already a number of similar milk substitutes on the market: Cerex, manufactured by Cow and Gate, was also based on malted cereal flour, and Allenbury's malted food was similar. Benger's Food was designed for the infirm, and, like Maltavena, it declared itself as "self-digested" and easy to absorb.[53] Maltavena built on these ideas, but was explicitly designed for humanitarian relief, representing a desire to treat malnutrition scientifically. Once nutrients had replaced foods, technical products like this could proliferate, reproducing nutrients in a seemingly cheap and practical manner.

On the other side of the world there was another humanitarian product based on a similar idea. It began a long way from devastated Rome: in downtown Los Angeles, at an establishment called Clifton's cafeteria. Clifton's was billed at the time as the world's largest café, a symbol of American abundance during this period of European shortage. Run by a colorful local figure called Clifford Clinton, the cafeteria was managed according to the principle of small margins and huge volumes; the food was plentiful and cheap. On his menu, Clinton included something he called the Vita-Meal: a plateful of soybeans, rice, meat, and vegetables, which was available for just five cents or free if you were unable to pay.[54] A self-consciously good citizen, Clinton decided that no one should be turned away from his establishment hungry, regardless of funds. The Vita-Meal, therefore, was often given as a free meal, making Clifton's cafeteria a curious business model: part soup kitchen, part café, and soon a wider humanitarian experiment.

Toward the end of the war, Clinton enlisted the assistance of a scientist from Caltech to convert his Vita-Meal into a cheaper, standardized product. Together, they came up with Multi-Purpose Food, or MPF, a powder made from precooked, dehydrated ingredients. MPF was described in promotional correspondence as "a compound of pricked, dehydrated flaked lima beans, tunnel dehydrated soya grits, potatoes, cabbage, parsley, tomatoes onions and leeks with a skillful blend of flavoring ingredients such as paprika, garlic powder, onion powder, sweet basil and bay leaf, and certain vitamins to increase nutrition."[55] The executive director of the US Food for Freedom campaign endorsed it, describing the product as perfect for feeding the hungry populations of Europe. When reconstituted in water it could "be served as a stew, a soup or an entrée [and] with such a meal under one's belt it is possible to perform a day's labor as well as if the person eating it had feasted at a modern restaurant."[56]

As MPF was under development in California, rumors about the product soon found their way to field workers like Francesca Wilson. With the same enthusiasm she lent to the "bomber loads of vitamins," Wilson wrote excitedly and misleadingly that "a good meal for a hungry man of meat, potatoes, carrots and greens, treated so they retain their vitamins and protective properties, is now the size of a crown piece."[57] The attraction, once again, was mobility, and the excitement originated in Clinton's claim that two ounces of MPF powder was equivalent to a quarter pound of beef, a glass of milk, a baked potato, and a dish of peas.[58] Although this ordered, militaristic approach to feeding captured the imagination of frontline aid workers, some UNRRA administrators were less impressed. Letters from Clinton and his backers were left in the UNRRA archives annotated with red crayon; their suggestion that this tasty and nourishing powder might "save humanity from starvation" met with three large exclamation marks and the financial backing of the California Dehydrators Association cynically circled.[59] Clifford Clinton may have managed to get his Multi-Purpose Food on the San Francisco Opera House menu, advertising the possibilities of science at the first meeting of the United Nations, but UNRRA remained "rather casual in expressing lack of approval."[60]

Like Maltavena, MPF had more significance as an idea. It was later distributed far more widely by a foundation called "Meals for Millions," but it never became a practical method for filling empty stomachs.[61] It generated excitement because it seemed somehow magical: a full meal reduced to a powder that arrived in a modernist silver can, and its white label proudly displaying huge futuristic letters: MPF.

Edible Immutable Mobiles

How do we make food mobile? The traditional technique is to preserve it, dry it, or seal it in tins. These were the techniques behind military rations, which were developed over hundreds of years, as armies found more effective ways of feeding people on the move. Sailors faced this problem even more acutely, spending weeks and weeks away from land, and their rations relied on hardtack: a ship's biscuit made from flour, salt and water, baked and left to harden and dry. Hardtack was around for as long as seafaring, but it only became a standardized element of navy life in the seventeenth century, its production monitored in Britain by Samuel Pepys.[62] The army later adopted hardtack and combined it with canned meat in the nineteenth century to become the classic military ration: "bully beef and biscuits." The canning techniques were still relatively new, but they got progressively cheaper and seeped into humanitarian practice after the First World War.[63]

Preserved food, however, was always too expensive to feed the starving on any kind of scale unless there were massive supplies of surplus combat rations, as there were in the Second World War. An alternative approach was to strip commodities back into their component parts, to reduce foods to nutrients and then manufacture these nutrients in isolation. This was the approach adopted by many aid agencies by the middle of the twentieth century. Vitamin C tablets were more portable than oranges. Casilan was more portable than milk. Getting grain, meat, and vegetables to a disaster zone was always a complex task, with a great many logistical elements and the constant danger of rotting and degradation, but getting a bomber load of vitamins was far simpler. Providing full meals of cooked food always had some advantages when aid workers want to see the food go "down the children's throats," to use Herbert Hoover's phrase, but it was also logistically very complicated. Reducing food to nutrients, in contrast, made the process more stable, standardized, and controllable.

Bruno Latour used the idea of *immutable mobiles* to describe how power can be exerted at a distance, how networks can be sustained over time. These, he explained, are objects that can move without degrading; they are items that can be transported without changing shape.[64] Latour used the concept to describe texts, images, maps, and books, which carried information from place to place in a stable form. Unlike verbal messages, he pointed out, immutable mobiles allow information to be passed around with relative stability; they do not deteriorate so easily into rumor or get corrupted when passed around. With a fixed representation of geography on a map, for example, people can travel and communicate their discoveries. With written instructions, individuals can take collective action simultaneously. With contracts and agreements, complicated human relationships can emerge over time. Immutable mobiles, Latour argued, are a modern achievement: they can facilitate the exercise of power in distant lands and manage basic needs around the world.

Immutable mobiles, Latour also explained, do not just take the form of written instructions and maps. They also transport parts of the world and include samples, artifacts, and objects. This became crucial to emerging scientific practices, as immutable mobiles helped scientists "act at a distance on unfamiliar events, places or people." They did so by bringing these distant events, places, and people into greater proximity with each other, transporting parts of the world back to the laboratory to be examined. The aim was to disaggregate things and then recombine them in other places "so that whatever stuff they are made of, they can be cumulated, aggregated or shuffled like a pack of cards."[65]

Nutritional emergencies—like scientific field sites—were also distant and diverse. Aid workers—like scientists—also needed to act on unfamiliar events. As a result, many ended up relying on *edible* immutable mobiles in their work: ration packs, portable commodities, and vitamin pills. These allowed relief workers act at a distance. They turned food into something mobile as well as immutable, lightweight as well as long lasting. By isolating and disaggregating the components of food they made sustenance more mobile and transportable. Nutrients were manufactured and recombined, shuffled like a pack of cards; at the same time they remained edible—or at least, they aspired to be edible, withstanding difficult journeys without rotting or degrading. These became crucial as humanitarians began to act over larger distances, building networks with a wider reach, and exerting control in difficult environments.

Medicalizing Hunger

At the very end of the Second World War, as allied troops moved through German territory, the true horror of the concentration camps began to emerge and soldiers were faced with thousands of seriously malnourished people in need of urgent care. Bergen-Belsen became particularly famous after a well-known broadcast by Richard Dimbleby describing a young girl, a "living skeleton" who had "practically no hair left on her head and her face was only a yellow parchment sheet with two holes left in it for eyes."[66] Photos soon arrived in the press illustrating piles of dead bodies, huts filled with withered torsos. This was an event that entered into the mythology of humanitarianism due to the conditions and the later revelation that the Red Cross had known about the camps and failed to speak out. Yet Bergen-Belsen was also significant because it was here, among these withered and skeletal bodies, that therapeutic feeding was first tested on a large scale.[67]

The initial response of first British soldiers was to offer their army rations to the victims, which contained an assortment of rich, dense, fatty, processed foods. The result was catastrophic. It led to a bout of refeeding syndrome, that, according to some reports, ended up with two thousand people dying in the first few days.[68] When the Royal Army Medical Corps (RAMC) arrived a few days later the situation was stabilized, but their famine treatments did not always improve things for the victims.[69] One procedure was described as "intravenous therapy," and it entailed administering plasma and glucose directly into the veins. The treatment was based on the idea that the protein levels in the blood were too low, and it was best to restore these proteins directly in the form of plasma, a protein reserve. According to one newspaper report, the entire plasma stock of the London Air Raid precaution services was offered for this experiment, in which the two powders—plasma and glucose—were given according to a strict schedule.[70] Another procedure involved feeding people with protein hydrolysates: partially digested proteins based on "casein from milk and extracts of lean beef."[71] These, again, were administered on the grounds that they would restore essential amino acids, and they had been devised as a treatment for starvation during the Bengal famine. Hopes for this treatment were particularly high, and just as rumors about MPF had seeped into Francesca Wilson's memoirs of frontline aid work, Marcus Smith, in Dachau, recorded a story about the great hopes of hydrolysates. A Red Cross worker he met started waxing lyrical about this "new wonder drug," which enabled "a starved person to eat normally in seventy-two hours."[72] This was pure hyperbole, but the experimental idea was that this food could do for nutrition what penicillin had done for infection: provide a magic bullet for a recurring problem.

Enthused by protein hydrolysates, the British Medical Research Council took many liters of from London to Belsen, but the treatment quickly turned out to be a failure. It was "foul," wrote one medical volunteer; it "smelt like vomit."[73] Even mixing it with Bovril or cocoa failed to disguise the flavor.[74] Relief workers resorted to nasal tubes or intravenous injections to get the hydrolysates into the wasted bodies, but the concentration camp survivors reacted dramatically to such procedures. Reminded of Nazi executions, they screamed and struggled, begging not to be taken to the crematorium as the medical workers approached them.[75] The persistence of some in the Medical Research Council surprised many doctors: "They are doing yet another trial of protein-hydrolysate," wrote one medical worker; "another round of tortures. . . . I watched the horror and loathing of the patients who had to drink two cup-fulls of the stuff—triple strength. We also had to put one or two nasal tubes down—another thing they don't like."[76] Physicians started calling for the practice to end as soon as possible.

The procedure did come to an end eventually, and after about a month, the leader of the Medical Research Council team admitted that the protein hydrolysates had failed.[77] Hundreds of liters were destroyed, and relief workers returned to older, more successful treatments, which involved giving frequent, small amounts of easily digestible food by mouth. Belsen, therefore, continued to be a testing ground for the most effective famine formula, or "F-treatment," as it had become known.[78] The mixture used in Bengal was brought to Belsen and offered to the concentration camp survivors, but despite high hopes, the Bengal famine gruel was considered far too sweet.[79] Some Red Cross workers tried to adapt it, but others declared that the inmates could not possibly be hungry if they were refusing food: "They are too bloody particular," said one.[80] In the memorable words of another Red Cross worker, "The pathetic, skeletal inmates who had sufficient strength to talk" nevertheless managed to communicate their "intense loathing" of the food:

> We tried for several days to persuade them of the nutritional value of the gruel and, at nightfall, would leave a full churn in every hut in the hope that they would help themselves.... This only resulted in the most active among them lugging the churn out into the darkness and tipping the contents over the ground. At first light when we re-entered the camp, each hut would be partly encircled by a lake of gleaming, white gruel. The occupants of the huts complained bitterly that the smell made them feel more unwell than the stench of death and excrement in which they had for so long existed.[81]

This was surely a low point for the relief workers, their confidence sinking into a pool of thick white soup surrounded by camp mud. At the very least, they learned that taste was important, which led them to try a more successful approach: a mixture of milk, with the addition of glucose and vitamins, which resembled real food. It looked and tasted like milk; indeed, it *was* milk, sweetened and served with the equivalent of a vitamin pill. It was much more acceptable than the hydrolysates or the Bengal famine mixture had ever been—primarily because it was familiar—yet even as it became the recommended recipe for therapeutic feeding, the humanitarian approach to hunger remained unchanged. Relief workers were still approaching the problem as if it were only a nutrient deficiency. One described the treatment as "a solution of . . . spray-dried skimmed milk powder 60g, glucose 40g, [and] water 500c.c combined with vitamin mixture (Protein 21.5g, Fat 4g, Carbohydrate 60g, Calories 396)."[82] This was precisely what the Belsen survivors had emphatically rejected. They had disliked the protein hydrolysates and saccharine-sodden famine mixtures because such foods prioritized nutrients over taste, illustrating Audrey Richards's point that food is always social and cultural, even when people are starving.

THE MEDICALIZATION OF HUNGER AND THE POSTWAR PERIOD

At the end of 1944, thirty-six men went to the University of Minnesota to voluntarily starve themselves. On arrival at the campus they were weighed, measured, given a psychological assessment, and they gradually ate less and less. Over the following six months they consumed ever smaller portions of what was described as a "poor European diet"—meals dominated by cabbage, potatoes and turnips—and as the experiment progressed, the volunteers were instructed to complete exercises to ensure that they were burning more calories than they were consuming. Eventually, once their bodies had become thin and wasted, their skin pale and translucent, and their energy drawing on its last reserves, they were put onto one of several recovery diets and monitored to track their response. The study, which became known as the Minnesota Starvation Experiment was devised and led by Ancel Keys, creator of the K-ration, and his aim was to create a laboratory simulation of famine. This, he hoped, would help understand how civilians in postwar Europe could cope with massive shortages of food.

At the end of the study, Keys published a lengthy, two-volume report that described what happened to his research subjects.[1] The initial effects of starvation, he explained, were relatively minor and quirky: the volunteers began playing with their food to make it last; they created "weird and distasteful concoctions" in order to create an illusion of variety; and they developed an obsession with collecting recipes, pinning them on their walls. Later, as their interpersonal relationships began to deteriorate, the volunteers experienced fatigue, irritability, "outbursts of temper," and "periods of sulking." They started complaining of cold, even in the middle of summer, and then depression set in. "What humor remained at the end of the semi-starvation period," Keys wrote in his report, "was mainly of the sarcastic variety."[2]

Once the starvation got more serious, psychologists began noting neurotic and psychotic reactions. These were often attributed to preexisting mental problems or a failure of discipline. One man was summarized as a "bisexual individual with poor personality integration and weak self-control." Another suffered from "indecisiveness, self-deprecation, feelings of guilt, restlessness, nervous tension, compulsive gum-chewing and eating off-diet." A third was so badly affected that he exhibited "fits of hysteria," "violent outbursts," and ended up mutilating himself, chopping off three fingers with an axe in an attempt to get discharged from the project.[3] The effect on the participants was huge: of the forty original volunteers, eight dropped out with severe trauma and many others experienced depression.[4]

The volunteers were placed under close observation throughout their starvation, and subjected to an array of medical tests. The researchers used a dye injection technique to examine circulation of the blood. They measured the venous pressure and respiration with new contraptions that were inserted into the veins and over the head. They undertook regular X-rays, fluoroscopes, and biochemical analyses of urine, semen, stool, blood, and gastric juices. They even tested the hearing by playing different frequencies in a soundproof room, and examined vision by conducting eye tests under flickering lamps. The study then extended to intelligence tests and tests of fine motor skills, which involved asking volunteers to play with miniature children's toys.[5] It was an intricate regime of close examination, designed to uncover exactly what happened to the bodies of starving people.

The volunteers involved in this study were mostly conscientious objectors from the historic peace churches of the United States, who had signed up to make a sacrifice for humanity.[6] The original advertisement for the study asked: "Will you starve that they be better fed?" and it was this question that motivated many of those involved.[7] They were later hailed as "the men who starved for science," a narrative that promoted their service to humanity, but it is important to remember that conscientious objectors were *required* to be part of a government "citizen service program" that ensured their sacrifice was similar to the armed forces.[8] Often this included mainstream jobs, such as firefighting, but a good number of conscientious objectors also became "human guinea pigs." Some experiments were even more unpleasant than semistarvation in Minnesota and included wearing lice infected underwear, living in decompression chambers that simulated high altitudes, and being infected with hepatitis after swallowing the body waste of infected patients.[9] Research ethics were loose, and despite the narrative of sacrifice there seemed to be an element of punishment in some of these experiments and a retaliation for the failure to fight.

The Minnesota Starvation Experiment was just one of a large number of similar studies into human starvation that took place in the 1930s and 1940s. It was not just volunteers that got involved in these studies, but the victims of

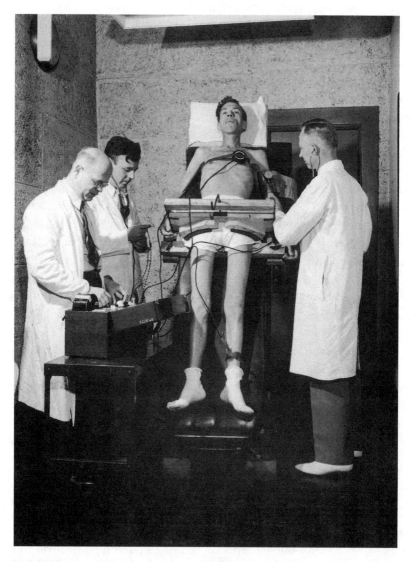

FIGURE 10.   The Minnesota Starvation Experiment. *Life Magazine*, July 30, 1945, 45. © Wallace Kirkland/LIFE Picture Collection/Getty Images.

battlefields, camps, and besieged towns in the Second World War. In Japanese prisoner of war camps, for example, British medical officers examined the effect of meager diets on their compatriots.[10] During the siege in Leningrad, physicians studied the collective impact of starvation on health and psychology.[11] After famine in the Low Countries, the government of the Netherlands commissioned a report into the medical effects of the crisis.[12] There were many other studies as well, from the refugee camps of the Far East to the university campuses of the American Midwest.[13] This chapter examines how they shared the same basic interest in the human biology of starvation, accumulating detailed information about starvation and its internal manifestations. In the process they reconfigured food as a medicine, hunger as a disease, and focused attention on the internal mechanics of the body.

Discovering Kwashiorkor

The "discovery" of kwashiorkor in the Gold Coast can be seen as an opening moment in the medicalization of hunger, when a colonial medical officer transformed a local, social problem into a specific form of "hunger disease." The story began in 1933, when reports about a new form of malnutrition in the Gold Coast first emerged in the *Lancet*. This condition was characterized not by wasting, but by swelling; rather than becoming thinner, patients became puffy. Cicely Williams wrote the first report, carefully noting edema in the limbs and stomach, thickening of skin, and a reddish tinge to the hair. The disease seemed most prevalent in children, especially those eating a low-protein diet, and it was often found in infants who had been recently weaned. Indeed, Williams noticed that babies were particularly vulnerable when they had been displaced from the breast by a younger sibling, since in such circumstances they were often given, instead of milk, a starchy pap made from maize flour.

Cicely Williams provided the first clinical description, which described the condition as "a nutritional disease of childhood associated with a maize diet." Two years later she gave the condition a more memorable name, taken from the local language: kwashiorkor, the "disease of the deposed child."[14] Over the next twenty years, kwashiorkor gradually gained medical acceptance and eventually became a big international cause. Descriptions of the condition had been trickling in from around the world for some years, but many commentators denied that these observations constituted anything new, interpreting them as either an existing disease or as an unrelated collection of symptoms.[15] The term *kwashiorkor* became widely adopted because Cicely Williams accumulated so much detail and then successfully defended her ideas from a variety of critics, the most vigorous of which were specialists in pellagra: a niacin deficiency disease that was also caused by a maize diet and that also led to similar patches of thickened skin. A physician called Hugh Stannus, for example, issued withering responses to Williams's articles, accusing her of failing to recognize what was really an infantile version of pellagra, and John Waterlow was another prominent nutritionist who refused to use the term *kwashiorkor*, preferring his term *fatty liver disease*.[16]

Much of this reluctance could be attributed to reflex sexism and the unfamiliarity of having a woman suggest a new disease in a male-dominated profession.[17] There was, however, another dynamic to these disputes. For Stannus and others, the use of a "West African native word" particularly rankled. Stannus complained that the word *kwashiorkor* was simply primitive, associated with the irrational superstition that "each successive child pushes the previous one into its grave."[18] This connection with weaning and the arrival of a new breastfeeding baby, in fact, was one of Cicely Williams's great achievements, but Stannus believed that "juju" terminology had to be rejected from science, not adopted as a descriptive label and brought into Western medicine.[19] Cicely Williams disagreed. She appreciated the significance of the "native word" and forcefully defended its use. The "disease of the deposed child," after all, had taught her a lot: it had informed her that kwashiorkor was caused by displacement from the breast, and therefore that it must have something to do with the absence of milk in the diet. She concluded it was basically down to a protein deficiency, and her biographers later praised her ability to "listen to the Ga" in this way, presenting it as a positive example of working from the bottom up.[20]

This interpretation, however, is misleading, because kwashiorkor turned out to be more complex than a simple protein deficiency. Williams did more than simply adopt a native word and a native understanding; she also transformed them both, altering the word and the understanding in profound and important ways. As Felix Konotey-Ahulu has explained, kwashiorkor had been a "sibling positional word" in the local vernacular. It connoted the social situation of the sufferer, emphasizing the risk of being a child, in a series of closely spaced siblings, in a resource-poor setting.[21] It eloquently identified a complex social problem—the ever-presence of death in communities that were characterized by entrenched poverty and large families—as well as an immediate cause: the arrival of a younger sibling, who displaced the previous child from the breast. To explain kwashiorkor, therefore, one needed to appreciate the wider environment, the social problems, and the structural situation of the suffering family.

After Williams published her *Lancet* article, however, kwashiorkor became medicalized. Williams took a vernacular word that had faced outward to society, and she turned it inward, focusing on the body and its biology. She took a word that had encapsulated a complex set of causes, and she reconfigured it to describe a single, overwhelming cause: a nutritional deficiency. Kwashiorkor, therefore, became characterized by absence rather than presence; by a lack of protein rather than the existence of many sociopolitical causes. This transformation had a profound impact on the way that the condition could be treated, especially as it became so central to hunger relief in the decades to come.

Intimate Anatomical Detail

It is often said of "discoveries" in Africa that they were no such thing: Europeans were simply finding things that Africans had always known about. There was certainly an element of this in the case of kwashiorkor, which was a common experience for Africans in the Gold Coast. The Ga had known about kwashiorkor long before a white medical officer published an account in the scholarly literature, and when Cicely Williams adopted the local term, she could be accused of appropriating it and changing its meaning. One clinician, when looking back at the discovery of kwashiorkor, noted with some irony that "the ignorant Africans [had long] recognized a disease that we had missed."[22] Another, Felix Konotey-Ahulu, pointed out that his "fellow tribespeople" had known "exactly what produces the syndrome and had no difficulty in diagnosing it."[23] A third, Guy Baily, put the point even more clearly: the cause of kwashiorkor, he wrote, was always "starkly simple and thoroughly understood," as it emerged from considerable poverty combined with a poor, restricted diet.[24] Cicely Williams may have been credited with discovering kwashiorkor, but its existence was widely known.

The point, however, must not detract from what was *produced* in this period. By writing to the *Lancet*, Cicely Williams launched something new, changing how the condition was framed and understood. This was not an isolated case: the process of identifying a disease never simply involves identifying preexisting facts that are waiting in the natural world since it is always a social process. It involves creating a new word, collecting signs and symptoms under that word, and then seeking wide acceptance of the new terminology. Richard Asher once described the discovery of a new disease as a process of creation. Charles Rosenburg, similarly, has explained how "disease does not exist until we have agreed that it does, by perceiving, naming, and responding to it."[25] Eric Cassell has moreover pointed out that disease is generated by medicine: "Illness is what the patient feels when he goes to the doctor; disease is what he feels on the way home from the doctor's office."[26] One does not need to be a Foucauldian or a Latourian, therefore, to accept that kwashiorkor was, in a crucial sense, being created anew by Cicely Williams in the Gold Coast.

Williams's definition was new in a number of respects as it prioritized biological over social causes, it focused on nutrients rather than rural poverty, and it explored the anatomy rather than political conditions. This was perhaps understandable—rural development is hardly the remit of the medical profession—but a number of practical implications followed once kwashiorkor had become medicalized. For one thing, blame for nutrient deficiencies could be more specifically attributed to certain people. In particular, mothers were blamed for failing to breastfeed according to a rigorous time schedule, blamed for failing to regulate the spacing of their babies, and blamed for failing to buy tinned milk or other high-protein weaning foods.[27] The British authorities then recommended a series of measures to tackle the disease, which generally focused on technical fixes such as the use of tinned milk. This illustrates Megan Vaughan's point about biomedicine being central to colonialism. Indeed, by this point kwashiorkor became a lever for modernization, used to promote the consumption of weaning foods and advocate smaller families.[28]

The medicalization of kwashiorkor also led to some shocking attempts to identify the missing nutrients and find new ways to deliver them. Various concoctions were tried as possible treatments: dehydrated liver, desiccated stomach, proteolyzed meats, casein hydrolysates, Marmite, and cod liver oil, to name just a few.[29] Rival physicians experimented with their own treatments, with those who believed the disease was a form of pellagra, for example, injecting children with nicotinic acid and those who thought it was related to iron deficiency administering desiccated stomach. All this was to the detriment of the kwashiorkor sufferers, many of whom died as a result.[30] The accumulation of information was nevertheless deemed necessary as kwashiorkor became stabilized as a medical fact. Different treatments could help identify the specific biological cause of the condition, and although Cicely Williams took fewer risks with her diets, she found other ways to study and understand the condition.

One of her techniques was the autopsy, which allowed her to establish one of the most important anatomical features of the disease: the presence of a fatty liver. This became so important to the definition of kwashiorkor that some commentators preferred the term *fatty liver disease* to the unusual local name. Autopsies, however, relied on the cooperation of local mothers, who viewed kwashiorkor rather differently. In an account given to her biographer, Cicely Williams spoke of the reluctance of mothers to provide their dead children for an autopsy, describing how they whisked their children away from the hospital as soon as they died or were close to death. She initially connected this with a local custom that demanded burial in the child's compound before sunset, but after talking with the mothers, however, Cicely Williams identified another possible cause. Apparently, bus drivers had been levying an extra charge for transporting corpses, which led the mothers of dead or dying children to take the bodies quickly away, hoping to pass them off as living. Williams found a solution that, in the view of her biographer, was "so simple, but [one that] no other European had thought of [before]."[31] She gained consent for autopsies by offering compensation to the mothers, which enabled them to pay the bus drivers and keep the bodies of the kwashiorkor victims a little longer in the hospital. She smoothed over an area where the medicalization of hunger was clashing with very different understandings of the world.

It is difficult to tell whether the reluctance of mothers was really down to the policy of bus drivers, or whether the mothers were just looking for a financial incentive to participate in what, to them, must have seemed a highly unusual practice. After all, the autopsy is likely to have seemed unnecessary to the Ga, who had always located the kwashiorkor in a social relationship rather than a biological one. There seemed no need to cut open dead bodies to discover why kwashiorkor occurred, if, to use the words of Felix Konotey-Ahulu again, one was convinced that kwashiorkor was "the result of a social pathology before it is the outcome of a biochemical pathology."[32] The local understanding of this condition explained kwashiorkor with reference to the position of the sibling, the circumstances of poverty, and the deposition from a breast. In other words, the causes of the condition were identified *outside* the body, not within it. The very opposite was true for Williams, who saw the intricate anatomical detail provided by autopsy as crucial to understanding how it was caused.[33]

The Postwar Starvation Studies

Intricate anatomical detail became a defining feature of hunger's medicalization, and opportunities to accumulate this detail expanded as the world descended into war. Civilians in many European countries were called up for military service in the 1940s, and many others lived in situations marked by siege and starvation. Even before the grim story of Bergen-Belsen unfolded, there were many other examples of physicians examining the empty stomach, and one of the first opportunities took place in Warsaw ghetto after it was sealed in 1941. Here, food for the Jewish population was restricted to only three hundred kilocalories per day. A group of physicians, stationed in a hospital overflowing with malnourished people, decided to study the effects on people's bodies, and they examined and recorded the situation in terrible detail. Calling on specialists in ophthalmology, metabolism, pathology, pediatrics, and the circulatory system to conduct hundreds of clinical examinations and thousands of autopsies, they built an account of physical deterioration that was unprecedented in its detail. As one commentator explained, "Nothing was too obscure or too trivial, nothing was overlooked in the investigator's searching descriptions" of starvation.[34] The study only lasted six months, but its intricacy remains remarkable.

As part of the many tests that were conducted in this period, the expert in circulatory system injected dye into the patients' arteries, retrieving blood with a second needle in order to examine its rate of return.[35] The ophthalmologist examined the intraocular pressure of the eye, using a primitive tonometer that placed weights on the eyeball.[36] Other physicians injected insulin and iron into patients' arms in order to see their effect on metabolism.[37] Bone marrow was extracted with a needle and examined; salt water was injected under the skin to see how long the resulting blisters remained.[38] The heart and circulation were examined by getting patients to do sit-ups, or by giving them hard-boiled eggs and measuring the response of their blood pressure to protein and exercise.[39] The reduction in body temperature, the weakness, the low red blood count, the skin pigmentation, the malfunction of the sweat glands, the abnormal hair growth, the slowing of circulation, the irritability and lack of energy were all examined and documented, with each observation supported by a mass of data. These tests were all used to build up a clinical description of hunger, which, in the opinion of some scholars, has never been surpassed.[40]

The studies of "hunger disease" in the Warsaw ghetto, however, leave a horrific impression because the research took place against the backdrop of the holocaust. The Jewish physicians were unable to improve the situation of the starving, and the Nazi blockade had left the Jewish physicians impotently conducting ghoulishly detailed research on the bodies of the dying. This generated a terrible subversion of the doctor's role. The experiments were cruel by today's standards, involving emaciated people subjected to injections, their internal workings illuminated by needles and dye, and the imaginative possibilities of this situation have been drawn out by Sherman Russell, who, in a fictitious enactment of a scene in the hospital, presents the research as a search for meaning amongst doctors and patients: "One more sit-up, the doctor's coaxed. One more needle. And from that, they promised, might come some meaning from this horror. . . . In our imagination, the woman on the hospital bed tried to understand. She might even feel reassured by this bit of meaning accomplished in fifteen sit-ups. What does it matter if she spends her last hoard of energy and lives a few minutes less? She is hungry for meaning too."[41]

If we look more closely at the physicians' reports, however, Russell's romanticism seems highly misplaced. There is no evidence to suggest the patients sought sense from the horror; indeed, it is a flight of imagination to suggest that they were even willing participants at all. The physicians' reports only mention the "negative attitude" of the patients, the need for more "goodwill and concentration."[42] Posterity, however, was certainly a motivation for the doctors. The initiator and coordinator of the research, Israel Milejkowski, stressed this clearly in his introduction to the study. The physicians, he emphasized, knew that the ghetto could be destroyed and emptied at any moment, and they conducted their tests in attempt to produce knowledge in the face of adversity.[43] They saw their work as an example of a heroic human endeavor, evidence of "courage under siege," a struggle on behalf of science.[44] The experiments, he wrote, were a bid for immortality by the physicians, showing how research conducted in the shadow of death can become "part of the immortal body of knowledge." Unable to help their patients, the doctors therefore sought meaning in "the reality of their grim, everyday life."[45] Dr. Milejkowski repeated these themes in the closing paragraph of his paper. Addressing colleagues, many of whom had already become victims of the death camps, he wrote: "Jewish physicians, you deserve some words of recognition. . . . You, too, were menaced by forced labor, starvation, deportation, by all the forms of death that stalked our ghetto. And you gave the murderers a bold answer with your work—'non omnis moriar' [I shall not wholly die]."[46]

The Warsaw studies of hunger disease have been held up as an example of resistance, but they really illustrate the failure of resistance. They are cited as evidence for the value of science, but they really illustrate its limitations. The story is so awful because the starvation was inflicted on the Warsaw ghetto as part of a fascist policy of extermination, to which there was no effective resistance for doctors, and these studies show how the quest for detailed anatomical information, realized through tests and autopsies, necessarily involved restricted political horizons. It was always optimistic to suppose that some practical good could come of studying intricate biological changes in such a circumstance, but just as the medicalization of kwashiorkor replaced a complex network of causes with singular deficiency, the studies of the Warsaw ghetto placed the root causes of suffering in parentheses. Fascism was less its focus than the biological changes of the body. The papers are filled with poignant realizations of this inevitable restriction, and perhaps the most powerful moment is when a doctor, testing people's responses to iron injections and a diet of raw animal blood, concluded that his patients' could only be helped "by supplying adequate food with an appropriate calorific value."[47] This, of course, was not just obvious, but it was the one thing that the doctors, despite all their scientific expertise, were completely unable to provide.

Death's Tragic Heaven

In her 1992 ethnography, *Death without Weeping,* Nancy Scheper-Hughes gave a detailed description of the medicalization of hunger in South America. Based on years of fieldwork in the favelas of Bom Jesus da Mata in northeastern

Brazil, she showed how persistent hunger could be diagnosed as *nervos*, a medical condition characterized by weakness, shaking, coldness, and trembling.[48] As Scheper-Hughes described it, the poor in Bom Jesus da Mata were visiting doctors for treatment of *nervos* when their true malady was persistent hunger. The pains of poverty were being transformed into a nervous condition, which was then managed through a cocktail of tonics, painkillers, and tranquilizers. Delving into the effects of this medicalization, Scheper-Hughes argued that it obscured the terrible conditions of the favelas and the inequality of everyday life. The implication was appalling. The poor were hungry, but they willingly took tranquillizers and forgot the root cause of their malady. Most tragically, they accepted and internalized the medical diagnosis, leading to a profound depoliticization of their condition.

Death without Weeping is a fascinatingly detailed description of medicalization in a particular time and place, but it does not help us understand the medicalization of hunger as a distinctive historical process. In Scheper-Hughes's example, the medical profession was not actually dealing with something they recognized as hunger: they were displacing the problem and treating *nervos* instead. As a result, they were not medicalizing food, but instead prescribing drugs that emphatically were not food. This chapter, however, has concerned a rather different process: a historical situation in which the problem of starvation was not displaced, but reframed. The story of Cicely Williams is crucial here, as it showed how the accumulation of anatomical detail and the identification of a nutrient deficiency became the hallmark of a medicalized paradigm. In some ways, this was far more successful than the medicalization of hunger described by Nancy Scheper-Hughes. Rather than offering painkillers and tranquilizers, the medicalization of hunger in the 1930s and 1940s offered nutrients as if they were drugs. In some ways, this was exactly what people needed, but the effect was still to transfer the problem of starvation over to medical professionals. Medicalization involved focusing on a narrow range of biological processes rather than wider social conditions, which stood as a remarkable contrast to the expansive wave of policies that had come out of social nutrition at the League of Nations just a decade earlier.

In thinking about this process of medicalization, Foucault's book, *The Birth of the Clinic*, is a common reference point. By tracing the emergence of the medical profession in the late seventeenth century, Foucault showed what happens when things enter the medical domain.[49] The rise of the autopsy was an important part of his account of how the medical profession emerged, as the practice of cutting open and examining dead bodies, Foucault pointed out, stopped being taboo in the Enlightenment; it emerged from religious and cultural prohibition to transform conceptions of death.[50] Before the autopsy, Foucault argued, death was represented as an external force. It came from outside the body. It arrived and "visited" someone. It overwhelmed life and led them to a different world. Death, in this reading, was everywhere: it affected everyone and could strike at any time. It was the great leveler of the medieval world, which came to anyone and everyone in the form of the grim reaper, whisking away rich and poor alike.

The autopsy transformed this understanding of death, and under the bright, cool lights of science and reason, human anatomy began to be illuminated. There was a new interest in the exact, internal cause of death, and illness became explicable. The arrival of death was no longer imminent; it was not a force that always waited in the wings, ready to take everyone away. Death could now be delayed. The rich could learn what was wrong inside their bodies, and death no longer affected everyone indiscriminately. It no longer visited the body from outside but came from the inside, associated with a particular illness. This was a transformation in our understanding of death and the body, which, to use Foucault's poetic phrase, involved death leaving its tragic heaven and becoming the "lyrical core of man."[51]

The autopsy, Foucault believed, was crucial in this transition, as it led to new knowledge about the body. Physicians could learn how the organs operated, what could go wrong and how problems could be fixed. The causes of death became more precise and detailed and reasons for mortality could be explained. The body was opened up, written about, and understood. Rather than the old system of a singular Death—personified in the grim reaper—who would affect everyone in the same way, there now emerged a multitude of deaths, attacking different people and different parts of the organism at different times. Medical textbooks became longer and more intricate as information was collected about the exact cause of a malady.[52]

In the history of humanitarian nutrition, we can see a similar process take place during the "hunger studies" of the 1930s and 1940s. Autopsies began to reveal the inner workings of the starving body and attention was refocused at the cellular level. Types of hunger disease proliferated and expanded as starvation took multiple forms. For hundreds of years there had been just one diagnosis for starvation, defined by the Greek word *marasmus*, which meant to waste or wither away. As studies of starvation proliferated, however, so did hunger diseases. First came the discovery of vitamins, creating new forms of deficiency, and then came the discovery of kwashiorkor as an edematous form of starvation. The accumulation of maladies and detailed descriptions culminated in the massive Minnesota Starvation Experiment, which stretched to thousands of pages of detail. Rather than simply concluding that people died from hunger, these studies demanded specificity and a much greater technical response.

By the end of World War II, a distinct change in focus had solidified, from starvation as a general experience to malnutrition as a specific experience. In the first two decades of the twentieth century hunger was most likely to be examined as a pervasive human problem, using the tools of political economy, sociology, or agriculture. Hunger's cause was located externally, in the political economy of wages, the failings of traditional agriculture, or the culture of the "savage tribe."[53] The medicalization of hunger, however, shifted attention inside the body, and starvation began to be understood as a medical problem, its causes found in cells and nutrients. In the terms of Foucault, hunger was no longer a horseman of the apocalypse: external, eternal, rooted in social conditions. It was a condition that could be known and tamed, residing in the lyrical core of man.

A Last Gasp for Social Nutrition

Social nutrition took one last breath before collapsing into the technical high modernist age, as it was kept alive for a few more years in the Food and Agricultural Organization (FAO). This organization's first director, John Boyd Orr, had been a prominent figure in the nutritional golden age, and he did everything in his power to realize the FAO's expansive founding agenda of freeing the world from hunger.[54] Among Orr's many proposals was a World Food Board, an international agency for food price regulation, which has been described as "one of the most ambitious designs for international action ever put forward."[55] The basic idea was to set maximum and minimum prices for staple commodities, buying and selling these foods on world markets in order to keep prices within established limits. When the price of wheat approached the upper boundary, for example, the World Food Board would release stocks and depress the price. When the price approached the lower limit, on the other hand, the Board would buy up the surplus and push prices back up again. The idea was to protect consumers from high prices and producers from low prices, while raising money to finance a credit facility for poor nations and a stockpile for famine relief.[56]

Orr's proposals for a World Food Board involved a comprehensive vision of an institution achieving many aims. By buying when prices were low and selling when they were high, the World Food Board could raise money for investment in developing nations. Simultaneously, the Board could use its large buffer stocks for famine relief in cases of regional crop failure. By stabilizing prices it would provide farmers with a stable income while also keeping food affordable and improving nutrition for food consumers. This constituted the last big attempt to cement social nutrition within international institutions, but unfortunately it came to nothing. Orr's proposal was too much of a threat to state sovereignty, and when the matter came to a final decision the member states rejected it.[57] FAO member states not only opposed the erosion of their sovereignty, but also registered their disagreement with Orr's whole approach to hunger. Whereas Orr believed that staple foods should be universally accessible, seeing full stomachs as a precondition for productivity and development, his opponents reversed the calculation. Rather than seeing good nutrition as the key to development, they saw development as the key to nutrition. They believed that free trade should not be interfered with, as it was precisely what was needed to generate growth and purchasing power. Noninterference and rising trade, they concluded, would ultimately enable people to buy the food they needed.

The Food and Agricultural Organization, in the end, followed this very different path, becoming an increasingly technocratic organization. Rather than intervening directly to stabilize the price of foods, it ended up collecting data and making recommendations. Orr was furious with the outcome. "The hungry people of the world wanted bread," he declared in his autobiography, "but they were to be given statistics."[58]

Statistics certainly dominated the FAO under the leadership of its next two directors, under whom the agency collected piles of data, from food supplies to legislative summaries.[59] A new FAO Nutrition Division was created in 1946, for example, which indicated how the medicalization of hunger had replaced social nutrition in the institutions of global governance. From the very beginning of this new Nutrition Division, its director, Wallace Aykroyd, shied away from the utopianism of Orr's proposals.[60] He retreated into technical data instead, commissioning new studies into the composition of different foods and the standardization of international tables. He launched dietary surveys and studied the intricacies of food fortification, examining the wartime hunger studies and exploring how malnutrition might be measured.[61]

Aykroyd believed that this kind of technical data was necessary for practical nutrition programs, but Orr railed against the move. Focusing the new organization's efforts in this way, he said, was "futile." "No research is needed to find out that half the people in the world lack sufficient food," he declared, arguing that interventionist international action was more important than any amount of data.[62]

The Nutrition Division at the FAO, meanwhile, recruited, trained and dispatched a whole new generation of nutritional experts to collect and analyze data. They were sent to "young and poor countries" to help new nations "reach a higher technical and economic level." They were "imbued with faith, the spirit of self-sacrifice" and "the qualities of pioneers . . . able to work under adverse circumstances."[63] Over the coming years the work of these technical experts would lead to a cadre of professionals that had learned from the wartime hunger studies: experimenting with diets, retreating into laboratory study, and assuming that hunger would be conquered by analyzing nutrients and measuring malnourishment.[64]

John Boyd Orr's vision of social nutrition died fast in this world. He had hoped that the FAO would involve member states pooling their resources and working together to end hunger, but instead the FAO became an organization shaped by experts pushing for top-down transfers of technical knowledge.[65]

There was an irony here. Nutritional science was held in very low esteem by the medical establishment of the 1940s and 1950s, yet international nutrition was becoming increasingly shaped by medicalization.[66] Doctors and clinicians had turned hunger into a nutritional disease, and this shaped global policy accordingly.

Central to this process was the Joint FAO/WHO Expert Committee, founded in 1949 to coordinate nutrition work, which promoted the study of malnutrition. In the wake of these new studies, diagnoses multiplied and complex typologies of hunger began to emerge. The first attempt was the Gomez classification, adopted by the Hospital Infatil de Mexico in 1946 to "simplify the nomenclature of a large group of diverse and confusing ailments, the common basis of which is deficient nutrition."[67] This divided malnourished children into "degrees" based on a statistical comparison: mild malnutrition (first degree), moderate malnutrition (second degree), and severe malnutrition (third degree). Later on there was the Protein-Energy Malnutrition pyramid, promoted by pediatrician Derrick Jelliffe, who pointed out that malnutrition consisted not just of degrees, but also forms. Jelliffe's pyramid showed how someone could suffer from the wasting that came with marasmus, the swelling that came with kwashiorkor, and then a "kaleidoscopic and bewildering variety of clinical pictures" that existed in between.[68]

The problem of hunger, therefore, had multiplied. Rather than an older system of a singular and widespread hunger that affected everyone in a similar way, humanitarians had now defined a much larger number of specific hungers, which attacked different people and different parts of the organism at different times. Nutritional researchers and food technologists flocked to study the new forms of hunger disease, while biochemical investigations explored the various types of edema and dermatitis. To respond to these more specific forms of hunger, humanitarians started experimenting with more specific forms of food. They became more concerned with technical realignments and complex products as a wave of high modernist fervor swept through the sector in the following two decades.

HIGH MODERNISM AND THE DEVELOPMENT DECADE

In the late 1950s British Petroleum started developing a new kind of food. It was called Single Cell Protein (SCP), and it was produced from fungi grown on oil. The process emerged when BP technicians tried to make oil easier to pour—they had realized that fungi consumed the wax that hardened in oil—but they soon became more interested in the byproduct than in the dewaxing itself. A recent United Nations report had declared protein deficiency to be the "most serious and widespread nutritional disorder known to nutritional and medical science," and it was found that the dewaxing process could produce fungi in the form of an edible, protein-rich biomass.[1] The stage was set, it seemed, for a high-protein food for a perceived global protein shortage. After some years of experimentation, a viable and inexpensive process had been devised for its production, and Single Cell Protein soon became a growth industry, with hundreds of millions of dollars invested in new industrial plants. Of the many enthusiastic newspaper reports, one article in the *New York Times* included a particularly vivid opening:

> In the dank basement of a laboratory on Long Island, a research scientist crouched before a glass cauldron filled with a yellowish translucent liquid that bubbled furiously beneath a bright light. "Grow my darlings, grow," he murmured. "Are you warm enough? Want some more ammonia?" . . . Hours later the liquid in the vat had changed to a deeper, creamier yellow, richly opaque. "Aha," the scientist exclaimed, "they're

growing!" He then skimmed off a cupful of the liquid, held it at arm's length, grinned and pronounced, "Food!"[2]

Much of this rhetoric was steeped in the grand ideals of the era. The glamour of technology was combined with Frankenstein-inflected imagery of muttering scientists nurturing life in isolated laboratories. Soon there were motivational speeches, appeals to the power of science, and a sense of historical destiny. One report declared Single Cell Proteins to be a "third age" in the history of man. At first, it said, humans had fed themselves through hunting and gathering, and then through husbandry and agriculture. The third age would be characterized by the production of biosynthetic foods, manufactured in industrial plants without dirt, work and weather.[3] Such food, BP emphasized, would be "entirely under [man's] control," growing with "no soil, sunlight, or even assistance from human labour."[4] Single Cell Protein, in other words, heralded nothing less than the beginning of a new era in food production, a transformation in our relationship to the environment.[5]

This was a classic example of high modernism: an approach that dominated international efforts from the 1950s to the middle of the 1970s. It emerged from the medicalization of hunger and was soon characterized by three central features. First of all it lionized science, adopting the idea that scientists could produce a superior and more rational diet. Second, it tamed nature, replacing natural processes with industrial production while bypassing the unpredictability and irrationality of agriculture. Third, it was preoccupied with elitist planning, breaking diets into precise nutritional formulae and making every element of their production more controllable. Humanitarians since World War II had been viewing hunger more and more as a technical problem, defining it as a mismatch between the biochemical needs of the body and the nutritional content of food. High modernism went further. It did not just reduce food to nutrients, but came with a commitment to industrial production and technical transfer to the Third World. This was very much in the spirit of the UN's first "development decade."[6] Whereas the earlier nutritional reductionists had believed technology to lead to bad diets, the high modernists believed that only man-made foods could free the world from hunger.[7] Repackaging and preserving familiar foods—as in the Second World War—was no longer sufficient; high modernism involved a radical remaking of the world. It sought a clean break from traditional practices, moving toward a bright, brave new future.

Single Cell Protein was the archetypal example of this approach, offering an unlimited supply of food from controlled and hygienic vats. It promised a source of nutrition that reproduced itself remarkably efficiently, largely through its own devices. "Where a calf may double its weight in four weeks, [and] a chicken in

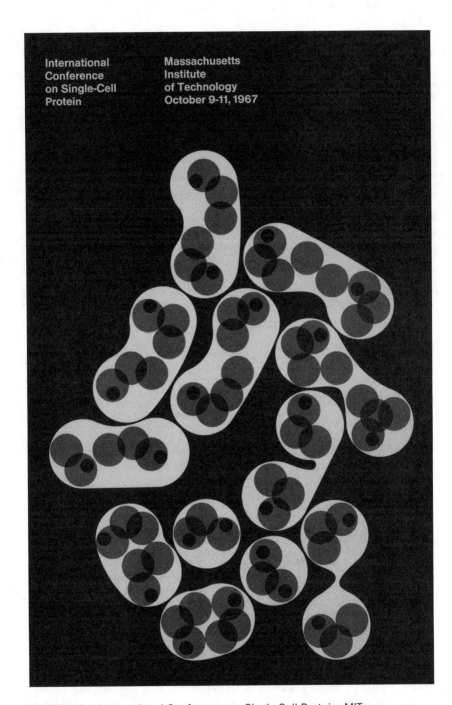

FIGURE 11. International Conference on Single-Cell Protein. MIT, October 9–11, 1967. Cover image © Dietmar Winkler. Reproduced with permission from Dietmar Winkler/Megan Verdugo.

four days," wrote one enthusiastic supporter of the new technique, "a micro-organism can double its weight in four hours."[8] Many similar schemes emerged in the 1950s and 1960s. As we will see in this chapter, in addition to fungi grown on oil, there were foods made from insects, biscuits made from fish offal, algae grown on sewage, and inedible leaves that had been pulped and boiled into a protein curd. The dream in all cases was to provide a cheap, efficient, mass-produced food that could sustain human bodies in extremis. This was a dream for the space age, which came associated with a vision of life emerging from waste, of human sustenance freed from irrationality.[9]

The high modernist approach dominated humanitarian nutrition in the 1950s and 1960s, and this chapter explores its manifestations. Beginning with Leaf Protein Concentrate, which emerged from postwar investigations into food shortage, high modernist hopes soon moved to less appetizing foods made from algae and junk fish, driven by an even more futuristic and top-down vision of life emerging from primordial sources. After this initial burst of enthusiasm came a different high modernist concept: the complete nutritional wonder-product, which was meant to offer a balanced meal in a simple powder or sachet. After generating great interest in aid agencies, this ideology began to go into decline by the early 1970s, limited by expense, complexity, and fundamental impracticality. As we see in the next chapter, high modernism then turned into low modernism. Stripped of its utopian fervor, the more workable ideas began to find a more commercially viable form.

Leaf Protein Concentrate

Single Cell Protein was a top-down foodstuff, emerging from the capital-intensive oil industry, but high modernism in nutrition also had some more modest beginnings. A good example is Leaf Protein Concentrate, or LPC. This was the work of a biochemist named N. W. Pirie who was based at the University of Cambridge during World War II.[10] Pirie had been pursuing unrelated research into plant viruses when an idea hit him. He had started a habit of tasting the protein he produced when centrifuging a mass of chloroplasts from the sap of their leaves, joking to colleagues that it could be a perfectly good source of food.[11] A British government official later visited the University of Cambridge to investigate solutions to postwar food shortage, and this provoked Pirie to take the idea more seriously. He began developing the idea that protein could be extracted from the leaves of many ordinary, nonedible plants, and the resulting product, which became the focus of his work, soon became known as LPC.

With government support, Pirie began devoting much of his professional life to this idea, which, at heart, was a relatively simple procedure: he mashed up the leaves, sieved off the pulp, then boiled the leftover liquid in a huge vat before finally skimming off the protein that coagulated on the surface.[12] By the 1950s, he had developed machines for large-scale production at Rothamsted, a government research station, and was manufacturing leaf protein in two different forms. One was a wet, bright green, jellylike curd, which perished easily but could be stored in cubes, like a "moist green cake."[13] The other was a dried green powder, gritty and sometimes difficult to reconstitute. Pirie preferred the former, emphasizing that he had consumed many pounds of it and found it perfectly acceptable as food. Given its texture and color, however, he recognized that it would be difficult to market this as a palatable and attractive product on its own.[14]

A number of Pirie's early papers were devoted to cooking this raw material into something more aesthetically pleasing. Pirie faced particular difficulty because leaf protein turned dishes an unappetizing dark green color and gave the feces a "greenish tinge."[15] He got around this problem by developing recipes that would be naturally green, suggesting that leaf protein might be added to "finely pulped fresh leaves with strong flavors, e.g. parsley, mint, spinach, mustard, cress," and arguing that green foods often led to green stools.[16] He also began packaging the result in familiar forms, for example enveloping it in pasta to make "leaf protein ravioli" and distributing this after his lectures.[17] He started arguing that leaf protein could be widely appreciated with the right preparation and advice.

Pirie took pride in his recipes, which were published in his articles. He made "leaf protein doughnuts," "deep fried leaf protein mixed with spice," and "flavored leaf protein paste on a wafer"—the last a particularly useful hors d'oeuvre when addressing "well-fed visitors from ministries, embassies and international organizations."[18] One address at the Royal Society of Arts ended with leaf protein biscuits, and Pirie repeated his fondness for leaf protein ravioli in a number of other articles.[19] His approach was "to dispense with apology and try flavour combinations without regard to colour." "Conventional cooking techniques," he wrote, "have a 50,000-year start, and it is hardly likely that we will catch up as a result of a few dozen trials." But, he concluded, "it is already clear that the protein blends excellently with small amounts of the more fatty types of fish or cheese, and that a mixture of egg and leaf protein scrambles well and has a pleasant flavour and texture."[20]

Alongside his experiments in the Cambridge laboratory, Pirie also became interested in making leaf protein work in developing nations. He enlisted the support from new funding agencies such as the International Biological Program, and later from Christian Aid.[21] The new projects were based around the same extraction process as in Cambridge, but with simpler equipment and community level production: they involved grinding green leaves into a juice by using local corn mills, before boiling them in local pots and then skimming off the green protein curd. The rustic machinery worked well enough, but there remained a problem about how to eat it. The dried form of the protein could be used as an additive, sprinkled on any meal like a condiment, but it was dark and gritty, and it unpleasantly roughened the consistency of food. The other option was to distribute the leaf protein as fresh curd, which had a nicer consistency, but this led to a different set of problems: the curd went off very quickly and so ideally needed to be frozen straight after production, but electricity in most developing countries was still sporadic. This meant that the product could only be distributed to a relatively small area and perishability made it hard to handle.[22]

The biggest problem, however, was that leaf protein required a huge change in people's daily diets, which was difficult to promote. Pirie's basic idea, after all, was to revolutionize the diet and overthrow tradition, a vision particularly well-illustrated in one of his lectures from 1958, entitled "World Hunger as a Biochemical Problem." In this address Pirie declared that the world was "bigoted about the colour of proteins" and suggested that opposition to the bright color of his product could be overcome if children in the developing world ate leaf protein from birth. "If the people we now have to cater for will not eat a green food, we must bring up a group who will!" he declared.[23] This was a classic example of the high modernist disregard for cultural practices and the desire to shape humans to fit with scientific order. Even a fifty-thousand-year history of dietary patterns was not enough to discourage Pirie from his work. Indeed, the central task soon became promotion rather than production: the need to convince consumers that Leaf Protein Concentrate could be a viable alternative to eggs, beans, and more traditional sources of food.[24]

Foods for the Future

Leaf Protein was an early and rather modest example of high modernist nutritional ambitions, but by the late 1950s there were a range of more expansive projects for making food from junk fish, algae, and insects. Food from algae was perhaps the most clearly high modernist idea, which was first mooted in 1947 and dominated technological visions of a world without hunger for over a decade. As with Single Cell Protein, the attraction came from efficiency. Here was a food that could be grown all year round, that multiplied rapidly, and that converted energy from the sun through photosynthesis at a far superior rate. The scientists involved lamented the inefficiency of more conventional crops because so much of the plant ended up being inedible: all those stalks, leaves, and flowers ended up wasted, they argued; all those seeds sat for so long in the ground before the plant appeared from the soil.[25] Proponents of algae-based foods, approaching food "as an engineer would," argued that these traditional crops were inefficient and primitive. Instead, they devised an alternative system that produced food from the very bottom of the food chain.[26]

The basic idea was that algae, as a primordial growth, could reproduce at over a hundred times the average yield of other crops. The preferred algae, Chlorella, was grown on sewage, skimmed off, concentrated to a paste in a centrifuge, spread on an aluminum sheet, heated until dry, and then pounded into a fine powder.[27] The seemingly revolting part of this process—the growth on sewage—was actually a key element of the modernist dream, for here was a food that did not produce waste so much as consume it. Chlorella was seen as ideal for long distance space travel, since it could convert sewage into food, *and* produce oxygen at the same time. In other words, it created a complete aeronautic support system.[28] The procedure was planned to solve global food shortages, since if food could be produced from waste, poor people could also benefit from scientific progress and efficiency. Funds poured in from the Carnegie Institution, and the progress report of 1953 was given a title that captures these aims: "Algae to Feed Starving."[29] A subsequent monograph gave a similar emphasis, claiming that algae could offer "respite from famine," providing "more salutary conditions for civilized living."[30]

Experiments with human subjects, however, soon revealed the unpalatable side of algae. By the end of the 1950s, only a few tests had taken place, with the most extensive experiments on malnourished Venezuelan lepers, providing a particularly vivid demonstration of the era's dubious research ethics.[31] The lepers did not seem to complain about the "plankton soup" they were served, even after being fed algae for five years, but later experiments in Japan, with algae noodles, and the United States, with algae milk-and-cookies, revealed considerable disgust—always mediated by the detached, ever-hopeful language of the scientific journal.[32] Foods made with algae, the journals reported, turned bitter and alarmingly green. They were described in one paper as appearing "foodlike," but leading to "a noticeable tightening at the back of the throat (gag factor)."[33] The taste lingered for several hours and led to "difficulties in digestive function," spelled out in another paper as "cramping pains," "increased flatulence," and "bowel excreta that had turned dark green in color."[34] Some articles suggested a way around this by recommending that algae should be treated as a garnish, since "its bright green color would add interest if it were sprinkled on certain foods," but this was blind optimism.[35] The problems with taste and digestion were clear, and algae was shelved relatively early in the modernist era.

Fish Protein Concentrate, or FPC, had more success. This was produced by mincing the unprofitable parts of a trawler's catch, then dehydrating and repeatedly centrifuging the result. This process initially produced something called "wet cake," which was then heated and ground into a powder.[36] The process yielded a fine dust, made from the whole of the "junk fish," which was seen to have an excellent nutritive profile, providing a great deal of protein, with a good balance of amino acids. It also had the advantage of fitting into a preexisting industry. Usually, when faced with a huge number of particularly small fish, industrial fishing fleets would destroy or waste the surplus. The idea of creating fishmeal by pulverizing the entire fish and turning it into a long-lasting dry powder, therefore, was attractive both practically and economically, using waste products to feed the starving. The FAO, UNICEF, and WHO promoted production plants around the world and invested a particularly large amount in establishing the industry in Chile, which had a long coastline, a large fishing industry, and high levels of malnutrition. A new production process removed much of the fat and oil from the fish, which avoided the intensely unpleasant "fishy" taste. Soon, both Chile and South Africa began incorporating fish flour into the manufacture of subsidized brown bread.[37]

Fish-enriched bread soon hit an obstacle, however, because the industry was being driven from the United States, where production had to be approved by the US Department of Food and Agriculture. This agency had long maintained hygiene and purity rules, systems to ensure, for example, that hamburgers did not contain cow dung or intestines. The US Department of Food and Agriculture was deeply concerned when they looked into Fish Protein Concentrate, because the product included the whole fish, including the scales, head, viscera, bones, as well as the guts and contents of the intestine. On the face of it, this was clearly unfit for human consumption. The government took steps to prevent the product from being sold within the United States, but still deemed it acceptable *outside* the United States: good enough to provide protein to the developing world. As a result, USAID continued to promote FPC as part of their drive for technical cooperation in the late-1960s, calling the initiative the "Food from the Sea Program."[38]

The label was misleading, of course, because, like foods from algae and oil, Fish Protein Concentrate started from the idea that malnutrition is a deficiency in nutrients rather than food. The product was too unclean to be a food in the United States, but could nevertheless be marketed as a source of nutrients overseas. Such a view fitted into the emerging humanitarian policy because FPC— like products made from oil and algae—was rich in protein, and protein was considered the most important nutrient of all. After kwashiorkor had become stabilized as a medical fact, a burgeoning literature had started suggesting that protein deficiency was "one of the most widespread nutritional disorders in tropical and sub-tropical areas."[39] This came accompanied by discussion of a worldwide "protein gap," a mismatch between the production and consumption of proteins, which would have serious implications.[40] High modernism shifted attention, therefore, from food manufacture to nutrient manufacture and then to protein manufacture. The new generation of foods, it was thought, would prevent a global catastrophe by focusing on the nutrients that people lacked in their everyday diets.

As the 1950s turned to the 1960s the scale of attention reduced still further. It was not just proteins that were missing in many people's diets, but specific kinds of protein; even the building blocks of protein. In response, humanitarian projects began not just to produce protein, but the essential amino acids *within* these proteins. Lysine, in particular, was thought to be a magical ingredient, a superior kind of protein that accelerated human growth and advancement.[41] Money was invested in projects to manufacture lysine synthetically and add it to basic foods like wheat flour or maize, which was presented as a way to convert the "low efficiency" protein found in bread, into the "high efficiency" protein found in meat.[42] Such ever-deeper methods of improving on the diet marked the very peak of high modernism, where basic staples were fortified and improved in line with the idea that nature could be tamed.[43]

Fortified Blended Foods

The trend toward lysine fortification and the manufacture of separate nutrients might be described as a process of nutritional involution, in which the scale of humanitarian nutritional intervention spiraled inward. It was a period in which humanitarian nutrition was pushing for greater internal complexity, ever-increasing intricacy, which continued even as it became clear that the process was delivering diminishing returns.[44] Nutritional involution was a significant feature of this era, but other high modernist schemes took a different strategy. Rather than breaking down nutrients into smaller components and manufacturing them in isolation, this strategy involved building them up, combining nutrients into products that approximated a balanced diet. This resulted in complete meals in the form of a powder or pill; products that were light and portable while meeting all the body's needs. This was, in many ways an extension of the World War II search for efficiency and mobility: developments that led to the K-ration, Pacific Packs, and vitamin pills. Now, however, these products became infused with the spirit of the space age. Rather than neatly arranged packets of preserved but everyday foodstuffs, the high modernist movement baked cutting edge science into the humble ration. It was an idea that became known as the Fortified Blended Food.

Unlike Single Cell Protein, or Leaf Protein Concentrate (LPC), Fortified Blended Foods were not based around a single nutrient, but motivated by the desire for comprehensiveness. Whereas SCP and LPC were just protein sources, Fortified Blended Foods were a full meal. Whereas SCP and LPC were a journalists' dream—fantastical, dramatic, conjuring the image of scientists creating edible substances from algae and petrol—Fortified Blended Foods were more banal. They received much less media coverage and were driven by pragmatic concerns: disposing of surpluses, increasing efficiency, and rationalizing aid. In many ways, this idea resembled Multi-Purpose Food, the powdered meal in a silver can promoted by Clifford Clinton, and Clinton's project became an important precursor to the Fortified Blended Food. Indeed, Clinton had set out a series of principles that soon became a perfect match for high modernist aims. He wanted a product that could supply the full nutritional requirements of an adult. He wanted a product that was quick to cook and that would keep for up to a year. He wanted a product that was light, compact, and transportable. Most crucially, he wanted a product that would cost no more than three cents a meal.[45]

The aim, therefore, was complete nutrition in a small, lightweight package, and after MPF this dream began to reappear in a number of other products as well. One of the earliest and most successful was Incaparina, developed in Central America in the early 1950s and made from a blend of maize, sorghum, and cottonseed flour. Like MPF, it was meant to be nutritionally balanced, cheap, long lasting, and compatible with local tastes.[46] It was, however, more clearly rooted in the Central American context. Whereas MPF emerged very much from the American wartime experience—promoted for bomb shelters as the equivalent to meat, potatoes and peas—Incaparina was designed to be made into *atole*, a hot, corn-based Latin American drink. It was also distinctive because it was the first major food conceived as an alternative to milk for those unable to afford it, which became a growth industry in the 1960s. Nevin Scrimshaw, founding director of the Institute of Nutrition for Central America and Panama (INCAP), articulated the central aim of this product as follows: it was, he wrote, "a weaning food that could be recommended for malnourished mothers and children in a country where milk was too costly and in short supply."[47]

INCAP went through eight different prototypes before a formula was found that had the correct nutritional balance, as well as being commercially viable. It quickly became far more complex than MPF (which was just soy grits combined with some flavorings and dehydrated vegetables), and far more ambitious. To produce Incaparina, four main ingredients had to be separately heated or boiled in calcium hydroxide, ground, dried, and prepared into flours: maize, sorghum, cottonseed, and kikuyu grass. They were then mixed with Torula yeast, rice polishing, and a vitamin mix, and blended and ground again. The mix was then slurried in water and dried in a double drum drier and air drier, then run through a flaker. Finally, it was ready for bagging.[48] The aim of all this was to produce an alternative to milk: a synthetic milk that would be cheaper, based on local cereals, and widely available in the tropics, where dairy farming was unsustainable. It would be more acceptable to different cultures, inserting itself into local traditions and dietary choices. One proponent of the project declared that cow's milk was "an unsophisticated approach" to gaining protein, disturbingly primitive and childlike. Technology, on the other hand, provided more "sophisticated" approaches, allowing Incaparina to offer something animals could not provide: a cheaper and more controllable source of food.[49]

Milk Alternatives

In its earliest days, UNICEF had, in the words of its official historian, been a "gigantic organizational udder": a proselytizer for milk, a worshipper of milk, which was presented as the key to nutrition.[50] After it was established from UNRRA in postwar Europe, UNICEF's main aim had been to provide milk to school children, and it achieved this by harnessing the power of milk drying, a new technology that allowed milk to be preserved and transported without refrigeration. Powdered milk could be taken from the vast dairy farms of North America to the ravaged areas of Europe and used as a staple of relief work. Many DPs remembered how UNICEF provided them and their children with essential milk in the early postwar years, and later UNICEF moved to support local milk production, transforming into a more development-focused organization. From providing milk for emergency feeding in the 1940s, therefore, the organization started funding cattle farming and the dairy industry in Europe. Later still, in the postcolonial world, they began promoting dairy industries worldwide. This was motivated by the idea, neatly summarized by one advisor, that "civilization follows the cow."[51]

For many reasons, supporting dairy industries in the global South proved rather limiting—cows do not thrive in tropical areas, and many cultures do not drink milk—but such was UNICEF's devotion that in the late 1950s they turned attention to supporting "milk alternatives" instead.[52] UNICEF started to pour money into Fortified Blended Foods, which were presented very much as a substitute for what remained, in many humanitarians' eyes, the ultimate nutritional tonic, and the Incaparina experiment soon led to a rash of imitations, as modernist ideas were taken up enthusiastically by humanitarian organizations around the world. The production of Fortified Blended Foods soon became the "main drive to prevent childhood malnutrition" in international organizations such as the FAO.[53] In Lebanon there was L'Aubina, based on chickpeas, parboiled wheat, dried milk and bone ash, providing the same amount of protein as "a roast leg of lamb."[54] In Algeria there was Superamine, a mix of wheat, lentils, dried milk, and sugar.[55] In Ethiopia, there was Faffa, based on wheat, soy, and chickpea flours.[56] Sri Lanka had Thriposha, made from corn, soya, and dried milk, and India had Bal-Ahar, made from soy, cottonseed flour, and peanut flour.[57] Most of these products emerged in the late 1960s: precooked, ground, and based on low-cost production. If civilization had previously followed the cow, it seemed that even higher civilizations would follow the Fortified Blended Food.

In many ways, these were classic development interventions in the modernist mold. They were designed to facilitate industrialization, create new factories, scale up agriculture, and develop new markets. Rather than using global hunger to leverage radical political changes as in the 1930s, these industries saw hunger as a technical problem; indeed, they were not as local and bottom-up as their names suggested. The projects were generally driven by a national government with funding and technical support from Western institutions: the Sri Lankan Ministry of Health, for example, instigated Thriposha with funding from USAID and CARE; Incaparina was created jointly by the Ministries of Health in six Central American countries and funded by the Rockefeller Foundation; Faffa was established at the Ethiopian Nutrition Institute with funding from Sweden; and Bal-Ahar was developed at a government-run research institute in Mysore with a range of donors from UNICEF to USAID.[58] The local names often revealed these alliances—such as L'Aubina deriving from the American University of Beirut, and Incaparina deriving from INCAP—but they also featured appeals to human improvement, such as Faffa, which means "to grow big and strong." Sometimes the name was simply bland, such as Bal-Ahar, which means "baby food."

Where the UN led, the NGOs followed. Oxfam, for example, maintained a strong interest in Fortified Blended Foods, and in 1963, its director, Leslie Kirkley, created links with N. W. Pirie.[59] A memo was circulated later that year, with a list of possible projects for Oxfam to support, and alongside Pirie's Leaf Protein Concentrate the charity considered putting money into the distribution of Clinton's Multi-Purpose Food and a British equivalent called LYPRO.[60] Oxfam were also approached by an industrial consultant at Cambridge University, backed by a "large industrial concern" to start a "Bacterial Protein Food" grown on oil.[61] They considered funding BP's research into Single Cell Proteins as well, although the memo, in a rather understated way, concluded that it was "unlikely any financial assistance will be needed."[62]

Oxfam ended up proceeding with two projects, each involving local production of Fortified Blended Foods: in India they supported Bal-Ahar—a product that was later used in the Bihar famine—and in Kenya they financed a new food called Supro, which became a key component of school feeding programs.[63] In the latter case, Oxfam also became a shareholder, the first time they had put money into a commercial operation, which became something of a failure. Such was Oxfam's commitment to high-protein foods that they chartered a cruise ship in 1966 to take British school children to Algeria to learn more about malnutrition. A significant component of this trip, named Operation Oasis, involved classes on nutrition. Indeed, Pirie's leaf protein was served in the ship's galley and grammar school girls learned how to cook banana fritters from Fortified Blended Foods.[64] This was perhaps the best use for a product whose practical relevance was increasingly coming into question.

Muscle-Bound Modernism

In *Seeing like a State*, James Scott examined how high modernist ideology represented an ambitious but ultimately doomed attempt to restructure society along rational lines. He showed how high modernism had its roots in the state's desire to map territories and populations, describing how governments made people and places "legible" in various ways. He explained how citizens were required by the modern state to have consistent surnames, attaching them to a particular address; he traced how weights and measures were standardized by the modern state, replacing a variety of regional variations; he explored how the natural world was managed by the modern state, parceled off into fields and plots. All of these processes, Scott argued, involved reducing complexity and making the world easier to "read." The drive toward greater legibility helped the modernist state rule more effectively, arranging the world in order to facilitate taxation, conscription, and the prevention of rebellion.[65]

Scott's book is a good source when theorizing the nutritional move toward high modernism, since he explained how it was "not so much the aspiration for comprehensive planning" that was new in high modernist ideology, but rather the extensive "administrative technology and social knowledge" that attempted to organize "an entire society in ways that only the barracks or the monastery had been organized before."[66] Scott owed an explicit debt to Foucault in these observations. High modernism, he stressed, was an extension of many previous instances of disciplinary power and biopower, but given a new and distinctive scale. It involved planning and monitoring whole societies with the kind of detail that had previously only been possible in narrow, disciplinary institutions. It involved collecting more and more data on citizens and recording their details in documents, grids, and organizing schemes.

High modernism in humanitarian nutrition also became a more intensive and ambitious manifestation of a much longer trend. In the 1850s Edward Smith had managed diets within the confines of institutions such as prisons and workhouses, and Wilbur Atwater had encouraged industrialists to monitor, plan, and manipulate the dietary intake of workers. All this was classically modernist, but the *high* modernist era, a hundred years later in the 1950s, extended these practices over entire societies. It was characterized by the industrial production of nutrients, the packaging of proteins in simple powders, and the dietary management of whole populations. This was an attempt to rationally engineer all aspects of social life; it was a "strong (one might even say muscle-bound) version of the beliefs in scientific and technical progress that were associated with industrialization in Western Europe and in North America from roughly 1830 until World War I."[67]

The whole aim of high modernism was to destroy tradition. Modernism had always been committed to progress, but high modernism constructed this edifice on a clean slate, a razed ground. Scott illustrated this with the Le Corbusien high modernist city, which rose in ordered, linear fashion from the ruins of the Second World War and in the rainforests of South America. In a similar way, high modernist nutrition sought to restructure society and tame the natural world with brutal efficiency and a remarkable commitment to rationalized aesthetic order. *Seeing Like a State* was peppered with pleasing images: the neat rows of trees in forestry plantations, the linear arrangement of buildings in urban designs, and a memorable cover image of square fields bordered by a road that tortuously skirted the plots in right angles to reach its destination. There may seem, at first glance, to be less concern for aesthetics in humanitarian nutrition—after all, fungi grown on oil, biscuits made from fish offal, and algae grown on sewage are disgusting concoctions on the surface—but the attractiveness of this movement lay in systematic and controlled production. The real aesthetic abomination, for high modernists, was the knobbly carrot surrounded by mud and harvested by a sweaty laborer. Algae and Single Cell Protein, in contrast, could be planned, predicted, and manufactured in hygienic environments.

Scott gave his book the subtitle: "How Certain Schemes to Improve the Human Condition Have Failed," which operated as a particularly succinct summary of the historical assessment. By the middle of the 1970s, indeed, many high modernist schemes were failing, not least in housing, where whole neighborhoods were marked for demolition. The Pruitt-Igoe housing project in St. Louis, Missouri, was one of the most famous. Built with great optimism in the middle of the 1950s, by 1972 it had ended up as a decrepit ghetto and its blocks were dynamited on television. In a number of accounts, this marked the moment that high modernism ended and the postmodern era began.[68] The image of a road winding at right angles on the cover of Scott's book captured why so many high modernist schemes failed dramatically. After all, who would relish driving along that road forever, violently lurching left and right, on a journey shaped more by aesthetic order than human practicality? Who would enjoy eating those ultra-rationalized and algae-based foods? The gleaming vats of protein, like the right angles in the road, were presented as though they had an intrinsic value independent of their actual function. It did not take long, however, before this utopia fell from favor.

The End of High Modernism

On the face of it, high modernism still seemed to be going strong in the early 1970s. In 1971 a whole new subsidiary within BP had been created to manage its nutrition work, called BP Proteins, and manufacturing plants were built in Grangemouth in the UK, Lavera in France, and Sardinia in Italy, with plans for the production of 700,000 tons every year. SCP initiatives appeared in other companies as well, including Standard Oil, Nestlé, ICI, Shell, and Rank Hovis McDougall.[69] There was competition from the other side of the Iron Curtain, as SCP plants were founded across the USSR, and the first Single Cell Proteins were soon brought to the market as an alternative to animal fodder.[70]

There seemed to be a similar momentum in the production of other fortified foods as well. In the early 1970s there were still more than a hundred different fortified foods in production, from South Africa to Lebanon, Panama to Hong Kong.[71] Food from algae may have lost its sheen, but there was more enthusiasm for foods from fish protein, with a new plant constructed in California in 1971. There was also interest in food from insects, a project led with enthusiasm by Dr. Ronald Taylor, author of the delightfully titled book, *Butterflies in My Stomach*.[72]

All was not well, however. Academic cliché has it that 1972 was a moment before the fall: the year when the modernist dream stood precariously, before crashing to earth along with the high-rise buildings of the Pruitt-Igoe housing project.[73] In some ways, the story of humanitarian nutrition mirrors this simplistic temporal scheme, with plenty of evidence to indicate a gradual ascent until 1972, followed by a rapid decline. In 1972, for example, major UN conferences were still referencing the protein gap, recommending "mass production of high-protein and multipurpose foods," but by 1974 the idea of a worldwide deficiency in proteins had been thoroughly undermined. This was encapsulated in McLaren's article, "The Great Protein Fiasco," which argued that the policy attention on high-protein food had been based on poor science and industrial lobbying from the very beginning.[74] Similarly, the use of milk substitutes was still seen as a progressive endeavor in 1972, with the local production of weaning foods promoted by the FAO and WHO. Again, however, this was soon undermined by another well-known article, "Commerciogenic Malnutrition," which criticized the introduction of commercial imperatives into infant feeding and was followed by the first stirrings of the Nestlé boycott.[75]

By the end of the 1970s, therefore, most of the new foods had failed dramatically. The factories for Fish Protein Concentrate and Single Cell Protein had become white elephants, the BP plant in Sardinia was mired in corruption and regulatory censure, and the fish protein plant in California failed to produce any viable product and was soon sold for scrap.[76] As if to underline this decline, by the end of the 1970s there were only a handful of fortified flours left on the market from the hundred plus that had been marketed at the beginning of the decade. Even Incaparina, the grandfather of fortified flours, ceased production in all but Guatemala by 1980.[77]

Alongside this decline was a wider cultural shift away from high modernist ideals. Schumacher's book *Small Is Beautiful* was published to great acclaim in 1973, and it elegantly criticized large-scale, top-down developmental planning.[78] The growth of the intermediate technology movement also promoted small-scale local solutions, and skepticism about industrial food permeated popular culture in big-budget blockbusters as well. The film *Soylent Green*, for example, was set in a resource-starved, overpopulated, dystopian future, where most of the population lived on processed food rations. These rations, including the eponymous Soylent Green, claimed to be made from algae, but were really manufactured from human corpses. It was this growing suspicion with high modernist foods, combined with their fundamental impracticality, that gradually led to a new phase in the history of humanitarian nutrition. High modernism had run out of steam, so humanitarian nutrition moved to a new and more commercially viable ideology: low modernism.

LOW MODERNISM AFTER BIAFRA

On May 30, 1967, the military governor of Nigeria's eastern region declared independence for a new state: Biafra, a homeland for the Igbo. This marked the beginning of the Nigerian civil war, a bitter three-year conflict in which food was a weapon of war. As the Nigerian army fought to retake the secessionist territory, they imposed a military blockade that prevented commodities from entering Biafra. Food supplies rapidly dwindled. By the start of 1968, photographs of emaciated Biafran children filled newspapers and television screens in the West, indicating an emerging famine and an impending humanitarian crisis. Many Europeans had not seen such images since the liberation of Belsen in 1945, and with the memory of skeletal concentration camp victims so raw and recent, a strong reaction soon followed.[1]

The humanitarian response was tentative at first, but soon became robustly pro-Biafran, with food sent directly into the breakaway territory.[2] This contravened the classical humanitarian principle of neutrality but was justified by the sense that a profound injustice was taking place against the Igbo. By this point in the war, Biafra was surrounded. The new state had been reduced to a landlocked, rainforest-dominated circle of land with no airport and very little food. Mindful of the pogroms that had taken place against the Igbo during the run-up to the war, many activists feared that genocide was inevitable if Biafra fell. As a result, they sided with the breakaway state in an attempt to prevent a repeat of the Red Cross inaction in the Second World War. Some even decided that the principle of neutrality was outdated and even immoral; certainly, it seemed wrong to stay neutral between the perpetrators and victims of what looked like genocide in Nigeria.

Relief in Biafra, when it came, centered on an airlift of food and medicine flown directly onto a straight stretch of road in the forest near Uli. This was, for a long time, the only way to get into the territory. The airlift helped sustain the nascent state and became an important lifeline for the regime—perhaps even prolonging the war by up to eighteen months—and this combination of famine, publicity, and negative consequences was a crucial moment in the history of relief.[3] Many of the Biafran war's features would reappear again and again in the coming years, as aid agencies operated across military lines, the media ran high-profile appeals, and aid workers questioned classical humanitarian principles. The "paradox" of humanitarian action, where aid agencies ended up creating even greater suffering, also became a recurring feature of the relief industry.[4]

When it came to food, however, Biafra is important for a more mundane reason, as it produced a generation of aid workers that had made relief into their profession. Attracted by the style and image of humanitarianism, this new cadre of aid workers became influenced by the counterculture and the idea of gaining "glory on the battlefield without having to kill anyone."[5] They sought tight, technical systems, which they could take around the world without friction. Indeed, over the next ten years these aid workers began refining the technical guidelines that were first developed in Biafra, carrying them from crisis to crisis, from Biafra to East Pakistan, Ethiopia to Cambodia, and adjusting as they went.[6] These techniques became the nutritional system that lasts to this day, and from the very start they were based around two crucial elements: first, anthropometric measuring tools; and second, Fortified Blended Food.

These two prongs of the contemporary nutritional system were adopted for mainly practical reasons, because they enabled aid workers to manage hunger on an extraordinary scale.[7] They were also grounded in the latest scientific discoveries, influenced by high modernism, and they allowed Biafra to become, in the words of Maggie Black, "one of the first instances where a child-nutrition program in emergency circumstances was run on a truly scientific basis."[8] They created a remarkably mobile system, "since no large, heavy, bulky equipment was needed," and they could be taken wherever they were required.[9] The basic approach will be familiar to anyone working in emergencies today, and it centered on an object called the "QUAC stick."[10] This was an early version of the MUAC procedure, and it was used to measure all the children in an area less than ten years of age, who had been asked by the local "village chief" to assemble "at a central place."[11] A team of humanitarian workers then compared every child's arm circumference with an anthropometric standard, and if the arm was too small they "marked the child on the forehead with gentian violet or some felt pen" to indicate their malnourishment with a capital "M."[12] These children, suitably branded and identified, were then referred to a food distribution, which was held under "a simple mat-covered shelter with rows of fixed bamboo benches," where fortified foods such as CSM (Corn-Soy-Milk) or a mixture called K-Mix-2, were provided in bowls.[13]

In this chapter I argue that this new system of humanitarian nutrition constituted a form of low modernism: a more pragmatic and business-friendly version of the high modernist ideals that had been percolating for some years when the Biafran crisis began. The approach contained a similar utopianism, but was directed toward smaller, more practical tools, which could be replicated and transported around the world. The MUAC tape and the product known as Corn-Soy-Milk became perhaps the most widespread and influential examples, and in this chapter I focus particularly on the evolution of Corn-Soy-Milk: a product composed of three of America's largest surplus commodities that were combined and exported overseas. The next chapter turns to a slightly different low modernist product—the MUAC band, which was less commercial, but driven by the call for newer, smaller-scale devices—but both objects constitute the low modernist turn in humanitarian nutrition, which took root from the 1970s and continues to dominate today.

Commerce and Starvation

To understand the rise of Corn-Soy-Milk, one has to appreciate the changing relationship between commerce and starvation. This goes back to the mid-nineteenth century, when Alexis Soyer furthered his fame through the Irish soup kitchen by selling a range of cookery books and proprietary sauces, and Justus Liebig demonstrated the early power of nutritional marketing by selling his Extract of Meat.[14] As starvation was reconfigured as a nutrient deficiency in the twentieth century, however, a number of more specific products emerged. These included iron-rich hog's stomach in proprietary formulae such as Extomak, milk proteins such as Casilan promoted for starvation diets, and protein hydrolysates such as Amigen, which were manufactured by Mead Johnson as "life-sustaining intravenous solution to nutrition."[15] The 1930s and 1940s, therefore, became dominated by specific, medicalized products, which, as one pediatrician lamented, were often uncritically accepted by clinicians. "Too frequently," he wrote, "one can find the pediatrician in a tropical, sun-drenched country, exhorting mothers to use cod liver oil to prevent non-existent rickets" or "the public health nurse from Europe advising mothers to feed their babies on orange juice when infantile scurvy does not exist."[16]

The reason for this, of course, was the power of marketing. Beginning with Extract of Meat, and continuing with a range of new vitamin supplements, food companies began to push the health claims of their products. Medical professionals were not immune from such promotions.[17] It was an issue that had reached the League of Nations Health Organization in the 1930s, where experts expressed deep concern about the "fantastic and confused ideas" taking root through the power of advertising: as one critic put it at the time, "the food industry endeavors by means of persuasive advertisements, garnished with incomprehensible catchwords and attractive presentation, to force what are often inferior, unnecessary or at least over-rated foodstuffs upon the public."[18] This trend intensified in the 1960s, with the growth of aid agencies and the move toward direct operations. The market for famine foods was rapidly expanding. Humanitarian organizations had previously been more likely to send money to local partners rather than flying expert staff out to disaster zones, but by the 1960s, more agencies were opening offices and managing projects directly. Instead of giving money to partners for local purchase, this meant maintaining warehouses, inventories, and buying food in bulk. The shift opened doors for Western food manufacturers, who exploited the opportunity for commerce.[19]

As a result of the Biafran war and the growth of direct operations, sales boomed in dried milk, fortified foods, and starvation treatments. Large corporations began to send samples to international aid agencies, making extravagant claims for new products. Christian Aid, for example, was offered several hundredweight of "Strong Arm" high-protein biscuits by the United Biscuit Company. UNICEF started working with large agricultural concerns in the United States to develop a fortified food for manufacture on a massive scale. Oxfam were approached by a company offering high-protein foods with high modernist names echoing the film *Soylent Green*: Polymine S (made from sesame), Polymine M (from soya), and Nutrimine C (from cottonseed).[20] Hundreds of other privately produced high-protein foods were also coming to market, many of them cushioned by significant public subsidies. Peruvita, for example, was made by Nestlé with support from the Peruvian government. Arlac was made by Unigate, supported by a government agency in Nigeria. Saci was produced by Coca-Cola in Brazil; Amama was manufactured by Glaxo in Nigeria; and Protea was made by General Mills in Mexico.[21] In 1972, Britain's Overseas Development Administration estimated that more than 70 percent of the high-protein mixtures were private operations.[22]

This growing market was assisted by the narrative of a worldwide protein gap, which created a perceived need for new, high-protein foods. Back in 1952, kwashiorkor had been declared the "most serious and widespread nutritional disorder known to medical and nutritional science," and this led to the widely accepted, if erroneous, notion that millions of people were lacking protein in

FIGURE 12. Cartoon by Mark Boxer. *The Times*, January 14, 1970, 10. © Mark Boxer. Reproduced with permission from the Mark Boxer Estate. Image supplied by the British Cartoon Archive, University of Kent.

their diet.[23] A meeting in 1955 brought experts together at Princeton to authorize the narrative, which then led to the establishment of a Protein Advisory Group (PAG). This was a body that began advising UN agencies on the "safety and suitability" of commercial high-protein foods.[24] Business became a crucial partner, and by the late 1960s the "protein gap" had become firmly embedded on the global agenda.[25] In 1968, the United Nations Advisory Committee on Science and Technology (ACST) disseminated a report entitled "International Action to Avert the Impending Protein Crisis," which presented the protein gap as not just a challenge for public health but a pressing issue for global security. Protein supply, it claimed, was "a threat to world peace and stability," which we "ignore at our peril."[26]

While responding to the problem of a "protein gap," businesses found inventive ways to profit. The most common technique was to design high-protein foods from unusual and untapped food sources, including the leftovers of other industries. The Strong Arm Biscuits sold to Christian Aid, for example, were promoted relatively benignly as "a new inexpensive source of high quality protein," but a closer look revealed that they were 40 percent fishmeal and had been made from the organs, skin, and small bones of fish.[27] The Strong Arm company had the chutzpah to describe the main ingredient of these biscuits as "fillet house by-products from white fish of the North Sea," but this was a rather disingenuous description of offal, and a Christian Aid director later admitted they tasted "somewhat fishy."[28] Incaparina, a far more successful product, was based around cottonseed protein, which was a cheap remainder from the cotton industry and one of America's biggest surplus products. Fish Protein Concentrate, like Strong Arm Biscuits, was manufactured from junk fish minced whole with their scales, fins, viscera and all.[29] Even Leaf Protein Concentrate, the more bottom-up and palatable of these new foods, was generated by the idea of gaining food from cheap and widely available green leaves. These were plants that were otherwise ignored as a source of nutrients, and could be productively converted into a marketable food source.

Making food from leftovers had long been a good commercial strategy. Dried skim milk (DSM), for example, was actually a byproduct of the butter and butter industry, preserved and distributed for relief. Its production had arguably benefited everyone: allowing farm surpluses to be stored and sold as well as filling UNICEF's great "organizational udder" in the 1940s and 1950s.[30] By the 1960s, however, idea of food from residue had become a less attractive facet of high modernism. It was not just the sources of residue that were the problem, but the dynamics of inequality that arrived as well. Many "miracle" foods for the malnourished, after all, were created from the leftovers of wealthy consumerism: Single Cell Protein, for example, emerged as a byproduct of oil refinement; cottonseed flour exploited a residue of clothing industry; even DSM was the poor relative of cream and butter. By the end of the 1960s, therefore, there were even proposals to make proteins from waste wood in the logging industry. These, as one article explained, could be "heated and treated with acid to convert the cellulose in the wood into sugar."[31]

The problem with high modernism went deeper than distaste and inequity, as these products had serious commercial failings. There were two issues, in particular, that regularly recurred: expense and acceptance. Many high modernists had developed complex production systems, which led to very costly products. In addition, they expected too much of consumers, producing foods that that nobody wanted to eat. In addressing these two issues, some schemes began to shift registers, taming their more utopian and unrealistic features. This was the beginning of low modernism, when fortified and high-protein protein foods become simplified and commercially viable.

From High to Low Modernism

A good example of the first tentative shift from high to low modernism can be found in the story of Leaf Protein Concentrate, which was taken from the airy dreams of a Cambridge biochemist and planted in the soil of everyday aid work. The process began when a young journalist read about Pirie's work in Elspeth Huxley's *Brave New Victuals* (1965) and began promoting the idea to friends at Christian Aid.[32] After conversations with Bill Pirie and a biochemist at the University of Ife in Nigeria, Christian Aid began to fund leaf protein production in West Africa. Pirie's utopian, ambitious scheme to feed the world, therefore, had to face up to practical challenges. The project tried to deal with the two core problems of high modernist schemes: first expense, then acceptance.

To face up to the challenge of cost, the staff tried to make production efficient. In the absence of Pirie's high-tech equipment, and in order to avoid a wholesale transfer of expensive technology from Britain to its former colony, the plan was to mash the leaves and produce their juice using an existing network of "Posho mills." These could be found across Nigeria to grind corn, cassava, and other staples, and it was thought that they could grind green leaves as well. The raw material, moreover, came from the local area: despite the optimistic narrative that any old grass and greenery could be transformed into a nutritious dish, only certain leaves really worked in the process. Leaf protein required a leaf that was abundant, quick to grow, while yielding a light and attractive protein. After experimenting with various local plants, the project workers settled on the Soto leaf, which met these requirements. Production was soon underway.[33]

Facing up to the challenge of acceptance was more difficult. It was obvious from the very beginning that if local people did not eat the leaf protein, the idea would get nowhere, yet there was no time to bring up a new generation of "green food eaters" as Pirie had desired.[34] To get around this problem the project workers dried leaf protein into a powder so that it could be added easily to soups, stews, and relishes, absorbing the nutrients and disguising the taste. This powder was presented in cellophane bags, with a bold, bright label and an attractive name. The idea was to gradually change attitudes amongst the population, and various branding ideas were considered. The name Agunmu was raised as a possibility, but was rejected on the basis of its "unfortunate local associations"—it referred to herbs used in traditional medicine, which did not match the modern image of the project. The name Milki Dudu, or black milk, was also considered, in the anticipation that this dark green powder might be associated with the white powder of dried milk. In the end, however, the product was named Sokotein, a portmanteau of the Soko plant and the protein extracted from its pulp. An attempt at publicity and marketing then followed.[35]

The strategy in Nigeria was to emphasize familiarity, so posters were drawn up declaring that Sokotein was made from "the concentrated goodness of the leaves that you like," the plants that "grow all around you."[36] Leaflets were conceived for schoolchildren, featuring a footballer and the claim that leaf protein will "make you strong!"[37] The project began working with local hospitals to help dispense the protein powder through local physicians, using promotional materials to ease fears about the unusual new product. This strategy was based on the successful marketing techniques of infant food manufacturers, and the project managers admitted in meeting minutes that they wanted to come up with a name as "recognized as Cow and Gate."[38] Through such small-scale tweaks and adjustments, the high modernist idea of grass from green leaves was given a more practical expression. Rather than production in gleaming laboratories, the product was now made in local mills. Rather than producing a new generation of green food eaters, the project made green food less obvious.

The transformation of leaf protein is a good illustration of an emerging trend toward low modernism, even though the project eventually failed. The production remained too costly and local people remained reluctant to eat the product, which still tasted "a bit like pond weed."[39] Perhaps the most damning critique of the whole scheme emerged in the late 1970s, when a scientist involved from the very start concluded that it was far too complicated and that "people might as well just grow a few more beans."[40] These issues of complexity, cost, and acceptance, therefore, had not been overcome, and they recurred in many other attempts as well. Incaparina, for example, enjoyed an extensive promotional push in the 1960s and became something of an aspirational infant food. Its lengthy production process, however, involved maize, sorghum, cottonseed, and kikuyu grass all boiled separately in calcium hydroxide before being ground, dried, and prepared into flours.[41] Given this process and the resulting cost, it was unsurprising that it never took off. It was proving difficult to make a product that was modernist and ambitious but also cheap, tasty, and commercially viable.

A good illustration of these challenges can be found in a project called Supro: a commercial venture by Oxfam in the 1960s that became an expensive and ineffective disaster. The idea of the scheme was that Oxfam would invest directly in a high-protein food for school feeding in Kenya, but within three months of the company's incorporation it was already making losses. Production was outstripping sales by three to one, and much of the flour had to be placed in storage, where it was attacked by rats and weevils.[42] Within four months, the company was seeking more capital, approaching Oxfam for a significant loan, and then the project was hit by a series of adverse reports.[43] Scientists at the University of Wisconsin first detected high ash content in the flour.[44] Another report by the World Food Program noted that the formula caused digestive problems due to its yeast.[45] Most seriously, the school feeding program, which was the main intended outlet for the flour, was beset by personality clashes and inertia. They failed to purchase as much Supro as had originally been anticipated, and the product continued to struggle.[46]

The new company resorted to promoting Supro to Kenyan prisons, corporations, large farms, estates, and mining compounds, with the aim of off-loading large quantities of the food. This, however, left Oxfam in the curious situation of pushing fortified flours on industrial canteens in the most exploitative Kenyan industries.[47] Their product was still ending up on the plates of the destitute via the kitchens serving low-paid workers in plantations and mines, but only by supporting the exploitative institutions that made people poor in the first place. The strangest part of this story emerged when a panel of experts declared that the nutritional contribution of Supro was actually rather poor. The product was justified on nutritional grounds, but a report concluded that its protein contribution was "negligible." In a reply, the Oxfam field director pointed out that the Supro was served with beans, but this raised the question why Oxfam needed to use Supro at all. Based on their figures, beans *alone* could have provided the necessary amount of protein, while coming in at a third of the price.[48]

The example of Supro shows the many challenges of producing a commercially viable humanitarian food, especially when the costs were so high and the alternatives so simple. In the end, Oxfam accepted the losses and sold their shares for the nominal price of five pounds. It seemed that people might as well have just grown a few more beans.

Corn-Soy-Milk

Low modernism only really took off with the production of Corn-Soy-Milk, which began in 1966 and was manufactured from two of America's most substantial agricultural surpluses: corn and soya. It fit into a preexisting food system that was already commercially successful and was distributed through America's Food for Peace program, which had been founded in 1954 to help American farmers by keeping production and prices high.[49] Corn-Soy-Milk, therefore, was very much a product of productivist agriculture and strategic motivations. The roots of Food for Peace had little to do with humanitarianism, as it was partly designed to facilitate American strategic interests by keeping countries reliant on US food, and partly designed to create new markets for US crops by flooding overseas countries with cheap commodities. Only after these rather self-interested motivations did the legislation mention world hunger.[50] The beauty of the Food for Peace program, at least for its proponents, was that it could meet many objectives at once. It could stabilize agriculture at home, open new markets abroad, *and* feed the hungry into the bargain as well.

In this context, Corn-Soy-Milk triumphed over the other fortified foods because the true cost was never fully calculated.[51] It could always undercut the alternatives because it was backed by the might of the American political elite. Like many other fortified foods, Corn-Soy-Milk was devised as an alternative to milk, which was at the time becoming too expensive. In early 1964, therefore, the American Corn Miller's Federation began working with the US Department of Agriculture to develop an American version of the increasingly common milk alternatives. Their first prototype was called Ceplapro, which was made from the same basic ingredients as CSM, but had been "extruded into a grainlike shape" to resemble rice.[52] A year later CSM appeared: initially known as Formula #2, it was a simpler product, cheaper to produce, and was first distributed in the Bihar famine during 1966.[53]

By the time of the Biafran war a year later sacks of CSM had become a mainstay of humanitarian relief. It was a dramatic rise to prominence, and shipments of the food went from zero in 1965 to 136,000 tons in 1967, 454,000 tons by 1971, and 1,270,000 tons by 1974.[54] Like the narrative of the "protein gap," the importance of this moment is difficult to exaggerate. Once CSM had been established as a humanitarian foodstuff it spawned a large variety of similar products, such as Wheat-Soy Blend (WSB), Wheat-Soy-Milk (WSM), and Soy-Fortified Bulgur (SFB) to name just three. The changing formulae reflected the balance of US surpluses, and when milk surpluses ran out, Corn-Soy Blend (CSB) was launched to replace the earlier CSM.[55] CSB then became the most significant and longstanding of all fortified foods, which is still widely procured by aid agencies today. Justified by its nutritional benefits, it emerged as a result of three key features of the US economy in the middle of the twentieth century: productivism in agriculture, vertical integration in the food industry, and the business-friendly changes made to the Food for Peace program in 1966.

Agricultural productivism had taken shape in the 1930s when the US government implemented a highly interventionist scheme to subsidize farms and stabilize prices. Part of this involved paying farmers to idle their land. When production was too high and prices began to fall, the government would pay farmers to leave their land fallow, ensuring that prices would go up the next season. The other part of the policy, however, involved buying excess output, as in the event of overproduction the government would commit to purchasing the excess, ensuring a minimum price for the farmers and building a stockpile of food. The idea was that this could be released in leaner years to prevent high prices, but the growing stockpiles eventually became too large, necessitating surplus disposal through Food for Peace. Such policies generated steady growth in the US farming sector, which was also assisted by new labor saving machinery and hybrid crops. The system rewarded overproduction. Since farmers were guaranteed a certain price for their produce, the rational thing was to produce as much as possible.[56]

By the late 1940s, US overproduction of food had become a recurring problem and stockpiling was no longer a viable solution. The postwar Marshall plan offered a temporary outlet for the huge scale of American surpluses, but by 1954 a new outlet was sought for the surplus commodities as well. Public Law 480 was passed in response. It was only later known as Food for Peace (the term was coined by President Kennedy in 1961), but its passing saw the final element of the "productivist" food system fall into place. Networks of production and consumption were globalized and American farms began to dominate the world food supply. These farms were now organized on increasingly corporate lines: wedded to Fordist production, dependent on exports for their sales, and specializing in a limited number of commodities, particularly rice, wheat, corn, and soy.[57]

This is where the second factor came in: vertical integration in the food industry. To grow their businesses, food companies started to combine the different stages between field and plate: planting, harvesting, processing, packaging, marketing, and engaging in storage and distribution through a single company. A Harvard Business School graduate coined a new term to describe this phenomenon in the late 1950s: agribusiness.[58] It was not a pejorative label because, in the view of many, it tackled the age-old problem of the fixed stomach, the inelastic demand for food. If food becomes cheaper, or consumers earn more money, people do not necessarily buy more of it. There is only so much food our stomachs can take. Food companies, as a result, have to "add value" at each stage of the production process to increase their profits.[59] They do this by processing and fortifying grains, pushing the nutritional advantages of commodities, and generating a sense of novelty by devising new products and packaging.

Crops such as corn and soy are particularly amenable to this process of "adding value," as they can be broken down into a variety of derivative products, becoming cheap inputs for a range of processed foods. Soy, for example, can be broken down into soy flour, pressed into oil, converted into milk, and transformed into lecithin, which is an extremely common emulsifier for food processing. Corn, similarly, can be turned into corn meal, corn starch, corn bran, and high fructose corn syrup, while also becoming the basis for a huge range of common ingredients in processing (such as baking powder, caramel, citric acid, dextrin, maltodextrin, xanthan gum, lactic acid, and monosodium glutamate). It has been estimated that 75 percent of the calories consumed worldwide comes from just four major commodities—wheat, rice, corn, and soy—and these are the crops that have dominated agribusinesses.[60] Corn-Soy-Milk, therefore, fit neatly into this system. As we have seen, it was manufactured from the most common crops in US agriculture, and then combined, processed, and enriched for a particular kind of consumer.[61]

Billions for US Business

On March 1, 1966, a new issue of *Forbes* hit the newsstands. It anticipated the rise of CSM and explored the implications of the new Food for Peace legislation, which had been rebranded under President Lyndon Johnson as "Food for Freedom." Johnson's phrase never took off, but his legislative changes were deeply significant, clearing the way for CSM to be produced on a massive scale. They also illustrated how emergency foods were not just driven by human need, but by commercial need. Indeed, *Forbes* led its March issue with the following memorable title: "Feeding the World's Hungry Millions: How It Will Mean Billions for U.S. Business."[62]

As *Forbes* reported, the 1966 Food for Peace amendments turned global hunger into a much larger business opportunity. Whereas the earlier legislation had stipulated that food aid could only come from surplus commodities, the 1966 changes allowed American farmers to grow extra crops *specifically* for the aid program, while paying companies to process, fortify, and blend foods.[63] The new law offered farms, food companies, and processing plants the opportunity to gain large new contracts, as well as allowing the development of new products—like CSM—to be paid for by the US government. Critics had long pointed out that the Food for Peace program was not really a benevolent act, geared as it was to disposing of surpluses. Senator McGovern even admitted that "it was almost as though the needy nations were doing us a favor by letting us give away or sell under concessional arrangements."[64] The 1966 move from "surplus liquidation" to "deliberate production," therefore, was meant to tackle this criticism head on, while also ensuring that the scheme as a whole could benefit from a much wider range of US industrial sectors.[65] It also, however, had the impact of stimulating US business.

Many companies were involved in lobbying for the new law, and the bill was strongly supported by Republican farm states. After the 1966 amendments were announced, prices rose sharply on soybean and wheat futures, and a year later a conference of wheat millers and producers reflected that they had "derived substantial economic dividends" from the new arrangement.[66] As the legislation came into force *Forbes* gave its readers detailed information about the forty-three major companies that would benefit most from the new law, describing their ability to fight hunger while "reap[ing] a harvest of their own." The editors appealed to the self-interest of its audience: "As a business executive or investor," their advertisement read, "you should read 'World Hunger': a revealing story in the new issue of *Forbes*."[67]

There was an immediate incentive for business here as well as a more structural one. The immediate incentive was the "tremendous opportunity" for commerce. The law meant that "smart farmers with capital" could "become rich," as Forbes explained: "Major segments of US Industry are going to benefit . . . [and] the menace of starvation will mean steadily mounting sales for the producers of fertilizers, farm machinery, seed and feed."[68] The magazine also explored potential growth for food processing and other industries: "The railroads will prosper," it noted, because "the food must be shipped from farm to seaport by rail. The steel industry will benefit because farm machinery is made of steel. Even the paper industry will profit," the article concluded, because crops and fertilizer end up in paper bags.[69]

These were the immediate benefits, but there was also a more distant, structural reason for supporting the law. A promotional insert for the new issue gave a particularly graphic illustration. It showed the image of a starving Asian man with his ribs sticking out, lying curled up on the floor. "Hey, Mister!" the caption read in large type, an unseen voice addressing the skeletal man in the photograph, "want to buy a shiny new car with white walls, air-conditioning, full power and stereo?"[70] In smaller type the advertisement explained the "joke," declaring that the world's 2 billion hungry people "are a very poor market for the things American business would like to sell them—cars, for instance."[71] Tackling world hunger, Forbes explained, would solve this problem by expanding markets everywhere.

The opportunity to promote specific foods to hungry people led to an even more tangible and dangerous connection between commerce and malnutrition: the baby milk scandal. This began in the early 1960s when food companies started more forcefully promoting dried milk and weaning foods to the poorest and most malnourished. Salespeople were often dressed up as nurses, mimicking medical language and playing on mothers' anxieties over the quality of their breast milk. Advertisements presented powdered milk as modern and progressive, describing breastfeeding as backward and traditional. Mothers who purchased the milk were unable to safely prepare the products, adding dirty water and placing the milk in unsterilized bottles, while taking on a huge financial burden on their families. In 1968, Derek Jelliffe coined a name for the result: "Commerciogenic Malnutrition," which he defined as malnutrition caused by the "thoughtless promotion" of milks and infant foods.[72]

This phrase, commerciogenic malnutrition, began to appear in medical textbooks, identifying a new and more complex relationship between commerce and malnutrition.[73] It had long been obvious that malnutrition generated commercial opportunities, but Jelliffe had pointed out that the relationship worked the other way around as well: commerce also generated malnutrition. The way that milk formulae and other foods were reconstituted, he observed, were causing illness and diarrhea. The resulting products, in his vivid description, resembled a "homeopathic dose of milk, administered with large quantities of bacteria."[74] The promotional materials, meanwhile, suggested that milk powder could offer "a method of instantaneous transport into the twenty-first century of satellites, moon probes and heart transplants."[75]

Low Modernism Defined

In 1989, Paul Rabinow developed the concept of "middling modernism"—a term he coined to describe a particular kind of administrative engineering that lay at the heart of French colonial rule.[76] Middling modernism, according to Rabinow, described what happened when ground-level bureaucrats implemented scientific visions; it was the result of high modernism percolating through the everyday work of officials. The administrative purveyors of middling modernism, Rabinow argued, were more concerned with arbitrating an effective social order than with transforming society wholesale. They shared high modernist concerns with efficiency and progress, but they were more concerned with practical issues such as meeting basic needs, administering colonial societies, and building effective forms of government.[77]

In humanitarian nutrition this form of middling modernism can be identified in the attempt to turn leaf protein into a more practical form of intervention. Bill Pirie had originally promoted high modernist values and worked to produce a light and jellied protein curd in his modern Cambridge laboratory. He cooked it as cocktail snacks for elite British audiences and packaged the whole scheme as a revolutionary and necessary change to dietary habits. Once it was transported to Nigeria, however, this scheme was given more "middling" characteristics by local project workers. Rather than producing a light smooth jelly in a high-tech laboratory, they created a gritty dark powder in a local corn mill. Rather than promoting cocktail snacks to the rich, they promoted it through clinics for the poor. Practicality, cost, and acceptance were being considered more seriously, even if this meant compromising the vision.

Leaf Protein eventually failed, but with the arrival of Corn-Soy-Milk in 1966, middling modernism turned to low modernism. A new, hard-edged pragmatism solidified around CSM, which treated fortified foods not simply as nutrients or medicine, but unapologetically as a commodity. This enthusiastic embrace of the commodity form shifted the register of modernism one step further. The new focus was on what was commercial, what was marketable, and what could make money.

Low modernism in the arts has come to mean an embrace of the kitsch and commercial, epitomized in portrayals of lipstick, diners, and dirty streets.[78] It is an art form that embraces the vernacular, the commonplace, and the routine. Whereas high modernism rejected commercialism, low modernism embraced it. Whereas high modernism opposed mass production, low modernism accepted it. Whereas high modernism proposed a radical break from quotidian capitalist society, low modernism represented it in a series of mundane artistic themes. Terry Eagleton described high modernism as "a strategy whereby the work of art resists commodification, [and] holds out by the skin of its teeth against those social forces which would degrade it into an exchangeable object."[79] Low modernism had no such concerns. It was not as revolutionary, but as a result it was far more marketable.

Low modernism in humanitarian nutrition captures this peculiar commercialized utopianism, maintaining the modernist orientation toward science and rational order, but in a more pragmatic form. Like middling modernism, low modernism is focused on bureaucratic action and universal responses, but it has a particular interest in commercial viability. Low modernists do not wait for the state to open industrial plants and invest in ambitious, capital-intensive nutrition schemes. They are not beholden to scientist-humanitarians for grand ideas. They have less commitment to transcendental principles, and so focus on more practical, smaller-scale solutions. This involves building commercial networks, working with businesses, but also devising new compact devices.

Low modernism has, until now, had a limited purchase beyond art and literature, although Jess Gilbert has applied the term to describe New Deal agricultural development schemes.[80] What he describes, however, is more akin to Rabinow's middling modernism, with its emphasis on bureaucratic interpretation of high modernist ideas. Low modernism in matters of development and humanitarianism, however, is similar to in the arts. It takes high modernist ideas, and mediates them through commercial channels; it adopts high modernist schemes, but it commits them to massive production.

The Radical Reaction

In 1974, the *Lancet* published an influential article entitled the "Great Protein Fiasco," which comprehensively undermined the idea that the world was threatened by an impending protein crisis. The fiasco had led to a massive industry, its author argued, with an interest in maintaining a set of spurious and dubious claims. The author, Donald McLaren, went on to describe the "long and disastrous chain of events which, once set in motion, led inexorably to the present crisis."[81] It had begun with undue attention on kwashiorkor, he argued, which had led to massive investments in high-protein food. Huge amounts of money, manpower, and global attention had then been devoted to a relatively marginal technical issue, while "children [were] lost in the unchecked scourge of malnutrition."[82] Scientists had become distracted by protein, McLaren went on, while people were dying from marasmus, or, to put it simply, starvation for want of food. This was a radical challenge to an established paradigm. After all, the search for protein sources had defined the previous years so much that the 1950s and 1960s are now often known as the "protein decades."[83]

The Great Protein Fiasco, in many ways, was a classic case of path dependency. In retrospect it was obvious that many people were dying from marasmus, but the specialists were more interested in kwashiorkor because it had become a "spectacular" disease.[84] Any questions raised about protein and kwashiorkor had simply become a justification for more research. Indeed, John Brock, who had coauthored a highly influential report, admitted that nutritionists had become preoccupied by scientific experiments in this way. Human needs, he lamented, were not really driving research. "We could have described many undernourished and marasmic African children," he said, "as they were all around us. But they did not represent what we had come to study."[85] Cicely Williams soon claimed that she had been trying to "debunk" kwashiorkor for decades, but biochemists and laboratory scientists were being listened to instead of clinicians with practical experience. "It is only the scientists who have any clout," she lamented. "Whoever heard of a Nobel Prize in medicine going to a clinician?"[86]

The Great Protein Fiasco encapsulated many problems with high modernism: the elite detachment from field-level practices, the unworkably grand ideas, the ignorance of lived experience. Clinicians on the ground plugged away "with their modest observations and their non-existent research grants," but scientists and managers unleashed a misguided utopianism that made "lamentable errors and wasted so much time, money, and personnel."[87] McLaren complained that any attempt to widen international focus beyond protein in the 1960s had been blocked by the establishment, who had an interest in the research grants and protein products and ended up "defending the party line."[88] His anger was particularly directed at waste, and he sarcastically suggested that a cost/detriment analysis could be undertaken of the protein fiasco rather than a cost/benefit analysis. How much had it cost to cause so much harm? How many resources were wasted in the pursuit of such misguided goals?

There was also a more troubling question concerning who benefited. Once high modernist ideas had percolated down into commercial practices, whole industries had been built on the protein fiasco. McLaren first identified the problem when he was working in the slums of Lebanon, realizing that the crucial issue was not kwashiorkor but "summer gastroenteritis": marasmus caused by bottle feeding, which "spread like wildfire" due to unhygienic milk preparation in hot and humid conditions. He noted that there was a real irony in protein-rich food mixtures being pedaled as a miracle cure when they were in fact causing a far bigger problem. There was "not a single study," McLaren complained, that could justify "the extravagant claims" made for these products.[89] One paper summarized the problem acidly: "There is still a general feeling that the giant food conglomerates are capable of great deeds," it sarcastically commented, "through various innovative techniques, imaginative advertising, demand manipulation, sophisticated packaging, skilled distribution, and other mystical techniques." Such aggressive forms of marketing, the author concluded, have been successful "in selling refrigerators to the Eskimos and spaghetti to the Italians."[90]

The role of businesses in infant feeding had already been questioned by Jelliffe's writings on commerciogenic malnutrition. In the 1970s, however, this campaign was furthered considerably when two incendiary reports burst onto the international scene. One, entitled *The Baby Killer*, was published by the British charity War on Want, and the other was a German translation with the more provocative title, *Nestlé Kills Babies*.[91] This dramatic discourse formed a backdrop to the 1974 World Food Conference in Rome, which became a scene of demands for radical action against the food business. Susan George, for example, published her well-known book, *How the Other Half Dies*, which criticized the connections between hunger and profit. She accused the conference in Rome of offering "purely technological" solutions that focused on production at the expense of equitable distribution.[92] Colin Tudge picked up some of these themes in another book called the *Famine Business*, which had its roots in a 1974 article in *World Medicine*.[93] The original article was accompanied by an illustration of Little Miss Muffet ("sat on a tuffet / eating the product of an inappropriate technology"), ending with a broadside against "modern food technologies, with their four apocalyptic horses": deep freezing, textured vegetable proteins, single cell proteins, and Unilever's "fish-heads, bulls' pizzles and chicken brains."[94] Tudge's language was reminiscent of William Cobbett's response to the Rumfordian soup kitchen, pointing out the irony of large multinational food corporations engaging in the problems of global hunger. It is as if they "really believe that they understand the world's problems," Tudge complained.

> They really believe that what they do is necessary; that all criticism is reactionary; that if we only understood their beneficence, how deeply they have probed and how subtly their have striven on our behalf, we would see that what they do is good. . . . I have looked at all their latest tricks and can find nothing that improves on what was done before . . . nothing that can, without drawing any comparisons, be said to be truly beneficial; nothing that does not take a cynical view of people's lives and aspirations; nothing that does not ignore totally the real issues, or follow a cruel and purblind path to their solution and by doing so make solutions ever more unlikely; nothing that does not ride rough-shod over every human aspiration, purely in the interest of ever-swifter commerce. They suggest that if only we knew about food, about agriculture, about the needs of people outside our middle class offices and our rich little island, we would raise no voice against them. Education, they say, is what we lack. Well, I am educated and I wish them all in hell.[95]

SMALL-SCALE DEVICES AND THE LOW MODERNIST LEGACY

There has long been an inverse relationship between what is practical and what is accurate when it comes to the measurement of malnutrition. Biochemical tests, for example, were meant to be the most accurate indicators of malnourishment, but they were also deeply impractical. As Derrick Jelliffe pointed out, they required a laboratory, sterilized lancets, sterile syringes, vacuum tubes and a system of refrigeration, which led to many problems in the field. Flies could pollute the blood samples, as could fleas and dust, he pointed out, and the whole assembly was bulky and complex. Many aid workers also feared "cross-cultural clashes" when taking biochemical samples, since drawing blood led to accusations of witchcraft.[1]

Anthropometry was far more practical: less invasive, less resource intensive, and more culturally acceptable, but also far less accurate. As Joel Glasman observed, the mid-upper arm circumference (MUAC) was frequently "accused of lacking accuracy," but "the more it has been criticized for inaccuracy, the more it has come to be used." This is because it absorbed the lessons of low modernism. As Glasman put it, "supporters of MUAC, rather than defending its accuracy, pushed for its materialization and industrialization."[2]

This sacrifice of idealism for practicality is a core feature of low modernism, which emerged particularly clearly in the mid-1970s. The high modernists had suggested that biochemical laboratories could be established around the world to identify the precise balance of nutrients in everyone's body. Practical problems, however, quickly accumulated.[3] Blood tests certainly offered the most accurate measure of malnutrition, but exporting equipment and teaching chromatogra-phy, enzyme assay, and amino-acid analysis proved just too complex and expen-sive. Simple anthropometric tools, therefore, emerged as a more practical alter-native. It was a preexisting idea, which had been documented in a 1930s League of Nations handbook, but nutritional anthropometry only really came to promi-nence after new World Health Organization guidelines were published in 1966.[4]

The WHO guidelines emphasized many reasons for adopting the mid-upper arm circumference. The upper arm, it pointed out, was an accessible and cultur-ally sensitive location, and, unlike the legs, not vulnerable to edema—that watery swelling that accompanies kwashiorkor. The decrease in muscle mass, moreover, was a much more sensitive indicator of malnutrition than the more traditional measures of weight and height, and perhaps more important, it did not require any specialist equipment, since it could be measured with a simple measuring tape and other lightweight tools.[5] Aid workers quickly saw the advantages of using this quick and dirty tool for nutritional assessment, particularly during the Biafran war. With so many individuals in need, aid workers were looking for a measuring tool that was "simple enough to be performed by unskilled Nigeri-ans under supervision."[6] With the new World Health Organization guidelines so recently published, anthropometry was tried on a larger scale.

The MUAC, of course, was not the only anthropometric method on offer, and the World Health Organization handbook suggested other more outdated measures such as the head circumference—reminiscent of racist colonial studies and *bertillonage*.[7] Like biochemical indicators, these were simply not appropri-ate in places like Biafra; nor were more high modernist versions of anthropom-etry, such as the Somatic Quotient, or SQ.[8] This was a complex amalgamation of measures, including both the arm and head circumferences, which had been designed as a counterpoint to the Intelligence Quotient, or IQ. The two scores, it was thought, would allow experts to track the full developmental picture of every child, with the mental development tracked with the IQ and the physical development with the SQ. It was all part of a high modernist dream of perfect legibility, but it was once again extremely impractical. In the end it proved more effective to embrace cruder tools such as the MUAC band, which represented the shift to a more pragmatic form of modernism: less accurate but also simpler, lightweight, and more transportable.

After experiments in Biafra, three key features standardized the MUAC tape in the early 1970s. First there was an insertion mechanism, introduced by Zerfas in 1975 with the idea to improve reliability.[9] Standard measuring tapes, which had previously been wrapped around the arm, ended up skewed and imprecise, and Zerfas dealt with this problem by suggesting a measuring tape that was inserted into itself with a small window for reading the circumference.[10] The second new

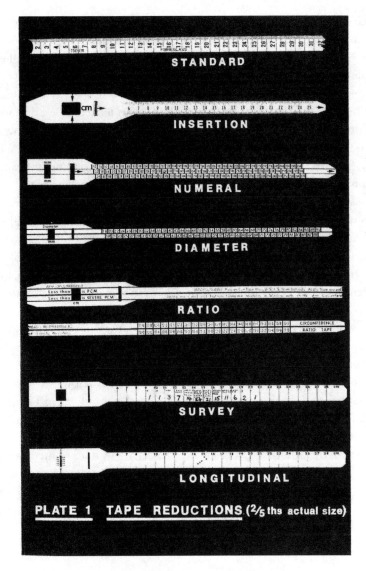

FIGURE 13. Early anthropometric measuring tapes. Alfred Zerfas, "The Insertion Tape: A New Circumference Tape for Use in Nutritional Assessment," *American Journal of Clinical Nutrition* 28, no. 7 (1975): 785. Reproduced with permission from Oxford University Press/American Society for Nutrition.

feature was a bold traffic light color scheme, with red indicating severe malnutrition and yellow indicating moderate malnutrition. A physician named David Morley had originally proposed this system as a way to monitor growth back in 1968: the red group showed "minimal or no growth," and the yellow group "were not achieving their growth potential."[11] By the early 1970s Morely began to apply the color-coding idea to MUAC screening as well, dividing the arm measurements into three categories: green to indicate a normal measurement, yellow to indicate "possible mild malnutrition," and red to designate malnutrition.[12] The third and final feature was the material itself. The MUAC band is today usually made from plastic, but it was only in the mid-1970s that suitable plastics were becoming cheap and widely available enough for mass production. Paper was no good for this measuring instrument, since it tore and got wet; fabric, meanwhile, stretched and created inaccuracies; PVC-coated fiberglass or linen was too expensive. The most effective material, it seemed, was cellulose acetate, which was either used to laminate paper, or to make MUAC strips out of old X-ray film. This had been adopted as a low-cost alternative in India during the 1970s and soon became a standard part of the toolkit.[13]

The three innovations made the MUAC band a bold and effective solution for nutritional screening, and by the late 1970s the insertion mechanism, color coding, and newly durable materials were combined in a version distributed by TALC (Teaching Aids at Low Cost).[14] The popularization of this simple object—which was later hailed by the Museum of Modern Art in New York as a classic design—showed how high modernist ideas could be made more practical, encapsulating modern, progressive ideas such as the universality of man and the commensurability of human needs in a more pragmatic form.[15] In this chapter I explore how the low modernist emphasis on small, practical devices spread throughout humanitarian nutrition in the 1970s and 1980s, arriving alongside a growing disillusionment with dominant paradigms. Indeed, after Donald McLaren had undermined the idea of a protein gap with his paper on the "Great Protein Fiasco" and Derrick Jelliffe had inspired suspicion of high modernist commerce and food technology, there was a concerted move toward smaller and more manageable interventions like the MUAC.

From Grand Narratives to Measurable Interventions

Alan Berg has confirmed that 1974 was a turning point away from high modernism: the year that humanitarian nutrition began recovering from its "enchantment with technological solutions," its obsession with "single-cell protein, fish protein concentrate, synthetic amino acid fortification and oilseed protein isolates." These "magic bullets" were based on an "excessive belief in the power of technology," which, in the end, failed to produce results.[16] The sector then moved through a relatively brief period of ambitious nutrition planning, based around

the idea that planning and management could succeed where the nutritional scientists had failed.[17] As the provocative slogan at the time had it, "Nutrition is too
important to be left to nutritionists."[18] There was a belief that nutritionists had
become "oblivious to the larger development context in which they functioned,"
and that solutions could be found by tying nutrition into the work of economists, agriculturalists, and planners.[19] This approach was known as Multisectoral
Nutrition Planning, and it was promoted by Alan Berg himself.[20]

Multisectoral Nutrition Planning was an idea that, on the face of it, resembled
the expansive push of social nutritionists of the 1930s. There was, however, a
crucial difference: this was a technical rather than political movement. One of
the policies, for example, was the establishment of "nutrition planning cells" in
national governments, which were meant to collect data, analyze the situation
in the country, and produce a coordinated response.[21] These bodies were soon
accused of collecting data for their own sake, collecting masses of statistics on
food supply, crop yield, income distribution, employment, consumer demand,
distribution, and consumption. As one critic of the movement put it, the planners had embarked on the "endless acquisition of data as an end unto itself." This
left them "mired in an analytical swamp of [their] own creation": collecting lots
of information but taking very little action.[22]

Within a few years the "holistic day dreaming" had come to an end, and
nutritional planning was bludgeoned into submission by "hypnotic but unman-
ageable" levels of information, which had become "mind-numbing more than
mind-liberating."[23] In retrospect, this short era can be seen as a last gasp of high
modernism, motivated by the same overambitious visions. As one insightful
article observed at the time, instead of solving malnutrition with small doses of
lysine, the nutritional planners wanted to solve it with large doses of data.[24] The
search for magic bullets continued, but the magician had changed. Some critics
recommended that humanitarian nutrition should take a more political turn in
response, advocating a new variety of social nutrition that was transformational
rather than technical.[25] Mainstream practice, however, took refuge in a different
approach, looking to smaller and more measurable interventions instead.

After Multisectoral Nutrition Planning came a period described by some as
"nutritional isolationalism."[26] This label, however, fails to highlight how small-
scale devices became so important in the 1980s and 1990s. True, the reaction
against large-scale planning was to isolate specific nutritional problems, but the
focus was very much on deficiencies that could be easily tackled. The shift in focus
began in 1975, with the foundation of the International Vitamin A Consultative
Group, which was later joined by another group focusing on international nutritional anemia.[27] These new bodies, with their focus on micronutrients, indicated
a shift away from big-picture programming. They were joined in the 1980s by
dedicated research on Severe Acute Malnutrition (SAM) and the development of

new treatment guidelines.[28] By this point, enthusiasm for multisectoral planning had faded and a postmortem was being played out in scientific journals.[29] Many humanitarians, in response, started to focus on specific nutritional disorders and the "big three" micronutrient deficiencies instead: vitamin A, iodine, and iron.

The advantage of focusing on the "big three" was that each could have a big impact and was relatively easy to address. Vitamin A deficiency was the biggest cause of blindness in children, but it could be easily managed by biannual high-dose supplements. Iodine deficiency was a cause of goiter and cretinism, but could be addressed by fortifying salt. Iron deficiency led to anemia and maternal death, but could be controlled through regular supplements and food fortification. All these approaches were simple and cheap, but it was iodine that most clearly captured the hopes of this period. By fortifying everyday salt a serious problem could be amenable to a cheap and targeted solution, distributed through commercial channels. The catchphrase "success in a pinch of salt" came to define the central idea: an era that looked to small-scale devices to deliver a large-scale impact on malnutrition.[30]

By the middle of the 1980s the micronutrient approach received a significant boost in profile and funding when the United Nations Standing Committee on Nutrition started taking micronutrients far more seriously.[31] In 1985 it developed a ten-year strategy for tackling vitamin A deficiency, and in the same year the International Council for the Control of Iodine Deficiency Disorders was founded, which led to a ten-year plan on salt iodization.[32] Iron deficiency, meanwhile, was the subject of a high-profile conference in 1988 and a workshop in 1990 to discuss international guidelines.[33] The agenda was driven by the accumulation of evidence, positive media reporting, and subsequent commitment at international institutions. The case of vitamin A is a good example. Alfred Sommer led the way with research into the benefits of supplementation, which led to meta-analyses and stories in the popular press.[34] By 1994 newspapers were making extravagant declarations, with the *Washington Post* describing vitamin A as a "wonder drug."[35] This led to international agencies taking up the call, with significant commitments made at the 1990 World Summit for Children. More generally, the early 1990s saw the foundation of an organization called "Micronutrient Initiative" and a 1991 conference in Montreal that gave the whole movement a memorable name: "hidden hunger."[36]

The idea of hidden hunger revealed a lot about the basic approach. After being sidelined by the planners, nutritionists were reiterating their ability to illuminate what was hidden to ordinary people. The problem, however, was that this presented a technical rather than political challenge, something forcefully pointed out by new generation of social nutritionists, who argued that improving nutrition should be an art more than a science. As one article put it, the job of tackling malnutrition ought to involve persuading governments to spend more of their finite resources on food and medical care, which required creativity, advocacy, and subtle persuasion. Tackling malnutrition could not be achieved purely scientifically, as it had to include redistributing power and resources away from those who controlled them, and toward those who were malnourished precisely because they did not.[37]

The new wave of social nutrition, however, was generally sidelined and the idea of "hidden hunger" prevailed. The attitude was one of charity rather than empowerment: as one commentator later put it, the attitude was "*they* lack something that *we* have—let us give it to them."[38] Of course, it was not power and resources being transferred but nutrients in a pill, supplement, or device, and the result was a top-down and outcome-focused set of programs: measurable but unambitious. Tackling micronutrients certainly reduced human suffering in a narrow and tangible way, but it supported rather than undermined the economic and political structures that caused such issues in the first place. As Stuart Gillespie put it in 2003, "The focus on reducing iodine, vitamin A, and iron deficiencies—through relatively quick-fix, topdown fortification and supplementation programs—diverted attention from more difficult problems."[39]

Small-Scale Devices

Devices such as iodized salt and vitamin A supplements gradually began to be more widely distributed, and there was an associated publicity push surrounding entrepreneurial new techniques. One of the most prominent was known as "Sprinkles": an additive to get iron into people's diet. Iron deficiencies were always less amenable to a simple solution than other micronutrient diseases, and supplements were much harder to distribute when compared to selling iodized salt or giving high-dose vitamin A supplements twice a year. Iron could be offered as a dose of syrup, but this had to be taken regularly and was inconvenient for aid agencies to distribute; the syrups also had a metallic taste, a short shelf life, and were heavy and expensive to transport. The other way to get iron into the diet was through fortification, as many processed foods could be enriched. Poor people, however, had no money to purchase such foods, and they could only afford to eat the same low-iron starchy cereals every day, which made the problem worse.

Sprinkles, or Micronutrient Powders (MNPs), were designed to overcome such challenges. The idea is generally attributed to a Canadian doctor named Stanley Zlotkin, who, in the 1990s, developed the basic product and then instigated a series of field trials. Sold in one-gram sachets, Sprinkles could be scattered onto a starchy diet to get micronutrients directly onto to the food.

Taking inspiration from the program for iodine—which had "success in a pinch of salt"—the idea was to fit a nutritional supplement seamlessly into daily habits.[40] This was soon being celebrated as a magical powder that could improve existing diets with a simple scattering of fairy dust; again, the structural cause of the poor diets was being obscured. In many ways Sprinkles also reflected the commercial mentality of the low modernist movement, because it was such a perfect commodity: small and lightweight, cheap and marketed for health and well-being, it had a long shelf life and was easy to stock at a very low cost in small shops even in the most rural locations. The ideal result, for Zlotkin and others, was that it would eventually be part of everyday purchases, reaching people at the "bottom of the economic pyramid."[41]

A similar set of characteristics could be found in another small-scale device: Plumpy'nut. According to most accounts, this was invented in the mid-1990s by the French pediatric nutritionist, André Briend, who had a "eureka moment" while looking at a jar of Nutella over breakfast.[42] Briend had been working on ways of improving therapeutic milk: a sweetened, fortified fluid that had been the main treatment for severe cases of malnutrition since it was first tried in Belsen.[43] Therapeutic milk, however, had a problem: it came as a powder and had to be reconstituted in water before it could be used. Given the shortage of clean water in many emergencies this could be dangerous, because when left uncovered in a hot and humid clinic or made with contaminated water therapeutic milk became a breeding ground for microbes. Therapeutic milk was also expensive, requiring not just the powder and a supply of clean water, but a set of sterilized receptacles, a clinic with beds, and a staff of medical professionals. Children had to be supervised around the clock.[44]

Briend was mulling over these issues at breakfast, considering how to develop a therapeutic food that did not require preparation in sanitary conditions, when, according to the standard account, inspiration hit. "His eyes locked on the jar of Nutella sitting on his kitchen table" and he studied the label, "comparing the contents to those of the famine foods recommended by the World Health Organization."[45] He suddenly realized that there was a striking similarity between Nutella and the requirements of therapeutic nutrition, and an idea came to him. Why not make therapeutic food into a paste? This could have low moisture content, making it difficult to spoil. It could be packaged safely, meaning no preparation on site. It could deliver nutrients surrounded by an oily, fatty product rather than a fluid, milky one, giving it a stable but moist and digestible form.[46] If the paste could be contained in an airtight foil sachet, moreover, then therapeutic feeding could take place at home. This would liberate the whole process from the costly and cumbersome feeding clinic, making treatment cheaper and easier.

Just as Sprinkles was the ideal small-scale device to treat micronutrient deficiencies, Plumpy'nut became the ideal equivalent for SAM. This search for a solution had been going on for some time, most notably in the standardized "F-100" formula developed by Michael Golden in the 1980s.[47] F-100 was a precise version of therapeutic milk, and it was designed to avoid inconsistencies, producing the right balance of nutrients in extreme cases of starvation. The idea was that a prepackaged formula could make the preparation of therapeutic milk much safer in the field, but the problem, of course, was that it still had to be reconstituted in water. Briend's inspiration was important in changing the stakes. The sticky form and attractive packaging became crucial to the narrative of innovation. Like Sprinkles, Plumpy'nut had a heroic nutritionist-inventor, an attractively packaged product, and a narrative of growing acceptance. Instead of success in a pinch of salt, however, this was success in a silvery packet.

The packet, indeed, became crucial to Plumpy'nut's success. To design it, Briend entered into alliance with a food technology company and manufacturer, Nutriset, who were instrumental in bringing the product to market. Briend stressed that there were always two key challenges in the development of Plumpy'nut: a nutritional challenge and technical challenge.[48] Briend and Golden had solved the nutritional challenge, but the technical challenge was to mass-produce the peanut paste and find suitable and long-lasting packaging. The oily, viscous paste made foil sachets difficult to seal because packets kept splitting, the glue kept failing, and Briend had no experience of mass manufacture. As a result, and because of its product manufacturing and marketing experience, Nutriset produced something that was visually arresting as well as nutritionally useful. Each portion of Plumpy'nut was surrounded by thick foil, with a satisfying bulk and firmness beneath the glinting exterior. The sachets were manufactured to weigh precisely 92 grams and were 12 centimeters long, 6 centimeters in width, and 1 centimeter deep. Slipped in the pocket, this offered a portable but powerful ration for emergencies, containing 500 kilocalories per portion: a great deal of energy for the weight. The paste was a light brown color with an orange tint—sugary in taste, oily in texture—and its wrapper was marked by the distinctive logo, which featured bouncing peanuts in place of the apostrophe, and the letters RUTF, an acronym for Ready-to-Use Therapeutic Food.

Much of the expertise in Plumpy'nut came congealed in the package itself. It was effectively invisible, replacing the very obvious modernist control of the huge therapeutic feeding center with individually wrapped portions of food. This was the opposite end of the scale from Soyer's enormous vats of soup, his gleaming meat digesters, and industrial-sized community kitchens. Emergency nutrition had shrunk into an eminently portable low modernist device, with clinicians prescribing Plumpy'nut for take-home care. It was, in other words, a micro-infrastructure—a feeding center in a packet—and it was also highly individualized.[49] Unlike a giant pot, this product could not be dipped into and measured out in a variety of ways; it was difficult to make into dishes and it was predisposed to remain in its packet. It was even distributed with warnings against sharing, and early versions of the packet were marked by the image of a doctor to illustrate this medicinal purpose, alongside the legend "Under Medical Supervision."

Ever since Plumpy'nut was born on Briend's breakfast table, the adoption of this simple peanut paste has been generally interpreted as a triumph for the treatment of malnutrition. These small, compact sachets can be easily transported into remote areas, and tests have proved their efficiency in treating the most malnourished. By the turn of the new millennium Plumpy'nut had been declared a "miracle" treatment for malnutrition, a "magic" commodity that could transform a child from "literally skin and bones to certain survival in just four to six weeks."[50] This, in many people's minds, had become the single biggest development in emergency humanitarian nutrition for decades. The first field trials took place in Chad in 1997, the Niger famine of 2005 allowed the product to be used in a serious emergency on a large scale, and as evidence began to accumulate, the process of acceptance gradually moved to completion.[51] By 2007 Plumpy'nut received international approval from the World Health Organization, the World Food Program, and UNICEF.[52]

Peanuts and Patents

There were, of course, critics of Plumpy'nut, and it was the commercialism that particularly rankled. Briend was clear that Nutriset's commercial expertise had been crucial in the development of his idea, and the patent, which had been filed back in the late 1990s, was justified by the need to cover the company's costs.[53] As the success of the product grew, however, the product was endorsed by the major UN agencies and the scene began to look different. Critics pointed out that if Plumpy'nut was as good as it claimed then it should be freely available and not restricted by patent. By the end of 2009, these denunciations went public. First the French aid agency Médecins Sans Frontières (MSF) published an open letter criticizing Nutriset for aggressively guarding its patent. Then a pair of US nonprofits took Nutriset to court, asserting their right to produce a similar product.[54] They all argued that the patent was limiting access to a lifesaving treatment and preventing other companies from meeting demand. This looked like a way to profit from other people's suffering, and, according to one MSF representative, the patent was so broad that an organization could be in violation by just adding a single additional micronutrient to a jar of Nutella.[55]

In response to the negative publicity, Nutriset soon developed a "Patent Usage Agreement": a simple online form that licensed companies to produce their own versions of the therapeutic food. This became a successful strategy for the company. Criticisms faded and the reputation of the company began to grow, but then a new wave of more radical criticism emerged from a slightly different direction. This time, it was not the medical humanitarians and rival corporations, but activists from the Right to Food movement in India objecting to the product—precisely those representatives of the poor and malnourished that the social nutritionists had argued were central to tackling malnutrition. The Right to Food movement mobilized a far more political line, arguing that Plumpy'nut did nothing to address poverty and powerlessness. They criticized the product for focusing on nutrients at the expense of structural injustices, and they argued that it was acting as a Trojan horse for the international food industry who were pushing "nutriceutricals" on the rural poor.[56] They condemned aid agencies for pushing Plumpy'nut as if it were a fetish, when it was just a packet of peanut butter wrapped in a silvery coating, and they objected to the way Plumpy'nut enabled treatment at home, arguing that any response to malnutrition should involve *increasing* points of contact between marginalized groups and the rest of society rather than decreasing them and pushing the malnourished back to their villages.[57]

Such powerful criticisms certainly gained an audience, but supporters of the product argued that these critics had missed the point. Plumpy'nut remained a useful device because it was simple to use, easy to store, and could be distributed to anyone so easily. Its simple form allowed feeding structures to be transformed and upended, and the fact that it was self-administered was an advantage. Rather than requiring a top-down clinic, with its beds, trained staff, and infrastructure, Plumpy'nut allowed malnutrition to be treated in the community—even by those affected. The product did not need to be prepared or cooked, and this enabled people to take it home, facilitating treatment of more people at a time. Perhaps most important, the product allowed aid workers to relinquish control over the feeding process, as they were now handing sachets directly over to those that needed it. The idea was that people could help themselves rather than being subjected to constant monitoring and an invasive regime of care. This was the essence of low modernist practicality: faith in science but without the top-down regimes of control.

Like Sprinkles and iodized salt, Plumpy'nut was connected to the rise of "bottom of the pyramid" interventions and other attempts to tackle nutrition through the private sector. The idea has been most clearly expressed in Prahalad's book, *The Fortune at the Bottom of the Pyramid*, which was published with the subtitle "Eradicating Poverty through Profits." This drew attention to the vast, untapped market of potential consumers living in the poorest parts of the world, which, Prahalad argued, presented a huge business opportunity as well as an opportunity to do good. His book contained a lengthy case study on iodized salt, which, he argued, was an example of how businesses can "do well by doing good," bringing solutions to nutritional problems.[58] As Prahalad put it, the private sector could help valuable products get to remote areas, channeling the formidable logistical powers of the market.[59] It could help poor people eat better foods, utilizing the powers of promotional persuasion. It could produce and distribute these products with much greater efficiency, using the incentive of profit to cut costs. All of this pointed to fertile new ground, on which microdevices such as Sprinkles, iodized salt, and other cheap, fortified foods were distributed through the market mechanism.

In 2002, the United Nations established the Global Alliance for Improved Nutrition (GAIN) to develop such commercial involvement. The aim of GAIN was to kick-start fortification programs, develop markets for new foods, and coordinate marketing and promotion campaigns. With a board that included representatives of many multinationals, such as Danone, Coca-Cola, and Unilever, GAIN began by encouraging each country to establish a National Fortification Alliance, which helped select and develop products for fortification and promotion.[60] Again, there were historical echoes here. The new national groupings resembled the 1930s national nutrition committees and 1970s nutrition planning cells, yet they reflected more contemporary concerns. While the 1930s was marked by political engagement and the 1970s by technocratic planning, these new bodies were marked by commerce. They promoted modest interventions and channeled commercial imperatives, facilitating the sale of products to school feeding programs, coordinating promotion between businesses, and in many cases, enabling close relationships in which aid agencies would run education programs while corporations distributed free samples.[61]

The growing involvement of the private sector is certainly one of the more durable trends of recent years, and it has led to an expanding market for nutriceuticals: "nutritionally fortified or engineered foods, beverages or supplements" that are "marketed for their health-giving properties." As Alice Street has pointed out, nutriceuticals have become a growth industry in places like India and South Africa, which are large markets with huge numbers of poor consumers.[62] The sector includes malt drink sachets made by Glaxo-Smith Kline, packets of fortified biscuits made by PepsiCo, as well as the "Growell" range by Nutriset. In addition to promoting these products for sale directly to the poor, many companies have invested in nutritional education campaigns and founded "research institutes" to build the evidence base.⁶³ The reach of the private sector has also extended backward along the production chain, promoting the sale of new biofortified crops such as "golden rice," enhanced with beta-carotene to address vitamin A deficiencies. As Aya Kimura has pointed out, this has added a new level to the food business's involvement in humanitarian nutrition. By genetically engineering the crops themselves, companies can now claim they are "doing well by doing good" by altering the very source of food rather than the outputs of industry.⁶⁴

Post-Humanitarianism?

With so many commercial innovations and small-scale devices on the market— not to mention the rise of cash transfer programs—it is tempting to describe our most recent era as postmodern. This term is often taken to mean a merging of forms and styles, the collapsing of high and low, and the end of unifying narratives. In the field of humanitarian nutrition, speaking of a postmodern turn would seem to indicate the end of grand narratives, the fizzling out of large-scale productivist agriculture, and the beginnings of an more ruptured approach to specific nutritional deficiencies. At first glance, humanitarian nutrition does seem to have moved in this direction, splitting into a variety of specialisms, with high modernism in decline and practitioners focusing on specific nutrients such as vitamin A, iron, and iodine. This has broken the big problem of global hunger down into ever smaller and more manageable interactions between nutrients and the body.

There have been numerous other attempts to connect humanitarianism to postmodernity on a wider scale. Mark Duffield, for example, has written how humanitarianism used to be connected to grandest narrative of all—the notion of human progress—with its central aim to "wall-off" disaster until the trajectory of progress could be resumed.⁶⁵ In this modernist vision, disaster was conceived as an aberration, something external to society that could be contained. Since the 1980s, however, the modernist conception of disaster has been replaced by a more dispersed and postmodern approach, which positions disaster as not external to society, but internal to it. Emergencies are no longer an aberration, but an ever-present possibility. Whereas humanitarian policy was once concerned with "protection"—offering an international safety net, which was modeled on the modern welfare state—the dominant policy rubric is now "resilience."⁶⁶ This is the doctrine of preparedness through entrepreneurship, making people ready to manage shocks and emergencies without relying on aid. Sometimes this approach is described as "post-humanitarianism," a term that has emerged in a number of recent texts.⁶⁷

The developments described in this chapter might be easily viewed through such a prism, but ultimately postmodernism is an unhelpful way of making sense of contemporary relief. Micronutrient supplements, it is true, reflect the narrow horizons of resilience and do not guarantee a good quality diet or address people's powerlessness. Plumpy'nut, moreover, does not depend on a functioning state and a large public health infrastructure. In many ways, top-down techniques have been replaced by consumer-centered and community-based approaches, and small-scale devices are now portable and distributed through the market. In Duffield's scheme, this all fits into a humanitarian worldview that is based not on human progress but on the need for individuals to begin to *help themselves*: a theme that appears in literature on "little development devices" and "humanitarian goods" as well. Such "micro-infrastructures" imagine life without the state, enabling individual survival without large infrastructural systems. Peter Redfield, for example, has written of the LifeStraw: a product that allows the user to drink safely from turbid river water through a simple tube that is light and compact enough to be carried around the neck.[68] This product replaces the need for piped water and large community treatment facilities—a theme that extends to many other recent devices as well. The photovoltaic panel is designed to supply a personal source of off-grid electricity; the PeePoo bag offers sanitation without the sewerage system; Plumpy'nut, meanwhile, can treat severe malnutrition at home.[69] When there is no clean piped water, no sanitation system, and no electricity network, the market can provide.[70]

The case for a postmodern turn in humanitarianism seems compelling, and it draws on a number of high-level policy changes for support. In addition to resilience, there has been a recent move toward "humanitarian innovation," which offers a similar vision of liberation: from camps, from bureaucracy, but also from the state itself.[71] "Innovation" begins with the view that aid bureaucracies have become complacent and inefficient, that new ideas from the private sector will bring life to an ailing sector. The future of aid is once again entrusted to entrepreneurial citizens, who embrace the opportunity that disaster affords them, turning emergencies into an opportunity for reinvention. Many scholars have pointed out that "innovation" and "resilience" are not just postmodern, but also fundamentally neoliberal ideas, shifting risk and responsibility onto individuals while introducing market forces into new areas of life.[72]

This certainly seems a convincing argument, but it ignores how everyday aid work remains practical and mundane. In most places, relief work remains dominated by sacks of Corn-Soy Blend, large tanks of clean water, and the careful organization of space. The more unusual and flashy designs—such as the LifeStraw and PeePoo bag—are not widely used, and humanitarian aid is more likely to be oriented around refugee camps with a strict, linear layout, registration systems organized around preset categories, and shelters designed as universal solutions. Humanitarian nutrition has long retained this modernist character, sharing the same commitment to efficiency and rationalization, the same belief in the power of technology, and the same orientation around a universal human dignity.

Devices such as Sprinkles and Plumpy'nut, therefore, do not represent the end of modernism, but simply its transformation into new, low modernist forms. Humanitarianism, in fact, has always been modern. From the bureaucratic techniques of early nutritional science to the more militaristic concerns with energy and efficiency, from the expanding role of medicine in the 1930s to the technology-intensive high-protein foods, its history has been entwined with modern transformations. The recent low modernist move toward pragmatism and commercialism is just the latest twist in this story.

CONCLUSION
On an Empty Stomach

This book began with Soyer's Irish soup kitchen, which was an archetypally Victorian approach to tackling the empty stomach. In the intervening century and a half we have seen humanitarians shift from a local to a global reach, from communal kitchens to individual rations, from patronage to anthropometry, and from a broadly "vernacular" menu to one that is highly technical in character. In the introduction to this book I used these rather schematic transformations to suggest a central argument: that aid reflects the age. Approaches to humanitarian nutrition, in other words, are profoundly shaped by historical conditions. These have been driven by the dynamics of modernity that were first visible in Soyer's soup kitchen back in the middle of the nineteenth century.

This focus on modern conditions has permeated all the chapters. Chapter 1, for example, examined the roots of the soup kitchen, explaining Count Rumford's classical worldview, which looked to harness natural laws and human nature to build an institution in Munich. Rumford was building on even older Renaissance legacies, such as notions of the moral economy and ideas of a great chain of being, but when Soyer took Rumford's ideas and scaled up the soup kitchen, he transformed this classical model into one that was marked by modernity. He detached the soup kitchen from its local contexts, exported it to Ireland, and fed more people per hour than ever before.

Chapter 2 introduced another central figure: Justus Liebig, the founder of modern biochemistry. Liebig developed a more scientific method for examining the empty stomach, which affected everything that came after. Classical dietetics had focused on balance and order, placing dietary advice within a holistic system of living. With the arrival of modern nutritional science, however, attention shifted to organic structures. The contrast between these systems was illustrated by comparing a pair of flavorful pastes that had been reduced by boiling beef in water: Osmazome Food and Extract of Meat. The products were essentially the same, but the former articulated its benefits through a language of humoral balance, whereas the latter drew instead on a more modern language of proteins and carbohydrates. The triumph of Extract of Meat showed that the terms of reference were changing. Food was now being judged in a different way, with implications for the management of hunger.

Chapter 3 turned to look at how these changes played out in the government of the diet. Liebig's biochemistry had made the diet measurable, but in Victorian prisons and industrial canteens it became governable. Focusing on the work of Edward Smith and Wilbur Atwater, this chapter showed how food could be valued as a source of energy for laborers and prisoners. Smith, for example, used nutritional science to set prison diets at a level that served the interests of reform; Atwater, meanwhile, contributed to a growing discourse of the "human motor," which compared the energy consumed and expended. Adherents of this approach reduced food to numbers and people into machines, sealing research subjects in airtight calorimeters. They began to measure what foods were worth. Rather than being a holistic philosophy of life, the diet was becoming, instead, a crucial instrument of state.

Chapter 4 examined how the government of diet became more ambitious in the early twentieth century, tasked with improving the strength of nations as well as improving the productivity of bodies. This approach, known as "dietary determinism," was underpinned by a simple but powerful notion: that collective weakness could be explained and solved by food. It was an explicitly modernist idea, which justified a generation of colonial development programs. David McCay and Robert McCarrison, for example, compared the diet of different "races" in India; Audrey Richards examined the "nutritional systems" of groups in Africa; John Gilks and John Boyd Orr linked the diet of Kikuyu and Masai in Kenya. If Wilbur Atwater's airtight container had represented the vision and scope of the early nutritional science—contained, abstract, and concerned with specifics— the open plains of the Kenyan landscape epitomized the scene by the 1930s. This was a period of growing ambition and expansive connections that drew out the wider implications of the diet.

Chapter 5 turned to the League of Nations, where this expansive approach was incubated, promoted, and applied. Better nutrition, the League argued, would lead to greater productivity, stimulating the economy and generating higher wages. International trade would follow, which would not just prevent future depression but promote peaceful diplomatic relations. It was a fundamentally optimistic vision that appealed to both left and right, and it soon became known as "social nutrition." Embracing parallel areas of expertise in public health, economics, and agriculture, social nutrition hit its high point with John Boyd Orr's proposals for a World Food Board in the 1940s. This was to have been an institution that aimed to stabilize the price of staples, provide a credit facility for agricultural investment, and maintain a stockpile of food for relief. World War II, however, had changed the terms of the debate.

Chapter 6 showed how the tragic scale of starvation during the war ended this ambitious vision. Orr's suggestions were rejected and humanitarianism became focused on the more practical issue of feeding the hungry masses. Aid agencies began stockpiling nonperishable, compact, and highly nutritious foods, which necessitated close connections with the military. Housed in former barracks, displaced people were fed surplus army rations, which were small, lightweight, and calorie dense. As humanitarians tried to feed as many people as possible, military handbooks became a useful reference point. "Enough to eat," read one, "does not mean enough bread, or enough soup, or enough potato; it means enough of each of the *nutrients* of which food is composed."[1] This became the mainstream approach. Efficiency and control began to characterize relief, and aid workers such as Kathryn Hulme described Spam-maddened adults chanting at the warehouse door. Humanitarians were forced to eschew expansive connections and refocus on intricate biological processes.

Chapter 7 examined the medicalization of hunger, which emerged from this postwar transformation. Humanitarians during World War II not only developed efficient new ways to feed the starving, but also conducted a range of studies on the process of starvation itself. In Minnesota, thirty-six volunteers were placed on a restricted diet and subjected to detailed tests as their bodies withered away. In Belsen, army medical officers examined skeletal concentration camp survivors and administered protein injections. In the Warsaw ghetto, the starving Jewish population had their respiration, circulation, and energy reserves closely examined. This interest in the deep, internal mechanics of starvation began with the "discovery" of kwashiorkor in the Gold Coast of Africa, where Cicely Williams took a word for a social condition and reconfigured it as a disease. Hunger was stripped back to its biological manifestations in the search for a technical fix.[2]

Chapter 8 showed how high modernism took up this challenge in the 1950s and 1960s. Single Cell Protein was perhaps the most dramatic example: a utopian product that involved the manufacture of nutrients in isolation. This was an approach that inspired many other new foods, defining starvation as a nutrient deficiency and manufacturing the missing nutrients in gleaming new laboratories. It was protein, in particular, that mattered most, and new sources were made from oil, algae, grass, junk fish and ordinary green leaves.[3] High modernism in humanitarian nutrition soon developed around three central features: a lionization of science, a taming of nature, and a commitment to elitist planning.

Chapter 9 looked at how high modernism turned to low modernism against the background of the Biafran war. This was the first time that the two central pillars of contemporary therapeutic feeding were developed in a nascent form: Corn-Soy Blend and the mid-upper arm circumference (MUAC) measuring tape. Focusing on Corn-Soy Blend, this chapter described how, in 1966, the Food for Peace legislation was adjusted to allow American companies to manufacture, process, and fortify foods for the poor. High modernist schemes had failed due to cost and acceptance, but Corn-Soy-Milk (CSM) and then Corn-Soy Blend (CSB) became more practical and profitable. As Forbes magazine put it that same year, feeding the world's hungry millions was generating billions for US businesses. Starvation was tied into large-scale agricultural production, commerce, and new innovations.

Chapter 10 examined another feature of low modernism, which was characterized not just by commercialism but also practicality. Beginning with the example of the MUAC band, it showed how accuracy was sacrificed in return for simplicity. With its three core features—an insertion mechanism, a traffic light color scheme, and a durable plastic material—this simple tool translated high modernist ideals of legibility into a more controllable and practical form. Other small-scale devices joined the field as an era of "nutritional isolationism" began in the 1980s. This led to products such as Plumpy'nut and Sprinkles, which emerged in a more fractured landscape. The modernist ambition, however, continued as small-scale devices were optimistically celebrated as a way to solve deep-rooted political problems.

The Faustian Pact of Modernity

It is easy to look back on this history and find a narrative of progress. Humanitarianism now relies on efficient, effective techniques that are much fairer than earlier methods. Relief is now more readily available, making use of a range of innovative new devices, and it has expanded in scale thanks to better funding, production, and logistics. Perhaps most significant, many mistakes have been rectified. In the distant past Count Rumford believed water made soup nourishing, Alexis Soyer treated paupers like pigs in a pen, Ellen Richards considered vegetables as an artistic addition to the plate, and David McCay promised to make "effeminate" Indians more "manly." These absurd beliefs became untenable in the light of modern science, but this does not necessarily point to a simple story of progress. Indeed, it is important to remember that contemporary techniques such as anthropometry and food fortification are just as rooted in sociopolitical systems as the work of Rumford, Soyer, or McCay.

In rejecting the story of progress, however, there is another trap to avoid: the narrative of decline. It is tempting to write a "Whig history in reverse," a story of growing control and surveillance, of modernist bureaucracy thwarting freedom and creativity.[4] I was certainly attracted to such an argument after my fieldwork in South Sudan, which left me depressed and despondent. I saw refugees shuffling through an education program, receiving amplified instructions on how to cook and clean in order to receive a couple of measly plastic bags filled with imported corn meal. I found nutritionists tinkering with the nutrient profile of food, justifying such mixes as more advanced and rational than local dietary choices. I witnessed aid workers wordlessly lining up refugees and measuring them with a strip of tape, reducing people to their physical measurements while silencing their voices. I saw corn and soy dominating the aid program—commodities that play an integral part in the global food system, erasing biodiversity and destroying the soil—while miles of fertile land around the camp went uncultivated and requests for seeds and tools went unanswered.

That trip to South Sudan illustrated some of the most damaging themes of contemporary nutritional relief—sidelining cultural practices, silencing beneficiary voices, and offering short-term solutions—but the problem with constructing a narrative of decline is that it is just as simplistic as the narrative of progress. A story of continual progression leaves out many failings in the aid industry, but a story of degeneration suggests that the whole system is corrupt.[5] In this book I have tried to navigate a path between these extremes, avoiding both a Panglossian celebration of progress and a Whig history in reverse. My alternative, meanwhile, has focused as much as possible on the wider intellectual changes within which humanitarianism takes place.

The first chapter of this book introduced the Faustian pact of modernity as a way to capture the balance of gains and losses that might be associated with the history of humanitarian nutrition. The idea comes from Marshall Berman, a sociologist who described modernization as story of construction and destruction, a drive for improvement that comes accompanied by a "terror of disorientation" and of "life falling apart."[6] Modernity, Berman wrote, is an experience that unites humankind. It offers universalism, economic growth, and a shared sense of progress, yet this is a "paradoxical unity," a "unity of disunity." It "pours us all into a maelstrom of perpetual disintegration and renewal, of struggle and contradiction," in which everyone loses what they have.[7] By drawing connections with Goethe's Faust, Berman casts humanity as benefiting from modernization but only "by radically transforming the whole physical and social and moral world."[8] Modernity produces incredible results, but exacts terrible costs. It generates wealth and opportunity, but leads to the destruction of tradition. It produces new freedoms, but imprisonment in bureaucratic machinery and self-ish individualism. It creates material comforts, but the destruction of the natural environment.

To be modern, Berman argues, is to live this "life of paradox and contradiction": "It is to be overpowered by the immense bureaucratic organizations that have the power to control and often to destroy all communities, values, lives; and yet to be undeterred in our determination to face these forces, to fight to change their world and make it our own." Modernity, in other words, "clears the decks of entanglements, so that the self and the world can be created anew."[9]

This account of modernity is an excellent description of humanitarianism and its history. Berman argues that the role of modernist is to "survive and create in the maelstrom's midst," which has long been the aim of relief work.[10] Promoting life, widening the circle of individuals being assisted, and constantly creating new ways to intervene more effectively is the central activity of relief work, while at the same time humanitarians end up caught in that maelstrom of destruction by silencing voices, sidelining cultures, and erasing the power of individuals. As it pertains to humanitarian nutrition, we can see this balance of gains and losses most clearly in the contrast that began this book. Whereas the soup kitchen was rooted in premodern notions of patronage, politics, and the moral economy—precisely the structures that then came into question with the rise of modernity—the emergence of biochemistry disrupted these systems of thought. The implication of this change was profound, and it led to four main areas where gains were accompanied by harm. First of all, it led to bureaucracy and rationalization, bringing efficiency at the expense of interpersonal concern. Second, it led to equality and universalism, bringing human rights at the expense of diversity. Third, it facilitated commerce and capitalism, generating huge quantities of food while rendering the hungry into an opportunity for profit. Fourth and finally, it brought medicine and science, which generated new knowledge about the empty stomach but created new forms of control in its wake.

These implications are all part of the Faustian bargain and we can look at each of them now in turn. Take, for example, the rise of bureaucracy and rationalization. This has allowed aid to grow in scope and size, but has also made it harder to realize any genuine interpersonal connection. It is a dynamic clearly illustrated by the MUAC procedure, which is enormously efficient but tends to objectify people, giving them little space to articulate their experiences, while generating a tension between breadth of reach and depth of engagement. This is a tragedy that has long been recognized by aid workers, who decry the impossibility of attending to so much suffering while extending care beyond the physique. It is also a problem that was expressed particularly clearly by Tony Vaux in his memoir of 2001, when he wrote:

> Aid that simply provides calories for the stomach and water for the throat is a reduction of people to things. How can there be human concern for such a mean objective? Concern for the person entails concern for the whole being. . . . It is a concern for every aspect of a person, including their loss of relatives and way of life, their disability, their love of children, their past and future. . . . It involves the aid worker infinitely in deeper and deeper understanding."[11]

In highlighting these valuable ideals, and lamenting the difficulty of realizing them, Vaux exposes the pressures of a bureaucratized system. Aid workers draw on the immense power of bureaucratic organizations to reach the most people in need, but they are forced to focus on what can be counted. The start of this book showed how, in the theory of classical dietetics, food was considered differently: not counted, but judged in relation to a broader philosophy of life and the complex particularities of the constitution. This was replaced by much greater attention on biology, whereby decisions about what to eat became managed by experts looking at the internal structures of the world. Governments took this opportunity to examine the diet of populations, ignoring their specificities and treating them as homogenous units. We were left with calories for the stomach, water for the throat, and bare lives to be saved and sustained. A wave of high modernist bureaucracy later attempted to rationally engineer these responses, manufacturing nutrients that could be counted and delivered.[12]

The second main theme of modernity is a commitment to humanitarian universalism. As Western aid organizations gradually widened their spheres of action, from small local projects to relief in colonial territories, more and more people were counted as fully human and treated as worthy of assistance. Principles such as humanity and impartiality became more readily accepted, institutionalizing the idea that all humans have equal worth and that assistance should be prioritized according to need.[13] What could be wrong with such universalism? The Faustian bargain in this case relates to the tension between universalism and culture. This, of course, is an old debate in human rights but it appears in relief work as well.[14] As humans are treated as members of a single group, their distinctive cultural practices tend to erode. As individual rights are enhanced and protected, some forms of communal existence become devalued. As the same standards are applied to everyone, a single set of norms become universal. This is in some ways a triumph for humanity but it ends up taking the experiences of some and applying them to all.

The issue, once again, can be illustrated by the MUAC band. This, after all, is an object that encapsulates the universal aims of humanitarianism by comparing each person to a "standard" or "normal" body. It is based on an idea of normality, which, as Ian Hacking has pointed out, became a hallmark of modernity just as human nature was the hallmark of the classical age. Nowadays, "we no longer ask, in all seriousness, what is human nature," Hacking wrote. "Instead we talk about normal people." Moreover, when we talk about what is normal, Hacking continued, we are never just mobilizing a descriptive term, defining what is average. We are also mobilizing an evaluative term, defining what is acceptable. What is normal is often taken to be normative—to be right. As Hacking put it, "We can use the word 'normal' to say how things are, but also to say how they ought to be"—and we can use it to say both things at once.[15]

The third theme of modernity is the role of commerce and capitalism. The private sector has been a long-standing feature of humanitarianism, generating huge quantities of food and effective new technologies, but it also renders the hungry into a market, an opportunity for profit. Looking back, it now seems rather obvious that the basic idea behind many high modernist schemes was that the malnourished could be fed on the leftovers of other industrial and agricultural processes—primarily those that met the needs of the very rich. This, it could be argued, was simple practicality and efficiency, yet one of the reasons these products seem so meager and limiting is precisely because of this connection with commerce. In many ways, these products offered little more than a slightly enhanced version of an already-awful diet. Their production tended to draw from, rather than challenge, the unequal economic structures that kept people poor. This was not just a failure to address inequalities and the systemic problems that cause malnutrition. In many ways, it contributed to them by making the production of famine foods reliant on surplus commodities and the profitability of food processing.

This reflects a wider problem with humanitarianism. Like the commercial imperative to short-term profits at the expense of longer-term sustainability, aid work often does little to address the wider structural causes of poverty and disadvantage. Again, the MUAC process illustrates the problem particularly well: by relying on anthropometric cutoff points it consistently identifies people who can be prioritized for nutritional assistance, but also risks abandoning people once they have recovered from extreme starvation. Even after being objectively identified as "adequately nourished," for example, people often remain hungry, have insufficient access to food, and suffer from the same social problems that accompany widespread malnourishment in society. Others, if fed back to strength and health, may find themselves ejected from humanitarian care in order to fend for themselves in circumstances of persistent poverty. This focus on short-term relief—met most practically through vast distribution of corn and soy—therefore comes at the expense of more structural concerns.

The fourth and final theme of modernity is the role of medicine and science. This has, without doubt, improved human understanding of starvation, swept away the inaccurately spiritual notions of osmazome, and debunked the ridiculous idea that water makes soup more nourishing. Yet the growth in scientific and medical expertise has also involved subtle and complex transformations in the governance of the diet. The earliest chapters of this book highlighted how the decline of the classical dietetic tradition left ordinary people with less and less faith in their ability to make truly informed judgments about their diet. This placed great power in the hands of experts, who applied their nutritional theories first in closed institutions like workhouses, then in industrial canteens, and later through other levers of the state. In this transformation, the poor were told that their dietary choices were "irrational," evidence of "conceit," and a central cause of their poverty. Knowledge about human digestion may have expanded in the process, but so did a paternalistic combination of care and control that has long become central to aid.

The government of the diet reached its apotheosis with the medicalization of hunger, which focused attention on the process of starvation itself. This was reconfigured as a disease, treated as a biological as much as a social process, and tied to wider transformations in society. The impact of "hunger studies" mirrored the way that autopsies and modern medicine had transformed understandings of the body over a century before. Foucault has pointed out how death was previously seen as an external force and how, until the eighteenth century, the grim reaper was the dominant metaphor for death, coming from the outside and striking at any moment. After the arrival of modern medicine, however, the inner workings of the body were exposed as death's proximate cause, which changed both conceptions and treatments of illness. In a similar way, the hunger studies of the 1930s and 1940s revealed the inner workings of the starving body and transformed our understanding of hunger. Attention thereafter was refocused at the cellular level, turning starvation into a technical condition.

Medicalization is often presented as an overwhelmingly negative process: a dangerous attempt by doctors to extend their power over everyday life. Ivan Illich, for example, has written one of the best-known critiques, pointing to the way that medics depoliticize social problems by turning them into biological conditions that are managed in technical ways.[16] Such populist denunciations of the "medical nemesis," however, neglect the *value* of medicalizing a problem. When it comes to hunger, medicalization may, in fact, lead to the most effective remedies, however insensitively applied.[17] Here, again, we can see the Faustian dynamic. The modern transformation of hunger into a medical condition has certainly made the issue more hierarchical and elitist, reducing its complexity, downplaying social contexts, and encouraging doctors to administer drugs and other magic bullets in place of genuine, structural change. Yet it has also saved many lives and brought the most absurd humanitarian treatments to an end.

Lessons and Recommendations

Since 2012 I have presented some of the arguments in this book at a number of contrasting conferences, but two of them particularly stay in my mind. Held just a few months apart, they involved very different audiences who reacted in very different ways. The first was a conference of anthropologists, who after I had presented a paper on the medicalization of hunger responded with barely disguised horror. In particular, they described the idea that "medicalization works" as "careless," and I was high-handedly informed that I should be seeking relativistic detachment rather than engaging in practical recommendations. The second presentation, which followed hot on the heels of the first, caused ire from the opposite direction. I gave exactly the same paper, but this time to an audience of humanitarian medical professionals, who disagreed with my analysis on different grounds. They argued that critique was largely pointless and that medicalizing hunger is the best solution in emergencies. It might exert paternalistic control and ignore structural conditions, they conceded, but *this is why it works.* Sometimes, they clarified, it helps to reduce complex social and cultural issues to a disease, since this can narrow the problem, maintain control, and target resources at treatable maladies.

The implications of these arguments—from the doctors and anthropologists respectively—can demonstrate the intricate balance between domination and effectiveness that lie at the heart of the Faustian bargain. The doctors' point was that, in the case of hunger, huge successes come from narrowing our target and focusing on severe acute malnutrition for those under two years of age. The anthropologists' point, however, was that triumphalism comes with risks: obscuring more structural issues, preventing critical thinking about power, and ignoring the way that humans can be treated as if they had no culture at all. The history of humanitarian nutrition, marked by a "maelstrom of perpetual disintegration and renewal," involves both of these dynamics. It is a story of "struggle and contradiction," which has generated huge successes, yet also destruction, paternalism, and control.[18]

Where does that leave future policy? Any nuanced account of the past should not be considered an evasive refusal to engage in practical discussions of improvement and change. It can, in fact, have practical implications. In the preface to this book I argued that history and anthropology offer us an inventory of alternatives, a way to question our taken-for-granted way of doing things. At the risk of appearing simplistic, this section summarizes four central lessons that emerge from these alternatives. They are provocations rather than solutions, and they can be summarized in the form of four imperatives: an insistence that form matters, that culture matters, that ambition matters, and that participation matters.

What does it mean to say that form matters? Throughout the long history of humanitarian nutrition there have been many attempts to design a perfect famine food, but the products that have come closest to success are the ones that are most satisfying to eat. Many foods have failed because, to put it bluntly, they were horrid. Rumford's soup was watery and inadequate, the Medical Research Council's protein hydrolysates tasted like "vomit," Pirie's Leaf Protein Concentrate turned stools alarmingly green, and there were other less vivid examples that failed because they were dry, powdery, fishy, or bland. The more successful foods, in contrast, have been appetizing. Liebig's extract of meat, for example, was delicious and eminently portable. Plumpy'nut has managed to appeal to sweet-toothed children around the world. Soup, for all its nutritional failings, has remained part of humanitarian response because it is so attuned to human aesthetic requirements: it requires only a pot and some heat to produce; it adapts to include any ingredient available; it can easily be made to scale; and it is capable of "almost infinite dilution" while still offering warmth and comfort.[19]

What counts as pleasant to eat, of course, changes with context, and this leads to the second lesson: that culture matters. Despite the high modernist desire to bring up a new generation of people who will eat unusual foods, it is important that nutritional relief fits with existing cultural practices. This matters even when people are close to death: as we saw in the response of Eastern European concentration camp victims, the sickly sweetness of the Bengal Famine gruel in 1945 generated disgust even though people were starving. The importance of culture in the foundation of taste has been well known for years, but its depth is unacknowledged as it becomes a tick-box exercise for relief workers. Audrey Richards, back in the 1930s, looked in great detail at the social and cultural side of human nutrition, but the twenty-first-century *Sphere Handbook* takes a more reductive line. By simply emphasizing that aid should offer "culturally important items" and that food should be "consistent with religious and cultural traditions," it turns this into a procedural matter.[20] Humanitarians, led by such guidelines, offer a nod to culture in order to improve effectiveness, while simplifying Richards's message.

In reality, human diets are deeply saturated by culture, and there are many good reasons to eat in "irrational" ways and control what goes into our stomachs.

To say that "culture matters," therefore, should mean that recipient decisions must be taken more seriously—perhaps as seriously as the nutritional content of food. Social and cultural awareness in medical practice has generated a useful refrain: "Ask not what disease the person has, but rather what person the disease has."[21] A similar slogan may be needed in humanitarianism. "Ask not what food the person consumes, but what person the food consumes." This encapsulates the need to think about who is eating the food as much as the food that is eaten. Humanitarians too often think that food delivers nutrients and that people eat primarily for their health, but food, in reality, can consume *us*. Recipient perspectives are often shaped by cultural predilections, by social pressures, by competing values, and they end up desiring and needing food for reasons that have little to do with biology.

This leads us to the third lesson: that ambition matters. It is not enough to say that the demands of emergency make culture irrelevant, because it is important to account for more complex situations. Humanitarians need to move beyond the narrow metrics of a crisis response, which sees foods as nutrients and humans as bodies to be sustained. Over the past three decades a number of initiatives have challenged us to think beyond this narrow framework, linking up humanitarianism and long-term development, but humanitarian ambitions should extend beyond extending one's *length* of engagement, to extend one's *breadth* of vision as well.[22] In the context of food and hunger, this means moving away from what I have called "nutritional involution"—the drive toward internal complexity and ever-increasing intricacy—in order to engage with politics and social structures as well. We have seen how this bubbles up at crucial moments in history, in movements advocating forms of social nutrition, but too often its supporters have been marginalized. Indeed, the only time that the political approach has been taken seriously by international policymakers was in the 1930s League of Nations.

Nutritional involution, as a mainstream humanitarian failing, can be seen in two principal areas: in the production of intricately constructed foodstuffs, and in the detailed studies of starvation. High modernism led to many examples of the former—complicated new foods that met physical needs while ignoring deep inequalities—but it also led to a great irony: although it *seemed* as though foods like Single Cell Protein were filled with ambition, such grand rhetoric delivered only modest results. Indeed, far from eradicating starvation, these high modernist foods condemned the poor to their existing, limited diets by tinkering and fortifying their gruels and offering little more than a value-added version of an already unacceptable meal. In the latter type of nutritional involution, studies of the starving body led to equally restricted visions. The intensive period of research into starvation over the middle decades of the twentieth century, for example, provided surprisingly little guidance for managing malnutrition in practice. In the 1,385-page final report that emerged from the Minnesota Starvation Experiment only five pages were devoted to practical issues of refeeding and rehabilitation, and a related "psychological manual for relief workers" failed to reveal anything beyond the depression, humorlessness, and irritability that had long been known to come from starvation.[23] This waste of resources was often publicly lamented, and one physician wrote to the *Lancet* to complain how research on malnutrition often involved "fiddling while children starve." "Third-world health," he concluded, "might be better served if the budgets of research institutes were distributed as ten dollar bills to the poor and undernourished."[24]

The fourth and final lesson follows from this point: that vast sums spent on "miracle" famine foods and fruitless biochemical studies are, at least in part, the result of an ingrained paternalism—even arrogance—on the part of humanitarians.[25] The theme has saturated this whole book, from Count Rumford's manipulation of the soup kitchen to Herbert Hoover's desire to see the grub go down the gullet; from the military rations in postwar Europe to the high modernist desire to launch a generation of green food eaters. As Harvey Levenstein noted in relation to late nineteenth-century nutritional reformers, there is a long-standing tendency to treat subjects as "ignoramuses," offering advice "with the smug assurance" that humanitarian recommendations are "far superior to that worked out by millions of people in their daily struggle to survive."[26] This tendency continues today. There remains a need for humanitarians to listen to people who are starving and to take their concerns and experiences more seriously. Being vaguely aware of cultural difference is simply not enough on its own.

In recent years a new generation of activists and campaigners have challenged the paternalistic control exerted by nutritional experts in other spheres of life. Michael Pollan is perhaps the most famous example. In a series of bestselling books he has argued that people all over the world have lost the ability to cater for themselves and trust their dietary decisions, deferring crucial decisions about this most basic of human acts—eating—to experts in cahoots with the food industry.[27] Pollan's campaign has stimulated a rethinking of our consumption habits in the West, but it has not crossed over into a concern about hunger and humanitarianism. His approach, however, with its neat slogans and simple manifesto might still have a role to play. Pollan implored the wealthy middle classes, to "eat food"—in other words, to buy whole foods rather than the amalgamations of dextrin, high fructose corn syrup, defatted soy flour, and other derivative ingredients that are central to so many products.[28] It might seem insensitive to implore those without anything to "eat food" as well, but asking humanitarians to "provide food" could be a start. After all, aid workers too often distribute imported, highly processed, low modernist products, which are rarely liked or desired. Instead they could provide more of what people eat every day, or more significantly, give recipients the power and resources to buy the foods they wish to eat through unconditional cash transfer schemes. Taking participation seriously means a genuine handover of power, a radical and unconditional restructuring of aid funds. Distributing ten-dollar bills to the poor and undernourished, may, in fact, be the best way to start.

Looking back on these four practical lessons, it might be said that much here is obvious. Is it really revolutionary to say that aid workers should avoid distributing foods that are unpleasant? That they should shun culturally intensive products and approaches? That they should be ambitious in their interventions and inclusive in their approach? In some ways these four recommendations are too vague, but the biggest lesson from this history is that certainty ends badly. The main problem with ending a lengthy scholarly monograph with policy recommendations is the risk of being arrogant, boiling all the complexity down into a few take-home bullet points. In reality, the main lesson from this book should be a rejection of oversimplification in all its forms. Cultural awareness in humanitarian nutrition cannot be reduced to a tick-box exercise oriented around eliminating food taboos. Ambition has to mean more than a passing fad for resilience or innovation. Participation must go far deeper than asking a few half-hearted questions in a focus group. Many aid agencies have taken steps in many of these areas, pursuing policies of cultural sensitivity, greater participation, and engagement in the structural causes of malnutrition, yet they are still framed by the modernist push for efficiency, profitability, and ever-greater technical expertise.

The most basic message of this book has been that, from classical dietetics to low modernism, humanitarian nutrition is shaped by its wider sociopolitical conditions. This makes the end of the story somewhat uncertain, because many new approaches are circulating in the aid sector that might turn out to be significant. At this point, however, it is difficult to know: without the benefit of hindsight it is hard to sort the profound from the perfunctory flash in the pan. We can be fairly certain of one thing, however: that notions of the empty stomach will continue to change. The title of this volume has been deliberately designed to capture that insight, resembling a classical treatise on hunger and the body. It is also a reminder that there have long been seemingly comprehensive solutions to hunger, which in the end are limited by our ideas. The way we frame and understand the empty stomach, in the end, may be the most important determinant of how we set about treating it.

Notes

PREFACE

1. Richards, *Hunger and Work*, 23–30.
2. Roth, "Foucault's History of the Present"; Fassin, *Humanitarian Reason*.
3. Vernon, *Hunger*; Mintz, *Sweetness and Power*. On the subject of condiments, see also Kurlansky, *Salt*.
4. Tosh, *The Pursuit of History*, 32. See also Davis, "The Possibilities of the Past."
5. Barnett, *Empire of Humanity*; Barnett and Weiss, "Humanitarianism."
6. Fiddian-Qasmiyeh and Daley, *Routledge Handbook of South-South Relations*.
7. Nader, "Up the Anthropologist."
8. Elias, *The Civilizing Process*. For another example of handbooks as historical sources, see Armstrong, *Political Anatomy of the Body*.
9. International Refugee Organization, "Operational Manual," c.1950, PW/PR/IRO/2, Weis Archive, Bodleian Library, Oxford.
10. Foucault, *The Order of Things*, xv. The taxonomy originally comes from an essay entitled "The Analytical Language of John Wilkins" in Borges, *Other Inquisitions*, 101–5.
11. Pietsch, *Dispensational Modernism*, vii.

INTRODUCTION

1. Morris, *Portrait of a Chef*, 32–36. See also "Kitchen Department of the Reform Club House," *Illustrated London News*, December 3, 1842. The Reform Club was built by Charles Barry, who had just won the competition to rebuild the Houses of Parliament.
2. Cowen, *Relish*, 323–24. Antonin Carême (1783–1833) has an alternative claim to be the first celebrity chef.
3. Soyer, *Charitable Cookery*.
4. "M. Soyer's Kitchen and Soup for the Poor," *The Times*, February 18, 1847. See also Soyer, *Memoirs*, 103–5. For some background on Soyer's foray into the soup kitchen, see Morris, *Portrait of a Chef*, 74–82; Cowen, *Relish*, 108–34.
5. Soyer, *Memoirs*, 105.
6. "M. Soyer's Kitchen and Soup for the Poor," *The Times*, February 18, 1847. See also Soyer, *Memoirs*, 105. The recipes Soyer proposed in the press were republished in *Charitable Cookery*.
7. "M. Soyer and the Soup Establishments for Ireland," *The Times*, February 22, 1847.
8. Ó Gráda, *Black '47*; Nally, *Human Encumbrances*; Woodham-Smith, *The Great Hunger*, 165–87.
9. Strang and Toomre, "Alexis Soyer and the Irish Famine," 67.
10. "M. Soyer's Model Soup Kitchen," *Illustrated London News*, April 17, 1847; "M. Soyer and the Soup Establishments for Ireland," *The Times*, February 22, 1847.
11. "M. Soyer's New Soup Kitchen," *The Times*, April 7, 1847. See also Cowen, *Relish*, 108–9; Soyer, *Charitable Cookery*, 39–46.
12. Kinealy, *Death-Dealing Famine*, 100–101.
13. "M. Soyer's New Soup Kitchen," *The Times*, April 7, 1847.

14. After the newspaper reports, various other correspondents weighed in with their own alchemical combination of ingredients. See, for example, letters to the editor, *The Times*, March 9, 1847.

15. Nicholson, *Annals of the Famine in Ireland*, 232.

16. Soyer, *Charitable Cookery*, 14–19. Soyer's original claim to feed the five thousand was published in *The Times*, April 7, 1847. The even higher figure of 8,750 meals per day appears in Morris, *Portrait of a Chef*, 78. Whatever the real figure, the *Times* confidently reported that, thanks to Monsieur Soyer, "there will soon be no more deaths from starvation in Ireland." See "M. Soyer and the Soup Establishments for Ireland," *The Times*, February 22, 1847.

17. Barnett, *Empire of Humanity*, 1–2; Hoffman and Weiss, *Humanitarianism*, 1–12; Moorehead, *Dunant's Dream*, 1–14; Forsythe, *Humanitarians*, 11–49. A much bigger body of work traces the history of more specific humanitarian institutions. See, for example, Reinisch, "Internationalism in Relief"; Hutchinson, *Champions of Charity*; Patenaude, *Big Show in Bololand*. For a different tradition, see Stamatov, *Origins of Global Humanitarianism*.

18. Collini, *Public Moralists*, 60–90; Haskell, "Capitalism and the Origins of Humanitarian Sensibility"; Thomas, *Man and the Natural World*, 173–75; Fiering, "Irresistible Compassion"; Harrison, "Philanthropy and the Victorians"; Himmelfarb, *Poverty and Compassion*; Cunningham and Innes, *Charity, Philanthropy, and Reform*.

19. Morris, *Portrait of a Chef*, 119–61.

20. Nicholson, *Annals of the Famine in Ireland*, 231.

21. Sphere Project, *Humanitarian Charter and Minimum Standards*. For background, see Walker and Purdin, "Birthing Sphere"; Buchanan-Smith, *Sphere Project*; Darcy, "Locating Responsibility."

22. For two more contemporary examples, see World Food Program, *Food and Nutrition Handbook*; World Health Organization, *Guiding Principles* and *Management of Nutrition*.

23. "Standing Operational Procedures for Disasters," January 1971, PRG/5/4/4; "Humanitarian Department Equipment Catalogue," May 2000, PRG/5/4/13, Oxfam Archives, Bodleian Library, Oxford.

24. "Oxfam Feeding Kits," April 1984; Sue Peel, "Selective Feeding Procedures," January 1979, PRG/5/4/25, Oxfam Archive, Bodleian Library, Oxford.

25. Redfield, "Doctors, Borders, and Life in Crisis," 345–48.

26. This account is based on fieldwork conducted in the refugee camps of Eastern Maban County, Upper Nile State, South Sudan, over the summer of 2012. A fuller description can be found in Scott-Smith, "Control and Biopower."

27. General rations ideally contained local staples such as sorghum and lentils, although often, due to availability, they were based around agricultural surpluses from other countries, such as maize.

28. Since birth certificates were rare, the height stick became a substitute for age. The aim was to focus on the youngest and most vulnerable.

29. Compare, for example, World Health Organization, *Management of Nutrition*, 66–67, with *Economy of an Institution*, 1–4.

30. Scott-Smith, "Control and Biopower."

31. Scott-Smith, "Sticky Technologies," 11–12.

32. Vernon, "Ethics of Hunger."

33. See also Barnett, *Empire of Humanity*, 9: "Humanitarianism," Barnett wrote, "is a creature of the world it aspires to civilize." He was referring to the institutional structure of the industry; this book concerns its technical practices.

34. Barnett, *Empire of Humanity;* Forsythe, *Humanitarians;* Loescher, *UNHCR and World Politics.*

35. Bloor, *Knowledge and Social Imagery,* 164–79. This idea was known as the Strong Program.

36. Shapin, "Phrenological Knowledge"; Gieryn, "Boundary-Work"; Cooter, *The Cultural Meaning of Popular Science.* Lysenkoism is another prominent example of 'bad science' corrupted by society.

37. Latour, *Science in Action,* 103–45.

38. Soyer, *Memoirs,* 103.

39. Latour, *We Have Never Been Modern,* 141.

CHAPTER 1. FROM THE CLASSICAL SOUP KITCHEN TO THE IRISH FAMINE

1. Wilson, "Count Rumford's Soup," 291; Maerker, "Political Order and the Ambivalence of Expertise," 219; Albala, *Cooking in Europe;* Poynter, *Society and Pauperism;* Rule, *Labouring Classes.*

2. Fideler, "Poverty, Policy and Providence"; Appleby, *Famine in Tudor and Stuart England;* Slack, *Poverty and Policy.*

3. Singer, "Soup and Sadaqa"; Kuran, "The Provision of Public Goods," 842; Peri, "Waqf and Ottoman Welfare Policy"; Singer, "Serving up Charity"; Li and Dray-Novey, "Beijing's Food Security"; Gal and Ajzenstadt, "From a Soup Kitchen to a Welfare State in Israel"; Singer, *Constructing Ottoman Beneficence.*

4. Sanborn Brown, *Benjamin Thompson;* Redlich, "Science and Charity," 186–88; Easton, "Charles Theodore of Bavaria," 150–57.

5. Maerker, "Political Order," 217; Fulford, Lee, and Kitson, *Literature, Science and Exploration,* 254–55. Berman, *Social Change,* 1–31.

6. Redlich, "Science and Charity," 189; Fulford, Lee, and Kitson, *Literature, Science and Exploration,* 254–57; Sherman, *Imagining Poverty,* 141–76.

7. Thompson, *Count Rumford's Experimental Essays,* 15.

8. Bulmer, Hatchard, and Becket, *Reports of the Society;* Bohstedt, *Politics of Provisions,* 237–38; Levene, *Childhood of the Poor,* 130–53; Clark, *British Clubs and Societies,* 106–9; Poynter, *Society and Pauperism,* 46.

9. Bohstedt, *Politics of Provisions,* 237; Owen, *English Philanthropy,* 109.

10. Heller, "'Let Them Eat Soup,'" 499–500; Gentilcore, *Italy and the Potato,* 3–4; Wilson, "Count Rumford's Soup," 294n36; Redlich, "Science and Charity," 196–97.

11. Maerker, "Political Order," 223–25.

12. Thompson, *Account of an Establishment,* 70. Italics in the original. See also Sherman, *Imagining Poverty,* 150.

13. Thompson, *Of the Fundamental Principles,* 193–95. Italics in the original. See also Maerker, "Political Order," 222; Sherman, *Imagining Poverty,* 165.

14. Thompson, *Essays,* 193–194. This particular pamphlet "Food; and Particularly of Feeding the Poor," was later printed in Dublin during the Irish famine.

15. Thompson, *Essays,* 196. See also Bohstedt, *Politics of Provisions,* 236; Poynter, *Society and Pauperism,* 88; Sokolow, "Count Rumford"; Innes, "On the 'Mixed Economy of Welfare.'"

16. Thompson, *Essays,* 206–8. See also Poynter, *Society and Pauperism,* 90; Sanborn Brown, *Count Rumford,* 64.

17. Sherman, *Imagining Poverty,* 167.

18. Thompson, *Essays,* 267. See also Bradley, *Count Rumford,* 15–16; Poynter, *Society and Pauperism,* 88–89. This is just part of a description that goes on for several pages.

19. Thompson, *Essays,* 255–56.

20. Maerker, "Political Order," 223; Wells, *Wretched Faces,* 301–11; Levene, *Childhood of the Poor,* 130–53; Clark, *British Clubs and Societies,* 106–9; Thompson, *Of the Fundamental Principles,* 140–43.

21. Thompson, *Of the Fundamental Principles,* 71; Maerker, "Political Order," 255.

22. Thompson, *Of the Fundamental Principles,* 71. Rumford concluded: "How sweet these tears were to me can easily be imagined."

23. Colquhoun, *Suggestions,* 3. See also Wells, *Wretched Faces,* 301–11; Roberts, "Head Versus Heart," 76; Levene, *Childhood of the Poor,* 130–53; Clark, *British Clubs and Societies,* 106–9.

24. Bohstedt, *Politics of Provisions,* 237.

25. Colquhoun, *Suggestions,* 3–4.

26. Colquhoun, *Account of a Meat and Soup Charity,* 14–17.

27. Colquhoun, *Account of a Meat and Soup Charity,* 17. The system was designed to exclude those "addicted to drinking and inebriety," those who would fail to "carry home the soup or meat for their children," and those who "shall not appear thankful for the benefits they enjoy." See also Colquhoun, *Suggestions,* 3.

28. Colquhoun, *Suggestions,* 18. See also Poynter, *Society and Pauperism,* 84–87; Wells, *Wretched Faces,* 214–15.

29. Colquhoun, *Account of a Meat and Soup Charity.* The grain merchant was William Allen and the magistrate was Patrick Colquhoun. The views of the latter played a part in Foucault's work on punishment. See Foucault, *Punitive Society,* 108–10.

30. Sherman, *Imagining Poverty,* 190, 207.

31. Bohstedt, *Riots and Community Politics,* 95.

32. Bohstedt, *Riots and Community Politics,* 97.

33. Colquhoun, *Account of a Meat and Soup Charity,* 15.

34. Sherman, *Imagining Poverty,* 148.

35. Bohstedt, *Politics of Provisions,* 272.

36. Miller, "The Chemistry of Famine," 459. Miller cites a nationalist newspaper, *The Freeman's Journal,* which expressed fury at the Union Jack "flaunted from the top of the soup kitchen," which told "a tale, as it flaps in the listless air, of a union with England brought about by force, stained by corruption, cemented in blood, and now consummated in famine."

37. *General Report of the Committee of Subscribers,* 8.

38. Colquhoun, *Suggestions,* 13.

39. Colquhoun, *Suggestions,* 13. The document also proposed more confidential soup houses on a smaller scale for "certain classes of people" who may not want to go to large soup houses because of "the delicacy they felt to expose their distresses."

40. Soyer, *Charitable Cookery,* 39–43.

41. "Soup Store at Cork," *Illustrated London News,* March 13, 1847. See also Hindle, *Provision for the Relief of the Poor,* 90–106.

42. Colquhoun, *Account of a Meat and Soup Charity,* 10, 15.

43. Cobbett, "Letter to the Luddites," 701.

44. Hammond, *Stories of Scientific Discovery,* 46; G. I. Brown, *Count Rumford,* 113.

45. Wells, *Wretched Faces,* 215. Rumford later became the basis for Jane Austin's mockery in the form of the pamphleteering reformer General Tilney in *Northanger Abbey* (1818). See Berman, *Social Change,* 11n37.

46. Colquhoun, *Suggestions,* 16–17. See also "The Soup Question," *All the Year Round,* June 6, 1863; Love, *Manchester,* 126–28.

47. Morris, *Portrait of a Chef,* 77. See also "Meagre Diet," *Punch* 12, 1847. *Punch* later compared Soyer's diet for the poor with the recently established Prussian Diet: a parliament that had no right to convene without permission from the King. The two were similar,

Punch declared, because neither contained anything of substance. "Soyer must have prepared the new Prussian Diet," the newspaper mused, "for it is so like his soup—there's nothing in it."

48. "Insufficiency of Soup for Nutriment," letter to the editor, *The Times*, February 24, 1847.

49. Fegan, *Literature and the Irish Famine*, 63.

50. "Scene from the Soup Boiler," *The Nation*, April 3, 1847; Strang and Toomre, "Alexis Soyer and the Irish Famine," 84n42.

51. Klancher, *Transfiguring the Arts and Sciences*, 59.

52. Wolcot, *Works of Peter Pindar*, 5:136–37.

53. Webb, "Wordsworth, Count Rumford, and Poverty Relief," 29–30.

54. Foucault, *Order of Things*, 81–82.

55. Dreyfus and Rabinow, *Michel Foucault*, 27; Gutting, *Michel Foucault's Archaeology*, 155; Lovejoy, *Great Chain of Being*.

56. Morus, *Frankenstein's Children*, 44.

57. Maerker, "Political Order," 221; Dreyfus and Rabinow, *Michel Foucault*, 20.

58. Berman, *Social Change*, 11n37; Sokolow, "Count Rumford," 76. According to Berman, Rumford's classical ideas were "typical of his era."

59. Dreyfus and Rabinow, *Michel Foucault*, 19–20.

60. Foucault, *Order of Things*, 29–30.

61. Foucault, *Order of Things*, 30–55; Gutting, *Michel Foucault*, 147; Cousins and Hussain, *Michel Foucault*, 33.

62. Sheridan, *Michel Foucault*, 72. Gutting, *Michel Foucault*, 190–92.

63. Foucault, *Order of Things*, 285–86.

64. Foucault, *Order of Things*, 338.

65. Dreyfus and Rabinow, *Michel Foucault*, 28.

66. Sherman, *Imagining Poverty*, 172.

67. "The Soup Question," *All the Year Round*, June 6, 1863: 354.

68. "The Soup Question," 354.

69. "The Soup Question," 354.

CHAPTER 2. JUSTUS LIEBIG AND THE RISE OF NUTRITIONAL SCIENCE

1. McGee, *Curious Cook*, 282–96; Davis, *Defining Culinary Authority*, 157–58; Spary, *Feeding France*, 229; McGee, "Osmazome." The word *osmazome* was first coined by Louis Jacques Thenard.

2. McGee, "Osmazome," 133. See also Brillat-Savarin, *Physiology of Taste*, 76–79.

3. Brillat-Savarin, *Physiology of Taste*, 15.

4. Barthes, *Rustle of Language*, 260–62; Weiss, *Feast and Folly*, 40–43.

5. Holmes, *Claude Bernard and Animal Chemistry*, 6–9; Brock, *Justus Von Liebig*, 221; Ackerknecht, *Medicine at the Paris Hospital*.

6. Spary, *Feeding France*, 230; Semba, *Vitamin A Story*, 20–39.

7. Spary, *Feeding France*, 204–20; Holmes, *Claude Bernard*, 6–9; Carpenter, *Protein and Energy*, 30; McGee, *The Curious Cook*, 290–91; de Vaux, *Mémoire Sur La Gelatin*, 13–17. For an image of Papin's digester, see Newcomb, *The World in a Crucible*, 61–63.

8. Spary, *Feeding France*, 230. In the words of Emma Spary, osmazome "became a rallying point for those opposed to the divorce of nourishment from flavour."

9. La Berge, *Mission and Method*, 29; Holmes, *Claude Bernard*, 8–9.

10. Spary, *Feeding France*, 230; Soyer, *The Modern Housewife*, 37.

11. Brillat-Savarin, *Physiology of Taste*, 75. Brillat-Savarin goes on, "It is the infallible goodness of osmazome which has inspired Canon Chevrier to invent a soup pot that locked with a key."

12. Simmons, *Vital Minimum*, 37; Holmes, *Claude Bernard*, 8–12; Semba, *Vitamin A Story*, 30–32.

13. Brock, *Justus Von Liebig*, 221; Simmons, *Vital Minimum*, 37; Carpenter, *Protein and Energy*, 29–31.

14. This has been described by some commentators as "nutritionism." See, for example, Scrinis, *Nutritionism*; Pollan, *In Defense of Food*.

15. Liebig, *Researches on the Chemistry of Food*. The key moment in the birth of modern nutritional science may have been the publication of Liebig's earlier book, *Animal Chemistry*. However, *Researches* was the more accessible text and had more impact. See Finlay, "Early Marketing of the Theory of Nutrition," 51.

16. Levere, *Transforming Matter*; Read, *From Alchemy to Chemistry*; Jaffe, *Crucibles*.

17. Brillat-Savarin, *Physiology of Taste*, 150. Brillat-Savarin assumed that people drink wine primarily to get drunk; it is a controversial theory, but after years of observation at Oxford University I have finally confirmed it.

18. Semba, *Vitamin A Story*, 30. See also Cadet de Vaux, *Mémoire Sur La Gelatin*, 11; "Is the Gelatine of Bones Alimentary?" 253. The original French reads "un étui, un manche de couteau, un douzaine de boutons d'os, sont autant de bouillons volés a l'indigence." This translation is from Semba, although the 1842 article "Is the Gelatine of Bones Alimentary?" contains a rather more extravagant translation: "A bone is a soup-cake formed from nature! A pound of bones yields as much soup as six pounds of butcher meat! A bone case, a knife handle, or a dozen knobs are just so many plates of soup robbed from the poor!!"

19. Carpenter, *Protein and Energy*, 31; Holmes, *Claude Bernard and Animal Chemistry*, 9. Krinsky, "Let Them Eat Horsemeat!" 88–113; Semba, *Vitamin A Story*, 30.

20. Holmes, *Claude Bernard and Animal Chemistry*, 8.

21. Simmons, *Vital Minimum*, 37.

22. Krinsky, "Let Them Eat Horsemeat!" 88–120; Semba, *Vitamin A Story*, 31. This process was patented by Joseph D'Arcet in 1817.

23. Holmes, *Claude Bernard and Animal Chemistry*, 9; Krinsky, "Let Them Eat Horsemeat!" 105, 113–14. The pharmacist was Jean-Nicolas Gannal.

24. Carpenter, *Protein and Energy*, 27–32; Holmes, *Claude Bernard and Animal Chemistry*, 11; Carpenter, "Nutritional Studies in Victorian Prisons," 3.

25. Brock, *Justus Von Liebig*, 221.

26. Prout, "Observations," 321–27; Rosenfeld, *Four Centuries of Clinical Chemistry*, 154. The word *carbohydrate* was coined by the chemist Carl Schmidt in 1844.

27. Hartley, "Origin of the Word 'Protein,'" 244–44; Carpenter, *Protein and Energy*, 43. Berzelius's word first appeared in a publication by Gerardus Johannes Mulder in 1838.

28. Prout, "On the Ultimate Composition of Simple Alimentary Substances." The term *nitrogenous foods* was also a synonym for protein. For an explanation, see Huff, "Corporeal Economies," 42.

29. Carpenter, *Protein and Energy*, 55. See also Holmes, Introduction to *Animal Chemistry*.

30. Ihde, *The Development of Modern Chemistry*. 178; Greenberg, *From Alchemy to Chemistry*, 425–56. The kaliapparat is now part of the logo of the American Chemical Society.

31. Liebig, *Animal Chemistry*, 275–78.

32. Beeton, *Book of Household Management*, 51–52.

33. This, *Molecular Gastronomy*, 23; Davis, *Defining Culinary Authority*, 157–58.

34. Morris, *Portrait of a Chef*, 57–59.

35. McGee, *The Curious Cook*, 294. Holmes, *Claude Bernard and Animal Chemistry*, 6–15. The French medical dictionary, *Materia Medica*, made this argument as early as 1837. The disappearance of the word *osmazome* can be traced through Ngram viewer.

36. Soyer, *Modern Housewife*, 39. Patent no. 520, entitled, "Improvements in Preparing and Preserving Soups." See also Morris, *Portrait of a Chef*, 57–59; Cowen, *Relish*, 232–82.

37. Soyer, *Modern Housewife*, 39.

38. Soyer, *Modern Housewife*, 171. See also Spary, *Feeding France*, 229.

39. "Review: Soyer's Modern Housewife," 202. Fraser's Magazine declared ironically, "We can imagine the proud consciousness of scientific comprehension with which fair young housewives will present basins of 'osmazome' to their invalid husbands and brothers."

40. Editorial, *Lancet* 49, February 27, 1847.

41. Medicus, "Insufficiency of Soup for Nutriment," letter to the editor, *The Times*, February 24, 1847.

42. Simpson, *On the More Effective Application*; Marsh, *On the Preparation of Food for the Labourer*. See also Miller, "Chemistry of Famine."

43. Editorial, *Lancet* 49, February 27, 1847.

44. Liebig, *Researches on the Chemistry of Food*, 133.

45. Liebig, *Researches on the Chemistry of Food*, 132. See also Spary, *Feeding France*, 229–30; McGee, *The Curious Cook*, 289; Finlay, "Quackery and Cookery," 406. "Tablettes de bouillon" had been marketed in France throughout the eighteenth century, and the British Navy also provided a "portable soup" for its ships from 1757. Other names for this product included "cake soup," "broth cakes," "solid soup" and "carry soup." Apparently these early stock cubes kept for years. In the 1930s Jack Drummond sampled a piece of portable soup kept in the Maritime Museum at Greenwich, which had been taken by James Cook on a voyage in 1772. He declared it still edible. See Clarkson, *Soup*, 68–70; Mamane, *Mastering Stocks and Broths*, 39–41.

46. Liebig, *Researches on the Chemistry of Food*, 129.

47. Beneke, "On Extractum Carnis."

48. Liebig, *Familiar Letters*, 426. See also Finlay, "Early Marketing," 53.

49. Brock, *Justus Von Liebig*, 227; Shephard, *Pickled, Potted and Canned*, 181–83; Critchell, *History of the Frozen Meat Trade*, 8.

50. Wynter, *Our Social Bees*, 203.

51. Wynter, *Our Social Bees*, 203. See also Brock, *Justus von Liebig*, 228; Finlay, "Quackery and Cookery," 409.

52. Swinburne, "Von Liebig Condensed," 249–50; Shephard, *Pickled, Potted and Canned*, 182.

53. Finlay, "Early Marketing," 61–62; Finlay, "Quackery and Cookery," 410. Later advertisements claimed that forty pounds of fresh beef went into every pound of extract. The recipe could have changed, or the marketing staff could have pulled these numbers from the lowest part of their digestive tract.

54. Finlay, "Quackery and Cookery," 409–10.

55. Boner, "Extract of Meat," 295–98. See also Finlay, "Quackery and Cookery," 409. Later Liebig began promoting products under the name Fray Bentos, after the port on the Uruguay River.

56. Nightingale, *Notes on Nursing*, 69–70.

57. Thudichum, *On the Origin, Nature, and Uses of Liebig's Extract of Meat*, 19–24; Swinburne, "Von Liebig Condensed," 249; Finlay, "Quackery and Cookery," 410; Advertisement for Liebig Company's Extract of Beef, 1899. Jay Paull/Getty Images. Editorial photo no. 159639427, available at https://www.gettyimages.fi

58. The word came from the Greek *diaita*, meaning "way of living" or "regular work."

59. Foucault, *Use of Pleasure*, 100.

60. Foucault, *Use of Pleasure*, 97–110. Foucault's *Use of Pleasure* was volume 2 of the anticipated, multivolume, *History of Sexuality*; it marks the start of his late period.

61. Foucault, *Use of Pleasure*, 105.

62. Foucault, *Hermeneutics of the Subject*, 43–106. See also Wall, *Recipes for Thought*, 8. Wendy Wall describes this as "food work": the use of food to care for the body and self.

63. Shapin, "'You Are What You Eat.'"

64. Wear, *Knowledge and Practice*, 169–84; Shapin, "Trusting George Cheyne," 263–97.

65. Hutchison, *Hutchison's Food and the Principles of Dietetics*, ix–xviii. Cannon, "The Rise and Fall of Dietetics," 701–5.

66. Shapin, "'You Are What You Eat,'" 378–79; Shapin, "Changing Tastes," 33–40. Steven Shapin has described this as a shift from "qualities" to "constituents." A similar argument can be found in Mikkeli, *Hygiene in the Early Modern*.

67. Shapin, "Trusting George Cheyne," 293–94. Shapin described this as a shift from "prudential expertise" to "ontological expertise."

68. Brillat-Savarin, *Physiology of Taste*, 15.

69. Shapin, "'You Are What You Eat,'" 380.

70. Shapin, "'You Are What You Eat,'" 380–85. This idea also appeared in popular attitudes to Soyer's Irish soup kitchen. See, for example, Strang and Toomre, "Alexis Soyer and the Irish Famine," 76–78.

71. Vester, *Taste of Power*, 1.

72. Shapin, "Trusting George Cheyne," 267.

73. Foucault, *Use of Pleasure*, 73, 105, 211.

CHAPTER 3. GOVERNING THE DIET IN VICTORIAN INSTITUTIONS

1. Miller, "Food, Medicine and Institutional Life," 212. See also Priestley, *Victorian Prison Lives*.

2. Carpenter, "Nutritional Studies in Victorian Prisons," 4. See also Chapman, "Edward Smith," 6. Chapman traces the origins of the treadmill to 1775.

3. Chapman, "Edward Smith," 6. See also Ignatieff, *A Just Measure of Pain*.

4. Carpenter, *Protein and Energy*, 62. Carpenter described the treadmill as "rather like the side paddle wheels of a Victorian steamship . . . a row of them were linked together on the same axle and connected to a sail on the roof of the prison to provide [wind] resistance." See also Priestly, *Victorian Prison Lives*; Mayhew and Binny, *Criminal Prisons of London*, 303–5; Chapman, "Edward Smith," 7.

5. Chapman, "Edward Smith," 8.

6. Cross and MacDonald, *Nutrition in Institutions*, 282. See also Miller, "Food, Medicine and Institutional Life," 210.

7. Carpenter, *Protein and Energy*, 60.

8. Chapman, "Edward Smith," 9.

9. Guy, "On Sufficient and Insufficient Dietaries," 279, 240.

10. Miller, "Food, Medicine and Institutional Life," 212; Chapman, "Edward Smith," 7–9.

11. Huff, "Corporeal Economies," 43–45.

12. Barker, Oddy, and Yudkin, *Dietary Surveys*, 14; Chapman, "Edward Smith," 10.

13. Vernon, *Hunger*, 326; Coveney, *Food, Morals and Meaning*, 82; Miller, "Feeding in the Workhouse," 943; Huff, "Corporeal Economies", 34n10; Vernon, "Ethics of Hunger," 701.

14. Huff, "Corporeal Economies," 30–32; Coveney, *Food, Morals and Meaning*, 81. The Reverend Milman put this more colorfully: "the workhouse should be a place of hardship, of coarse fare, of degradation and humility," he wrote, and "as repulsive as is consistent with humanity." Anstruther, *The Scandal of the Andover Workhouse*, 16.

15. The appalling levels of neglect were made evident in reports from the 1830s and 1840s, which described workhouse inmates forced to eat rotten potatoes and rancid

meat, gnawing candles and putrid bones. Johnston, *Diet in Workhouses and Prisons*, 19; Anstruther, *The Scandal of the Andover Workhouse*, 133. For a more subtle appraisal, see Miller, "Feeding in the Workhouse."

16. Cullather, "The Foreign Policy of the Calorie," 340.

17. Aronson, "Nutrition as a Social Problem," 476.

18. Cullather, *Hungry World*, 11. Neswald and Smith, *Setting Nutritional Standards*, 38–39.

19. Scrinis, *Nutritionism*, 59.

20. Hargrove, "History of the Calorie," 2959. In Hargrove's words, "the Calorie probably entered U.S. English because W.O. Atwater learned the term during studies in Germany, and not because it was defined in a newly translated physics text."

21. Cullather, "The Foreign Policy of the Calorie," 343–5. Cullather points out that between 1885 and 1910 nutritionists conducted more than five hundred investigations into the nutritional intake of English blacksmiths, Swedish soldiers, Silesian peasants, and the inhabitants of slums, Indian reservations, and Chinese railroad camps. See also Rabinbach, *Human Motor*, 131; Neswald and Smith, *Setting Nutritional Standards*, 33; Carpenter, "Protein"; Jaffa, *Study of Human Foods*.

22. Rabinbach, *Human Motor*.

23. Rabinbach, *Human Motor*, 142–5. The story of Wilhelm Weichardt's claim to have found a vaccine against fatigue is one of the highlights of Rabinbach's book.

24. Kanigel, *One Best Way*; Milles, "Working Capacity and Calorie Consumption."

25. Aronson, "Nutrition as a Social Problem"; Aronson, "Social Definitions of Entitlement."

26. Aronson, "Nutrition as a Social Problem," 478.

27. Neswald and Smith, *Setting Nutritional Standards*, 41.

28. Atkinson, "Food Question," 242. These precise words were written in an introduction to Atwater's work by his patron, Edward Atkinson. See also Aronson, "Nutrition as a Social Problem", 478.

29. Mendel, *Changes in the Food Supply*, 26; Aronson, "Social Definitions of Entitlement," 53.

30. Levenstein, "The New England Kitchen," 371. See also Atwater, "Chemistry of Foods," 72–73; Atwater. "Pecuniary Economy," 445; Levenstein, *Revolution at the Table*, 47.

31. Aronson, "Nutrition as a Social Problem," 478. See also Atwater, "How Food Nourishes the Body," 238.

32. Lusk, "Introduction," 24. See also Aronson, "Social Definitions of Entitlement," 53–4; Scrinis, *Nutritionism and Functional Foods*, 61; Veit, *Modern Food, Moral Food*, 47–8.

33. *Nutrition and Relief Work*, 14. Another fantastic example of the metaphor can be found in Long, *Food and* Fitness, 1–2.

34. Marx and Engels, *Collected Works*, 30:46.

35. Luxemburg, *Complete Works*, 1:276.

36. Levenstein, *Revolution at the Table*, 56.

37. Cowan, "Ellen Swallow Richards"; Douty, *America's First Woman Chemist*.

38. Wessell, "Alimentary Products," 116.

39. Richards, *Plain Words About Food*, 21; Levenstein, *Revolution at the Table*, 49.

40. Shapiro, *Perfection* Salad, 150.

41. DuPuis, *Dangerous Digestion*, 68.

42. Colt, *Big House*, 23. For a detailed description, see Atkinson, "Art of Cooking." See also Levenstein, *Revolution at the Table*, 49; Shapiro, *Perfection Salad*, 141–3; Aronson, "Nutrition as a Social Problem," 479; Levenstein, "Perils of Abundance," 519.

43. Colt, *Big House*, 23. This fascinating memoir also explains how Atkinson insisted on using the Aladdin Oven at home. "I do not remember what we had," recalled one of his guests, "but it all took a very long time."

44. Levine, *School Lunch Politics*, 17; Levenstein, "The New England Kitchen."

45. Richards, *Plain Words About Food*, 12.

46. Richards, *Plain Words About Food*, 16.

47. *Report of the Massachusetts Board*, 41–2; Richards, *Plain Words About Food*, 15.

48. Richards, *Plain Words About Food*, 29. Presumably this did not include Rumford's writings on how to humiliate children, how water was the most nourishing part of a soup, or how people should eat pudding very slowly.

49. *Letters of Eugene V. Debs*, 1:41. See also DuPuis, *Dangerous Digestion*, 69–70.

50. American Federation of Labor, *Some Reasons for Chinese Exclusion*. By the late 1890s the New England Kitchen was winding up for lack of momentum. See Douty, *America's First Woman Chemist*, 155.

51. Turner, *Regulating Bodies*, 193. For an alternative view, see Earle, "Food, Colonialism," 170–93. Rebecca Earle suggests that the idea of creating a vigorous population through diet has a much longer history.

52. Foucault, "On Governmentality"; Burchell, Gordon and Miller, *Foucault Effect*, 87–104. The most authoritative version can now be found in Foucault, *Security, Territory, Population*, 87–114. For context, see Elden, "Rethinking Governmentality."

53. See also Sherman, "Tensions of Colonial Punishment," 665.

54. Foucault, *Security, Territory, Population*, 115. For a delightful skewering of the jargon, see Billig, *Learn to Write Badly*, 143–175.

55. Burchell, Gordon, and Miller, *The Foucault Effect*, 102–103. Foucault spoke of governmentality as (1) the "calculations, and tactics" that facilitate the exercise of power, (2) the historical "tendency" in the West to consolidate power as government, and (3) the *result* of this historical process, in which the state becomes "governmentalized."

56. For an example of this attempt at systemization, see Dean, *Governmentality*.

57. Foucault, *Birth of Biopolitics*, 77.

58. Geertz, Clifford. "Stir Crazy," 6. See also Berman, *All That Is Solid Melts into Air*, 34. In one of his earlier lectures, Foucault described his method in *Madness and Civilization* as supposing that madness does not exist, and then "see[ing] what history can make of these different events and practices which are apparently organised around something that is supposed to be madness." His approach to government was the same. Rather than simply saying that there is more and more of it, Foucault was suggesting that its nature had changed profoundly. See Foucault, *Birth of Biopolitics*, 3.

59. Summers, "Militarism in Britain," 111.

60. Maurice, "Where to Get Men." Maurice published this under the pseudonym "Miles." He was not, in fact, the first to make these arguments about the strength of new recruits, although his article was the most influential. See Shee, "Deterioration in the National Physique"; Gilbert, "Health and Politics," 145; Searle, *Quest for National Efficiency*.

61. Gilbert, "Health and Politics," 145–6; Soloway, "Counting the Degenerates."

62. Maurice, "Where to Get Men," 81.

63. Kipling, *Land and Sea Tales*, v.

64. *Report of the Inter-Departmental Committee on Physical Deterioration*. See also Gorst, "Physical Deterioration"; Gilbert, "Health and Politics"; Smyth, *Physical Deterioration*.

65. Vernon, *Hunger*, 161–2.

66. Dwork, *War Is Good for Babies*.

67. Major-General Henderson, "Food: Cooking, Pests, Principles, Deficiency Diseases, Metabolism, Rations, Service," c.1920, RAMC/1138/3/5, Royal Army Medical Corps Muniments Collection, Wellcome Library, London. This and other handbooks in the

Muniments Collection include a comparison of rations from different countries and tests on army ration biscuits to reveal durability.

CHAPTER 4. COLONIALISM AND COMMUNAL STRENGTH

1. McCay, *Standards*, 34, 59, 62. For context, see Barton, "Imperialism, Race, and Therapeutics," 508; O'Connor, *British Physiologists*, 523–24.

2. McCay, *Standards*, 29–31, 55–56.

3. First, McCay studied jail dietaries and physiques in Bengal; then he studied jail dietaries and physiques in the United Provinces. See McCay, *Investigations on Bengal Jail Dietaries*; McCay, *Investigations into the Jail Dietaries of the United Provinces*. As with Edward Smith, prison studies were considered particularly reliable and controllable.

4. McCay, *Investigations into the Jail Dietaries of the United Provinces*, 188–90. See also McCarrison, *Nutrition and National Health*, 19; Arnold, "Malnutrition and Diet in Colonial India," 13–15.

5. Arnold, "British India," 311; Arnold, "Malnutrition and Diet in Colonial India," 9–23. Criticism of Indian rice diets continued into the high modernist era. See Kimura, *Hidden Hunger*, 139–61.

6. McCay, *Protein Element*, 178.

7. Chevers, *Commentary*, 568–69. See also Arnold, "British India," 310–14; Arnold, "Malnutrition and Diet in Colonial India," 9–13, 23–24.

8. McCay, *Standards*, 32. My emphasis.

9. McCay, *Standards*, 30.

10. McCay, *Investigations into the Jail Dietaries of the United Provinces*, 189–90.

11. Bonarjee, *Handbook*; MacMunn, *Martial Races*. See also Arnold, "Malnutrition and Diet in Colonial India," 14–16; Arnold, "British India," 311–12; Vernon, *Hunger*, 106–11; Vernon, "Ethics of Hunger," 704–5; Arnold, *Colonizing the Body*; McCay, *Standards*, 31.

12. McCay, *Standards*, 31. McCay often examined the chest circumference precisely because it "furnishes a very good idea of the state of development, and is made use of in every country in the physical examination of [military] recruits."

13. Vernon, *Hunger*, 104–12. Arnold, "Malnutrition and Diet in Colonial India," 17. Worboys, "Discovery of Colonial Malnutrition."

14. Arnold, "Malnutrition and Diet in Colonial India," 15.

15. Arnold, "Malnutrition and Diet in Colonial India," 15.

16. McCay, *Investigations into the Jail Dietaries of the United Provinces*, 186. For a more modern example, see Moradi, "Towards an Objective Account."

17. Like McCay (1873–1948), Robert McCarrison (1878–1960) had a medical training in Ireland followed by a long period of service in the subcontinent. For more biographical detail see Aykroyd, "Major-General Robert McCarrison"; McCarrison, "Adventures in Research."

18. McCarrison, *Nutrition and National Health*, 18.

19. Aykroyd, "Major-General Robert Mccarrison," 416–17.

20. McCarrison, *Nutrition and National Health*, 18–19.

21. McCay, *Protein Element*, 154.

22. McCarrison, *Studies in Deficiency Disease*, 9.

23. Hilton, *Lost Horizon*; Wrench, *Wheel of Health*. See also Hussain, *Remoteness and Modernity*, 96–99.

24. Kamminga, "Axes to Grind"; Weatherall, "Bread and Newspapers."

25. McCarrison, *Nutrition and National Health*, 24.

26. Arnold, "British India," 300–301; Worboys, "Discovery of Colonial Malnutrition," 211.

27. Orr, *As I Recall*, 123–25. Vernon, *Hunger*, 109–10.

28. Huxley, *Nine Faces of Kenya*, 91.

29. Horne, *Mau Mau in Harlem*, 46–47; Campbell, *Race and Empire*, 43–86; Campbell, "Eugenics in Colonial Kenya," 290–91. According to Campbell the KSSRI was "the centerpiece of the colonial eugenic movement." See also Tilley, *Africa as a Living Laboratory*, 235–40.

30. Gilks, "Medical Safari." See also Crozier, *Practising Colonial Medicine*, 83–84.

31. Orr and Gilks, *Studies of Nutrition*, 9, 11, 30–31.

32. Brantley, "Orr and Gilks Revisited," 74, 81; Cullather, *Hungry World*, 30–31. The concern over Carrier Corps recruits was similar to the "physical deterioration" crisis after the Boer War. Soloway, "Counting the Degenerates."

33. Orr, *As I Recall*, 125. The result of this research was Orr and Gilks, *Studies of Nutrition*. For context to this study, see Brantley, "Orr and Gilks Revisited"; Vernon, *Hunger*, 109–17; Wylie, "Disease, Diet and Gender," 280–82; Worboys, "The Discovery of Colonial Malnutrition," 210–13.

34. Orr, *As I Recall*, 125. Orr's hunch was seemingly supported by the observation that Kikuyu women consumed more minerals in the form of "salt licks from special spring water and from ashes they produced by burning swamp plants." See Brantley, "Orr and Gilks Revisited," 65.

35. Walter Elliot, "The New Empire," *The Times*, May 7, 1929. This paragraph is quoted in Brantley, "Orr and Gilks Revisited," 81.

36. McCarrison, *Nutrition and National Health*, 20. See also Deniker, *Races of Man*, 495–500; Arnold, "Malnutrition and Diet in Colonial India," 15. When it came to the implications of this dietary advice McCarrison at least practiced what he preached. As Wallace Aykroyd put it in his obituary, "He regarded refined white flour as a defective food and for many years breakfasted on whole-wheat chappaties. His distinguished appearance, of which he was agreeably aware, was a valuable asset; the abundant wavy hair, clear complexion, and Irish accent made an attractive ensemble." Aykroyd, "Major-General Robert McCarrison," 417.

37. Kevles, *In the Name of Eugenics*, 164.

38. Baker and Green, *Julian Huxley*. Weindling, "Julian Huxley." Huxley's social concerns were also evident in his narration of Anstey's film *Housing Problems*. See Vernon, *Hunger*, 135.

39. Kevles, *In the Name of Eugenics*, 164. These are Jacob Landman's words.

40. Horne, *Mau Mau in Harlem*, 47. See also Campbell, *Race and Empire*, 91.

41. Kevles, *In the Name of Eugenics*, 164–74. See also Hasian, *Rhetoric of Eugenics*, 112–38. For an alternative view, see Mazumdar, "'Reform' Eugenics." A version of this argument was promoted in Titmuss, *Poverty and Population*, who argued that public health improvements meant the better "stock" surviving and reproducing. See also Hanson, *Eugenics*, 9.

42. "Softer" eugenic policies included selectively offering contraception rather than enforcing sterilization. Hasian, *Rhetoric of Eugenics*, 114–16. Spektorowski and Saban, *Politics of Eugenics*; Currell, "Introduction."

43. McCarrison, *Nutrition and National Health*, 19, 25. The photographs originally came from McCay, *Protein Element*, 58, 86, 108, 156, 172, 186, 194, 204, 177. See also McCarrison, "Adventures in Research," 71.

44. McCay, *Investigations into the Jail Dietaries of the United Provinces*, 186.

45. Foucault, *Will to Knowledge*, 149–50. Race is mentioned at a few other points in the book, but developed in a manner that Ann Laura Stoler describes as "muted." Stoler, *Race and the Education of Desire*, x. See also Hacking, *Social Construction of What?* 16–18; Mitchell, *Rule of Experts*, 2–3.

46. These lectures appeared first in Italian, then in French in 1997, and finally in English as *Society Must Be Defended*. The first two lectures of this series also appeared in Foucault, *Power/Knowledge*. Note that Foucault also tackled racism, albeit in a more limited manner, in the lectures of 1975. See Foucault, *Abnormal*, 133, 316–18.

47. Foucault, *Society Must Be Defended*, 239–64.

48. Foucault was planning a whole volume of the anticipated six-volume *History of Sexuality* to be devoted to race, but after a sabbatical in 1977 he returned to the lecture theatre with a very different set of preoccupations. Stoler suggests that Foucault had become "deadlocked" in his thinking. Stoler, *Race and the Education of Desire*, 25.

49. Foucault, *Society Must Be Defended*, 254–55.

50. Foucault, *Society Must Be Defended*, 254–55.

51. Stoler, *Race and the Education of Desire*, viii, 21. Stoler became one of the first scholars to study and develop the 1976 Foucault lectures, drawing on audio tape. For more on the history of the lectures, see Ewald and Fontana, "Foreword."

52. Stoler, "Rethinking Colonial Categories," 138. See also Mamdani, *Citizen and Subject*.

53. An instructive example is the comparison between colonial responses to the Mau Mau in Kenya and black nationalism in South Africa. Berman, "Nationalism"; Lonsdale, "Mau Maus of the Mind"; Elkins, "Mau Mau Rehabilitation."

54. Vaughan, *Curing Their Ills*, 11, 202.

55. Foucault, *Society Must Be Defended*, 256. This was the beginning of a long expansion in humanitarian techniques of care and control, which many scholars have since linked with race. Ticktin, *Casualties of Care*; Benton, "African Expatriates"; Duffield, "Racism, Migration and Development," 73; Redfield, "Doctors, Borders, and Life in Crisis," 344, 361.

56. Adam Kuper has described functionalism as an elaborate "guessing game," which involves deducing the function of a social practice, no matter how bizarre or extraordinary. See Kuper, *Among the Anthropologists*, 118. For Audrey Richards's account of functionalism, see *Hunger and Work*, 21.

57. Richards, *Hunger and Work*, 1.

58. Richards, *Hunger and Work*, 1. See also Goody, *Cooking, Cuisine, and Class*, 15.

59. Richards, *Hunger and Work*, 38–54.

60. Richards, *Hunger and Work*, 187.

61. Richards, *Hunger and Work*, 162.

62. Richards, *Hunger and Work*, 85–114, 174–82, 190–93.

63. Richards, *Hunger and Work*, 213.

64. Richards, *Hunger and Work*, 31.

65. Hailey, *An African Survey*.

66. Vernon, *Hunger*, 111.

CHAPTER 5. SOCIAL NUTRITION AT THE LEAGUE OF NATIONS

1. Poppendieck, *Breadlines*, xvi, 33, 255; Averbeck, "'Want in the Midst of Plenty.'"

2. Barona, *Problem of Nutrition*; Borowy, *Coming to Terms with World Health*, 361–94. Clavin, *Securing the World Economy*, 164–75. Gibson, *Feeding of Nations*, 179–83. Cullather, "The Foreign Policy of the Calorie," 360–63.

3. Weindling, "Role of International Organizations."

4. Carpenter, "Work of Wallace Aykroyd," 874.

5. Passmore, "Wallace Ruddell Aykroyd," 246. The London Economic Conference, properly called the World Monetary and Economic Conference, met from June 12 to July 27, 1933, at the Geological Museum in London.

6. Hofstadter, *American Political Tradition*, 333.

7. Burnet and Aykroyd, *Nutrition and Public Health*; Walters, *History of the League of Nations*, 753.

8. Sen, *Poverty and Famines*.

9. Clavin, *Securing the World Economy*, 164–71; Borowy, *Coming to Terms with World Health*, 387. Weindling, "Moral Exhortation," 113–30. Hodge, *Triumph of the Expert*, 166–75. The Burnet-Aykroyd report elevated nutrition to the status of a serious world problem, examining the relationship of hunger with food production, supply, preservation, education, and wages. Weindling, "Role of International Organizations," 323.

10. Walters, *History of the League of Nations*, 753–54; Staples, *Birth of Development*, 73; O'Brien, "McDougall and the Origins of the FAO"; Way, *New Idea Each Morning*.

11. Waldorf Astor, the 2nd Viscount Astor (1879–1952), owner of the London *Observer*.

12. Waldorf Astor, "Mixed Committee on the Problem of Nutrition: Opening Speech by the President," February 7, 1936, File 50/22394/20095, Box R6747, League of Nations Archives, United Nations Library, Geneva.

13. This four-part definition comes from Vernon, *Hunger*, 134–35. See also "Introductory Note on the League and its Achievements in the Field of Nutrition," October 28, 1934, File 8A/2133/2133, Box 6074, League of Nations Archives, United Nations Library, Geneva.

14. The policies that encapsulate the social nutrition movement are most clearly reflected in the *Final Report of the Mixed Committee*. They included public education, higher wages, free school meals, the subsidization of vitamin rich foods, agricultural credits for small farmers, and the liberalization of trade.

15. Waldorf Astor, "Mixed Committee on the Problem of Nutrition: Opening Speech by the President," February 7, 1936, File 50/22394/20095, Box R6747, League of Nations Archives, United Nations Library, Geneva.

16. Claud Cockburn, "The Best People's Front," *The Week*, June 17, 1936. See also Goldman, "Claud Cockburn"; Rose, *Cliveden Set*; McDonough, *Neville Chamberlain*, 96–103.

17. Waldorf Astor, "Mixed Committee on the Problem of Nutrition: Opening Speech by the President," February 7, 1936, File 50/22394/20095, Box R6747, League of Nations Archives, United Nations Library, Geneva. See also Waldorf Astor, "A Nutrition Policy," *Spectator*, November 12, 1937.

18. Ludwik Rajchman (1881–1965) was a Polish citizen and antifascist who headed the Health Secretariat from its inception in 1921 until he was dismissed by the appeaser Joseph Avenol in 1938. He went on to help found the WHO and UNICEF. See Balinska, *For the Good of Humanity*.

19. Barona, *The Problem of Nutrition*, 23; Barona, "Nutrition and Health," 88. Astor was well connected and ensured that the final report did not end up like so many others in the League: "Received with words of praise, and then buried in official pigeon holes." See Walters, *History of the League of Nations*, 755. Way, *New Idea Each Morning*, 171–72. Peterson, "International Interest Organizations," 173.

20. Worboys, "Discovery of Colonial Malnutrition," 210–19.

21. *Final Report of the Mixed Committee*. An interim report from the Mixed Committee had been released a year earlier, in the summer of 1936.

22. Borowy, *Coming to Terms with World Health*, 392.

23. Walters, *History of the League of Nations*, 754–55; Cullather, "Foreign Policy of the Calorie," 361. See also Clavin, *Securing the World Economy*, 164–71; Orr, *As I Recall*, 120; Shaw, *World Food Security*, 8; Gibson, *The Feeding of Nations*, 180–81; Jean Kain, "Your Figure, Madame! League of Nations Group Reports World-Wide Diet Principles," *Washington Post*, October 30, 1937.

24. "A Nutrition Policy," *Spectator*, July 24, 1936. See also Cullather, "Foreign Policy of the Calorie," 361–62.

25. "The Staff of Nations," *New York Times*, September 4, 1937.

26. "Nutrition Study: League Committee of Experts, Headed By Lord Astor, Issues Significant Report Dealing with Problem of Food and its Uses," *Washington Post*, September 30, 1937.

27. George Newman, "The Health of Nations," *Observer*, September 26, 1937.

28. "Nutrition Study: League Committee of Experts, Headed By Lord Astor, Issues Significant Report Dealing with Problem of Food and its Uses," *Washington Post*, September 30, 1937.

29. "A Disappointing Report: Committee on Nutrition," *Manchester Guardian*, June 9, 1936.

30. Weindling, "From Sentiment to Science," 203–12. See also Cabanes, *Great War and the Origins of Humanitarianism*, 82–94.

31. Patenaude, *Big Show in Bololand*, 591.

32. Wilson, *Advice to Relief Workers*, 11. Unsurprisingly, this was an unpopular regulation, not least because the most malnourished children did not have the strength to leave home and many others lacked the proper clothes and shoes for the icy walk to canteens. Patenaude, *Big Show in Bololand*, 86–89.

33. Patenaude, *Big Show in Bololand*, 89; Weindling, "Role of International Organizations," 320; Weindling, "From Sentiment to Science," 204. Paul Weindling seems to identify him as Ralph Kellogg but it is more likely to be biologist and entomologist Vernon Kellogg (1867–1937) who was an administrator in the ARA and author of Kellogg, Taylor, and Hoover, *The Food Problem*.

34. Cabanes, *Origins of Humanitarianism*, 286–87; Kelly, *British Humanitarian Activity in Russia*, 159–213.

35. Benjamin Robertson, "Descriptive Notes on Tour in Saratov and Samara Provinces," January 1922, EJ198, Box A0410, Save the Children Fund Archive, Cadbury Research Library, University of Birmingham.

36. "Details of Kitchens," c.1922, EJ200, Box A0410, Save the Children Fund Archive, Cadbury Research Library, University of Birmingham.

37. "Resolution of Vienna," October 8, 1924, EJ258, Box A0415, Save the Children Fund Archive, Cadbury Research Library, University of Birmingham.

38. "Machine Age Humanitarianism," *The New Near East*, December 1923, File 48/28978/23735, Box 1757, League of Nations Archives, United Nations Library, Geneva.

39. MacCollum, *Newer Knowledge of Nutrition*. See also Kamminga, "'Axes to Grind'"; Aronson, "Social Definitions of Entitlement."

40. Lusk, "Introduction," 24. Aronson, "Social Definitions of Entitlement," 53–54. See also Scrinis, *Nutritionism*, 61.

41. Drummond, "Nomenclature," 660. For an accessible account of this history, see Price, *Vitamania*.

42. "Minutes of the First Meeting of the Technical Committee," November 25, 1936, File 8a/22155/20883, Box R6134, League of Nations Archives, United Nations Library, Geneva.

43. "Report on Standardisation for Dietary Surveys," c.1932, File 8a/36440/1409, Box R5866, League of Nations Archives, United Nations Library, Geneva.

44. "Minutes of the First Meeting of the Technical Committee," November 25, 1936, File 8a/22155/20883, Box R6134, League of Nations Archives, United Nations Library, Geneva.

45. Wallace Aykroyd, "Note on Official Family Budget Enquiries," June 30, 1932, File 8a/36440/1409, box R5866, League of Nations Archives, United Nations Library, Geneva.

46. Wallace Aykroyd gives the example of New Zealand where 1,800 books were distributed but only 69 returned satisfactorily completed. Surveys required the researcher to make judgments on whether the mother was "thrifty, wasteful, or hopeless," as well as rating her standard of cooking. "Nutrition Investigation," c.1932, File 8a/20879/20879, Box R6131, League of Nations Archives, United Nations Library, Geneva.

47. Vernon, *Hunger,* 130. Vincent, *Poor Citizens,* 75–79.

48. "Directions for Filling in the Questionnaire Concerning Nutrition," c.1932, File 8a/1409/1409, Box 5865, League of Nations Archives, United Nations Library, Geneva. The handbook recommends that "the teacher put these questions to the children unexpectedly, without giving them any previous warning," so no one could prepare answers in advance.

49. Jelliffe and Jelliffe, *Community Nutritional Assessment,* 13–126; Millman and DeRose, "Measuring Hunger," 21–46; Jelliffe, *Assessment of Nutritional Status,* 10–94.

50. Bigwood, *Guiding Principles.*

51. Henri Laugier, "General Programme of Research into Biological Measurements and Tests for the Definition of States of Malnutrition," May 5, 1936, File 8a/20879/20879, Box R6131; Stephani to Ranchman, Nov 30, 1932, File /8A/39809/39676, Box R5936, League of Nations Archives, United Nations Library, Geneva. See also Borowy, *Coming to Terms with World Health,* 383.

52. "Assessment of the Nutritional State of Children: Remarks by Dr. C. Schlotz," May 5, 1936, File 8a/20879/20879, Box R6131, League of Nations Archives, United Nations Library, Geneva.

53. Turmel, *Historical Sociology of Childhood.*

54. Pirquet's technique was called the Pelidisi index, and it involved looking at the ratio between the weight of the child and its sitting height. It was a complicated—and ultimately inaccurate—measure developed in Vienna and used in Russia during the famine. See Abbott, *From Relief to Social Security,* 365; Borowy, *Coming to Terms,* 384; Patenaude, *Big Show in Bololand,* 87.

55. Latour, *Pasteurization of France.*

56. Callon and Latour, "Unscrewing the Big Leviathan," 278–79.

57. Cullather, "Foreign Policy of the Calorie."

58. McCarrison, *Nutrition and National Health,* 19.

59. Orr, *Food, Health and Income,* 48–49.

60. Veit, *Modern Food, Moral Food,* 37–77.

61. Aykroyd to Podzimkova, Feb 9, 1933, File 8a/1409/1409, Box 5865, League of Nations Archives, United Nations Library, Geneva.

62. Borowy, "Crisis as Opportunity," 46. See also Walters, *History of the League of Nations,* 755; Clavin, *Securing the World Economy,* 164. Patricia Clavin describes this moment as "the rediscovery of hunger as a major international issue from the obscurity in which it had languished since 1919."

63. "Advice on the Feeding of Refugees in Spain and China," c.1938; "Suggested Emergency Diets for Famine Relief," September 9, 1938, File 8a/35164/20883, Box R6139, League of Nations Archives, United Nations Library, Geneva.

64. Wilson, *Advice to Relief Workers,* 6, 20.

65. Wilson, *Advice to Relief Workers,* 11; Thornhill, "Britain's Political Humanitarians."

66. Verzar to Gaultier, May 28, 1942, File 50/41418/41418, Box R5809, League of Nations Archives, United Nations Library, Geneva.

67. Osborn to Gorvin, March 3, 1942, File 50/41418/41418, Box R5809, League of Nations Archives, United Nations Library, Geneva.

68. Lester to Chrystal, March 16, 1942; Verzar to Gaultier, 28 May 1942; Osborn to Gorvin, 3 March 1942, File 50/41418/41418, Box R5809, League of Nations Archives, United Nations Library, Geneva.

69. "Postwar Food Relief: Note by the Health Section," September 16, 1942, File 50/41418/41418, Box R5809, League of Nations Archives, United Nations Library, Geneva.

70. Verzar to Gaultier, May 28, 1942, File 50/41418/41418, Box R5809, League of Nations Archives, United Nations Library, Geneva.

71. Osborn to Gorvin, March 3, 1942, File 50/41418/41418, Box R5809, League of Nations Archives, United Nations Library, Geneva.

72. "Vitamin (A and C) Extract from Orange Peel," c.1938; "Suggested Minimum Dietary for Chinese Refugees," August 1938, File 8a/35164/20883, Box R6139, League of Nations Archives, United Nations Library, Geneva.

CHAPTER 6. MILITARY FEEDING DURING WORLD WAR TWO

1. Hulme, *Nun's Story*; Hulme, *Wild Place*; "Real-Life Sister Luke Found World Full of Surprises," *Life Magazine,* June 8, 1959. Hulme's papers are kept at the Beinecke Rare Book and Manuscript Library, Yale University.

2. Hulme, *Wild Place*, 6.

3. Hulme, *Wild Place*, 29.

4. Hulme, *Wild Place*, 105.

5. Hulme, *Wild Place*, 51–52.

6. Hulme, *Wild Place*, 53–54.

7. Hulme, *Wild Place*, 49–63.

8. Smith, *Dachau*, 182–84.

9. Bryan, *Healing the Wounds,* 12.

10. McNeill, *By the Rivers of Babylon*, 78–86.

11. McNeill, *By the Rivers of Babylon*, 82.

12. McNeill, *By the Rivers of Babylon*, 78–86.

13. Malkki, "Refugees and Exile," 498; Cohen, "Between Relief and Politics"; Steinert, "British Humanitarian Assistance"; Reinisch, "Internationalism in Relief."

14. Malkki, "Refugees and Exile," 498–99.

15. Bryan, *Healing the Wounds*; Guest, *Broken Images;* McClelland, *Embers of War*; McNeill, *By the Rivers of Babylon*; Pettiss and Taylor, *After the Shooting Stopped*; Wilson, *In the Margins of Chaos*. A particularly good description of the criteria for selecting the location of DP camps, which usually meant army barracks, can be found in Smith, *Dachau*, 3–40.

16. Levi, *Reawakening*, 202. See also Reinisch, "Introduction: Relief in the Aftermath of War," 377.

17. Wilson, *Advice to Relief Workers*, 25. See also "One Day Course in Nutrition in Postwar Europe," 28 June 1942, FRS/1992/30, Friends Relief Service Archives, Library of the Religious Society of Friends in Britain, London.

18. "Notes on an Informal Talk given to the Friends' Emergency Relief Training Centre by Arthur Koestler," September 1943, FRS/1992/28, Friends Relief Service Archives, Library of the Religious Society of Friends in Britain, London.

19. "Notes for Relief Workers: the Phoenix Park Lectures," September 1943, FRS/1992/28, Friends Relief Service Archives, Library of the Religious Society of Friends in Britain, London. See particularly "the Administration of Refugee Camps," "Camp Psychology," and "Some Administrative Problems in Temporary Communities."

20. Wilson, *Advice to Relief Workers*, 9, 11, 27.

21. *Nutrition and Relief Work*, 90–98.

22. "Notes for Relief Workers: the Phoenix Park Lectures," September 1943, FRS/1992/28, Friends Relief Service Archives, Library of the Religious Society of Friends in Britain, London. See particularly "Course I: Nutrition," "Elementary Cooking," and "European Peasant Diets."

23. Judt, *Postwar*, 13.

24. "UNRRA Request to Supply (number UA-1240)," 29 November 1945; Office of the Quartermaster General, Press Release, 11 October 1945; Gustavus Tuckerman, "Procurement of Surplus Army Foods in Continental United States and Their Allocation," c.1947, File S-1021–0013–20, Box S-1021–0013, United Nations Relief and Rehabilitation Administration Archive, New York.

25. Gustavus Tuckerman, "Procurement of Surplus Army Foods in Continental United States and Their Allocation," c.1947, File S-1021–0013–20, Box S-1021–0013, United Nations Relief and Rehabilitation Administration Archive, New York.

26. Penuel and Statler, *Encyclopedia of Disaster Relief*, 1:85–86; Wieters, *NGO CARE and Food Aid from America*, 21–23, 49; Kruger, *Logistics Matters*, 134. The aid agency CARE was originally formed in 1945 as the Cooperative for American Remittances to Europe.

27. War Department Technical Bulletin, "Emergency Feeding of Infants, Children and other Special Groups of Civil Populations," 12 June 1944, File S-1271–0000–0115, Box S-0520–0395, United Nations Relief and Rehabilitation Administration Archive, New York.

28. Vernant, *Refugee*, 162. See also Cohen, "Between Relief and Politics," 443.

29. Trentmann, "Coping with Shortage," 30.

30. Cullather, "Foreign Policy of the Calorie." See also Grossmann, "Grams, Calories, and Food"; Weinreb, "For the Hungry Have No Past."

31. *Nutrition and Relief Work*, 19.

32. "The Illusion of the German Calories," *Manchester Guardian*, December 13, 1946.

33. Steege, *Black Market*, 48.

34. "The Miracle of Vitamins," *Hindustan Times*, November 7, 1943. Reproduced in Vernon, *Hunger*, 150.

35. Borgwardt, *New Deal for the World*, 116. David Weintraub, "Request for Allocation: Vitamins," 14 July 1944, File S-1227–0000–0278, Box S-0519–0287, United Nations Relief and Rehabilitation Administration Archive, New York.

36. Wilson, *Advice to Relief Workers*, 13. See also Apple, "Vitamins and the War."

37. Williams, "Relief and Research," 104. The humanitarian combination of Marmite and milk probably began with the work of the Birthday Trust Fund.

38. Shephard, *After Daybreak*, 99; Trepman, "Rescue of the Remnants," 287.

39. Anthony Aspinall, "The Strange Case of Bengal Famine Gruel," letter to the editor, *The Independent*, January 30, 1993.

40. Thompson, *Practical Dietetics*, 303–4. See also Watson, *Food and Feeding*, 564–65.

41. Trowell, "Infantile Pellagra," 403; Trowell, "Beginning of the Kwashiorkor Story," 3.

42. Carpenter, *Protein and Energy*, 148; "Desiccated Stomach Substance."

43. Dean, "Treatment and Prevention of Kwashiorkor"; Huehns, "Kwashiorkor."

44. Raimondi and Goetzl, "Treatment"; "Desiccated Stomach Substance."

45. Memorandum, Moran to Ritchie, 21 March 1945, MAF 256/93, Ministry of Food Records, National Archives, London.

46. Egon Larsen, "Maltavena: the Story of a New Milk Substitute," *Chamber's Journal*, December 1946; "Our London Correspondence," *Manchester Guardian*, May 14, 1946.

47. M. Pyke to A. Bour, 11 November 1946, MAF 256/93, Ministry of Food Records, National Archives, London.

48. Perkins correspondence, 1945–1948, File S-1448–0000–0195, Box S-0523–0577, United Nations Relief and Rehabilitation Administration Archive, New York.

49. R. F. A. Dean lecture notes, January 1949; "Background Letter," 9 December 1948, FO 943/470, Foreign Office Records, National Archives, London.

50. Memorandum, "The Caprino Formula for Baby Food," c.1945; O. J. Virden, "Suggested Procedure for Making Malt Extract and Cereal Product Suitable for Emergency

Infant Feeding," c.1945, MAF 256/93, Ministry of Food Records, National Archives, London.

51. "Brewing 'Milk' for Babies: Ruhr Experiment with Malted Wheat and Soya Flour," *Manchester Guardian*, April 8, 1946. Chick and Slack, "Malted Foods for Babies"; McClelland, *Embers of War*, 101–23.

52. Smith to Laurie, 23 November 1949; R. F. A. Dean lecture notes, January 1949, FO 943/470, Foreign Office Records, National Archives, London.

53. Apple, *Mothers and Medicine*, 23–28, 106–11; Valenze, *Milk*, 178–98.

54. "Life Visits Clifton's Cafeteria," *Life*, November 27, 1944.

55. Harold Weston to UNRRA, May 18, 1945, File S-1227–0000–0158, Box S-0519–0276, United Nations Relief and Rehabilitation Administration Archive, New York.

56. Memorandum on Multi-Purpose Food, c.1945, File S-1227–0000–0158, Box S-0519–0276, United Nations Relief and Rehabilitation Administration Archive, New York.

57. Wilson, *Advice to Relief Workers*, 13.

58. Gladwin Hill, "3-cent 'Meals' Aid in Famine Areas," *New York Times*, August 21, 1955.

59. Harold Weston to UNRRA, May 18, 1945, File S-1227–0000–0158, Box S-0519–0276, United Nations Relief and Rehabilitation Administration Archive, New York.

60. "Report of Opinions of the Food and Nutrition Board and the Committee on Food Habits," July 18, 1945; Harold Weston to UNRRA, May 18, 1945; File S-1227–0000–0158, Box S-0519–0276, United Nations Relief and Rehabilitation Administration Archive, New York. See also Paul de Kruif, "How We Can Feed Europe's Hungry," *Reader's Digest*, September 1945.

61. "5-ton Food Shipment Sent to Starving Congo," *Los Angeles Times*, Feburary 21, 1961; Fred Hafner, "Multi-Purpose Food: Valuable Aid to Improved Nutrition," *Soybean Digest*, June 1961.

62. Tanner, *Samuel Pepys and the Royal Navy*.

63. Save the Children Fund, "Reports of meetings held at Hotel Rome, Riga," 30 March 1922, EJ255, Box A0413, Save the Children Fund Archive, Cadbury Research Library, University of Birmingham. Bully beef and biscuits also became part of the "Nansen" rations for refugees in Eastern Europe.

64. Latour, "Drawing Things Together," 26–27; Latour, *Science in Action*, 227.

65. Latour, *Science in Action*, 223. A particularly clear example of this process can be found in Latour, *Pandora's Hope*, 24–79.

66. Shephard, *After Daybreak*, 3–4. These images, and the power of the Dimbleby broadcast, remained prominent in the British public mind until the time of Biafra. See Harrison and Palmer, *News out of Africa*, 31–33.

67. For more on the Red Cross and World War II, see Favez, *Red Cross and the Holocaust*; Steinacher, *Humanitarians at War*. For more on Belsen and historical memory, see Reilly et al., *Belsen in History and Memory*; Bardgett and Cesarani, *Belsen 1945*.

68. Shephard, "Medical Relief Effort at Belsen," 37; Steinert, "British Relief Teams in Belsen," 65–69; Vaughan, Dent, and Rivers, "Physiology and Treatment of Starvation"; Hughes, "Medical Students and Belsen"; Paton, "Mission to Belsen."

69. Trepman, "Rescue of the Remnants," 286; Lipscomb, "Medical Aspects"; Walker, "Feeding Problem." Many detailed treatments and experimental diets are recorded in "Sick Diets submitted by Conference of Doctors," 26 April 1945, RAMC/792/3/3, Royal Army Medical Corps Muniments Collection, Wellcome Library, London.

70. David Anderson, "Nutrition Experts Arrive in Holland: Eight-Man Team, with Plasma and Diet for Starving Populace," *New York Times*, April 10, 1945.

71. F. M. Lipscomb, "Belsen Camp: Use of Proteolysates, Plasma and Serum in Starvation," May 18, 1945, RAMC 792/3/4, Royal Army Medical Corps Muniments Collection,

Wellcome Library, London. For a detailed summary of the procedure, see Narayanan, Krishnan, and Sankaran, "Protein Hydrolysates."

72. Smith, *Dachau*, 208.

73. Shephard, *After Daybreak*, 100.

74. Cordell and Forsdick, "Symposium," 29.

75. Collis, "Belsen Camp," 815. The link between injections and the crematorium probably originated in rumours that the Nazis were putting flammable liquids into people's veins immediately before sending them to the crematorium. This was was one of the many sadistic practices used by the doctor Aribert Heim at Mauthausen concentration camp.

76. Shephard, *After Daybreak*, 101 and 224n21. The doctor was Alex Paton. See also Paton, "Mission to Belsen."

77. Janet Vaughan, "Treatment of Starvation: A Report to the War Office and the Medical Research Council," May 24, 1945, RAMC 792/3/4, Royal Army Medical Corps Muniments Collection, Wellcome Library, London. See also Shephard, *After Daybreak*, 224n20.

78. The term "F-treatment" is still in widespread use, appearing in the names of F-100 and F-75 therapeutic formulae.

79. Shephard, *After Daybreak*, 98–100.

80. Shephard, *After Daybreak*, 99. See also Shephard, "Medical Relief Effort at Belsen," 42.

81. Anthony Aspinall, "The Strange Case of Bengal Famine Gruel," letter to the editor, *The Independent*, January 30, 1993.

82. Janet Vaughan, "Treatment of Starvation: a Report to the War Office and the Medical Research Council," May 24, 1945, RAMC 792/3/4, Royal Army Medical Corps Muniments Collection, Wellcome Library, London.

CHAPTER 7. THE MEDICALIZATION OF HUNGER AND THE POSTWAR PERIOD

1. Keys et al., *Biology of Human Starvation*.

2. Keys et al., *Biology of Human Starvation*, 837.

3. Keys et al., *Biology of Human Starvation*, 880–900.

4. Stark, *Behind Closed Doors*, 94; Taylor, *Acts of Conscience*, 73–103; Krehbiel, *Lewis B. Hershey*, 8–9; Russell, *Hunger*, 119–20.

5. Keys et al., *Biology of Human Starvation*, 1071–1150. The intelligence tests followed the US Army General Classification technique.

6. The volunteers included Quakers, Mennonites, and members of the Church of the Brethren.

7. Kalm and Semba, "They Starved So That Others Be Better Fed."

8. Tucker, *The Great Starvation Experiment*.

9. Stark, *Behind Closed Doors*, 94. As Laura Stark put it, "The great virtue of religious objectors was that they were healthy, pliant and cheap."

10. Stanley Willimott, "Food and Nutrition Conditions in POW Camps in Java and Japan," c. 1945, NUT/11/03, Nutrition Collection, London School of Hygiene and Tropical Medicine Archives, University of London. See also "Famine Disease in Internment Camps and its Treatment," c.1944, File 8A/41882/2133, Box R6077, League of Nations Archives, United Nations Library, Geneva.

11. Brozek et al., "Medical Aspects of Semi-starvation"; Kirschenbaum, *Legacy of the Siege of Leningrad*, 42–76; Vasilyev, "Alimentary and Pellagra Psychoses."

12. Drummond et al., *Malnutrition and Starvation in Western Netherlands*; Stein, *Famine and Human Development*.

13. Rosencher, "Medicine in Dachau"; Lipscomb, "Medical Aspects of Belsen"; Mollison, "Observations."

14. Williams, "Kwashiorkor"; Williams, "Nutritional Disease of Childhood." For a fuller account of the origins of kwashiorkor, see Craddock, *Retired Except on Demand*; Dally, *Cicely*; Williams, "Story of Kwashiorkor"; Trowell, "Beginning of the Kwashiorkor Story."

15. Trowell, Davies, and Dean, *Kwashiorkor*, 2–9, 13. Waterlow, *Protein-Energy Malnutrition*. This condition had a variety of names, from the colloquial ("red baby"), to the medical ("dyschronic oedematous syndrome"). The earliest description emerged in Mexico in 1908.

16. Stannus, "Kwashiorkor"; Stannus, "Nutritional Disease"; Waterlow, *Fatty Liver Disease*; Ruxin, "Hunger, Science, and Politics," 67–71.

17. Discrimination dogged Cicely Williams throughout her life, even amongst her eventual supporters, one of whom patronizingly attributed her success to "being a lady, and a very gracious lady" that meant she could "arrive by instinct at the correct answer." See Trowell, "Kwashiorkor Story in Africa," 1.

18. Stannus, "Kwashiorkor," 1207.

19. Craddock, *Retired Except on Demand*, 62.

20. Stanton, "Listening to the Ga."

21. Konotey-Ahulu, "Kwashiorkor," 180. See also Konotey-Ahulu, "Issues in Kwashiorkor."

22. Trowell, "Beginning of the Kwashiorkor Story," 3.

23. Konotey-Ahulu, "Issues in Kwashiorkor," 548.

24. Baily, "Fiddling While Children Starve?," 1490.

25. Asher, *Talking Sense*, 42–53. Rosenberg, "Framing Disease," xiii. See also Rosenberg, "Disease and Social Order."

26. Cassell, *The Healer's Art*, 48. See also Helman, "Disease versus Illness"; Freidson, *Profession of Medicine*, 223. Freidson observed that "when a physician diagnoses a human's condition as illness, he changes the man's behavior by diagnosis; a social state is added to a biophysiological state by assigning the meaning of illness to disease. It is in this sense that the physicians creates illness."

27. Brock and Autret, *Kwashiorkor in Africa*, 32, 66. Williams, "Nutritional Disease"; Stanton, "Listening to the Ga," 160; Ruxin, "Hunger, Science and Politics," 69. See also Wylie, *Starving on a Full Stomach*, 1–19; Vernon, *Hunger*, 196–235. Diana Wylie offers a comprehensive treatment of the tendency to blame malnutrition on African ignorance and tradition; Vernon describes how hunger in Britain was blamed on the ignorance of working-class housewives.

28. Vaughan, *Curing Their Ills*, 1–28. Kwashiorkor would later be used as a pretext for dietary and industrial modernization, but Cicely Williams was not implicated; in fact, she vigorously opposed many elements of this agenda. For more, see Williams, "Milk and Murder."

29. Carpenter, *Protein and Energy*, 146–48; Trowell, "Malignant Malnutrition"; Gillman and Gillman, *Perspectives in Human Malnutrition*; Gillman and Gillman, "Hepatic Damage in Infantile Pellagra."

30. Trowell, "Infantile Pellagra," 403; Trowell, "Beginning of the Kwashiorkor Story," 3.

31. Craddock, *Retired Except on Demand*, 63.

32. Konotey-Ahulu, "Issues in Kwashiorkor," 548.

33. Dally, *Cicely*, 48–53; Ruxin, "Hunger, Science, and Politics," 235; Williams, "On that Fiasco"; Konotey-Ahulu, "Kwashiorkor," 180–81.

34. Tushnet, *The Uses of Adversity*, 51.

35. Apfelbaum, "Pathophysiology of the Circularatory System," 131–54. This technique resembles modern angiograms and was almost certainly based on the procedure set out in Gibson and Evans, "Clinical Studies."

36. Fajgenblat, "Ocular Disturbances in Hunger Disease," 200–205.

37. Fliederbaum, "Metabolic Changes in Hunger Disease," 77. Szejnman, "Changes in Peripheral Blood," 183.

38. Szejnman, "Changes in Peripheral Blood," 183. Braude-Heller et al., "Clinical Aspects of Hunger Disease," 49. The blister experiment became known as the Aldrich McClure skin water test.

39. Apfelbaum, "Pathophysiology of the Circularatory System," 142–43.

40. Winick, "Preface."

41. Russell, *Hunger*, 104.

42. Fajgenblat, "Ocular Disturbances in Hunger Disease," 155. "Some of the techniques," he dryly observed, "were not without risk to the patient."

43. Milejkowski, "Introduction," 4.

44. Roland, *Courage under Siege*; Tushnet, *Uses of Adversity*.

45. Milejkowski, "Introduction," 4.

46. Tushnet, *Uses of Adversity*, 96. See also Milejkowski, "Introduction," 5. The Latin is from Horace's Ode 3.30. *Non omnis moriar multaque pars mei vitabit Libitinam*. I shall not wholly die and the greater part of me shall avoid the goddess of death.

47. Szejnman, "Changes in Peripheral Blood," 185.

48. Scheper-Hughes, *Death without Weeping*. Bom Jesus da Mata was a pseudonym; Scheper-Hughes later revealed the town to be Timbaúba, in Pernambuco state in North-Eastern Brazil.

49. Foucault, *Birth of the Clinic*. This text was first published in French in 1963 and was Foucault's second major work after *Madness and Civilization* in 1960.

50. Foucault, *Birth of the Clinic*, 146–55.

51. Foucault, *Birth of the Clinic*, 176.

52. Armstrong, *Political Anatomy of the Body*.

53. Richards, *Hunger and Work*.

54. Phillips, *FAO*, 1–35; O'Brien, "McDougall and the Origins of the FAO," 164–74.

55. Staples, "To Win the Peace," 504. See also Shaw, *World Food Security*, 15.

56. Staples, *Birth of Development*, 86, 228n8; Phillips, *FAO*, 15–35.

57. Phillips, *FAO*, 16.

58. Orr, *As I Recall*, 162. Orr had a variation on this phrase: "The people are crying out for bread, and we offer them pamphlets." See John Boyd Orr, "Draft Script," c. 1948, RG0.1.1, Series H1, Food and Agricultural Organization Archives, David Lubin Memorial Library, Rome.

59. The next two directors of the FAO were Norris Dodd and Philip Cardon. See also Staples, *Birth of Development*, 77.

60. Ruxin, "Hunger, Science, and Politics," 58.

61. "Work of the Nutrition Division FAO in 1946–7," c.1948, RG0–57.0, Series D1, Food and Agricultural Organization Archives, David Lubin Memorial Library, Rome. See also Ruxin, "Hunger, Science, and Politics," 83.

62. Orr, *As I Recall*, 163.

63. Autret, Teulon, and de Crescenzo, "Guide for the Use of Experts of the Nutrition Division of FAO," February 1964, ACC/689072, Food and Agricultural Organization Archives, David Lubin Memorial Library, Rome.

64. Ritchie, *Teaching Better Nutrition*, 143–44; *Joint FAO/WHO Expert Committee On Nutrition*, 15. The new wave of nutrition researchers included Gomez in Mexico, Brock in South Africa, Bhattachariyya in Calcutta, McLaren in Lebanon, and Calvo in Venezuela. See also Ruxin, "Hunger, Science, and Politics," 50.

65. Orr, *White Man's Dilemma*, 102.

66. Ruxin, "Hunger, Science, and Politics," 74.

67. McLaren, "Fresh Look," 275.

68. Jelliffe, "Protein-Calorie Malnutrition," 242.

CHAPTER 8. HIGH MODERNISM AND THE DEVELOPMENT DECADE

1. Brock and Autret, *Kwashiorkor in Africa*, 72.

2. Sandra Blakeslee, "High-Protein Food, Created in Laboratories, Is Starting to Enter the Consumer's Diet," *New York Times*, March 1, 1970. See also Yvonne Freita, "Microbes Help Solve Protein Shortages," *Times of India*, February 9, 1969. J. W. Murray, "A Nice, Tasty Wooden Steak," *Observer*, March 1, 1970; Martin Sherwood, "Single-Cell Protein Comes of Age," *New Scientist*, November 28, 1974; Victor McElheny, "1-Cell Protein Sought for Food," *Washington Post*, October 12, 1967.

3. Bamberg, *British Petroleum*, 434.

4. James Nagle, "U.S. Industry Set to Feed the Poor," *New York Times*, August 13, 1967.

5. Mateles and Tannenbaum, *Single-Cell Protein*; Goldberg, *Single Cell Protein*; Bamberg, *British Petroleum*, 425–31.

6. Arndt, *Economic Development*, 49–114; Stokke, *UN and Development*, 131–56.

7. For more on "nutritional reductionism" see Cook, "Production, Ecology and Economic Anthropology"; Pollan, *In Defence of Food*, 62–63; Scrinis, "Nutritionism," 271. In the 1960s it was still quite possible to be a nutritional reductionist without becoming a high modernist. For a good example see Latham, *Human Nutrition*.

8. Colin Tudge, "Food for the Unthinking," *World Medicine*, June 5, 1974. Quoting J. H. Sheldon of Birds Eye.

9. Many of these schemes emerged from the experience of the Second World War, when scientists were asked to investigate new foods in the context of wartime shortage. See Bamberg, *British Petroleum*, 427–29; Kapsiotis, "Single Cell Protein."

10. Fowden and Pierpoint, "Norman Pirie."

11. The process is described particularly well in Pirie, "Leaf Protein as a Human Food [1958]." See also Pirie, "Leaf Proteins"; Pirie, "Leaf Protein as Human Food [1960]."

12. N. W. Pirie in Conversation with W.S. Pierpoint, 27 June 1988, at Biochemical Society Collection, Film and Sound Online, University of Edinburgh Library. See also Fowden and Pierpoint, "Norman Pirie."

13. Pirie, "Leaf Protein as a Human Food [1958]," 19.

14. Morrison and Pirie, "Presentation of Leaf Protein," 8.

15. Morrison and Pirie, "Presentation of Leaf Protein," 8. See also Byers, Green and Pirie, "Presentation of Leaf Protein"; Morrison and Pirie, "Large-Scale Production."

16. Pirie, "Leaf Protein as a Human Food [1958]," 20.

17. Pirie, "World Hunger," 523–24; Pirie, "Leaf Protein as a Human Food [1958]" 20.

18. Pirie, "Present Position," 512.

19. Pirie, "World Hunger," 523; Jane Brody, "The Search for Food," *New York Times*, July 24, 1966.

20. Pirie, "Leaf Protein as a Human Food [1958]," 20. Despite Pirie's optimism, the fresh LPC was not very versatile and, unlike eggs, could not be baked, whipped, fried or boiled to produce different dishes.

21. Pirie, "Production and Use," 86. See also Box CA4/A/1, CA4/A/2, CA4/A/3, CA2/D/26, CA4/D/27, Christian Aid Archive, School of Oriental and African Studies (SOAS) Library, University of London.

22. Scott-Smith, "How Projects Rise and Fall."

23. Pirie, "World Hunger," 526.

24. Justin Phipps to Sarah Hughes, 24 November 1980, CA4/A/2/12, Christian Aid Archive, SOAS Library, University of London.

25. Powell, Nevels, and McDowell, "Algae Feeding in Humans," 7. See also Spoehr, "Need for a New Source of Food," 26.

26. Spoehr, "Need for a New Source of Food," 26. The language of engineering is used in Burlew, *Algal Culture*. See also Belasco, "Algae Burgers."

27. Cook, "Nutritive Value," 244; Borgstrom, *Too Many,* 96–98, 270–87.

28. Spoehr, "Chlorella as a Source of Food"; Burlew, *Algal Culture,* iii; Lubitz, "Protein Quality."

29. "Algae to Feed Starving," *Science News Letter,* July 18, 1953. See also Belasco, "Algae Burgers," 620.

30. Burlew, *Algal Culture,* v.

31. Jorgensen and Convit, "Cultivation of Complexes," 195.

32. Tamiya, "Mass Culture of Algae," 328; Powell, Nevels, and McDowell, "Algae Feeding in Humans." Plankton soup was a slightly different product. See Borgstrom, *Too Many,* 274–77; Burlew, *Algal Culture,* 21.

33. Fisher and Burlew, "Nutritional Value of Microscopic Algae," 310.

34. Krauss, "Mass Culture of Algae," 432; Powell, Nevels, and McDowell, "Algae Feeding in Humans," 9–10.

35. Fisher and Burlew, "Nutritional Value of Microscopic Algae," 310. See also Powell, Nevels, and McDowell, "Algae Feeding in Humans," 11; Belasco, *Meals to Come,* 166–218.

36. M. L. Windsor, "Fish Protein Concentrate," c.1970, AY 9/39. Torry Research Station Records, National Archives, London.

37. Between 1956 and 1959 more than eight hundred tons of fish flour were incorporated into the manufacture of brown bread in South Africa, but the scheme was eventually stopped when it became clear that the poorest communities did not even eat bread. See Pariser et al., *Fish Protein Concentrate*; Black, *Children First,* 159; Carpenter, *Protein and Energy,* 162–68.

38. Roels, "Fish Protein Concentrate"; Wallerstein and Pariser, "Fish Protein Concentrate." Food From the Sea was the name of a section within the Office of the War on Hunger at USAID.

39. *Joint FAO/WHO Expert Committee On Nutrition,* 15.

40. Waterlow and Payne, "Protein Gap."

41. "The Enrichment of Whole Wheat Flour and Iranian Bread with Lysine and Vitamins," May 1969, NUT/17/02/06/02, Nutrition Collection, London School of Hygiene and Tropical Medicine Archives, University of London. See also Orr, *Use of Protein-Rich Foods,* 2.

42. Lysine enriched staple foods were soon pioneered on a particularly large scale in India, where wheat was chemically engineered to contain new amino acids, thus "doubling their food value." See "High-Efficiency Protein to Attack Malnutrition," *New York Times,* November 17, 1957; Carpenter, *Protein and Energy,* 177–78. The magical reputation of Lysine rubbed off on the creators of the film *Jurassic Park,* in which dinosaurs were kept dependent on lysine pills.

43. "Doubling the Food Value of Cereals," *Times of India,* August 17, 1958; "Food Value of Rice Can Be Raised," *Times of India,* November 10, 1957; "Fighting Malnutrition in Tropical Lands," *Times of India,* January 12, 1958. By 1974 experts had heartily dismissed the hopes for Lysine. See McLaren, "Great Protein Fiasco," 94.

44. The anthropological notion of involution (the process of becoming ever more intricately involved or entangled) began in the work of the Boasian scholar Alexander Goldenweiser in relation to art; Clifford Geertz then applied the notion to Javanese agriculture and Miriam Ticktin has more recently examined "biological involution" in relation to asylum claims. See Kuper, *Culture,* 86–87; Geertz, *Agricultural Involution*; Ticktin, *Casualties of Care,* 192–220.

45. Borsook, "We Could Feed the World," 9.

46. Jensen, "Protein-Calorie Malnutrition," 224. See also Pernet, "Between Entanglements and Dependencies."

47. Scrimshaw, "Background and History of Incaparina," 1.

48. "Progress Report on Development of Vegetable Mixtures 9 and 10," September 1958, NUT/18/20/04, Nutrition Collection, London School of Hygiene and Tropical Medicine Archives, University of London.

49. Shaw, "The Flour of San Vicente," 3. For more on the "sophistication" of milk alternatives, see Valenze, *Milk*; Atkins, *Liquid Materialities*.

50. Black, *Children First*, 141.

51. Black, *Children First*, 146. The advisor was Joseph Edwards. It is probably no coincidence that, with such sentiments, Edwards also worked for the Milk Marketing board of the UK.

52. In addition to Scrimshaw and Incaparina, another inspiration was the work of R.F.A Dean, who took Maltavena to the tropics. "Proposed fieldwork in Uganda by R.F.A. Dean and Assistant," c.1949, CO 859/233/2, Colonial Office Records, National Archives, London.

53. McLaren, "Great Protein Fiasco," 94.

54. Jane Brody, "Protein Supplement Developed to Fight Malnutrition in Young," *New York Times*, November 30, 1967.

55. DeMaeyer, "Processed Weaning Foods," 402.

56. Taba, "Nutritional Problems," 217–18; Hofvander, "North–South Collaboration," 323; Jensen, "Protein-Calorie Malnutrition." For a fuller report on Faffa, see Hofvander, *50 Years Of Ethio-Swedish Collaboration*.

57. Hornstein, *Thriposha*; Tandon, "Supplementary Nutrition"; Siegel, *Hungry Nation*, 206–8; Brown and Eckholm, *By Bread Alone*, 164–76.

58. Siegel, *Hungry Nation*, 206–8; Berg, *Famine Contained*, 108–30; DeMaeyer, "Processed Weaning Foods," 402; Taba, "Nutritional Problems," 217–18.

59. Frank Wokes, "Report on Operation Oasis," c.1965, DIR/2/3/2/57, Oxfam Archive, Bodleian Library, Oxford.

60. Patrick Cooney to the Director General of Oxfam, 30 December 1963; Memorandum, "Nutrition Research Project," May 1963, DIR/2/3/2/57, Oxfam Archive, Bodleian Library, Oxford.

61. R. M. Belbin, "Notes on a project to develop a Bacterial Protein Food," 3 April 1963, DIR/2/3/2/57, Oxfam Archive, Bodleian Library, Oxford.

62. Memorandum, "Nutrition Research Project," May 1963, DIR/2/3/2/57, Oxfam Archive, Bodleian Library, Oxford.

63. Black, *A Cause for our Times*, 111–16. Prasannappa, "Precooked Bal-Ahar"; Rowntree to Ezra, September 12, 1966, DIR/2/3/2/54, Oxfam Archive, Bodleian Library, Oxford.

64. Frank Wokes, "Report on Operation Oasis," c.1965, DIR/2/3/2/57, Oxfam Archive, Bodleian Library, Oxford. See also Scott-Smith, "How Projects Rise and Fall."

65. Scott, *Seeing Like a State,* 1–8. The notion of "high modernism" had been around for some time, referring to an experimental form of literary modernism, but Scott innovatively applied the term to politics and governance. See also Huyssen, *After the Great Divide*.

66. Scott, *Seeing Like a State*, 78, 378n11.

67. Scott, *Seeing Like a State*, 89.

68. Jencks, *Language of Post-modern Architecture*, 22–23. Grenz, *Primer on Postmodernism*, 11; Killen, *1973 Nervous Breakdown*, 3, 211; Jameson, *Postmodernism*, 41–50.

69. Bamberg, *British Petroleum*, 424–35; Bud, *Uses of Life*, 135–36; Frazer Imrie, "Single-Cell Protein from Agricultural Wastes," *New Scientist*, May 22, 1975.

70. "Soviet Increasing Output of Fodder: It Uses Petroleum to Grow Single Cell Protein," *New York Times*, June 23, 1973. Bud, *Uses of Life*, 136.

71. Mitzner, Srimshaw, and Morgan, "Improving the Nutritional Status."

72. Taylor and Tweed, *Butterflies in My Stomach*. The closure of the fish protein plant is described in Carpenter, *Protein and Energy*, 165. See also Black, *Children First*, 159.

73. Jencks, *Language of Post-Modern Architecture*, 22–23; Grenz, *Primer on Postmodernism*, 11; Killen, *1973 Nervous Breakdown*, 3, 211; Sim, *Routledge Companion to Postmodernism*, 63; Jameson, *Postmodernism*, 41–50.

74. *Report of the 1972 United Nations Conference*. 8; McLaren, "Great Protein Fiasco."

75. "Travelling Seminar on Protein Foods"; Jelliffe, "Commerciogenic Malnutrition?"

76. Bamberg, *British Petroleum*, 434; Carpenter, *Protein and Energy*, 165. Single Cell Protein left its legacy in the meat-substitute Quorn.

77. Orr, *Use of Protein-Rich Foods*, 47–48; Carpenter, *Protein and Energy*, 174; Mitzner, Scrimshaw and Morgan, "Improving the Nutritional Status of Children."

78. Schumacher, *Small is Beautiful*. For more on the way this reaction fed into the countercultural whole foods movement, see Belasco, *Appetite for Change*.

CHAPTER 9. LOW MODERNISM AFTER BIAFRA

1. Harrison and Palmer, *News out of Africa*, 33. The association with World War II was particularly powerful given that the Igbo were often referred to as the "Jews of Africa." Bruder, *Black Jews of Africa*, 142–46. Heerten, *Biafran War*, 63, 186.

2. De Waal, *Famine Crimes*, 72–77. Not all aid agencies took such a pro-Biafran line, and the Red Cross movement adopted a more cautious approach. See Forsythe, *Humanitarians*, 63–68.

3. De Waal, *Famine Crimes*, 73; Fast, *Aid in Danger*, 71; Moses and Heerten. *Postcolonial Conflict*, 189.

4. Forsythe, *Humanitarians*, 62–68; Benthall, *Disasters*, 92–108; Harrison and Palmer, *News out of Africa*, 5–39; Chandler, "Road to Military Humanitarianism," 678–700; Chandler, *From Kosovo to Kabul*, 29–31; Terry, *Condemned to Repeat?* 42–43.

5. Philip Gourevitch, "Alms Dealers: Can You Provide Humanitarian Aid without Facilitating Conflicts?" *New Yorker*, October 11, 2010. See also De St. Jorre, *Nigerian Civil War*, 233–53; Stremlau, *International Politics*, 238–52.

6. Berman, *Power and the Idealists*, 193–246; De Waal, *Famine Crimes*, 65–79.

7. One aid worker stated that he was able to assist 250 children every hour in Biafra through a combination of arm circumference measurements and nutritionally fortified foods. Rainer, "Arm Circumference," 244–45.

8. Black, *Children First*, 280.

9. Rainer, "Arm Circumference," 245.

10. The QUAC stick was makeshift wooden ruler held against a child to measure their height. Instead of being marked in centimetres or inches, however, it was inscribed with the limit measurements of a healthy arm circumference. The name was abbreviated from 'Quaker Arm Circumference'. Sommer and Loewenstein, "Nutritional Status and Mortality"; Ifekwunigwe, "Recent Field Experiences."

11. Rainer, "Arm Circumference," 244.

12. Rainer, "Arm Circumference," 245.

13. Gans, "Biafran Relief Mission," 661; Black, *Children First*, 280. K-Mix 2 was an abbreviation of "kwashiorkor mixture," and it contained skim milk powder, sugar, and casein.

14. Finlay, "Early Marketing," 59n55; Calkins, "Florence Nightingale."

15. Williams, "On That Fiasco," 793.

16. Jelliffe, "Commerciogenic Malnutrition?" 199.

17. For the example of Marmite, which was promoted as a source of B vitamins, see Frankenburg, *Vitamin Discoveries*, 57–58; Gamgee, "Yeast Extracts"; Marsh, *Back to the Land*, 187–204.

18. "Communication from the International Council of Women to the League of Nations, with a View to the Establishment of an International Institute for Nutrition," c.1930. 8A/21523/1409, League of Nations Archive, United Nations Library, Geneva.

19. Black, *Cause for Our Times*, 109–12

20. Arnold Bender to Janet Lacey, 14 September 1967, CA/C/13/10, Christian Aid Archive, SOAS Library, University of London. Patrick Cooney to the Director General of Oxfam, 30 December 1963, DIR/2/3/2/57, Oxfam Archive, Bodleian Library, Oxford.

21. Orr, "Contribution of New Food Mixtures," 4–10; Orr, *Use of Protein-Rich Foods*, 7–32; Jensen, "Protein-Calorie Malnutrition," 231; Carpenter, *Protein and Energy*, 172–75; Semba, "Rise and Fall of Protein Malnutrition," 83; Brown and Eckholm. *By Bread Alone*, 164–76.

22. Orr, *Use of Protein-Rich Foods*, 34. Pronutro began as a soya and maize weaning food for the black urban poor in 1940s South Africa, but was then relaunched for white consumers; it is still a popular breakfast cereal. Vitasoy was conceived in the 1940s as a cheap soymilk for malnourished refugees in Hong Kong, but it later became a popular beverage across in the Far East. Thriposha, originally established in 1972 for public-sector feeding programs, was privatized and relaunched in 1980 by Lever brothers. See also Carpenter, *Protein and Energy*, 172–73; Orr, *Use of Protein-Rich Foods*, 15–24; Brown and Eckholm, *By Bread Alone*, 169; Hornstein, *Thriposha*; Porter and Shafritz, *Packaged Foods for Complementary Feeding*, 30.

23. Brock and Autret, *Kwashiorkor in Africa*, 72.

24. Ruxin, "United Nations Protein Advisory Group," 152.

25. Semba, "Rise and Fall of Protein Malnutrition," 80–81; George, *How the Other Half Dies*, 160–61.

26. *International Action to Avert the Impending Protein Crisis*, 5. See also Jensen, "Protein-Calorie Malnutrition," 226–67; Ruxin, "United Nations Protein Advisory Group," 155–56. Two years later FAO echoed this language with their own report, entitled *Lives in Peril*, and by 1971 the *Impending Protein Crisis* was repackaged as a UN Strategy Statement, complete with a foreword by UN secretary general claiming that the protein crisis was no longer "impending," but "real."

27. Promotional Leaflet "Strong Arm High Protein Food," c. 1967; Laboratory Reports, "Ministry of Technology Torry Research Station and the Central Institute for Nutrition and Food Research," CA/C/13/10, Christian Aid Archive, SOAS Library, University of London.

28. "Strong Arm High Protein Food: General Description," c.1968; B. J Dudbridge to Helmut Reuschle, 24 March 1969, CA/C/13/10, Christian Aid Archive, SOAS Library, University of London.

29. Pariser et al., *Fish Protein Concentrate*, 19–74

30. Black, *Children First*, 141.

31. J. W. Murray, "A Nice, Tasty Wooden Steak," *Observer*, March 1, 1970.

32. Huxley, *Brave New Victuals*, 98.

33. "Preliminary Report of the Leaf Protein Trials," July 1977; Peter Fellows, "The Construction of a Processing Unit for the Production of Dried Leaf Protein Concentrate," c.1977, CA4/A/3/1, Christian Aid Archive, SOAS Library, University of London. Peter Fellows, interview with the author, January 11, 2011.

34. Pirie, "World Hunger," 526.

35. John Nightingale, "Some Questions of Distribution," 1977; Committee Minutes, 22 June 1973 and 2 March 1977, CA4/A/2/11, Christian Aid Archive, SOAS Library, University of London.

36. Committee Minutes, 22 June 1973 and 2 March 1977, CA4/A/2/11; Peter Fellows, "Leaf Protein project report," 1977, CA4/A/3/1, Christian Aid Archive, SOAS Library, University of London.

37. Committee Minutes, 15 September 1973, CA4/A/2/10, Christian Aid Archive, SOAS Library, University of London.

38. Committee Minutes, 2 March 1977, CA4/A/2/11, Christian Aid Archive, SOAS Library, University of London.

39. Committee Minutes, "Posho Mill Project for the Production of Leaf Protein," 22 June 1973, CA4/A/2/10, Christian Aid Archive, SOAS Library, University of London.

40. Justin Phipps to Sarah Hughes, 24 November 1980, CA4/A/2/12, Christian Aid Archive, SOAS Library, University of London.

41. "Progress Report on Development of Vegetable Mixtures 9 and 10," September 1958, NUT/18/20/04, Nutrition Collection, London School of Hygiene and Tropical Medicine Archives, University of London. See also Paddock and Paddock, *Famine,* 66.

42. T. F Betts to Leslie Kirkley, 18 March 1967, DIR/2/3/2/54, Oxfam Archive, Bodleian Library, Oxford.

43. "Circular Memorandum to Members of Council: the Supro Project in East Africa," September 1966; Memorandum, "Supro: a Digest of Correspondence and Minutes up to 30.6.1967"; T. F Betts to Leslie Kirkley, 18 March 1967, DIR/2/3/2/54, Oxfam Archive, Bodleian Library, Oxford.

44. "Wisconsin Alumni Research Foundation Laboratories, Assay report on Supro," June 27, 1967; Memorandum, "To the Board of Supro Laboratories, Kenya limited: Tour of Mr. T. F. Betts to Uganda, Rwanda and Burundi." January/February 1967, DIR/2/3/2/54, Oxfam Archive, Bodleian Library, Oxford.

45. Memorandum, "Supro: a Digest of Correspondence and Minutes up to 30.6.1967," DIR/2/3/2/54, Oxfam Archive, Bodleian Library, Oxford.

46. T. F Betts to Leslie Kirkley, 18 March 1967; Memorandum, "Supro, Oxfam and Oxfam Activities ltd.," 1967, DIR/2/3/2/54, Oxfam Archive, Bodleian Library, Oxford.

47. M. Murimi to M. Ronaldson, 19 December 1967; T. F. Betts to Leslie Kirkley, 8 October 1967, DIR/2/3/2/54, Oxfam Archive, Bodleian Library, Oxford. On industrial feeding canteens in Africa, see Wylie, *Starving on a Full Stomach*; Popkin and Latham, "Limitations and Dangers," 1016n7.

48. T. F. Betts to Leslie Kirkley, 8 October 1967; Memorandum, "Supro Scheme for Karamoja," 1968, DIR/2/3/2/54, Oxfam Archive, Bodleian Library, Oxford.

49. Shaw and Clay, *World Food Aid,* 221; Singer, Jennings, and Wood, *Food Aid,* 22–23.

50. Ball and Johnson, "Political, Economic, and Humanitarian Motivations," 516; Clapp, *Hunger in the Balance,* 18; Ruttan, "Politics of U.S. Food Aid"; George, *How the Other Half Dies,* 199; Paddock and Paddock, *Famine,* 170.

51. This caused some consternation, not least on the part of the Oxfam field director in Kenya, who blamed the failure of Supro on the arrival of American Corn-Soy-Milk. Memorandum, "To the Board of Supro Laboratories, Kenya limited: Tour of Mr. T. F. Betts to Uganda, Rwanda and Burundi," January/February 1967, DIR/2/3/2/54, Oxfam Archive, Bodleian Library, Oxford.

52. Bert Tollefson, "New Milled Corn Products, including CSM" (presentation, Fifth National Conference On Wheat Utilization Research, Fargo, North Dakota, November 1–3, 1967).

53. Combs, "Development of a Supplementary Food Mixture"; Senti et al., "Protein-Fortified Food."

54. Webb et al., *Improving the Nutritional Quality,* 21–24, 119; Brown and Eckholm, *By Bread Alone,* 170; Black, *Children First,* 268.

55. Dexter, "Requirements for Effective Fortification," 78. Brown and Eckholm, *By Bread Alone,* 169–70.

56. Roberts, *End of Food,* 117; Shaw and Clay, *World Food Aid,* 221; Clapp, *Hunger in the Balance,* 15–21; Wallerstein, *Food for War,* 3–17.

57. Friedmann and McMichael, "Agriculture and the State"; Goodman and Redclift, *Refashioning Nature,* 87–132; Friedmann, "Remaking 'Traditions'"; Friedmann, "International Political Economy."

58. Davis and Goldberg, *Concept of Agribusiness*; George, *How the Other Half Dies,* 58.

59. I have placed this in scare quotes because value accrues to the producer rather than the consumer. See Nestle, *Food Politics,* 298–316.

60. Roberts and Schlenker, "World Supply and Demand"; Cassman, "Ecological Intensification."

61. The flexibility of this system can be illustrated by comparing CSM with a very different product: the 1960s slimming food, Metrecal, which had the same basic ingredients. In Metrecal, corn, soy, and milk were packaged for losing weight; in CSM, they were packaged for gaining weight. The similarity between the two products even led some humanitarian agencies to distribute Metrecal as a famine food. See Melvin Myers to Janet Lacey, 21 June 1968, CA/C/13, Christian Aid Archive, SOAS Library, University of London.

62. "Feeding the World's Hungry Millions: How It Will Mean Billions for US Business," *Forbes,* March 1, 1966, 19–26. See also Paddock, *Famine,* 187. Shlomo Reutlinger, "Value of PL480."

63. F. Belair, "Johnson Calls for a 5-Year 'Food for Freedom' Program," *New York Times,* Feb 11, 1966. See also Marchione, "Foods Provided," 2106.

64. George, *How the Other Half Dies,* 197.

65. Ahlberg, *Transplanting the Great Society,* 92.

66. James Nagle, "Commodities: Soybean and Wheat Futures Rally," *New York Times,* March 31, 1966. See also Amstutz, Daniel, "Wheat And Food For Peace: An Exporter's Viewpoint" (presentation, Fifth National Conference On Wheat Utilization Research, Fargo, North Dakota, November 1–3, 1967).

67. Advertisement for the new Forbes issue, *New York Times,* 27 Feb and 5 March 1966. See also Marchione, "Foods Provided"; Ahlberg, *Transplanting the Great Society*, 92; Ball and Johnson, "Political, Economic, and Humanitarian Motivations."

68. "Feeding the World's Hungry Millions: How It Will Mean Billions for US Business," *Forbes,* March 1, 1966.

69. "Feeding the World's Hungry Millions: How It Will Mean Billions for US Business," *Forbes,* March 1, 1966. See also "Excerpts From Johnson's Foreign Aid Message," *New York Times,* Feb 2, 1966; Paddock, *Famine,* 191–201.

70. Praed, "American Dilemma," 4.

71. Praed, "American Dilemma," 4.

72. Jelliffe, "Commerciogenic Malnutrition: Time For a Dialogue?" 56.

73. Jelliffe, "Impact of the Food Industry."

74. Jelliffe, "Commerciogenic Malnutrition?" 200.

75. Chetley, *Baby Killer Scandal,* 41.

76. Rabinow, *French Modern,* 320–57.

77. Rabinow, "On the Archaeology of Late Modernity," 402. See also Walker, "Institutional Audience and Architectural Style," 146.

78. DiBattista and McDiarmid, *High and Low Moderns*; Potter and Trotter, "Low Modernism."

79. Eagleton, *Against the Grain,* 140. See also Adamson, *Embattled Avant-Gardes.* For a contrasting view, see Huyssen, *After the Great Divide.*

80. Gilbert, "Low Modernism." See also Miller, *Misalliance,* 58–59, 67–80.

81. McLaren, "Great Protein Fiasco," 93.

82. McLaren, "Great Protein Fiasco," 95. As one expert put it later, when you cure a headache with aspirin, would you ever say that the cause was an aspirin deficiency? Waterlow, *Protein-Energy Malnutrition,* 4. See also Golden, "Development of Concepts of Malnutrition," 2118.

83. See, for example, Gillespie and Harris, "How Nutrition Improves," 4–5.

84. Waterlow, *Protein-Energy Malnutrition,* 4. See also Carpenter, *Protein and Energy,* 198.

85. Brock and Hansen, "Protein Requirement," 713. See also Carpenter, *Protein and Energy*, 198.

86. Williams, "On That Fiasco," 794. See also McLaren, "Great Protein Fiasco Revisited," 464. Diener, "Humanism and Science," 13–20; Newman, "Case of Protein-Energy Malnutrition."

87. Williams, "On That Fiasco," 794.

88. McLaren, "Great Protein Fiasco," 94. See also Waterlow and Payne, "Protein Gap," 113, 117; Ruxin, "United Nations Protein Advisory Group," 159.

89. McLaren, "Great Protein Fiasco," 94. See also McLaren, "Great Protein Fiasco Revisited," 464.

90. Popkin and Latham, "Limitations and Dangers," 1017.

91. Muller, "Baby Killer." The German translation was published by the Bern Third World Action Group and entitled *Nestlé Tötet Babys* (Bern: Arbeitsgruppe Dritte Welt Bern, 1974). See also Hugh Geach, "The Baby Food Tragedy," *New Internationalist*, August 6, 1973. Problems with infant formula had been raised many years earlier by Cicely Williams. See Williams, "Milk and Murder"; Valenze, *Milk*, 281. For more on the 1970s campaign, see Sasson, "Milking the Third World?"; Baumslag and Michels, *Milk, Money, and Madness*; Richter, *Holding Corporations Accountable*, 44–59; Chetley, *Politics of Baby Foods*.

92. George, *How the Other Half Dies*, 15.

93. Tudge, *Famine Business*; Tudge, "Food for the Unthinking."

94. Tudge, "Food for the Unthinking," 15.

95. Tudge, "Food for the Unthinking," 15–16.

CHAPTER 10. SMALL-SCALE DEVICES AND THE LOW MODERNIST LEGACY

1. Jelliffe, *Assessment of Nutritional Status*, 160.

2. Glasman, "Measuring Malnutrition," 21.

3. McLaren, "Great Protein Fiasco," 95.

4. Bigwood, *Guiding Principles*; Glasman, "Measuring Malnutrition"; Jelliffe, *Assessment of Nutritional Status*. When Bigwood included these measurements as part of his handbook in the 1930s he considered it as a way to survey *groups* of people; Jelliffe's 1960s handbook, however, applied it to individual assessment. Glasman identifies the use of MUAC in Jamaica as an important precursor.

5. Jelliffe and Jelliffe, "Arm Circumference as a Public Health Index," 182; Standard, Wills, and Waterlow, "Indirect Indicators of Muscle Mass."

6. Davis, "Epidemiology of Famine," 359.

7. Jelliffe, *Assessment of Nutritional Status*, 70–71. Named after Alphonse Bertillon, *bertillonage* involved comparing the heads of convicted criminals. See Rafter, *Origins of Criminology*, 220–35; Beirne, *Inventing Criminology*, 65–110. For more on the colonial origins of anthropometry, see Caspari, "From Types to Populations"; Lindqvist, *Skull Measurer's Mistake*.

8. McLaren and Kanawati, "Somatic Quotient."

9. Zerfas, "Insertion Tape."

10. Alternatives to the insertion mechanism included the "Shakir string" and the "anthropometric Quipu," which were based on a thin piece of string rather than measuring tape. These, however, were hard to measure in standard units and often became stretched and distorted. See Shakir and Morley, "Measuring Malnutrition."

11. Morley, "Prevention of Protein-Calorie Deficiency." In other words, the traffic light system was first designed as a preventative measure, when monitoring a single child's growth over time, rather than in nutritional screening. It was later reapplied.

12. Shakir, "Surveillance"; Shakir and Morley, "Measuring Malnutrition"; Glasman, "Measuring Malnutrition," 32–33.

13. Ramachandran et al., "Limitations of Film Strip." See also Jelliffe and Jelliffe, "Quipu"; Laugesen, "Child's Bangle." A comprehensive summary of MUAC methods can be found in Jelliffe and Jelliffe, *Community Nutritional Assessment*, 91–103.

14. Glasman, "Measuring Malnutrition," 32.

15. "Safe: Design Takes on Risk," exhibition at the Museum of Modern Art in New York, October 16, 2005, until January 2, 2006.

16. Berg and Austin, "Nutrition Policies and Programmes," 305.

17. Berg and Austin, "Nutrition Policies and Programmes," 304–5; Levinson, "Vital to the Creation," 26; Berg, Scrimshaw, and Call, *Nutrition, National Development, and Planning*. For a comprehensive genealogy and critique, see Escobar, *Encountering Development*, 113–20.

18. World Bank, *Learning from World Bank History*, 11.

19. Gillespie, McLachlan, and Shrimpton, *Combating Malnutrition*, 102.

20. Perhaps the founding document in this approach was Berg, *The Nutrition Factor*. His concern was that nutrition had become a narrow and technical issue, the exclusive domain of nutritionists and clinicians. For context, see Levinson, "Vital to the Creation"; Gillespie, McLachlan, and Shrimpton, *Combating Malnutrition*, 81.

21. United States Agency for International Development, *Planning National Nutrition Programs*; Gillespie, McLachlan, and Shrimpton, *Combating Malnutrition*, 102–3; Joy and Payne, *Nutrition and National Development*; Payne, "Nutrition Planning."

22. Field, "Multisectoral Nutrition Planning," 20.

23. McLaren, "Nutrition Planning," 742; Field, "Multisectoral Nutrition Planning," 20. For further criticisms of this movement, see Harriss and Payne, "Magic Bullets"; Field, "Soft Underbelly." For a rejoinder, see Berg, "Nutrition Planning Is Alive and Well," 365.

24. Harriss and Payne, "Magic Bullets," 313–14.

25. For an illustration of the new social nutrition movement, see McKenzie, "What Is Social Nutrition?"; Harriss and Payne, "Magic Bullets." For analysis, see Escobar, *Encountering Development*, 146–53.

26. Gillespie, McLachlan and Shrimpton, *Combating Malnutrition*, 103–6; Kimura, *Hidden Hunger*, 29. See also Levinson and McLachlan, "How Did We Get Here?"; Jonsson, "Rise and Fall of Paradigms"; Gillespie and Harris, "How Nutrition Improves"; World Bank, *Learning from World Bank History*; Golden, "Development of Concepts of Malnutrition."

27. Underwood and Smitasiri, "Micronutrient Malnutrition"; Underwood, "Vitamin A Deficiency Disorders"; Kimura, *Hidden Hunger*.

28. Lusty and Diskett, *Selective Feeding Programmes*.

29. Field, "Multisectoral Nutrition Planning: A Post-Mortem"; Berg, "Nutrition Planning Is Alive and Well, Thank You."

30. Hodge, "Hidden Hunger," 36.

31. Longhurst, *Global Leadership for Nutrition*, 37–38. The United Nations Standing Committee on Nutrition (SCN) was formerly known as the UN Sub-Committee on Nutrition, and it emerged from the Protein Advisory Group of the 1960s. The changing name and activity of this body says a lot about the decline of grand paradigms and the rise of low modernism.

32. Longhurst, *Global Leadership for Nutrition*, 33–38; Gillespie, McLachlan, and Shrimpton, *Combating Malnutrition*, 95.

33. The conference was held at the WHO in Geneva on October 10–12, 1988. The proceedings were published in the American Journal of Clinical Nutrition 50, no. 3 (1989):

565–705. Proceedings of the 1990 workshop were written up as Gillespie, Kevany, and Mason, *Controlling Iron Deficiency*.

34. Sommer, "Vitamin A Deficiency"; Sommer, Katz, and Tarwotjo, "Increased Risk"; Sommer et al., "Impact of Vitamin A Supplementation." An influential meta-analysis was written up in Beaton et al., "Vitamin A Supplementation."

35. Kimura, *Hidden Hunger*, 27–28.

36. Underwood, "Overcoming Micronutrient Deficiencies," 356; Gillespie, McLachlan, and Shrimpton, *Combating Malnutrition*, 95; Kimura, *Hidden Hunger*, 19–21. Micronutrient Initiative was later rechristened "Nutrition International."

37. Harriss and Payne, "Magic Bullets," 313. See also McKenzie, "What is Social Nutrition?"; Escobar, *Encountering Development*, 146–53. These more radical critiques reemerged in the 1990s, rebranded as Public Nutrition. See Mason et al., "Public Nutrition."

38. Jonsson, "Rise and Fall of Paradigms," 144.

39. Gillespie, McLachlan and Shrimpton, *Combating Malnutrition*, 97.

40. Zlotkin et al., "Treatment of Anemia"; Schauer and Zlotkin, "Home Fortification with Micronutrient Sprinkles."

41. Prahalad, *Fortune at the Bottom of the Pyramid*, 4, 11, 29. The idea of "bottom of the pyramid" interventions is for companies and entrepreneurs to tap into the 4 billion consumers living on less than two dollars per day. See also Elyachar, "Next Practices"; Cross and Street, "Anthropology at the Bottom of the Pyramid."

42. Andrew Rice, "The Peanut Solution," *New York Times*, September 5, 2010; Michael Wines, "Hope for Hungry Children, Arriving in a Foil Packet," *New York Times*, August 8, 2005; Jeffrey Sachs, "Saying 'Nuts' to Hunger," *Huffington Post*, September 6, 2010; Andre Briend, interview by Ian Simpson, "Peanut Butter for Malnourished Children," World Health Organization Media Centre, October 22, 2007.

43. After first tests in Belsen the basic idea of therapeutic, sweetened, fortified milk was refined and formalized in Biafra, and as Michael Golden put it, as late as the 1990s "the humanitarian movement largely used the methods that were developed empirically during the Biafran war." Golden, "Development of Concepts," 2121.

44. In situations of dire poverty and numerous children it was particularly difficult for families to come to a clinic with their malnourished relative and stay for the many days required for recovery. Very often, the family was already on the breadline: crops needed harvesting, money needed to be earned, and other children needed looking after. Since clinics were often in large towns, where infrastructure was good and electricity more reliable, they were a long way from remote areas, where malnutrition could be found. Not surprisingly, many parents with malnourished children were forced to withdraw their children and return to their homes to make ends meet, which made default rates very high and survival rates very low. Clinics and therapeutic milk are now less common, but they are still used for the most malnourished as well as people with medical complications. For some recent medical protocols, see Médecins Sans Frontières, *Clinical Guidelines*, 42–43.

45. Tim Anderson, "André Briend," Science Heroes, accessed 21, 2019, http://www.scienceheroes.com/article&id=148. See also Ian Simpson, "Peanut Butter for Malnourished Children: Interview with André Briend," World Health Organization Media Centre, October 22, 2007. There was not really a "eureka moment": Briend had long been experimenting with solid therapeutic foods and had slowly realized that a peanut paste could be produced at an affordable price. For more, see Scott-Smith, "Sticky Technologies," 14–15.

46. Chaparro and Dewey, "Use of Lipid-Based Nutrient Supplements."

47. There were two main formulae developed by Golden: F-100 and F-75, whose numbers indicated the quantity of kilocalories contained in 100ml of fluid. One humanitarian nutritionist recalled how, before the premix, the standard approach involved "mixing dry

skimmed milk with oil and sugar" onsite, which left "the oil floating on the surface" in a very unattractive manner. See Valerie Captier, "New Approaches to Nutrition," *Dialogue 6*, published by Médecins Sans Frontières, 2007.

48. André Briend in discussion with the author, June 15, 2016. Nutriset was founded in 1986 to find new solutions for humanitarian nutrition and by the early 1990s the company was already manufacturing sachets of Golden's F-100 formula. See also Enserink, "Peanut Butter Debate," 36–38.

49. As Peter Redfield put it, this was a "microworld" of humanitarian design. See Redfield, "Fluid Technologies."

50. Andrew Rice, "The Peanut Solution," *New York Times*, September 5, 2010.

51. Briend et al., "Ready-to-Use Therapeutic Food"; Tectonidis, "Crisis in Niger"; Linneman at al., "Large-Scale Operational Study."

52. "Community-Based Management of Acute Malnutrition: a Joint Statement," Geneva: World Health Organization, World Food Programme, United Nations System Standing Committee on Nutrition, and United Nations Children's Fund, May 2007.

53. As a small, family-run company, Nutriset designed the patent to prevent large multinational food corporations from undercutting it. The patent is registered at WIPO as "High Energy Complete Food or Nutritional Supplement, Method for Preparing Same and Uses Thereof," patent number WO2002034077.

54. Tido von Schoen-Angerer to Isabelle Lescanne, Campaign for Access to Essential Medicines, Médecins Sans Frontières International, Geneva, November 13, 2009. Enserink, "Peanut Butter Debate"; Scott-Smith, "Sticky Technologies." The lawsuit was brought by Breedlove Foods and the Mama Cares Foundation at the U.S District Court of Columbia.

55. "Making Peanut Butter Gets Stickier," *IRIN News*, November 11, 2009.

56. Street, "Food as Pharma."

57. Doyon, "India." These criticisms also appeared in other places, such as in Niger, where the dominance of Plumpy'nut was described by one author as a "medical coup." See Jézéquel, "Staging a 'Medical Coup'?"

58. Prahalad, *Fortune*, 169–206. The phrase 'doing well by doing good' has become something of a cliché in corporate social responsibility, and appears on page 2 of Prahalad's book.

59. For a more critical reflection on the private sector's logistical powers, see Hopgood, "Saying 'No' to Wal-mart."

60. In 2005 these companies came together with others in an even more business-friendly organization called the Business Alliance for Food Fortification (BAFF).

61. Powell, "Childhood Obesity, Corporate Philanthropy."

62. Street, "Food as Pharma," 361. See also Pentecost and Cousins, "Temporary as the Future."

63. Two good examples are the Horlicks Nutritional Academy, founded in 2011 by GlaxoSmith Kline, and the Beverage Institute for Health and Wellness, founded in 2004 by Coca Cola. Street, "Food as Pharma," 367; Nestle, *Food Politics*, 173–294.

64. Kimura, *Hidden Hunger*, 5–6.

65. Duffield, "Challenging Environments"; Mark Duffield, "How Did We Become Unprepared? From Modernist to Postmodernist Conceptions of Disaster" (keynote lecture, Humanitarianism: Past, Present and Future conference, University of Manchester, November 10, 2012).

66. Scott-Smith, "Paradoxes of Resilience."

67. Duffield, *Post-Humanitarianism*; Chouliaraki, "Post-Humanitarianism"; Chouliaraki, *Ironic Spectator*; Chandler, *Resilience*; Hopgood and Vinjamuri, "Faith in Markets."

68. Redfield, "Fluid Technologies."

69. Redfield, "Bioexpectations"; Cross, "The 100th Object."

70. Scott-Smith, "Fetishism of Humanitarian Objects," 916–20; Redfield, "Bioexpectations," 166–70.

71. Scott-Smith, "Humanitarian Neophilia."

72. Joseph, "Resilience as Embedded Neoliberalism"; Corry, "From Defense to Resilience"; Dean, "Rethinking Neoliberalism"; Evans and Reid. *Resilient Life.*

CONCLUSION

1. *Nutrition and Relief Work*, 19. See also Wilson, *Advice to Relief Workers*, 14.

2. For comparison, see Biehl, "Pharmaceuticalization"; Petryna, Lakoff, and Kleinman, *Global Pharmaceuticals.*

3. Brock and Autret, *Kwashiorkor in Africa*, 72. *International Action to Avert the Impending Protein Crisis*, 5.

4. Geertz, "Stir Crazy," 6.

5. Polman, *War Games;* Maren, *Road to Hell.*

6. Berman, *All That Is Solid*, 13.

7. Berman, *All That Is Solid*, 15.

8. Berman, *All That Is Solid*, 40.

9. Berman, *All That Is Solid*, 13, 345.

10. Berman, *All That Is Solid*, 346.

11. Vaux, *Selfish Altruist*, 7–8. This theme reappears in other memoirs of aid workers. For a good recent example, see Maskalyk, *Six Months in Sudan,* 35. For a historical example, see Nightingale, *Notes on Nursing,* 74.

12. Scott, *Seeing Like a State,* 88.

13. For a more critical look at humanitarian universalism, see Benton, "African Expatriates and Race"; Benton, "Risky Business"; Fassin, "Humanitarianism as a Politics of Life"; Ticktin, "Where Ethics and Politics Meet."

14. Cowan, Dembour and Wilson, *Culture and Rights*; Parekh, *Rethinking Multiculturalism.*

15. Hacking, *Taming of Chance*, 161, 163.

16. Illich, *Medical Nemesis.* See also Illich, "The Medicalization of Life."

17. Weindling, "Medicine and Modernization," 277; Lupton, "Foucault and the Medicalization Critique"; Lantz, Lichtenstein, and Pollack, "Health Policy Approaches." There are "soft" and "hard" definitions of medicalization; Paul Weindling describes the process relatively neutrally as "the extension of rational, scientific values in medicine to a wide range of social activities."

18. Berman, *All That Is Solid*, 15.

19. Clarkson, *Soup*, 49.

20. Sphere, *Humanitarian Charter and Minimum Standards*, 184–85.

21. Sacks, *Anthropologist on Mars*, 1. William Ostler's original version of the phrase was: "It is much more important to know what sort of a patient has a disease than what sort of a disease a patient has."

22. Scott-Smith, "Paradoxes of Resilience." Initiatives include Disaster Risk Reduction (DRR), Disaster Mitigation and Preparedness (DMP), Linking Relief, Rehabilitation and Development (LRRD), and Resilience.

23. Golden, "Development of Concepts of Malnutrition," 2121; Guetzkow and Bowman, *Men and Hunger.*

24. Baily, "Fiddling While Children Starve?" 1490. Even now, the causes of kwashiorkor are not very well understood. See Krawinkel, "Kwashiorkor"; Golden, "Oedematous Malnutrition."

25. Barnett, *Empire of Humanity,* 12. Michael Barnett wrote that "humanitarianism is partly paternalism," and that "a world without paternalism might be a world without an ethics of care."

26. Levenstein, *Revolution at the Table,* 55.

27. Pollan, *Omnivore's Dilemma;* Pollan, *In Defence of Food;* Pollan, *Food Rules.*

28. Pollan, *Food Rules,* 41–88.

Bibliography

ARCHIVES

Christian Aid Archive. School of Oriental and African Studies (SOAS) Library, University of London.
Colonial Office, Records. National Archives, London.
Food and Agricultural Organization Archives, David Lubin Memorial Library, Rome.
Foreign Office, Records. National Archives, London.
Friends Relief Service Archive, Library of the Religious Society of Friends in Britain, London.
League of Nations Archive. United Nations Library, Geneva.
Oxfam Archive. Bodleian Library, Oxford.
Ministry of Food, Records, National Archives, London.
Nutrition Collection. London School of Hygiene and Tropical Medicine Archives, University of London.
Royal Army Medical Corps Muniments Collection. Wellcome Library, London.
Save the Children Fund Archive. Cadbury Research Library, University of Birmingham.
Torry Research Station, Records. National Archives, London
United Nations Relief and Rehabilitation Administration Archive. United Nations Archives and Record Management, New York.
Weis Archive. Bodleian Library, Oxford.

WORKS CITED

Abbott, Grace. *From Relief to Social Security: The Development of the New Public Welfare Services and their Administration.* Chicago: University of Chicago Press, 1941.
Ackerknecht, Erwin H. *Medicine at the Paris Hospital, 1794–1848.* Baltimore: Johns Hopkins Press, 1967.
Adamson, Walter. *Embattled Avant-Gardes: Modernism's Resistance to Commodity Culture in Europe.* Berkeley: University of California Press, 2007.
Agier, Michel. *Managing the Undesirables: Refugee Camps and Humanitarian Government.* Cambridge: Polity, 2011.
Ahlberg, Kristin. *Transplanting the Great Society: Lyndon Johnson and Food for Peace.* London: University of Missouri Press, 2008.
Albala, Ken. *Cooking in Europe, 1250–1650.* Westport, CT: Greenwood Press, 2006.
American Federation of Labor. *Some Reasons for Chinese Exclusion. Meat vs. Rice. American Manhood against Asiatic Coolieism. Which Shall Survive?* Washington, DC: Government Print Office, 1902.
Anstruther, Ian. *The Scandal of the Andover Workhouse.* London: Bles, 1973.
Apfelbaum, Emil. "Pathophysiology of the Circulatory System in Hunger Disease." In *Hunger Disease: Studies by the Jewish Physicians in the Warsaw Ghetto*, 125–60. New York: Wiley, 1979.

Apple, Rima. *Mothers and Medicine: A Social History of Infant Feeding, 1890–1950.* Madison: University of Wisconsin Press, 1987.

Apple, Rima. "Vitamins and the War: Nutrition, Commerce, and Patriotism in the United States During the Second World War." In *Food, Science, Policy and Regulation in the Twentieth Century: International and Comparative Perspectives,* edited by David Smith and Jim Phillips, 135–49. London: Routledge, 2000.

Appleby, Andrew. *Famine in Tudor and Stuart England.* Stanford: Stanford University Press, 1978.

Armstrong, David. "Bodies of Knowledge/Knowledge of Bodies." In *Reassessing Foucault: Power, Medicine, and the Body,* edited by Colin Jones and Roy Porter, 17–28. London: Routledge, 1994.

Armstrong, David. *Political Anatomy of the Body: Medical Knowledge in Britain in the Twentieth Century.* Cambridge: Cambridge University Press, 1983.

Arndt, Heinz Wolfgang. *Economic Development: The History of an Idea.* Chicago: University of Chicago Press, 1987.

Arnold, David. "British India and the 'Beriberi' Problem, 1798–1942." *Medical History* 54, no. 3 (2010): 295–314.

Arnold, David. *Colonizing the Body: State Medicine and Epidemic Disease in Nineteenth-Century India.* Berkeley: University of California Press, 1993.

Arnold, David. "The 'Discovery' of Malnutrition and Diet in Colonial India." *Indian Economic and Social History Review* 31, no. 1 (1994): 1–26.

Aronson, Naomi. "Nutrition as a Social Problem: A Case Study of Entrepreneurial Strategy in Science." *Social Problems* 29, no. 5 (1982): 474–87.

Aronson, Naomi. "Social Definitions of Entitlement: Food Needs 1885–1920." *Media, Culture and Society* 4, no. 1 (1982): 51–61.

Asher, Richard. *Talking Sense: A Collection of Papers.* London: Pitman Medical, 1972.

Atkins, Peter. *Liquid Materialities: A History of Milk, Science, and the Law.* Farnham, UK: Ashgate, 2010.

Atkinson, Edward. "The Art of Cooking." *Popular Science Monthly* 36 (1889): 1–14.

Atkinson, Edward. "The Food Question in America and Europe." *Century Magazine* 33 (1886): 238–48.

Atwater, Wilbur. "Chemistry of Foods and Nutrition." *Century Magazine* 34 (1887): 59–74.

Atwater, Wilbur. "How Food Nourishes the Body." *Century Magazine* 34 (1887): 237–52.

Atwater, Wilbur. "Pecuniary Economy of Food." *Century Magazine* 35 (1888): 437–46.

Averbeck, Robin Marie. "'Want in the Midst of Plenty': Social Science, Poverty, and the Limits of Liberalism." Ph.D. diss., University of California Davis, 2013.

Aykroyd, Wallace Ruddell. "Obituary Notice: Major-General Robert McCarrison." *British Journal of Nutrition* 14 (1960): 413–18.

Baily, Guy. "Fiddling While Children Starve?" *The Lancet* 342, no. 8885 (1993): 1490.

Baker, John, and Jens-Peter Green. *Julian Huxley, Scientist and World Citizen, 1887 to 1975: A Biographical Memoir.* Paris: Unesco, 1978.

Balinska, Marta Aleksandra. *For the Good of Humanity: Ludwik Rajchman, Medical Statesman.* Budapest: Central European University Press, 1998.

Ball, Richard, and Christopher Johnson. "Political, Economic, and Humanitarian Motivations for PL480 Food Aid: Evidence from Africa." *Economic Development and Cultural Change* 44, no. 3 (1996): 515–37.

Bamberg, James. *British Petroleum and Global Oil, 1950–1975: The Challenge of Nationalism.* Cambridge: Cambridge University Press, 1982.

Banton, Michael. *The International Politics of Race.* Cambridge: Polity Press, 2002.

Bardgett, Suzanne, and David Cesarani, eds. *Belsen 1945: New Historical Perspectives.* Edgware, UK: Vallentine Mitchell, 2006.

Barkan, Elazar. *The Retreat of Scientific Racism: Changing Concepts of Race in Britain and the United States between the World Wars.* Cambridge: Cambridge University Press, 1992.

Barker, Theodore, Derek Oddy, and John Yudkin. *The Dietary Surveys of Dr. Edward Smith, 1862–63: A New Assessment.* London: Staples Press, 1970.

Barnett, Michael. *Empire of Humanity: A History of Humanitarianism.* Ithaca: Cornell University Press, 2011.

Barnett, Michael, and Thomas George Weiss. "Humanitarianism: A Brief History of the Present." In *Humanitarianism in Question: Politics, Power, Ethics*, edited by Michael Barnett and Thomas George Weiss, 1–49. Ithaca: Cornell University Press, 2008.

Barona, Josep. "Nutrition and Health: The International Context During the Inter-War Crisis." *Social History of Medicine* 21, no. 1 (2008): 87–105.

Barona, Josep. *The Problem of Nutrition: Experimental Science, Public Health, and Economy in Europe, 1914–1945.* Oxford: Peter Lang, 2010.

Barthes, Roland. *The Rustle of Language.* Oxford: Basil Blackwell, 1986.

Barton, Patricia. "Imperialism, Race, and Therapeutics: The Legacy of Medicalizing the 'Colonial Body.'" *Journal of Law, Medicine, and Ethics* 36, no. 3 (2008): 506–16.

Baumslag, Naomi, and Dia Michels. *Milk, Money, and Madness: The Culture and Politics of Breastfeeding.* London: Bergin & Garvey, 1995.

Beaton, George, Reynaldo Martorell, Kristan Aronson, and Barry Edmonston. "Vitamin A Supplementation and Child Morbidity and Mortality in Developing Countries." *Food and Nutrition Bulletin* 15 (1994): 282–89.

Beeton, Isabella Mary. *The Book of Household Management.* London, 1861.

Beirne, Piers. *Inventing Criminology: Essays on the Rise of Homo Criminalis.* Albany: State University of New York Press, 1993.

Belasco, Warren. "Algae Burgers for a Hungry World? The Rise and Fall of Chlorella Cuisine." *Technology and Culture* 38, no. 3 (1997): 608–34.

Belasco, Warren. *Appetite for Change: How the Counterculture Took on the Food Industry.* London: Cornell University Press, 2007.

Belasco, Warren. "Dietary Modernization." *Reviews in American History* 18, no. 2 (1990): 262–66.

Belasco, Warren. *Meals to Come: A History of the Future of Food.* London: University of California Press, 2006.

Beneke, William. "On Extractum Carnis. Recommended for Admission into the London Pharmacopoeia, as a Most Valuable Remedy in the Treatment of Disease." *The Lancet* 57, no. 1427 (1851): 6–8.

Benthall, Jonathan. *Disasters, Relief, and the Media.* London: I. B. Tauris, 1993.

Benton, Adia. "African Expatriates and Race in the Anthropology of Humanitarianism." *Critical African Studies* 8, no. 3 (2016): 266–77.

Benton, Adia. "Risky Business: Race, Nonequivalence, and the Humanitarian Politics of Life." *Visual Anthropology* 29, no. 2 (2016): 187–203.

Berg, Alan. *Famine Contained: Notes and Lessons from the Bihar Experience.* Washington, DC: Brookings Institution, 1971.

Berg, Alan. *The Nutrition Factor: Its Role in National Development.* Washington, DC: Brookings Institution, 1973.

Berg, Alan. "Nutrition Planning Is Alive and Well, Thank You." *Food Policy* 12, no. 4 (1987): 365–75.

Berg, Alan, and James Austin. "Nutrition Policies and Programmes: A Decade of Redirection." *Food Policy* 9, no. 4 (1984): 304–12.

Berg, Alan, Nevin Scrimshaw, and David Call. *Nutrition, National Development, and Planning: Proceedings of an International Conference Held at Cambridge, Massachusetts, October 19–21, 1971.* Cambridge: MIT Press, 1973.

Berman, Bruce. "Nationalism, Ethnicity, and Modernity: The Paradox of Mau Mau." *Canadian Journal of African Studies* 25, no. 2 (1991): 181–206.

Berman, Marshall. *All That Is Solid Melts into Air: The Experience of Modernity.* London: Verso, 1983.

Berman, Morris. *Social Change and Scientific Organization: The Royal Institution, 1799–1844.* London: Heinemann, 1978.

Berman, Paul. *Power and the Idealists: Or, the Passion of Joschka Fischer, and Its Aftermath.* New York: Norton, 2007.

Biehl, João Guilherme. "Pharmaceuticalization: AIDS Treatment and Global Health Politics." *Anthropological Quarterly* 80, no. 4 (2007): 1083–126.

Bigwood, Edouard Jean. *Guiding Principles for Studies on the Nutrition of Populations.* Geneva: League of Nations Health Organization, 1939.

Billig, Michael. *Learn to Write Badly: How to Succeed in the Social Sciences.* Cambridge: Cambridge University Press, 2013.

Black, Maggie. *A Cause for Our Times: Oxfam, the First 50 Years.* Oxford: Oxford University Press, 1992.

Black, Maggie. *Children First: The Story of Unicef, Past and Present.* Oxford: Oxford University Press, 1996.

Bloor, David. *Knowledge and Social Imagery.* Chicago: University of Chicago Press, 1991.

Boas, Franz. "Changes in the Bodily Form of Descendants of Immigrants." *American Anthropologist* 14, no. 3 (1912): 530–62.

Bohstedt, John. *The Politics of Provisions: Food Riots, Moral Economy, and Market Transition in England, C. 1550–1850.* The History of Retailing and Consumption. Farnham, UK: Ashgate, 2010.

Bohstedt, John. *Riots and Community Politics in England and Wales, 1790–1810.* Cambridge: Harvard University Press, 1983.

Bonarjee, P. D. *A Handbook of the Fighting Races of India.* Calcutta: Thacker, Spink & Company, 1899.

Boner, Charles. "Extract of Meat." *Popular Science Monthly* (1865): 295–98.

Borges, Jorge Luis. *Other Inquisitions, 1937–1952.* Translated by Ruth Simms. London: Souvenir Press, 1973.

Borgstrom, Georg. *Too Many: A Study of Earth's Biological Limitations.* New York: Macmillan, 1969.

Borgwardt, Elizabeth. *A New Deal for the World: America's Vision for Human Rights.* Cambridge: Belknap Press, 2005.

Borowy, Iris. *Coming to Terms with World Health: The League of Nations Health Organisation 1921–1946.* Frankfurt am Main: Lang, 2009.

Borowy, Iris. "Crisis as Opportunity: International Health Work During the Economic Depression." *Dynamis* 28 (2008): 29–51.

Borsook, Henry. "We Could Feed the World." *Engineering and Science* 12, no. 3 (1948): 7–9.

Bradley, Duane. *Count Rumford.* Princeton: Van Nostrand, 1967.

Brantley, Cynthia. "Kikuyu-Maasai Nutrition and Colonial Science: The Orr and Gilks Study in Late 1920s Kenya Revisited." *International Journal of African Historical Studies* 30, no. 1 (1997): 49–86.

Braude-Heller, Anna, Israel Rotbalsam, and Regina Elbinger. "Clinical Aspects of Hunger Disease in Children." In *Hunger Disease: Studies by the Jewish Physicians in the Warsaw Ghetto*, edited by Myron Winick, 45–68. New York: Wiley, 1979.

Briend, André, Radandi Lacsala, Claudine Prudhon, Béatrice Mounier, Yvonne Grellety, and Michael Golden. "Ready-to-Use Therapeutic Food for Treatment of Marasmus." *The Lancet* 353, no. 9166 (1999): 1767–68.

Brillat-Savarin, Jean Anthelme *The Physiology of Taste: Or, Meditations on Transcendental Gastronomy.* Translated and edited by M.F.K. Fisher. London: Random House, 2009.

Brock, W. H. *Justus Von Liebig: The Chemical Gatekeeper.* Cambridge: Cambridge University Press, 1997.

Brock, J. F., and M. Autret. *Kwashiorkor in Africa.* Geneva: World Health Organization, 1952.

Brock, J. F., and J. Hansen. "Protein Requirement." *The Lancet* 304, no. 7882 (1974): 712–14.

Brown, G. I. *Count Rumford: Scientist, Soldier, Statesman, Spy.* Stroud: Sutton, 1999.

Brown, Lester, and Erik Eckholm. *By Bread Alone.* Oxford: Pergamon, 1974.

Brown, Sanborn. *Count Rumford, Physicist Extraordinary.* London: Heinemann, 1964.

Brown, Sanborn. *Benjamin Thompson, Count Rumford.* Cambridge: MIT Press, 1979.

Brozek, J., S. Wells, and A. Keys. "Medical Aspects of Semi-starvation in Leningrad (Siege 1941–1942)." *American Review of Soviet Medicine* 4, no. 1 (1946): 70–86.

Bruder, Edith. *The Black Jews of Africa: History, Religion, Identity.* Oxford: Oxford University Press, 2008.

Bryan, Alex. *Healing the Wounds: Quaker Relief Work During World War Two and Its Aftermath.* London: Quaker Home Service, 1986.

Buchanan-Smith, Margie. *How the Sphere Project Came into Being: A Case Study of Policy-Making in the Humanitarian Aid Sector and the Relative Influence of Research.* London, Overseas Development Institute, 2003.

Bud, Robert. *The Uses of Life: A History of Biotechnology.* Cambridge: Cambridge University Press, 1993.

Bulmer, William, John Hatchard, and Thomas Becket. *The Reports of the Society for Bettering the Condition and Increasing the Comforts of the Poor.* London: Bulmer and Company, 1798.

Burchell, Graham, Colin Gordon, and Peter Miller, eds. *The Foucault Effect: Studies in Governmentality.* London: Harvester Wheatsheaf, 1991.

Burlew, John, ed. *Algal Culture: From Laboratory to Pilot Plant.* Washington, DC: Carnegie Institution, 1953.

Burnet, Etienné, and Wallace Ruddell Aykroyd. *Nutrition and Public Health.* Geneva: League of Nations, 1935.

Byers, M., S. H. Green, and Norman Wingate Pirie. "The Presentation of Leaf Protein on the Table—II." *International Journal of Food Sciences and Nutrition* 19, no. 2 (1965): 63–70.

Cabanes, Bruno. *The Great War and the Origins of Humanitarianism, 1918–1924.* Cambridge: Cambridge University Press, 2014.

Cadet de Vaux, Antoine-Alexis. *Mémoire Sur La Gelatine Des Os Et Son Application À L'économie Alimentaire, Privée Et Publique, Et Principalement À L'économie De L'homme Malade Et Indigent.* Paris: Marchant, 1792.

Calkins, Beverly. "Florence Nightingale: On Feeding an Army." *American Journal of Clinical Nutrition* 50, no. 6 (1989): 1260–65.

Callon, Michael, and Bruno Latour. "Unscrewing the Big Leviathan: How Actors Macro-Structure Reality and How Sociologists Help Them to Do So." In

Advances in Social Theory and Methodology, edited by Karin Knorr-Cetina and Aaron Victor Cicourel, 277–303. Boston: Routledge & Kegan Paul, 1981.

Campbell, Chloe. "Eugenics in Colonial Kenya." In *The Oxford Handbook of the History of Eugenics*, edited by Alison Bashford and Philippa Levine, 289–300. Oxford: Oxford University Press, 2010.

Campbell, Chloe. *Race and Empire: Eugenics in Colonial Kenya*. Manchester: Manchester University Press, 2007.

Cannon, Geoffrey. "The Rise and Fall of Dietetics and of Nutrition Science, 4000 BCE–2000 CE." *Public Health Nutrition* 8, no. 6 (2007): 701–5.

Carpenter, Kenneth. "Nutritional Studies in Victorian Prisons." *Journal of Nutrition* 136, no. 1 (2006): 1–8.

Carpenter, Kenneth. "Protein." In *The Cambridge World History of Food*, edited by Kenneth F. Kiple and Kriemhild Coneè Ornelas, 882–88. Cambridge: Cambridge University Press, 2000.

Carpenter, Kenneth. *Protein and Energy*. Cambridge: Cambridge University Press, 1994.

Carpenter, Kenneth. "The Work of Wallace Aykroyd: International Nutritionist and Author." *Journal of Nutrition* 137, no. 4 (2007): 873–78.

Caspari, Rachel. "From Types to Populations: A Century of Race, Physical Anthropology, and the American Anthropological Association." *American Anthropologist* 105, no. 1 (2003): 65–76.

Cassell, Eric. *The Healer's Art: A New Approach to the Doctor-Patient Relationship*. Harmondsworth, UK: Penguin, 1978.

Cassman, Kenneth. "Ecological Intensification of Cereal Production Systems: Yield Potential, Soil Quality, and Precision Agriculture." *Proceedings of the National Academy of Sciences* 96, no. 11 (1999): 5952–59.

Chandler, David. *From Kosovo to Kabul and Beyond: Human Rights and International Intervention*. London: Pluto Press, 2006.

Chandler, David. *Resilience: The Governance of Complexity*. London: Routledge, 2014.

Chandler, David. "The Road to Military Humanitarianism: How the Human Rights NGOs Shaped a New Humanitarian Agenda." *Human Rights Quarterly* 23, no. 3 (2001): 678–700.

Chaparro, Camila, and Kathryn Dewey. "Use of Lipid-Based Nutrient Supplements (LNS) to Improve the Nutrient Adequacy of General Food Distribution Rations for Vulnerable Sub-Groups in Emergency Settings." *Maternal and Child Nutrition* 6 (2010): 1–69.

Chapman, Carleton. "Edward Smith (?1818–1874), Physiologist, Human Ecologist, Reformer." *Journal of the History of Medicine and Allied Sciences* 22, no. 1 (1967): 1–26.

Chetley, Andrew. *The Baby Killer Scandal: A War on Want Investigation into the Promotion and Sale of Powdered Baby Milks in the Third World*. London: War on Want, 1979.

Chetley, Andrew. *The Politics of Baby Foods: Successful Challenges to an International Marketing Strategy*. Global Politics. London: Pinter, 1986.

Chevers, Norman. *A Commentary on the Diseases of India*. London: Churchill, 1886.

Chick, Harriette, and E. B. Slack. "Malted Foods for Babies: Trials with Young Rats." *The Lancet* 248, no. 6426 (1946): 601–3.

Chouliaraki, Lilie. *The Ironic Spectator: Solidarity in the Age of Post-Humanitarianism*. Cambridge: Polity, 2013.

Chouliaraki, Lilie. "Post-Humanitarianism: Humanitarian Communication Beyond a Politics of Pity." *International Journal of Cultural Studies* 13, no. 2 (2010): 107–26.

Clapp, Jennifer. *Hunger in the Balance: The New Politics of International Food Aid.* Ithaca: Cornell University Press, 2012.

Clark, Peter. *British Clubs and Societies 1580–1800: The Origins of an Associational World.* Oxford: Clarendon Press, 2000.

Clarkson, Janet. *Soup: A Global History.* Edible. London: Reaktion Books, 2010.

Clavin, Patricia. *Securing the World Economy: The Reinvention of the League of Nations, 1920–1946.* Oxford: Oxford University Press, 2013.

Cloke, Paul, and Mark Goodwin. "Conceptualizing Countryside Change: From Post-Fordism to Rural Structured Coherence." *Transactions of the Institute of British Geographers* 17, no. 3 (1992): 321–36.

Cobbett, William. "A Letter to the Luddites." *Cobbett's Weekly Political Register* 31, no. 22 (1816): 674–704.

Cohen, Gerald Daniel. "Between Relief and Politics: Refugee Humanitarianism in Occupied Germany 1945–1946." *Journal of Contemporary History* 43, no. 3 (2008): 437–49.

Cohen, Gerald Daniel. *In War's Wake: Europe's Displaced Persons in the Postwar Order.* Oxford Studies in International History. Oxford: Oxford University Press, 2012.

Collini, Stefan. *Public Moralists: Political Thought and Intellectual Life in Britain 1850–1930.* Oxford: Clarendon Press, 1991.

Collis, W. R. F. "Belsen Camp: A Preliminary Report." *British Medical Journal* 1, no. 4405 (1945): 814–16.

Colquhoun, Patrick. *An Account of a Meat and Soup Charity, Established in the Metropolis, in the Year 1797, with Observations Relative to the Situation of the Poor.* London: H. Fry, 1797.

Colquhoun, Patrick. *Suggestions Offered to the Consideration of the Public, and in Particular to the More Opulent Classes of the Community, for the Purpose of Reducing the Consumption of Bread Corn, and Relieving at the Same Time the Labouring People, by the Substitution of Other Cheap, Wholesome and Nourishing Food, and Especially by Means of Soup Establishments.* London: His Majesty's Press, 1800.

Colt, George Howe. *The Big House: A Century in the Life of an American Summer Home.* New York: Scribner, 2003.

Combs, G. "Development of a Supplementary Food Mixture (CSM) for Children." *Protein Advisory Group Bulletin* 7 (1967): 15–24.

Cook, Bessie. "The Nutritive Value of Waste-Grown Algae." *American Journal of Public Health and the Nations Health* 52, no. 2 (1962): 243–51.

Cook, Scott. "Production, Ecology and Economic Anthropology: Notes toward an Integrated Frame of Reference." *Social Science Information* 12, no. 1 (1973): 25–52.

Cooter, Roger. *The Cultural Meaning of Popular Science: Phrenology and the Organization of Consent in Nineteenth-Century Britain.* Cambridge: Cambridge University Press, 1984.

Cordell, R. F., and D. H. Forsdick. "Symposium: Commemoration of the Liberation of the Bergen-Belsen Concentration Camp and Medical Management of Disasters." *Journal of the Royal Army Medical Corps* 145 (1999): 28–30.

Corry, Olaf. "From Defense to Resilience: Environmental Security Beyond Neo-Liberalism." *International Political Sociology* 8, no. 3 (2014): 256–74.

Cousins, Mark, and Athar Hussain. *Michel Foucault.* London: Macmillan, 1984.

Coveney, John. *Food, Morals, and Meaning: The Pleasure and Anxiety of Eating.* London: Routledge, 2000.

Cowan, Jane, Marie-Bénédicte Dembour, and Richard Wilson, eds. *Culture and Rights: Anthropological Perspectives.* Cambridge: Cambridge University Press, 2001.

Cowan, Ruth. "Ellen Swallow Richards: Technology and Women." In *Technology in America: A History of Individuals and Ideas,* edited by Carroll W. Pursell, 142–50. Cambridge: MIT Press, 1990.

Cowen, Ruth. *Relish: The Extraordinary Life of Alexis Soyer, Victorian Celebrity Chef.* London: Phoenix, 2007.

Craddock, Sally. *Retired Except on Demand: The Life of Dr. Cicely Williams.* Oxford: Green College, 1983.

Critchell, James Troubridge. *A History of the Frozen Meat Trade: An Account of the Development and Present Day Methods of Preparation, Transport, and Marketing of Frozen and Chilled Meats.* London: Constable, 1912.

Cross, Jamie. "The 100th Object: Solar Lighting Technology and Humanitarian Goods." *Journal of Material Culture* 18, no. 4 (2013): 367–87.

Cross, Jamie, and Alice Street. "Anthropology at the Bottom of the Pyramid." *Anthropology Today* 25, no. 4 (2009): 4–9.

Cross, Maria, and Barbara MacDonald. *Nutrition in Institutions.* Chichester, UK: Wiley-Blackwell, 2009.

Crozier, Anna. *Practising Colonial Medicine: The Colonial Medical Service in British East Africa.* London: I. B. Tauris, 2007.

Cullather, Nick. "The Foreign Policy of the Calorie." *American Historical Review* 112, no. 2 (2007): 337–64.

Cullather, Nick. *The Hungry World: America's Cold War Battle against Poverty in Asia.* Cambridge: Harvard University Press, 2010.

Cunningham, Hugh, and Joanna Innes, eds. *Charity, Philanthropy, and Reform: From the 1690s to 1850.* Basingstoke: Macmillan, 1998.

Currell, Susan. "Introduction." In *Popular Eugenics: National Efficiency and American Mass Culture in the 1930s,* edited by Susan Currell and Christina Cogdell, 1–16. Athens, Ohio: Ohio University Press, 2006.

Dally, Ann. *Cicely: The Story of a Doctor.* London: Gollancz, 1968.

Darcy, James. "Locating Responsibility: The Sphere Humanitarian Charter and Its Rationale." *Disasters* 28, no. 2 (2004): 112–23.

Davis, Jennifer. *Defining Culinary Authority: The Transformation of Cooking in France, 1650–1830.* Baton Rouge: Louisiana State University Press, 2013.

Davis, John Herbert, and Ray A. Goldberg. *A Concept of Agribusiness.* Boston: Harvard University Graduate School of Business Administration, 1957.

Davis, Larry. "Epidemiology of Famine in the Nigerian Crisis: Rapid Evaluation of Malnutrition by Height and Arm Circumference in Large Populations." *American Journal of Clinical Nutrition* 24, no. 3 (1971): 358–64.

Davis, Lennard. *Enforcing Normalcy: Disability, Deafness, and the Body.* London: Verso, 1995.

Davis, Natalie Zemon. "The Possibilities of the Past." *Journal of Interdisciplinary History* 12, no. 2 (1981): 267–75.

Dean, Mitchell. *Governmentality: Power and Rule in Modern Society.* London: Sage, 1999.

Dean, Mitchell. "Rethinking Neoliberalism." *Journal of Sociology* 50, no. 2 (2014): 150–63.

Dean, Reginald Francis Alfred. "Treatment and Prevention of Kwashiorkor." *Bulletin of the World Health Organization* 9, no. 6 (1953): 767–83.

Debs, Eugene Victor. *Letters of Eugene V. Debs.* Edited by J. Robert Constantine. 3 vols. Urbana: University of Illinois Press, 1990.

DeMaeyer, E. M. "Processed Weaning Foods." In *Nutrition in Preventive Medicine: The Major Deficiency Syndromes, Epidemiology, and Approaches to Control,* edited by G. H. Beaton and J. M. Bengoa, 389–405. Geneva: WHO, 1976.

Deniker, Joseph. *The Races of Man: An Outline of Anthropology and Ethnography.* London: Walter Scott, 1900.

"Desiccated Stomach Substance." *British Medical Journal* 1, no. 4554 (1948): 759.

De St. Jorre, John. *The Nigerian Civil War.* London: Hodder and Stoughton, 1972.

De Waal, Alex. *Famine Crimes: Politics and the Disaster Relief Industry in Africa.* Oxford: James Currey, 1997.

Dexter, Patricia. "Requirements for Effective Fortification in Food Aid Programmes." In *Food Fortification: Technology and Quality Control.* Rome: FAO, 1995.

DiBattista, Maria, and Lucy McDiarmid, eds. *High and Low Moderns: Literature and Culture, 1889–1939.* Oxford: Oxford University Press, 1996.

Diener, Paul. "Humanism and Science in Cultural Anthropology: The Great Protein Fiasco." *Journal of Social Philosophy* 15, no. 1 (1984): 13–20.

Diener, Paul, Kurt Moore, and Robert Mutaw. "Meat, Markets, and Mechanical Materialism: The Great Protein Fiasco in Anthropology." *Dialectical Anthropology* 5, no. 3 (1980): 171–92.

Douty, Esther Morris. *America's First Woman Chemist: Ellen Richards.* New York: Messner, 1961.

Doyon, Stéphane. "India: The Expert and the Militant." In *Humanitarian Negotiations Revealed: The MSF Experience*, edited by Claire Magone, Michael Neuman, and Fabrice Weissman, 147–60. London: Hurst, 2011.

Dreyfus, Hubert, and Paul Rabinow. *Michel Foucault: Beyond Structuralism and Hermeneutics.* Brighton: Harvester, 1982.

Drummond, Jack Cecil. "The Nomenclature of the So-Called Accessory Food Factors (Vitamins)." *Biochemical Journal* 14, no. 5 (1920): 660–60.

Drummond, Jack Cecil, H. R. Sandstead, and G.C.E. Burber. *Malnutrition and Starvation in Western Netherlands.* 2 vols. The Hague: Allied Forces Supreme Headquarters Netherlands Mission, 1948.

Duffield, Mark. "Challenging Environments: Danger, Resilience, and the Aid Industry." *Security Dialogue* 43, no. 5 (2012): 475–92.

Duffield, Mark. *Post-Humanitarianism: Governing Precarity in the Digital World.* Cambridge: Polity, 2019.

Duffield, Mark. "Racism, Migration, and Development: The Foundations of Planetary Order." *Progress in Development Studies* 6, no. 1 (2006): 68–79.

DuPuis, Erna Melanie. *Dangerous Digestion: The Politics of American Dietary Advice.* Oakland: University of California Press, 2015.

Dwork, Deborah. *War Is Good for Babies and Other Young Children: A History of the Infant and Child Welfare Movement in England, 1898–1918.* London: Tavistock, 1987.

Eagleton, Terry. *Against the Grain: Essays 1975–1985.* London: Verso, 1986.

Earle, Rebecca. "Food, Colonialism, and the Quantum of Happiness." *History Workshop Journal* 84 (2017): 170–93.

Easton, J. C. "Charles Theodore of Bavaria and Count Rumford." *Journal of Modern History* 12, no. 2 (1940): 145–60.

Economy of an Institution, Established in Spitalfields, London, for the Purpose of Supplying the Poor with a Good Meat Soup, at One Penny Per Quart. London: Society for the Relief of the Industrious Poor, printed by W. Phillips, 1799.

Elden, Stuart. "Rethinking Governmentality." *Political Geography* 26, no. 1 (2007): 29–33.

Elias, Norbert. *The Civilizing Process.* Oxford: Basil Blackwell, 1978.

Elkins, Caroline. "The Struggle for Mau Mau Rehabilitation in Late Colonial Kenya." *International Journal of African Historical Studies* 33, no. 1 (2000): 25–57.

Ellenbogen, Josh. *Reasoned and Unreasoned Images: The Photography of Bertillon, Galton, and Marey*. University Park: Pennsylvania State University Press, 2012.

Elyachar, Julia. "Next Practices: Knowledge, Infrastructure, and Public Goods at the Bottom of the Pyramid." *Public Culture* 24, no. 1 (2012): 109–29.

Enserink, Martin. "The Peanut Butter Debate." *Science* 322, no. 5898 (2008): 36–38.

Escobar, Arturo. *Encountering Development: The Making and Unmaking of the Third World*. Princeton: Princeton University Press, 1995.

Evans, Brad, and Julian Reid. *Resilient Life: The Art of Living Dangerously*. Cambridge: Polity, 2014.

Ewald, François, and Alessandro Fontana. "Foreword." In *Society Must Be Defended: Lectures at the Collège De France, 1975–76*, by Michel Foucault, ix–xiv. London: Allen Lane, 2003.

Fajgenblat, Szymon. "Ocular Disturbances in Hunger Disease." In *Hunger Disease: Studies by the Jewish Physicians in the Warsaw Ghetto*, edited by Myron Winick, 197–206. New York: Wiley, 1979.

Fassin, Didier. *Humanitarian Reason: A Moral History of the Present*. Berkeley: University of California Press, 2012.

Fassin, Didier. "Humanitarianism as a Politics of Life." *Public Culture* 19, no. 1 (2007): 499–520.

Fast, Larisa. *Aid in Danger: The Perils and Promise of Humanitarianism*. Philadelphia: University of Pennsylvania Press, 2014.

Favez, Jean-Claude. *The Red Cross and the Holocaust*. Translated by John Fletcher and Beryl Fletcher. Cambridge: Cambridge University Press, 1999.

Fegan, Melissa. *Literature and the Irish Famine 1845–1919*. Oxford: Clarendon Press, 2002.

Fiddian-Qasmiyeh, Elena, and Patricia Daley. *Routledge Handbook of South-South Relations*. Abingdon: Routledge, 2019.

Fideler, Paul. "Poverty, Policy and Providence: The Tudors and the Poor." In *Political Thought and the Tudor Commonwealth: Deep Structure, Discourse and Disguise*, edited by Paul Fideler and Thomas Mayer, 199–228. London: Routledge, 1992.

Field, John Osgood. "Multisectoral Nutrition Planning: A Post-Mortem." *Food Policy* 12, no. 1 (1987): 15–28.

Field, John Osgood. "The Soft Underbelly of Applied Knowledge: Conceptual and Operational Problems in Nutrition Planning." *Food Policy* 2, no. 3 (1977): 228–39.

Fiering, Norman. "Irresistible Compassion: An Aspect of Eighteenth-Century Sympathy and Humanitarianism." *Journal of the History of Ideas* 37, no. 2 (1976): 195–218.

Final Report of the Mixed Committee of the League of Nations on the Relation of Nutrition to Health, Agriculture, and Economic Policy. Geneva: League of Nations, 1937.

Finlay, Mark. "Early Marketing of the Theory of Nutrition: The Science and Culture of Liebig's Extract of Meat." In *The Science and Culture of Nutrition, 1840–1940*, edited by Harmke Kamminga and Andrew Cunningham, 48–74. Amsterdam: Rodopi, 1995.

Finlay, Mark. "Quackery and Cookery: Justus Von Liebig's Extract of Meat and the Theory of Nutrition in the Victorian Age." *Bulletin of the History of Medicine* 66, no. 3 (1992): 404–18.

Fisher, A. W., and J. Burlew. "Nutritional Value of Microscopic Algae." In *Algal Culture*, edited by John Burlew, 303–10. Washington, DC: Carnegie Institution, 1953.

Fliederbaum, Julian. "Metabolic Changes in Hunger Disease." In *Hunger Disease: Studies by the Jewish Physicians in the Warsaw Ghetto*, edited by Myron Winick, 69–124. New York: Wiley, 1979.

Forsythe, David. *The Humanitarians: The International Committee of the Red Cross*. Cambridge: Cambridge University Press, 2005.

Foucault, Michel. *Abnormal: Lectures at the Collège De France 1974–1975*. Edited by Valerio Marchetti and Antonella Salomoni. Translated by Graham Burchell. London: Verso, 2003.

Foucault, Michel. *The Birth of Biopolitics: Lectures at the Collège De France, 1978–79*. Edited by Michel Senellart. Translated by Graham Burchell. Basingstoke: Palgrave Macmillan, 2008.

Foucault, Michel. *The Birth of the Clinic: An Archaeology of Medical Perception*. London: Tavistock, 1976.

Foucault, Michel. *The Hermeneutics of the Subject: Lectures at the Collège De France, 1981–1982*. Edited by Frédéric Gros. Translated by Graham Burchell. New York: Palgrave-Macmillan, 2005.

Foucault, Michel. *The History of Sexuality, I: The Will to Knowledge*. Translated by Robert Hurley. London: Penguin, 1979.

Foucault, Michel. *The History of Sexuality, II: The Use of Pleasure*. Translated by Robert Hurley. London: Penguin, 1986.

Foucault, Michel. "On Governmentality." *Ideology and Consciousness* 6 (1979): 5–22.

Foucault, Michel. *The Order of Things: An Archaeology of the Human Sciences*. London: Tavistock, 1970.

Foucault, Michel. *Power/Knowledge: Selected Interviews and Other Writings, 1972–1977*. Edited and Translated by Colin Gordon. Brighton: Harvester, 1980.

Foucault, Michel. *The Punitive Society: Lectures at the Collège De France 1972–1973*. Edited by Bernard Harcourt. Translated by Graham Burchell. New York: Palgrave Macmillan, 2015.

Foucault, Michel. *Security, Territory, Population: Lectures at the Collège De France, 1977–78*. Edited by Michel Senellart. Translated by Graham Burchell. Basingstoke: Palgrave Macmillan, 2007.

Foucault, Michel. *Society Must Be Defended: Lectures at the Collège De France, 1975–76*. Edited by Mauro Bertani and Alessandro Fontana. Translated by David Macey. New York: Picador, 2003.

Fowden, Leslie, and Stan Pierpoint. "Obituary: Norman Pirie (1907–97)." *Nature* 387, no. 6633 (1997): 560–60.

Frankenburg, Frances Rachel. *Vitamin Discoveries and Disasters: History, Science, and Controversies*. Oxford: Praeger, 2009.

Freidson, Eliot. *Profession of Medicine: A Study of the Sociology of Applied Knowledge*. New York: Dodd Mead, 1970.

Friedmann, Harriet. "The International Political Economy of Food: A Global Crisis." In *Food in the USA: A Reader*, edited by Carole Counihan, 325–46. New York: Routledge, 2002.

Friedmann, Harriet. "Remaking 'Traditions': How We Eat, What We Eat and the Changing Political Economy of Food." In *Women Working the NAFTA Food Chain: Women, Food and Globalization*, edited by Deborah Barndt, 35–60. Toronto: Sumach Press, 2004.

Friedmann, Harriet, and Philip McMichael. "Agriculture and the State System: The Rise and Decline of National Agricultures, 1870 to the Present." *Sociologia Ruralis* 29, no. 2 (1989): 93–117.

Fulford, Tim, Debbie Lee, and Peter J. Kitson. *Literature, Science, and Exploration in the Romantic Era: Bodies of Knowledge*. Cambridge: Cambridge University Press, 2004.

Gal, John, and Mimi Ajzenstadt. "The Long Path from a Soup Kitchen to a Welfare State in Israel." *Journal of Policy History* 25, no. 2 (2013): 240–63.

Gamgee, Arthur. "Are Yeast Extracts Justifiable as Substitutes for Extract of Meat?" *British Medical Journal* 2, no. 2486 (1908): 449–53.

Gans, Bruno. "A Biafran Relief Mission." *The Lancet* 293, no. 7596 (1969): 660–65.

Garza, Cutberto, and Mercedes de Onis. "Rationale for Developing a New International Growth Reference." *Food and Nutrition Bulletin* 25, no. 1 (2004): 5–14.

Geertz, Clifford. *Agricultural Involution: The Process of Ecological Change in Indonesia*. Berkeley: University of California Press, 1963.

Geertz, Clifford. "Stir Crazy: Review of Discipline and Punish." *New York Review of Books*, January 26, 1978.

George, Susan. *How the Other Half Dies: The Real Reasons for World Hunger*. Harmondsworth, UK: Penguin, 1986.

General Report of the Committee of Subscribers to a Fund for the Relief of the Industrious Poor, Resident in the Cities of London and Westminster, the Borough of Southwark and Several out Parishes of the Metropolis. London: J. Richardson, 1800.

Gentilcore, David. *Italy and the Potato: A History, 1550–2000*. London: Continuum, 2012.

Gibson, John, and William Evans. "Clinical Studies of the Blood Volume." *Journal of Clinical Investigation* 16, no. 3 (1937): 301–16.

Gibson, Mark. *The Feeding of Nations: Re-Defining Food Security for the 21st Century*. London: CRC Press, 2012.

Gibson, Rosalind. *Principles of Nutritional Assessment*. Oxford: Oxford University Press, 2005.

Gieryn, Thomas. "Boundary-Work and the Demarcation of Science from Non-Science: Strains and Interests in Professional Ideologies of Scientists." *American Sociological Review* 48, no. 6 (1983): 781–95.

Gilbert, B. B. "Health and Politics: The British Physical Deterioration Report of 1904." *Bulletin of the History of Medicine* 39 (1965): 143–53.

Gilbert, Jess. "Low Modernism and the Agrarian New Deal: A Different Kind of State." In *Fighting for the Farm: Rural America Transformed*, edited by Jane Adams, 129–46. Philadelphia: University of Pennsylvania Press, 2003.

Gilks, John. "A Medical Safari in a Native Reserve." *Kenya Medical Journal* 1 (1924): 270–74.

Gillespie, Stuart, and Jody Harris. "How Nutrition Improves: Half a Century of Understanding and Responding to the Problem of Malnutrition." In *Nourishing Millions: Stories of Change in Nutrition*, edited by Stuart Gillespie, Judith Hodge, Sivan Yosef, and Rajul Pandya-Lorch, 1–16. Washington, DC: IFPRI, 2016.

Gillespie, Stuart, J. Kevany, and J. Mason. *Controlling Iron Deficiency: A Report Based on an ACC/SCN Workshop*. Nutrition Policy Discussion Paper 9. Geneva: United Nations Sub-Committee on Nutrition, 1991.

Gillespie, Stuart, Milla McLachlan, and Roger Shrimpton. *Combating Malnutrition: Time to Act*. Washington, DC: World Bank, 2003.

Gillman, Joseph, and Theodore Gillman. *Perspectives in Human Malnutrition: A Contribution to the Biology of Disease from a Clinical and Pathological Study of Chronic Malnutrition and Pellagra in the African Interior*. New York: Grune and Stratton, 1951.

Gillman, Theodore, and Joseph Gillman. "Hepatic Damage in Infantile Pellagra and Its Response to Vitamin, Liver, and Dried Stomach Therapy." *Journal of the American Medical Association* 129, no. 1 (1945): 12–19.

Glasman, Joël. "Measuring Malnutrition: The History of the MUAC Tape and the Commensurability of Human Needs." *Humanity: An International Journal of Human Rights, Humanitarianism, and Development* 9, no. 1 (2018): 19–44.

Goldberg, Israel. *Single Cell Protein.* Berlin: Springer-Verlag, 1985.

Golden, Michael. "The Development of Concepts of Malnutrition." *Journal of Nutrition* 132, no. 7 (2002): 2117–22.

Golden, Michael. "Oedematous Malnutrition." *British Medical Bulletin* 54, no. 2 (1998): 433–44.

Goldman, Aaron. "Claud Cockburn, the Week and the 'Cliveden Set.'" *Journalism Quarterly* 49, no. 4 (1972): 721–28

Goodman, David, and Michael Redclift. *Refashioning Nature: Food, Ecology, and Culture.* London: Routledge, 1991.

Goody, Jack. *Cooking, Cuisine, and Class: A Study in Comparative Sociology.* Cambridge: Cambridge University Press, 1982.

Gorst, John E. "Physical Deterioration in Great Britain." *North American Review* 181, no. 584 (1905): 1–10.

Gorstein, J., K. Sullivan, R. Yip, M. de Onis, F. Trowbridge, P. Fajans, and G. Clugston. "Issues in the Assessment of Nutritional Status Using Anthropometry." *Bulletin of the World Health Organization* 72, no. 2 (1994): 273–83.

Greenberg, Arthur. *From Alchemy to Chemistry in Picture and Story.* Hoboken: Wiley, 2007.

Grenz, Stanley. *A Primer on Postmodernism.* Cambridge: W. B. Eerdmans, 1996.

Grossmann, Atina. "Grams, Calories, and Food: Languages of Victimization, Entitlement, and Human Rights in Occupied Germany, 1945–1949." *Central European History* 44, no. 1 (2011): 118–48.

Guest, John. *Broken Images: A Journal.* London: Green, 1949.

Guetzkow, Harold, and Paul Bowman. *Men and Hunger: A Psychological Manual for Relief Workers.* Elgin: Brethren, 1946.

Gutting, Gary. *Michel Foucault's Archaeology of Scientific Reason.* Cambridge: Cambridge University Press, 1989.

Guy, William A. "On Sufficient and Insufficient Dietaries, with Special Reference to the Dietaries of Prisoners." *Journal of the Statistical Society of London* 26, no. 3 (1863): 239–80.

Hacking, Ian. *The Social Construction of What?* Cambridge: Harvard University Press, 1999.

Hacking, Ian. *The Taming of Chance.* Cambridge: Cambridge University Press, 1990.

Hailey, William Malcolm. *An African Survey: A Study of Problems Arising in Africa South of the Sahara.* London: Oxford University Press, 1938.

Hammond, D. B. *Stories of Scientific Discovery.* Cambridge: Cambridge University Press, 1923.

Hanson, Clare. *Eugenics, Literature, and Culture in Post-War Britain.* New York: Routledge, 2013.

Haraway, Donna. "Remodelling the Human Way of Life: Sherwood Washburn and the New Physical Anthropology, 1950–1980." In *Bones, Bodies, Behavior: Essays on Biological Anthropology,* edited by George Stocking, 206–59. Madison: University of Wisconsin Press, 1988.

Hargrove, James. "History of the Calorie in Nutrition." *Journal of Nutrition* 136, no. 12 (December 1, 2006): 2957–61.

Harris, James Arthur, and Francis Gano Benedict. *A Biometric Study of Basal Metabolism in Man*. Washington, DC: Carnegie Institution, 1919.

Harrison, Brian. "Philanthropy and the Victorians." *Victorian Studies* 9, no. 4 (1966): 353–74.

Harrison, Paul, and Robin Palmer. *News out of Africa: Biafra to Band Aid*. London: Shipman, 1986.

Harriss, Barbara, and Philip Payne. "Magic Bullets and the Nutrition Agenda." *Food Policy* 9, no. 4 (1984): 313–16.

Hartley, Harold. "Origin of the Word 'Protein.'" *Nature* 168, no. 4267 (1951): 244–44.

Hasian, Marouf Arif. *The Rhetoric of Eugenics in Anglo-American Thought*. Athens: University of Georgia Press, 1996.

Haskell, Thomas. "Capitalism and the Origins of Humanitarian Sensibility." *American Historical Review* 90, no. 2 (1985): 339–61.

Heerten, Lasse. *The Biafran War and Postcolonial Humanitarianism: Spectacles of Suffering*. Cambridge: Cambridge University Press, 2017.

Heller, R. A. "'Let Them Eat Soup': Count Rumford and Napoleon Bonaparte." *Journal of Chemical Education* 53, no. 8 (1976): 499–500.

Helman, Cecil. "Disease Versus Illness in General Practice." *Journal of the Royal College of General Practitioners* 31, no. 230 (1981): 548–52.

Higgins, Margot. "Soy Products in National and International Programs: Field and Emergency Programs." *Journal of the American Oil Chemists' Society* 51 (1974): 143–45.

Hilton, James. *Lost Horizon*. London: Macmillan, 1933.

Himmelfarb, Gertrude. *Poverty and Compassion: The Moral Imagination of the Late Victorians*. New York: Knopf, 1991.

Hindle, Gordon Bradley. *Provision for the Relief of the Poor in Manchester, 1754–1826*. Manchester: Manchester University Press for the Chetham Society, 1975.

Hodge, Joseph Morgan. *Triumph of the Expert: Agrarian Doctrines of Development and the Legacies of British Colonialism*. Athens: Ohio University Press, 2007.

Hodge, Judith. "Hidden Hunger: Approaches to Tackling Micronutrient Deficiencies." In *Nourishing Millions: Stories of Change in Nutrition*, edited by Stuart Gillespie, Judith Hodge, Sivan Yosef, and Rajul Pandya-Lorch, 35–44. Washington, DC: International Food Policy Research Institute, 2016.

Hoffman, Peter, and Thomas Weiss. *Humanitarianism, War, and Politics: Solferino to Syria and Beyond*. Lanham: Rowman & Littlefield, 2017.

Hofstadter, Richard. *The American Political Tradition and the Men Who Made It*. New York: Vintage, 1948.

Hofvander, Yngve. *50 Years Of Ethio-Swedish Collaboration In Child Health And Nutrition: A Chronicle With Recollections And Personal Experiences*. Stockholm: SIDA, 2010.

Hofvander, Yngve. "North-South Collaboration: A Success Story." *Journal of Tropical Pediatrics* 57, no. 5 (2011): 323.

Holmes, Frederic Lawrence. *Claude Bernard and Animal Chemistry: The Emergence of a Scientist*. Cambridge: Harvard University Press, 1974.

Holmes, Frederic Lawrence. Introduction to *Animal Chemistry: Or, Organic Chemistry in Its Application to Physiology and Pathology*, by Justus Liebig. Edited by William Gregory. New York: Appleton, 1964.

Hopgood, Stephen. "Saying 'No' to Wal-Mart? Money and Morality in Professional Humanitarianism." In *Humanitarianism in Question: Politics, Power, Ethics*, edited by Michael Barnett and Thomas George Weiss, 98–123. Ithaca: Cornell University Press, 2008.

Hopgood, Stephen, and Leslie Vinjamuri. "Faith in Markets." In *Sacred Aid: Faith and Humanitarianism*, edited by Michael Barnett and Janice Gross Stein, 37–64. Oxford: Oxford University Press, 2012.

Horne, Gerald. *Mau Mau in Harlem? The U.S. and the Liberation of Kenya.* Basingstoke: Palgrave Macmillan, 2009.

Hornstein, Irwin. *Thriposha: Product and Program.* Washington, DC: USAID, 1986.

Horrocks, Sally. "The Business of Vitamins: Nutrition Science and the Food Industry in Inter-War Britain." In *The Science and Culture of Nutrition, 1840–1940,* edited by Harmke Kamminga and Andrew Cunningham, 235–58. Amsterdam: Rodopi, 1995.

Huehns, Ernst Reinhard. "Kwashiorkor." *British Medical Journal* 1, no. 4821 (1953): 1220.

Huff, Joyce. "Corporeal Economies: Work and Waste in Nineteenth-Century Constructions of Alimentation." In *Cultures of the Abdomen: Diet, Digestion, and Fat in the Modern World,* edited by Christopher Forth and Ana Carden-Coyne, 31–50. Basingstoke: Palgrave Macmillan, 2005.

Hughes, Glyn. "Medical Students and Belsen Concentration Camp." *The Lancet* 245, no. 6355 (1945): 769.

Hulme, Kathryn. *The Nun's Story.* London: Muller, 1956.

Hulme, Kathryn. *The Wild Place.* London: Frederick Muller, 1954.

Hussain, Shafqat. *Remoteness and Modernity: Transformation and Continuity in Northern Pakistan.* New Haven: Yale University Press, 2015.

Hutchinson, John. *Champions of Charity: War and the Rise of the Red Cross.* Boulder: Westview Press, 1996.

Hutchison, Robert, Vernon Henry Mottram, and Graham George. *Hutchison's Food and the Principles of Dietetics.* 9th ed. London: Edward Arnold, 1940.

Hutton, George. "International Programs Utilizing Soy Foods: The World Food Program." *Journal of the American Oil Chemists' Society* 51 (1974): 146–48.

Huxley, Elspeth. *Brave New Victuals: An Inquiry into Modern Food Production.* London: Chatto & Windus, 1965.

Huxley, Elspeth. *Nine Faces of Kenya.* London: Collins Harvill, 1990.

Huyssen, Andreas. *After the Great Divide: Modernism, Mass Culture, Postmodernism.* Bloomington: Indiana University Press, 1986.

Ifekwunigwe, Aaron. "Recent Field Experiences in Eastern Nigeria (Biafra)." In *Famine: A Symposium Dealing with Nutrition and Relief Operations in Times of Disaster,* edited by Gunnar Blix, Yngve Hofvander, and Bo Conradsson Vahlquist, 144–54. Uppsala: Almqvist & Wiksell, 1971.

Ignatieff, Michael. *A Just Measure of Pain: The Penitentiary in the Industrial Revolution, 1750–1850.* London: Macmillan, 1978.

Ihde, Aaron. *The Development of Modern Chemistry.* New York: Harper & Row, 1964.

Illich, Ivan. *Medical Nemesis: The Expropriation of Health.* London: Calder & Boyars, 1975.

Illich, Ivan. "The Medicalization of Life." *Journal of Medical Ethics* 1, no. 2 (1975): 73–77.

Innes, Joanna. "On the 'Mixed Economy of Welfare' in Early Modern England." In *Charity, Self-Interest, and Welfare in Britain: 1500 to the Present,* edited by Martin Daunton, 104–34. London: UCL Press, 1996.

International Action to Avert the Impending Protein Crisis, New York: United Nations Advisory Committee on the Application of Science and Technology to Development, 1968.

"Is the Gelatine of Bones Alimentary?" *American Journal of the Medical Sciences* 3, no. 5 (1842): 253–55.

Jackson, John. "In Ways Unacademical: The Reception of Carleton S. Coon's the Origin of Races." *Journal of the History of Biology* 34, no. 2 (2001): 247–85.

Jaffa, M. E. *The Study of Human Foods and Practical Dietetics*. Sacramento, CA: State Printing, 1896.

Jaffe, Bernard. *Crucibles: The Story of Chemistry from Ancient Alchemy to Nuclear Fission*. New ed. London: Hutchinson, 1949.

Jameson, Fredric. *Postmodernism, or, the Cultural Logic of Late Capitalism*. London: Verso, 1991.

Jelliffe, Derrick Brian. *The Assessment of the Nutritional Status of the Community: With Special Reference to Field Surveys in Developing Regions of the World*. Geneva: World Health Organization, 1966.

Jelliffe, Derrick Brian. "Commerciogenic Malnutrition: Time for a Dialogue?" *Food Technology* 25 (1971): 55–56.

Jelliffe, Derrick Brian. "Commerciogenic Malnutrition?" *Nutrition Reviews* 30, no. 9 (1972): 199–205.

Jelliffe, Derrick Brian. "Protein-Calorie Malnutrition in Tropical Preschool Children: A Review of Recent Knowledge." *Journal of Pediatrics* 54, no. 2 (1959): 227–56.

Jelliffe, Derrick Brian, and Eleanore Patrice Jelliffe. *Community Nutritional Assessment: With Special Reference to Less Technically Developed Countries*. Oxford: Oxford University Press, 1989.

Jelliffe, Derrick Brian, and Eleanore Patrice Jelliffe. "The Quipu in Measuring Malnutrition." *American Journal of Clinical Nutrition* 28, no. 3 (1975): 203–4.

Jelliffe, Eleanore Patrice. "The Impact of the Food Industry on the Nutritional Status of Young Children in Developing Countries." In *Food and Nutrition Policy in a Changing World*, edited by Jean Mayer and Johanna Dwyer, 197–222. New York: Oxford University Press, 1979.

Jelliffe, Eleanore Patrice, and Derrick Brian Jelliffe. "The Arm Circumference as a Public Health Index of Protein-Calorie Malnutrition of Early Childhood: Background." *Journal of Tropical Pediatrics* 15, no. 4 (1969): 179–88.

Jencks, Charles. *The Language of Post-Modern Architecture*. London: Academy Editions, 1978.

Jensen, Jorgen. "Protein-Calorie Malnutrition and Industrially Processed Weaning Foods." In *Food and Nutrition Policy in a Changing World*, edited by Jean Mayer and Johanna Dwyer, 223–40. New York: Oxford University Press, 1979.

Jézéquel, Jean-Hervé. "Staging a 'Medical Coup'? Médecins Sans Frontières and the 2005 Food Crisis in Niger." In *Medical Humanitarianism: Ethnographies of Practice*, edited by Sharon Alane Abramowitz and Catherine Panter-Brick, 119–36. Philadelphia: University of Pennsylvania Press, 2015.

Johnson, Jim [Bruno Latour]. "Mixing Humans and Nonhumans Together: The Sociology of a Door-Closer." *Social Problems* 35, no. 3 (1988): 298–310.

Johnston, Francis. "Anthropometry and Nutritional Status." In *Assessing Changing Food Consumption Patterns*, edited by National Research Council (US) Committee on Food Consumption. Washington, DC: National Academies Press, 1981.

Johnston, Valerie J. *Diet in Workhouses and Prisons, 1835–1895*. London: Garland, 1985.

Joint FAO/WHO Expert Committee On Nutrition, Report on the First Session, Geneva 24–28 October 1949. Geneva: WHO, 1950.

Jonsson, Urban. "The Rise and Fall of Paradigms in World Food and Nutrition Policy." *World Nutrition* 1, no. 3 (2010): 128–58.

Jorgensen, Jorgen, and Jacinto Convit. "Cultivation of Complexes of Algae with Other Fresh-Water Microorganisms in the Tropics." In *Algal Culture: From Laboratory to Pilot Plant*, edited by John Burlew, 190–96. Washington, DC: Carnegie Institution, 1953.

Joseph, Jonathan. "Resilience as Embedded Neoliberalism: A Governmentality Approach." *Resilience* 1, no. 1 (2013): 38–52.

Joy, Leonard, and Philip Payne. *Nutrition and National Development Planning: Three Papers*. Brighton: Institute of Development Studies, 1975.

Judt, Tony. *Postwar: A History of Europe since 1945*. London: William Heinemann, 2005.

Kalm, Leah, and Richard Semba. "They Starved So That Others Be Better Fed: Remembering Ancel Keys and the Minnesota Experiment." *Journal of Nutrition* 135, no. 6 (2005): 1347–52.

Kamminga, Harmke. "'Axes to Grind': Popularising the Science of Vitamins, 1920s and 1930s." In *Food, Science, Policy and Regulation in the Twentieth Century: International and Comparative Perspectives*, edited by David Smith and Jim Phillips, 83–100. London: Routledge, 2000.

Kamminga, Harmke, and Andrew Cunningham. "Introduction: The Science and Culture of Nutrition, 1840–1940." In *The Science and Culture of Nutrition, 1840–1940*, edited by Harmke Kamminga and Andrew Cunningham, 1–14. Amsterdam: Rodopi, 1995.

Kanigel, Robert. *The One Best Way: Frederick Winslow Taylor and the Enigma of Efficiency*. Cambridge: MIT Press, 2005.

Kapsiotis, G. D. "Single Cell Protein: Review and Assessment." *Food and Nutrition Quarterly* 4, no. 1–2 (1978): 2–7.

Kellogg, Vernon, Alonzo Englebert Taylor, and Herbert Hoover. *The Food Problem*. New York: Macmillan, 1917.

Kelly, Luke. *British Humanitarian Activity in Russia, 1890–1923*. London: Palgrave Macmillan, 2018.

Kevles, Daniel J. *In the Name of Eugenics: Genetics and the Uses of Human Heredity*. Cambridge: Harvard University Press, 1995.

Keys, Ancel, Ernst Simonson, Angie Sturgeon Skinner, and Samuel M. Wells. *The Biology of Human Starvation*. Minneapolis: University of Minnesota Press, 1950.

Killen, Andreas. *1973 Nervous Breakdown: Watergate, Warhol, and the Birth of Post-Sixties America*. New York: Bloomsbury 2006.

Kimura, Aya Hirata. *Hidden Hunger: Gender and the Politics of Smarter Foods*. Ithaca: Cornell University Press, 2016.

Kinealy, Christine. *A Death-Dealing Famine: The Great Hunger in Ireland*. London: Pluto Press, 1997.

Kipling, Rudyard. *Land and Sea Tales for Scouts and Guides*. London: Macmillan, 1923.

Kirschenbaum, Lisa. *The Legacy of the Siege of Leningrad, 1941–1995*. Cambridge: Cambridge University Press, 2006.

Klancher, Jon. *Transfiguring the Arts and Sciences: Knowledge and Cultural Institutions in the Romantic Age*. Cambridge: Cambridge University Press, 2013.

Konotey-Ahulu, Felix. "Issues in Kwashiorkor." *The Lancet* 343, no. 8896 (1994): 548–49.

Konotey-Ahulu, Felix. "Kwashiorkor." *British Medical Journal* 302, no. 6769 (1991): 180–81.

Krauss, Robert. "Mass Culture of Algae for Food." *American Journal of Botany* 49, no. 4 (1962): 425–35.

Krawinkel, Michael. "Kwashiorkor Is Still Not Fully Understood." *Bulletin of the World Health Organization* 81, no. 12 (2003): 910–11.

Krehbiel, Nicholas. *Lewis B. Hershey and Conscientious Objection During World War Two*. Columbia: University of Missouri Press, 2012.

Krinsky, Alan, "Let Them Eat Horsemeat! Science, Philanthropy, State, and the Search for Complete Nutrition in Nineteenth-Century France." Ph.D. diss., University of Wisconsin, 2001.

Kruger, Linda Lee. *Logistics Matters and the U.S. Army in Occupied Germany, 1945–1949*. New York: Palgrave Macmillan, 2016.

Kuper, Adam. *Among the Anthropologists: History and Context in Anthropology*. London: Athlone, 1999.

Kuper, Adam. *Culture: The Anthropologists' Account*. Cambridge: Harvard University Press, 1999.

Kuran, Timur. "The Provision of Public Goods under Islamic Law: Origins, Impact, and Limitations of the Waqf System." *Law and Society Review* 35, no. 4 (2001): 841–98.

Kurlansky, Mark. *Salt: A World History*. London: Jonathan Cape, 2002.

La Berge, Ann. *Mission and Method: The Early Nineteenth-Century French Public Health Movement*. Cambridge: Cambridge University Press, 1992.

Lantz, Paula M., Richard L. Lichtenstein, and Harold A. Pollack. "Health Policy Approaches to Population Health: The Limits of Medicalization." *Health Affairs* 26, no. 5 (2007): 1253–57.

Lasker, G. W. "The Place of Anthropometry in Human Biology." In *Anthropometry: The Individual and the Population*, edited by Stanley J. Ulijaszek and C.G.N. Mascie-Taylor, 1–6. Cambridge: Cambridge University Press, 1994.

Latham, Michael. *Human Nutrition in Tropical Africa: A Textbook for Health Workers with Special Reference to Community Health Problems in East Africa*. Rome: Food and Agriculture Organization, 1965.

Latour, Bruno. "Drawing Things Together." In *Representation in Scientific Practice*, edited by Michael Lynch and Steve Woolgar, 19–68. Cambridge: MIT Press, 1990.

Latour, Bruno. *Pandora's Hope: Essays on the Reality of Science Studies*. Cambridge: Harvard University Press, 1999.

Latour, Bruno. *The Pasteurization of France*. Cambridge: Harvard University Press, 1988.

Latour, Bruno. "The Powers of Association." In *Power, Action, and Belief: A New Sociology of Knowledge?* edited by John Law, 264–80. London: Routledge & Kegan Paul, 1986.

Latour, Bruno. *Science in Action: How to Follow Scientists and Engineers through Society*. Milton Keynes: Open University Press, 1987.

Latour, Bruno. *We Have Never Been Modern*. Cambridge: Harvard University Press, 1993.

Latour, Bruno. "Where Are the Missing Masses? The Sociology of a Few Mundane Artefacts." In *Shaping Technology/Building Society: Studies in Sociotechnical Change*, edited by Wiebe Bijker and John Law, 225–58. Cambridge: MIT Press, 1992.

Laugesen, M. "Child's Bangle for Nutrition Screening." *Indian Journal of Pediatrics* 12 (1975): 1261.

Lee, David. *Stanley Melbourne Bruce: Australian Internationalist*. London: Continuum, 2010.

Lerner, Natan. "New Concepts in the UNESCO Declaration on Race and Racial Prejudice." *Human Rights Quarterly* 3, no. 1 (1981): 48–61.

Levene, Alysa. *The Childhood of the Poor: Welfare in Eighteenth-Century London*. Basingstoke: Palgrave Macmillan, 2012.

Levenstein, Harvey. *Fear of Food: A History of Why We Worry About What We Eat*. Chicago: University of Chicago Press, 2012.

Levenstein, Harvey. "The New England Kitchen and the Origins of Modern American Eating Habits." *American Quarterly* 32, no. 4 (1980): 369–86.

Levenstein, Harvey. *Paradox of Plenty: A Social History of Eating in Modern America*. Berkeley: University of California Press, 2003.

Levenstein, Harvey. "The Perils of Abundance: Food, Health, and Morality in American History." In *Food: A Culinary History from Antiquity to the Present*, edited by Jean Louis Flandrin, Massimo Montanari, and Albert Sonnenfeld, 516–29. New York: Columbia University Press, 1999.

Levenstein, Harvey. *Revolution at the Table: The Transformation of the American Diet*. Berkeley: University of California Press, 2003.

Levere, Trevor Harvey. *Transforming Matter: A History of Chemistry from Alchemy to the Buckyball*. Baltimore: Johns Hopkins University Press, 2001.

Levi, Primo. *The Reawakening*. New York: Touchstone Books, 1993.

Levine, Susan. *School Lunch Politics: The Surprising History of America's Favorite Welfare Program*. Princeton: Princeton University Press, 2008.

Levinson, James. "Vital to the Creation: Interview with Alan Berg." *Development* 56, no. 1 (2013): 24–36.

Levinson, James, and Milla McLachlan. "How Did We Get Here? A History of International Nutrition." In *Scaling up, Scaling Down: Overcoming Malnutrition in Developing Countries*, edited by Thomas Marchione, 41–49. Amsterdam, Netherlands: Gordon & Breach Publishers, 1999.

Li, Lillian, and Alison Dray-Novey. "Guarding Beijing's Food Security in the Qing Dynasty: State, Market, and Police." *Journal of Asian Studies* 58, no. 4 (1999): 992–1032.

Liebig, Justus. *Animal Chemistry: Or, Chemistry in Its Applications to Physiology and Pathology*. London: Taylor and Walton, 1843.

Liebig, Justus. *Familiar Letters on Chemistry in Its Relations to Physiology, Dietetics, Agriculture, Commerce, and Political Economy*. London: Taylor, Walton & Maberly, 1851.

Liebig, Justus. *Researches on the Chemistry of Food*. London: Taylor and Walton, 1847.

Lindqvist, Sven. *The Skull Measurer's Mistake: And Other Portraits of Men and Women Who Spoke out against Racism*. New York: New Press, 1997.

Linneman, Zachary, Danielle Matilsky, MacDonald Ndekha, Micah Manary, Ken Maleta, and Mark Manary. "A Large-Scale Operational Study of Home-Based Therapy with Ready-to-Use Therapeutic Food in Childhood Malnutrition in Malawi." *Maternal and Child Nutrition* 3, no. 3 (2007): 206–15.

Lipscomb, F. M. "Medical Aspects of Belsen Concentration Camp." *The Lancet* 246, no. 6367 (1945): 313–15.

Lives in Peril: Protein and the Child. Rome: Food and Agriculture Organization, 1970.

Loescher, Gil. *The UNHCR and World Politics: A Perilous Path*. Oxford: Oxford University Press, 2001.

Long, James. *Food and Fitness: Or, Diet in Relation to Health*. London: Chapman and Hall, 1917.

Longhurst, Richard. *Global Leadership for Nutrition: The UN's Standing Committee on Nutrition (SCN) and Its Contributions*. IDS Discussion Paper 390. Brighton: Institute of Development Studies, 2010.

Lonsdale, John. "Mau Maus of the Mind: Making Mau Mau and Remaking Kenya." *Journal of African History* 31, no. 3 (1990): 393–421.

Love, Benjamin. *Manchester as It Is, or, Notices of the Institutions, Manufactures, Commerce, Railways, Etc. Of the Metropolis of Manufactures Interspersed with Much Valuable Information Useful for the Resident and Stranger*. Manchester, England: Love and Barton, 1839.

Lovejoy, Arthur O. *The Great Chain of Being: A Study of the History of an Idea*. William James Lectures. Cambridge, Mass: Harvard University Press, 1936.

Lubitz, Joseph A. "The Protein Quality, Digestibility, and Composition of Algae, Chlorella 71105a." *Journal of Food Science* 28, no. 2 (1963): 229–32.

Lupton, Deborah. "Foucault and the Medicalization Critique." In *Foucault, Health and Medicine*, edited by Alan R. Petersen and Robin Bunton, 94–111. London: Routledge, 1997.

Lusk, Graham. "Introduction." In *Analysis and Cost of Ready-to-Serve Foods*, edited by Frank Curtis Gephart and Graham Lusk. Chicago: Press of American Medical Association, 1915.

Lusty, Tim, and Pat Diskett. *Selective Feeding Programmes*. Oxford: Oxfam, 1984.

Luxemburg, Rosa. *The Complete Works of Rosa Luxemburg*. Vol. 1. *Economic Writings*. London: Verso, 2013.

MacCollum, Elmer Verner. *The Newer Knowledge of Nutrition: The Use of Food*. New York: Macmillan, 1919.

MacMunn, George Fletcher. *The Martial Races of India*. London: Low, Marston & Company, 1933.

Maerker, Anna. "Political Order and the Ambivalence of Expertise: Count Rumford and Welfare Reform in Late Eighteenth-Century Munich." *Osiris* 25, no. 1 (2010): 213–30.

Malkki, Liisa. "Refugees and Exile: From "Refugee Studies" to the National Order of Things." *Annual Review of Anthropology* 24, no. 1 (1995): 495–523.

Mamane, Rachael. *Mastering Stocks and Broths: A Comprehensive Culinary Approach*. White River: Chelsea Green, 2017.

Mamdani, Mahmood. *Citizen and Subject: Contemporary Africa and the Legacy of Late Colonialism*. London: James Currey, 1996.

Marchione, Thomas. "Foods Provided through U.S. Government Emergency Food Aid Programs: Policies and Customs Governing Their Formulation, Selection and Distribution." *Journal of Nutrition* 132, no. 7 (2002): 2104–11.

Maren, Michael. *The Road to Hell: The Ravaging Effects of Foreign Aid and International Charity*. London: Free Press, 1997.

Marsden, Terry. "Exploring a Rural Sociology for the Fordist Transition." *Sociologia Ruralis* 32, no. 2–3 (1992): 209–30.

Marsh, Henry. *On the Preparation of Food for the Labourer*. Dublin: James McGlashan, 1847.

Marsh, Jan. *Back to the Land: The Pastoral Impulse in England, from 1880 to 1914*. London: Quartet Books, 1982.

Marx, Karl, and Friedrich Engels. *Collected Works*. Vol. 30. *Marx 1861–63*. London: Lawrence and Wishart, 2010.

Maskalyk, James. *Six Months in Sudan: A Young Doctor in a War-Torn Village*. Edinburgh: Canongate, 2010.

Mason, J. B., J. P. Habicht, J. P. Greaves, U. Jonsson, J. Kevany, R. Martorell, and B. Rogers. "Public Nutrition." *American Journal of Clinical Nutrition* 63, no. 3 (1996): 399–400.

Mateles, Richard, and Steven Tannenbaum. *Single-Cell Protein.* Cambridge: MIT Press, 1968.

Maurice, John Frederick [Miles]. "Where to Get Men." *Contemporary Review* 81 (1902): 78–86.

Mayhew, Henry, and John Binny. *The Criminal Prisons of London, and Scenes of Prison Life.* London: Griffin Bohn, 1862.

Mayhew, Madeleine. "The 1930s Nutrition Controversy." *Journal of Contemporary History* 23, no. 3 (1988): 445–64.

Mazumdar, Pauline M. H. "'Reform' Eugenics and the Decline of Mendelism." *Trends in Genetics* 18, no. 1 (2002): 48–52.

McCarrison, Robert, "Adventures in Research: Lloyd Roberts Lecture at the Medical Society of London, November 19, 1936." *Transactions of The Medical Society of London* 60 (1937): 46–71.

McCarrison, Robert. *Nutrition and National Health: Being the Cantor Lectures Delivered before the Royal Society of Arts, 1936.* London: Faber and Faber Limited, 1936.

McCarrison, Robert. *Studies in Deficiency Disease.* London: Hodder & Stoughton, 1921.

McCay, David. *Investigations on Bengal Jail Dietaries, with Some Observations on the Influence of Dietary on the Physical Development and Well-Being of the People of Bengal.* Calcutta: Superintendent of Government Printing, 1910.

McCay, David. *Investigations into the Jail Dietaries of the United Provinces with Some Observations on the Influence of Dietary on the Physical Development and Well-Being of the People of the United Provinces.* Calcutta: Superintendent Government Printing, 1912.

McCay, David. *The Protein Element in Nutrition.* International Medical Monographs. London: Edward Arnold, 1912.

McCay, David. *Standards of the Constituents of the Urine and Blood and the Bearing of the Metabolism of Bengalis on the Problems of Nutrition.* Calcutta: Superintendent of Government Printing, 1908.

McClelland, Grigor. *Embers of War: Letters from a Quaker Relief Worker in War-Torn Germany.* London: British Academic Press, 1997.

McDonough, Frank. *Neville Chamberlain, Appeasement and the British Road to War.* Manchester: Manchester University Press, 1998.

McFarlane, H., K. J. Adcock, A. Cooke, M. I. Ogbeide, H. Adeshina, G. O. Taylor, S. Reddy, J. M. Gurney, and J. A. Mordie. "Biochemical Assessment of Protein-Calorie Malnutrition." *The Lancet* 293, no. 7591 (1969): 392–95.

McGee, Harold. *The Curious Cook.* London: HarperCollins, 1992.

McGee, Harold. "Osmazome, the Maillard Reaction, and the Triumph of the Cooked." In *Taste: Proceedings of the Oxford Symposium on Food and Cookery 1987*, edited by Tom Jaine, 133–35. London: Prospect Books, 1988.

McKenzie J. C. "What Is Social Nutrition?" *Nutrition Bulletin* 5, no. 6 (1980): 309–25.

McLaren, Donald. "A Fresh Look at Anthropometric Classification Schemes in Protein-Energy Malnutrition." In *Anthropometric Assessment of Nutritional Status*, edited by John Himes, 273–86. New York: Wiley-Liss, 1991.

McLaren, Donald. "The Great Protein Fiasco." *The Lancet* 304, no. 7872 (1974): 93–96.

McLaren, Donald. "The Great Protein Fiasco Revisited." *Nutrition* 16, no. 6 (2000): 464–65.

McLaren, Donald. "Nutrition Planning: The Poverty of Holism." *Nature* 267 (1977): 742.

McLaren, Donald, and Abdallah Kanawati. "A Somatic Quotient." *American Journal of Clinical Nutrition* 25, no. 4 (1972): 363–64.

McNeill, Margaret. *By the Rivers of Babylon: A Story of Relief Work among the Displaced Persons of Europe.* London: Bannisdale Press, 1950.

Médecins Sans Frontières. *Clinical Guidelines: Diagnosis and Treatment Manual,* Paris: MSF, 2016.

Megill, Allan. "The Reception of Foucault by Historians." *Journal of the History of Ideas* 48, no. 1 (1987): 117–41.

Mendel, Lafayette Benedict. *Changes in the Food Supply and Their Relation to Nutrition.* New Haven: Yale University Press, 1916.

Metcoff, J. "Biochemical Effects of Protein-Calorie Malnutrition in Man." *Annual Review of Medicine* 18, no. 1 (1967): 377–422.

Mikkeli, Heikki. *Hygiene in the Early Modern Medical Tradition.* Helsinki: Academia Scientiarum Fennica, 1999.

Milejkowski, Israel. "Introduction." In *Hunger Disease: Studies by the Jewish Physicians in the Warsaw Ghetto,* edited by Myron Winick, 1–6. New York: Wiley, 1979.

Miller, Ian. "The Chemistry of Famine: Nutritional Controversies and the Irish Famine, c.1845–7." *Medical History* 56, no. 4 (2012): 444–62.

Miller, Ian. "Feeding in the Workhouse: The Institutional and Ideological Functions of Food in Britain, C.1834–70." *Journal of British Studies* 52, no. 4 (2013): 940–62.

Miller, Ian. "Food, Medicine, and Institutional Life in the British Isles, C.1790–1900." In *The Routledge History of Food,* edited by Carol Helstosky, 200–219. London: Routledge, 2015.

Miller, Edward Garvey. *Misalliance: Ngo Dinh Diem, the United States, and the Fate of South Vietnam.* Cambridge: Harvard University Press, 2013.

Milles, Dietrich. "Working Capacity and Calorie Consumption: The History of Rational Physical Economy." In *The Science and Culture of Nutrition, 1840–1940,* edited by Harmke Kamminga and Andrew Cunningham, 75–97. Amsterdam: Rodopi, 1995.

Millman, Sara, and Laurie DeRose. "Measuring Hunger." In *Who's Hungry? And How Do We Know? Food Shortage, Poverty, and Deprivation,* edited by Laurie DeRose, Ellen Messer and Sara Millman, 20–51. New York: United Nations University, 1998.

Mintz, Sidney Wilfred. *Sweetness and Power: The Place of Sugar in Modern History.* New York: Penguin, 1986.

Mitchell, Timothy. *Rule of Experts: Egypt, Techno-Politics, Modernity.* Berkeley: University of California Press, 2002.

Mitzner, Karen, Nevin Scrimshaw, and Robert Morgan. *Improving the Nutritional Status of Children during the Weaning Period: A Manual for Policymakers.* Washington, DC: USAID, 1984.

Mol, Annemarie. *The Body Multiple: Ontology in Medical Practice.* Durham, NC: Duke University Press, 2002.

Mollison, P. L. "Observations on Cases of Starvation at Belsen." *British Medical Journal* 1, no. 4435 (1946): 4–8.

Moorehead, Caroline. *Dunant's Dream: War, Switzerland and the History of the Red Cross.* London: HarperCollins, 1998.

Moradi, Alexander. "Towards an Objective Account of Nutrition and Health in Colonial Kenya: A Study of Stature in African Army Recruits and Civilians, 1880–1980." *Journal of Economic History* 69, no. 3 (2009): 719–54.

Morley, David. "Prevention of Protein-Calorie Deficiency Syndromes." *Transactions of The Royal Society of Tropical Medicine and Hygiene* 62, no. 2 (1968): 200–208.

Morris, Helen Soutar. *Portrait of a Chef: The Life of Alexis Soyer, Sometime Chef to the Reform Club*. Cambridge: Cambridge University Press, 1938.

Morrison, J., and Norman Wingate Pirie. "The Presentation of Leaf Protein on the Table." *International Journal of Food Sciences and Nutrition* 14, no. 1 (1960): 7–11.

Morrison, J., and Norman Wingate Pirie. "The Large-Scale Production of Protein from Leaf Extracts." *Journal of the Science of Food and Agriculture* 12, no. 1 (1961): 1–5.

Morus, Iwan Rhys. *Frankenstein's Children: Electricity, Exhibition, and Experiment in Early-Nineteenth-Century London*. Princeton: Princeton University Press, 1998.

Moses, A. Dirk, and Lasse Heerten. *Postcolonial Conflict and the Question of Genocide: The Nigeria-Biafra War, 1967–1970*. London: Routledge, 2017.

Muller, Mike. *The Baby Killer: A War on Want Investigation into the Promotion and Sale of Powdered Baby Milks in the Third World*. London: War on Want, 1974.

Nader, Laura. "Up the Anthropologist: Perspectives Gained from Studying Up." In *Reinventing Anthropology*, edited by Dell H. Hymes, 284–311. New York: Pantheon Books, 1972.

Nally, David. *Human Encumbrances: Political Violence and the Great Irish Famine*. Notre Dame, IN: University of Notre Dame Press, 2011.

Narayanan, E. K., K. Krishnan, and G. Sankaran. "Protein Hydrolysates in the Treatment of Inanition." *Indian Medical Gazette* 79 (1944): 160–62.

Nestle, Marion. *Food Politics: How the Food Industry Influences Nutrition and Health*. Berkeley: University of California Press, 2002.

Neswald, Elizabeth, and David Smith. *Setting Nutritional Standards: Theory, Policies, Practices*. Rochester: University of Rochester Press, 2017.

Newcomb, Sally. *The World in a Crucible: Laboratory Practice and Geological Theory at the Beginning of Geology*. Boulder: Geological Society of America, 2009.

Newman, James. "From Definition, to Geography, to Action, to Reaction: The Case of Protein-Energy Malnutrition." *Annals of the Association of American Geographers* 85, no. 2 (1995): 233–45.

Nicholson, Asenath. *Annals of the Famine in Ireland, in 1847, 1848 and 1849*. Dublin: Lilliput Press, 1851.

Nightingale, Florence. *Notes on Nursing: What It Is, and What It Is Not*. London: Harrison, 1859.

Nutrition and Relief Work: A Handbook for the Guidance of Relief Workers. London: Council of British Societies for Relief Abroad (COBSRA), 1945.

O'Brien, John. "F. L. McDougall and the Origins of the FAO." *Australian Journal of Politics and History* 46, no. 2 (2000): 164–74.

O'Connor, W. J. *British Physiologists, 1885–1914: A Biographical Dictionary*. Manchester: Manchester University Press, 1991.

Ó Gráda, Cormac. *Black '47 and Beyond: The Great Irish Famine in History, Economy and Memory*. Princeton: Princeton University Press, 1999.

Orr, Elizabeth. "The Contribution of New Food Mixtures to the Relief of Malnutrition: A Second Look." *Food and Nutrition Quarterly* 3, no. 2 (1977): 2–10.

Orr, Elizabeth. *The Use of Protein-Rich Foods for the Relief of Malnutrition in Developing Countries: An Analysis of Experience*. London: Tropical Products Institute, 1972.

Orr, John Boyd. *As I Recall*. London: MacGibbon & Kee, 1966.

Orr, John Boyd. *Food Health and Income: Report on a Survey of Adequacy of Diet in Relation to Income*. London: Macmillan, 1936.

Orr, John Boyd. *The White Man's Dilemma; Food and the Future.* London: Allen and Unwin, 1953.

Orr, John Boyd, and John Langton Gilks. *Studies of Nutrition: The Physique and Health of Two African Tribes.* London: H. M. Stationery Office, 1931.

Owen, David Edward. *English Philanthropy, 1660–1960.* Cambridge: Harvard University Press, 1965.

Paddock, William, and Paul Paddock. *Famine - 1975!* London: Weidenfeld & Nicolson, 1968.

Parekh, Bhikhu. *Rethinking Multiculturalism: Cultural Diversity and Political Theory.* Basingstoke: Palgrave Macmillan, 2006.

Pariser, Ernst, M. B. Wallerstein, C. J. Corkery, and N. L Brown. *Fish Protein Concentrate: Panacea for Protein Malnutrition?* Cambridge: MIT Press, 1978.

Passmore, R. "Wallace Ruddell Aykroyd." *British Journal of Nutrition* 43, no. 2 (1980): 245–50.

Patenaude, Bertrand. *The Big Show in Bololand: The American Relief Expedition to Soviet Russia in the Famine of 1921.* Stanford: Stanford University Press, 2002.

Paton, Alex. "Mission to Belsen 1945." *British Medical Journal* 283, no. 6307 (1981): 1656–59.

Payne, Philip. "Nutrition Planning and Food Policy." *Food Policy* 1, no. 2 (1976): 107–15.

Pentecost, Michelle, and Thomas Cousins. "The Temporary as the Future: Ready-to-Use Therapeutic Food and Nutraceuticals in South Africa." *Anthropology Today* 34, no. 4 (2018): 9–13.

Penuel, K. Bradley, and Matthew Statler. *Encyclopedia of Disaster Relief.* London: Sage, 2011.

Peri, Oded. "Waqf and Ottoman Welfare Policy. The Poor Kitchen of Hasseki Sultan in Eighteenth-Century Jerusalem." *Journal of the Economic and Social History of the Orient* 35, no. 2 (1992): 167–86.

Pernet, Corinne. "Between Entanglements and Dependencies: Food, Nutrition, and National Development at the Central American Institute of Nutrition (INCAP)." In *International Organizations and Development, 1945–1990*, edited by Marc Frey, Sönke Kunkel and Corinna Unger, 101–25. London: Palgrave, 2014.

Peterson, Martin. "International Interest Organizations and the Transmutation of Postwar Society." Ph.D. diss., University of Gothenburg, 1979.

Petryna, Adriana, Andrew Lakoff, and Arthur Kleinman, eds. *Global Pharmaceuticals: Ethics, Markets, Practices.* Durham, NC: Duke University Press, 2006.

Pettiss, Susan, and Lynne Taylor. *After the Shooting Stopped: The Story of an UNRRA Welfare Worker in Germany 1945–1947.* Victoria: Trafford, 2004.

Phillips, Ralph W. *FAO: Its Origins, Formation and Evolution, 1945–1981.* Rome: Food and Agriculture Organization of the United Nations, 1981.

Pietsch, Brendan. *Dispensational Modernism.* New York: Oxford University Press, 2015.

Pirie, Norman Wingate. "Leaf Protein as a Human Food." *International Journal of Food Sciences and Nutrition* 12, no. 1 (1958): 17–22.

Pirie, Norman Wingate. "Leaf Protein as Human Food." *Nutrition Reviews* 18, no. 7 (1960): 218–19.

Pirie, Norman Wingate. "Leaf Proteins." *Annual Review of Plant Physiology* 10, no. 1 (1959): 33–52.

Pirie, Norman Wingate. "The Present Position and Future Needs of Research on Leaf Protein." In *Progress in Meeting Protein Needs of Infants and Preschool Children,* edited by LeRoy Voris, 509–16. Washington, D. C.: National Academy of Sciences, 1961.

Pirie, Norman Wingate. "The Production and Use of Leaf Protein." *Proceedings of the Nutrition Society* 28, no. 1 (1969): 85–91.

Pirie, Norman Wingate. "World Hunger as a Biochemical Problem." *Journal of the Royal Society of Arts* 106, no. 5053 (1958): 511–28.

Pollan, Michael. *In Defense of Food: An Eater's Manifesto*. New York: Penguin Press, 2008.

Pollan, Michael. *Food Rules: An Eater's Manual*. London: Penguin, 2010.

Pollan, Michael. *The Omnivore's Dilemma: The Search for a Perfect Meal in a Fast-Food World*. London: Bloomsbury, 2006.

Polman, Linda. *War Games: The Story of Aid and War in Modern Times*. London: Penguin, 2011.

Popkin, Barry, and Michael Latham. "The Limitations and Dangers of Commerciogenic Nutritious Foods." *American Journal of Clinical Nutrition* 26, no. 9 (1973): 1015–23.

Poppendieck, Janet. *Breadlines Knee-Deep in Wheat: Food Assistance in the Great Depression*. Berkeley: University of California Press, 2014.

Porter, Robert, and Lonna Shafritz. *Packaged Foods for Complementary Feeding: Marketing Challenges and Opportunities*. Washington, DC: Center for Nutrition, 1999.

Potter, Rachel, and David Trotter. "Low Modernism: Introduction." *Critical Quarterly* 46, no. 4 (2004): iii–iv.

Powell, Darren. "Childhood Obesity, Corporate Philanthropy, and the Creeping Privatisation of Health Education." *Critical Public Health* 24, no. 2 (2014): 226–38.

Powell, Richard, Elizabeth Nevels, and Marion McDowell. "Algae Feeding in Humans." *Journal of Nutrition* 75, no. 1 (1961): 7–12.

Poynter, John Riddoch. *Society and Pauperism: English Ideas on Poor Relief, 1795–1834*. London: Routledge & Kegan Paul, 1969.

Praed, Max. "An American Dilemma." *Australian Left Review* 1, no. 13 (1968): 36–41.

Prahalad, Coimbatore Krishnarao. *The Fortune at the Bottom of the Pyramid: Eradicating Poverty through Profits*. Upper Saddle River, NJ: Wharton, 2005.

Prasannappa, G. "Precooked Bal-Ahar and Indian Multi Purpose Food." *Journal of Food Science and Technology* 9, no. 4 (1972): 174–78.

Price, Catherine. *Vitamania: Our Obsessive Quest for Nutritional Perfection*. New York: Penguin Press, 2015.

Priestley, Philip. *Victorian Prison Lives: English Prison Biography, 1830–1914*. London: Methuen, 1985.

Prout, William. "Observations on the Application of Chemistry to Physiology, Pathology, and Practice." *London Medical Gazette* 8 (1831): 321–27.

Prout, William. "On the Ultimate Composition of Simple Alimentary Substances; with Some Preliminary Remarks on the Analysis of Organized Bodies in General." *Philosophical Transactions of the Royal Society of London* 2 (1815): 324–26.

Quetelet, Adolphe. *A Treatise on Man and the Development of His Faculties*. Edinburgh: W&R Chambers, 1842.

Rabinbach, Anson. *The Human Motor: Energy, Fatigue, and the Origins of Modernity*. New York: Basic Books, 1990.

Rabinow, Paul. "On the Archaeology of Late Modernity." In *Nowhere: Space, Time, and Modernity*, edited by Deirdre Boden and Roger Friedland, 402–18. Berkeley: University of California Press, 1994.

Rabinow, Paul. *French Modern: Norms and Forms of the Social Environment.* Cambridge: MIT Press, 1989.

Rafter, Nicole Hahn. *The Origins of Criminology.* Abingdon: Routledge, 2009.

Raimondi, P. J., and F. R. Goetzl. "Treatment of Idiopathic Ulcerative Colitis with Desiccated, Defatted Duodenal Powder." *Permanente Foundation Medical Bulletin* 7, no. 1 (1949): 1–11.

Rainer, Arnhold. "The Arm Circumference as a Public Health Index of Protein-Calorie Malnutrition of Early Childhood: The QUAC Stick." *Journal of Tropical Pediatrics* 15, no. 4 (1969): 243–47.

Ramachandran, K., B. S. Parmar, J. K. Jain, B. N. Tandon, and P. C. Gandhi. "Limitations of Film Strip and Bangle Test for Identification of Malnourished Children." *American Journal of Clinical Nutrition* 31, no. 8 (1978): 1469–72.

Read, John. *From Alchemy to Chemistry.* New York: Dover, 1995.

Redfield, Peter. "Bioexpectations: Life Technologies as Humanitarian Goods." *Public Culture* 24, no. 1 (2012): 157–84.

Redfield, Peter. "Doctors, Borders, and Life in Crisis." *Cultural Anthropology* 20, no. 3 (2005): 328–61.

Redfield, Peter. "Fluid Technologies: The Bush Pump, the Lifestraw® and Microworlds of Humanitarian Design." *Social Studies of Science* 46, no. 2 (2016): 159–83.

Redlich, Fritz. "Science and Charity: Count Rumford and His Followers." *International Review of Social History* 16, no. 2 (1971): 184–216.

Reilly, Joanne, David Cesarani, Tony Kushner, and Colin Richmond, eds. *Belsen in History and Memory.* London: Frank Cass, 1997.

Reinisch, Jessica. "Internationalism in Relief: The Birth (and Death) of UNRRA." *Past and Present* 210, no. 6 (2011): 258–89.

Reinisch, Jessica. "Introduction: Relief in the Aftermath of War." *Journal of Contemporary History* 43, no. 3 (2008): 371–404.

Reinisch, Jessica. "'We Shall Rebuild Anew a Powerful Nation': UNRRA, Internationalism and National Reconstruction in Poland." *Journal of Contemporary History* 43, no. 3 (2008): 451–76.

Report of the 1972 United Nations Conference on the Human Environment, Stockholm, 5–16 June 1972. New York: United Nations, 1973.

Report of the Inter-Departmental Committee on Physical Deterioration. London: HMSO, 1904.

Report of the Massachusetts Board of World's Fair Managers. Boston: Wright and Potter, 1894.

Reutlinger, Shlomo. "The Value of PL480: A Fresh Look." *Food Policy* 8, no. 3 (1983): 246–52.

"Review: Soyer's Modern Housewife." *Fraser's Magazine for Town and Country* 44 (1851): 201–3.

Richards, Audrey. *Hunger and Work in a Savage Tribe: A Functional Study of Nutrition among the Southern Bantu.* London: Routledge, 1932.

Richards, Audrey. *Land, Labour, and Diet in Northern Rhodesia: An Economic Study of the Bemba Tribe.* London: Oxford University Press, 1939.

Richards, Ellen. *Plain Words about Food: The Rumford Kitchen Leaflets.* Boston: Rockwell and Churchill Press, 1899.

Ritchie, Jean. *Teaching Better Nutrition: A Study of Approaches and Techniques.* Washington, DC: Food and Agricultural Organization, 1950.

Richter, Judith. *Holding Corporations Accountable: Corporate Conduct, International Codes, and Citizen Action.* London: Zed Books, 2001.

Roberts, Michael. "Head Versus Heart? Voluntary Associations and Charity Organization in England, c.1700–1850." In *Charity, Philanthropy and Reform: From the 1690s to 1850*, edited by Hugh Cunningham and Joanna Innes, 66–86. Basingstoke: Macmillan, 1998.

Roberts, Michael, and Wolfram Schlenker. "World Supply and Demand of Food Commodity Calories." *American Journal of Agricultural Economics* 91, no. 5 (2009): 1235–42.

Roberts, Paul. *The End of Food*. Boston: Houghton Mifflin, 2008.

Roels, O. A. "Fish Protein Concentrate: History and Trends in Production." In *Production of Fish Protein Concentrate: Report and Proceedings*, 3–11. New York: United Nations, 1972.

Roland, Charles. *Courage under Siege: Starvation, Disease, and Death in the Warsaw Ghetto*. New York: Oxford University Press, 1992.

Rose, Norman. *The Cliveden Set: Portrait of an Exclusive Fraternity*. London: J. Cape, 2000.

Rosenberg, Charles. "Disease and Social Order in America: Perceptions and Expectations." *The Milbank Quarterly* 64, no. 1 (1986): 34–55.

Rosenberg, Charles. "Framing Disease: Illness, Society, and History." In *Framing Disease: Studies in Cultural History*, edited by Charles Rosenberg and Janet Lynne Golden, xiii–xxvi, New Brunswick: Rutgers University Press, 1992.

Rosencher, Henri. "Medicine in Dachau." *British Medical Journal* 2, no. 4485 (1946): 953–55.

Rosenfeld, Louis. *Four Centuries of Clinical Chemistry*. New York: Routledge, 1999.

Roth, Michael. "Foucault's 'History of the Present.'" *History and Theory* 20, no. 1 (1981): 32–46.

Rule, John. *The Labouring Classes in Early Industrial England, 1750–1850*. London: Longman, 1986.

Russell, Sharman Apt. *Hunger: An Unnatural History*. New York: Basic Books, 2005.

Ruttan, Vernon. "The Politics of U.S. Food Aid Policy: A Historical Review." In *Why Food Aid?* edited by Vernon Ruttan, 2–36. Baltimore: Johns Hopkins University Press, 1993.

Ruxin, Josh. "Hunger, Science, and Politics: FAO, WHO, and UNICEF Nutrition Policies, 1945–78." Ph.D. diss., University College London, 1996.

Ruxin, Josh. "The United Nations Protein Advisory Group." In *Food, Science, Policy and Regulation in the Twentieth Century: International and Comparative Perspectives*, edited by David Smith and Jim Phillips, 151–66. London: Routledge, 2000.

Sacks, Oliver. *An Anthropologist on Mars: Seven Paradoxical Tales*. London: Picador, 1995.

Sasson, Tehila. "Milking the Third World? Humanitarianism, Capitalism, and the Moral Economy of the Nestlé Boycott." *American Historical Review* 121, no. 4 (2016): 1196–224.

Schauer, Claudia, and Stanley Zlotkin. "Home Fortification with Micronutrient Sprinkles—A New Approach for the Prevention and Treatment of Nutritional Anemias." *Paediatrics and Child Health* 8, no. 2 (2003): 87–90.

Scheper-Hughes, Nancy. *Death without Weeping: The Violence of Everyday Life in Brazil*. Berkeley: University of California Press, 1992.

Scheurich, James Joseph, and Kathryn Bell McKenzie. "Foucault's Methodologies: Archeology and Genealogy." In *The Sage Handbook of Qualitative Research*, edited by Norman Denzin and Yvonna Lincoln, 841–68. London: Sage, 2005.

Schumacher, Ernst Friedrich. *Small Is Beautiful: A Study of Economics as If People Mattered*. London: Blond and Briggs, 1973.

Scott, James. *Seeing Like a State: How Certain Schemes to Improve the Human Condition Have Failed*. London: Yale University Press, 1998.

Scott-Smith, Tom. "Control and Biopower in Contemporary Humanitarian Aid: The Case of Supplementary Feeding." *Journal of Refugee Studies* 28, no. 1 (2015): 21–37.

Scott-Smith, Tom. "The Fetishism of Humanitarian Objects and the Management of Malnutrition in Emergencies." *Third World Quarterly* 34, no. 5 (2013): 913–28.

Scott-Smith, Tom. "How Projects Rise and Fall: The Lifecycle of a Dietary Modernisation Scheme." *Development in Practice* 24, no. 7 (2014): 785–96.

Scott-Smith, Tom. "Humanitarian Neophilia: The 'Innovation Turn' and Its Implications." *Third World Quarterly* 37, no. 12 (2016): 2229–51.

Scott-Smith, Tom. "Paradoxes of Resilience: A Review of the World Disasters Report 2016." *Development and Change* 49, no. 2 (2018): 662–77.

Scott-Smith, Tom. "Sticky Technologies: Plumpy'nut®, Emergency Feeding and the Viscosity of Humanitarian Design." *Social Studies of Science* 48, no. 1 (2018): 3–24.

Scrimshaw, Nevin. "The Background and History of Incaparina." *Food and Nutrition Bulletin of the United Nations University* 2, no. 2 (1980): 1–2.

Scrinis, Gyorgy. "Nutritionism and Functional Foods." In *The Philosophy of Food*, edited by David Kaplan, 269–91. Berkeley: University of California Press, 2012.

Scrinis, Gyorgy. *Nutritionism: The Science and Politics of Dietary Advice*. New York: Columbia University Press, 2013.

Searle, Geoffrey Russell. *The Quest for National Efficiency: A Study in British Politics and Political Thought, 1899–1914*. Oxford: Basil Blackwell, 1971.

Semba, Richard. "The Rise and Fall of Protein Malnutrition in Global Health." *Annals of Nutrition and Metabolism* 69, no. 2 (2016): 79–88.

Semba, Richard. *The Vitamin A Story: Lifting the Shadow of Death*. Basel: Karger, 2012.

Sen, Amartya. *Poverty and Famines: An Essay on Entitlement and Deprivation*. Oxford: Clarendon Press, 1981.

Senti, F. R., M. J. Copley, and J. W. Pence. "Protein-Fortified Food Grain Products for World Uses." *Cereal Science Today* 12, no. 10 (1967): 426–30.

Shakir, Adnan. "The Surveillance of Protein-Calorie Malnutrition by Simple and Economical Means." *Journal of Tropical Pediatrics* 21, no. 2 (1975): 69–85.

Shakir, Adnan, and David Morley. "Measuring Malnutrition." *The Lancet* 303, no. 7860 (1974): 758–59.

Shapin, Steven. "Changing Tastes: How Things Tasted in the Early Modern Period and How They Taste Now." Hans Rausing Lecture 2011. Salvia Sm<å>skrifter Series. Uppsala: University of Uppsala, 2011.

Shapin, Steven. "Phrenological Knowledge and the Social Structure of Early Nineteenth-Century Edinburgh." *Annals of Science* 32, no. 3 (1975): 219–43.

Shapin, Steven. "Trusting George Cheyne: Scientific Expertise, Common Sense, and Moral Authority in Early Eighteenth-Century Dietetic Medicine." *Bulletin of the History of Medicine* 77, no. 2 (2003): 263–97.

Shapin, Steven. "'You Are What You Eat': Historical Changes in Ideas About Food and Identity." *Historical Research* 87, no. 237 (2014): 377–92.

Shapiro, Laura. *Perfection Salad: Women and Cooking at the Turn of the Century*. Berkeley: University of California Press, 2009.

Shaw, D. John. *World Food Security: A History since 1945*. Basingstoke, UK: Palgrave Macmillan, 2007.

Shaw, D. John, and Edward J. Clay. *World Food Aid: Experiences of Recipients and Donors*. London: James Currey, 1993.

Shaw, Richard. "The Flour of San Vicente." *Américas* 12, no. 2 (1960): 3–7.

Shee, George. "The Deterioration in the National Physique." *Nineteenth Century and After* 53 (1903): 797–805.

Shephard, Ben. *After Daybreak: The Liberation of Belsen, 1945*. London: Pimlico, 2006.

Shephard, Ben. "Becoming Planning Minded: The Theory and Practice of Relief 1940–1945." *Journal of Contemporary History* 43, no. 3 (2008): 405–19.

Shephard, Ben. *The Long Road Home: The Aftermath of the Second World War*. London: Vintage, 2011.

Shephard, Ben. "The Medical Relief Effort at Belsen." In *Belsen 1945: New Historical Perspectives*, edited by Suzanne Bardgett and David Cesarani, 31–50. Edgware: Vallentine Mitchell, 2006.

Shephard, Sue. *Pickled, Potted, and Canned: The Story of Food Preserving*. London: Headline, 2001.

Sheridan, Alan. *Michel Foucault: The Will to Truth*. London: Routledge, 1990.

Sherman, Sandra. *Imagining Poverty: Quantification and the Decline of Paternalism*. Columbus: Ohio State University Press, 2001.

Sherman, Taylor. "Tensions of Colonial Punishment: Perspectives on Recent Developments in the Study of Coercive Networks in Asia, Africa and the Caribbean." *History Compass* 7, no. 3 (2009): 659–77.

Shurtleff, William, and Akiko Aoyagi. *Soymilk Industry and Market: Worldwide and Country by Country Analysis*. Lafayette: Soyfoods Center, 1984.

Siegel, Benjamin Robert. *Hungry Nation: Food, Famine, and the Making of Modern India*. Cambridge: Cambridge University Press, 2018.

Sim, Stuart. *The Routledge Companion to Postmodernism*. London: Routledge, 2001.

Simmons, Dana. *Vital Minimum: Need, Science, and Politics in Modern France*. Chicago: University of Chicago Press, 2015.

Simpson, James. *On the More Effective Application of the System of Relief by Means of Soup Kitchens*. London: Whittaker, 1847.

Singer, Amy. *Constructing Ottoman Beneficence: An Imperial Soup Kitchen in Jerusalem*. Albany: State University of New York Press, 2002.

Singer, Amy. "Serving up Charity: The Ottoman Public Kitchen." *Journal of Interdisciplinary History* 35, no. 3 (2005): 481–500.

Singer, Amy. "Soup and Sadaqa: Charity in Islamic Societies." *Historical Research* 79, no. 205 (2006): 306–24.

Singer, Hans, Anthony Jennings, and John Wood. *Food Aid: The Challenge and the Opportunity*. Oxford: Clarendon Press, 1987.

Slack, Paul. *Poverty and Policy in Tudor and Stuart England*. London: Longman, 1988.

Smith, Marcus. *Dachau: The Harrowing of Hell*. Albany: State University of New York Press, 1995.

Smyth, A. Watt. *Physical Deterioration, Its Causes and the Cure*. London: Murray, 1904.

Sokolow, Jayme. "Count Rumford and Late Enlightenment Science, Technology and Reform." *The Eighteenth Century* 21, no. 1 (1980): 67–86.

Soloway, Richard. "Counting the Degenerates: The Statistics of Race Deterioration in Edwardian England." *Journal of Contemporary History* 17, no. 1 (1982): 137–64.

Sommer, Alfred. "Vitamin A Deficiency and Mortality Risk." *The Lancet* 323, no. 8372 (1984): 347–48.

Sommer, Alfred, Edi Djunaedi, A. Loeden, I. Tarwotjo, Keith West, Robert Tilden, and Lisa Mele. "Impact of Vitamin A Supplementation on Childhood Mortality: A

Randomised Controlled Community Trial." *The Lancet* 327, no. 8491 (1986): 1169–73.

Sommer, Alfred, J. Katz, and I. Tarwotjo. "Increased Risk of Respiratory Disease and Diarrhea in Children with Preexisting Mild Vitamin A Deficiency." *American Journal of Clinical Nutrition* 40, no. 5 (1984): 1090–95.

Sommer, Alfred, and Matthew Loewenstein. "Nutritional Status and Mortality: A Prospective Validation of the QUAC Stick." *American Journal of Clinical Nutrition* 28, no. 3 (1975): 287–92.

Soyer, Alexis Benoît. *Charitable Cookery; or, the Poor Man's Regenerator*. London, 1848.

Soyer, Alexis Benoît. *Memoirs of Alexis Soyer; with Unpublished Receipts and Odds and Ends of Gastronomy*. Edited by F. Volant and J. R. Warren. London: W. Kent, 1859.

Soyer, Alexis Benoît. *The Modern Housewife or Ménagère*. London: Simpkin Marshall, 1849.

Spary, Emma. *Feeding France: New Sciences of Food, 1760–1815*. Cambridge: Cambridge University Press, 2014.

Spektorowski, Alberto, and Liza Ireni Saban. *Politics of Eugenics: Productionism, Population, and National Welfare*. Abingdon: Routledge, 2014.

Sphere Project. *Humanitarian Charter and Minimum Standards in Humanitarian Response*. Geneva: Sphere Project, 2011.

Spoehr, Herman Augustus. "Chlorella as a Source of Food." *Proceedings of the American Philosophical Society* 95, no. 1 (1951): 62–67.

Spoehr, Herman Augustus. "The Need for a New Source of Food." In *Algal Culture: From Laboratory to Pilot Plant*, edited by John Burlew, 24–30. Washington, DC: Carnegie Institution, 1953.

Stamatov, Peter. *The Origins of Global Humanitarianism: Religion, Empires, and Advocacy*. Cambridge Studies in Social Theory, Religion and Politics. Cambridge: Cambridge University Press, 2014.

Standard, K. L., V. G. Wills, and J. C. Waterlow. "Indirect Indicators of Muscle Mass in Malnourished Infants." *American Journal of Clinical Nutrition* 7, no. 3 (1959): 271–79.

Stannus, Hugh. "'Kwashiorkor.'" *The Lancet* 226, no. 5856 (1935): 1207–8.

Stannus, Hugh. "A Nutritional Disease of Childhood Associated with a Maize Diet - and Pellagra." *Archives of Disease in Childhood* 9, no. 50 (1934): 115–18.

Stanton, Jennifer. "Listening to the Ga: Cicely Williams' Discovery of Kwashiorkor on the Gold Coast." In *Women and Modern Medicine*, edited by Lawrence Conrad and Anne Hardy, 149–72. Amsterdam: Rodopi, 2001.

Staples, Amy. *The Birth of Development: How the World Bank, Food and Agriculture Organization, and World Health Organization Changed the World, 1945–1965*. Kent: Kent State University Press, 2006.

Staples, Amy. "To Win the Peace: The Food and Agriculture Organization, Sir John Boyd Orr, and the World Food Board Proposals." *Peace and Change* 28, no. 4 (2003): 495–523.

Stark, Laura. *Behind Closed Doors: IRBs and the Making of Ethical Research*. Chicago: University of Chicago Press, 2012.

Steege, Paul. *Black Market, Cold War: Everyday Life in Berlin, 1946–1949*. Cambridge: Cambridge University Press, 2007.

Stein, Zena. *Famine and Human Development: The Dutch Hunger Winter of 1944–1945*. London: Oxford University Press, 1975.

Steinacher, Gerald. *Humanitarians at War: The Red Cross in the Shadow of the Holocaust*. Oxford: Oxford University Press, 2017.

Steinert, Johannes-Dieter. "British Humanitarian Assistance: Wartime Planning and Postwar Realities." *Journal of Contemporary History* 43, no. 3 (2008): 421–35.

Steinert, Johannes-Dieter. "British Relief Teams in Belsen Concentration Camp: Emergency Relief and the Perception of Survivors." In *Belsen 1945: New Historical Perspectives*, edited by Suzanne Bardgett and David Cesarani, 62–86. Edgware: Vallentine Mitchell, 2006.

Steinert, Johannes-Dieter. "Food and the Food Crisis in Post-War Germany, 1945–1948: British Policy and the Role of British NGOs." In *Food and Conflict in Europe in the Age of the Two World Wars*, edited by Frank Trentmann and Flemming Just, 266–88. New York: Palgrave Macmillan, 2006.

Stigler, Stephen. *The History of Statistics: The Measurement of Uncertainty before 1900.* Cambridge: Belknap Press, 1986.

Stokke, Olav. *The UN and Development: From Aid to Cooperation.* Bloomington: Indiana University Press, 2009.

Stoler, Ann Laura. *Race and the Education of Desire: Foucault's History of Sexuality and the Colonial Order of Things.* Durham, NC: Duke University Press, 1995.

Stoler, Ann Laura. "Rethinking Colonial Categories: European Communities and the Boundaries of Rule." *Comparative Studies in Society and History* 31, no. 1 (1989): 134–61.

Strang, Jillian, and Joyce Toomre. "Alexis Soyer and the Irish Famine: Splendid Promises and Abortive Measures." In *The Great Famine and the Irish Diaspora in America*, edited by Arthur Gribben, 66–84. Amherst: University of Massachusetts Press, 1999.

Street, Alice. "Food as Pharma: Marketing Nutraceuticals to India's Rural Poor." *Critical Public Health* 25, no. 3 (2015): 361–72.

Stremlau, John. *The International Politics of the Nigerian Civil War, 1967–1970.* Princeton: Princeton University Press, 1977.

Summers, Anne. "Militarism in Britain before the Great War." *History Workshop Journal* 2, no. 1 (1976): 104–23.

Swinburne, Layinka. "Von Liebig Condensed." In *Cooks and Other People: Proceedings of the Oxford Symposium on Food and Cookery 1995*, edited by Harlan Walker, 247–58. Totnes, UK: Prospect Books, 1996.

Szejnman, Michal. "Changes in Peripheral Blood and Bone Marrow in Hunger Disease." In *Hunger Disease: Studies by the Jewish Physicians in the Warsaw Ghetto*, 161–96. New York: Wiley, 1979.

Taba, A. H. "Nutritional Problems in the Weaning Period: Report on a Seminar in Addis Ababa, Ethiopia 3–15 March 1969." *Journal of Tropical Pediatrics* 16, no. 4 (1970): 211–42.

Tamiya, Hiroshi. "Mass Culture of Algae." *Annual Review of Plant Physiology* 8, no. 1 (1957): 309–34.

Tandon, Badri. "Supplementary Nutrition: A Case Study from India." In *Nutrition Policy Implementation: Issues and Experience*, edited by Nevin Scrimshaw and Mitchel Wallerstein, 141–50. New York: Plenum, 1982.

Tanner, James Mourilyan. *A History of the Study of Human Growth.* Cambridge: Cambridge University Press, 1981.

Tanner, Joseph Robson. *Samuel Pepys and the Royal Navy.* Cambridge: Cambridge University Press, 1920.

Taylor, Ronald, and John Tweed. *Butterflies in My Stomach: Insects in Human Nutrition.* Santa Barbara: Woodbridge Press, 1975.

Taylor, Steven. *Acts of Conscience: World War II, Mental Institutions, and Religious Objectors.* Syracuse: Syracuse University Press, 2009.

Tectonidis, Milton. "Crisis in Niger: Outpatient Care for Severe Acute Malnutrition." *New England Journal of Medicine* 354, no. 3 (2006): 224–27.

Terry, Fiona. *Condemned to Repeat? The Paradox of Humanitarian Action.* London: Cornell University Press, 2002.

This, Hervé. *Molecular Gastronomy: Exploring the Science of Flavor.* New York: Columbia University Press, 2006.

Thomas, Keith. *Man and the Natural World: Changing Attitudes in England, 1500–1800.* London: Allen Lane, 1983.

Thompson, Benjamin. *An Account of an Establishment for the Poor at Munich: Together with a Detail of Various Public Measures.* London: Cadell and Davies, 1795.

Thompson, Benjamin. *Count Rumford's Experimental Essays, Political, Economical, and Philosophical.* London: printed for T. Cadell Jun. and W. Davies, 1795.

Thompson, Benjamin. *Essays: Political, Economical, and Philosophical.* 3rd ed. London: Cadell and Davies, 1797.

Thompson, Benjamin. *Of the Fundamental Principles on Which General Establishments for the Relief of the Poor May Be Formed.* London: Cadell and Davies, 1796.

Thompson, William Gilman. *Practical Dietetics: With Special Reference to Diet in Disease.* London: Henry Kimpton, 1902.

Thornhill, Kerrie. "Britain's Political Humanitarians: The National Joint Committee for Spanish Relief and the Spanish Refugees of 1939." Ph.D. diss., Queen Mary University of London, 2017.

Thudichum, John Louis William. *On the Origin, Nature, and Uses of Liebig's Extract of Meat; with an Analytical Comparison of Other Essences and Preparations of Meat.* London, 1869.

Ticktin, Miriam. *Casualties of Care: Immigration and the Politics of Humanitarianism in France.* Berkeley: University of California Press, 2011.

Ticktin, Miriam. "Where Ethics and Politics Meet: The Violence of Humanitarianism in France." *American Ethnologist* 33, no. 1 (2006): 33–49.

Tilley, Helen. *Africa as a Living Laboratory: Empire, Development, and the Problem of Scientific Knowledge, 1870–1950.* Chicago: University of Chicago Press, 2011.

Titmuss, Richard Morris. *Poverty and Population: A Factual Study of Contemporary Social Waste.* London: Macmillan, 1938.

Tosh, John. *The Pursuit of History: Aims, Methods, and New Directions in the Study of Modern History.* Harlow: Pearson Longman, 2006.

"Travelling Seminar on Protein Foods in Africa Organised by FAO and WHO." *Protein Advisory Group Bulletin* 2, no. 1 (1972): 36–38.

Trentmann, Frank. "Coping with Shortage: The Problem of Food Security and Global Visions of Coordination, C.1890s-1950." In *Food and Conflict in Europe in the Age of the Two World Wars,* edited by Frank Trentmann and Flemming Just, 13–48. New York: Palgrave Macmillan, 2006.

Trepman, Elly. "Rescue of the Remnants: The British Emergency Medical Relief Operation in Belsen Camp, 1945." *Journal of the Royal Army Medical Corps* 147 (2001): 281–93.

Trowell, Hubert Carey. "The Beginning of the Kwashiorkor Story in Africa." *Central African Journal of Medicine* 21, no. 1 (1975): 1–5.

Trowell, Hubert Carey. "Infantile Pellagra." *Transactions of the Royal Society of Tropical Medicine and Hygiene* 33, no. 4 (1940): 389–404.

Trowell, Hubert Carey. "Malignant Malnutrition (Kwashiorkor)." *Transactions of the Royal Society of Tropical Medicine and Hygiene* 42, no. 5 (1949): 417–42.

Trowell, Hubert Carey, Jack Neville Phillips Davies, and Reginald Francis Alfred Dean. *Kwashiorkor.* London: Arnold, 1954.

Tucker, Todd. *The Great Starvation Experiment: Ancel Keys and the Men Who Starved for Science*. Minneapolis: University of Minnesota Press, 2007.

Tucker, William. *The Science and Politics of Racial Research*. Champaign: University of Illinois Press, 1994.

Tudge, Colin. *The Famine Business*. London: Faber and Faber, 1977.

Tudge, Colin. "Food for the Unthinking." *World Medicine* 9, no. 15 (1974): 15–37.

Turmel, André. *A Historical Sociology of Childhood: Developmental Thinking, Categorization, and Graphic Visualization*. Cambridge: Cambridge University Press, 2008.

Turner, Bryan. *Regulating Bodies: Essays in Medical Sociology*. London: Routledge, 1992.

Tushnet, Leonard. *The Uses of Adversity*. New York: Yoseloff, 1966.

Ulijaszek, Stanley, and John Komlos. "From a History of Anthropmetry to Anthropometric History." In *Human Variation: From the Laboratory to the Field*, edited by C. G. N. Mascie-Taylor, Akira Yasukouchi, and Stanley J. Ulijaszek, 183–97. London: CRC Press, 2010.

Underwood, Barbara. "Overcoming Micronutrient Deficiencies in Developing Countries: Is There a Role for Agriculture?" *Food and Nutrition Bulletin* 21, no. 4 (2000): 356–60.

Underwood, Barbara. "Vitamin A Deficiency Disorders: International Efforts to Control a Preventable 'Pox.'" *Journal of Nutrition* 134, no. 1 (2004): 231–36.

Underwood, Barbara, and Suttilak Smitasiri. "Micronutrient Malnutrition: Policies and Programs for Control and Their Implications." *Annual Review of Nutrition* 19, no. 1 (1999): 303–24.

United States Agency for International Development. *Planning National Nutrition Programs: a Suggested Approach*, Washington, DC: USAID, 1973.

Valenze, Deborah. *Milk: A Local and Global History*. New Haven: Yale University Press, 2011.

Vasilyev, Pavel. "Alimentary and Pellagra Psychoses in Besieged Leningrad." In *Food and War in Twentieth Century Europe*, edited by Ina Zweiniger-Bargielowska, Rachel Duffett, and Alain Drouard, 111–24. Farnham, UK: Ashgate, 2011.

Vaughan, J., C. Dent, and R. P Rivers. "The Physiology and Treatment of Starvation." *Proceedings of the Royal Society of Medicine* 38, no. 7 (1945): 388–98.

Vaughan, Megan. *Curing Their Ills: Colonial Power and African Illness*. Cambridge: Polity, 1991.

Vaux, Tony. *The Selfish Altruist: Relief Work in Famine and War*. London: Earthscan, 2001.

Veit, Helen Zoe. *Modern Food, Moral Food: Self-Control, Science, and the Rise of Modern American Eating in the Early Twentieth Century*. Chapel Hill: University of North Carolina Press, 2013.

Vernant, Jacques. *The Refugee in the Post-War World*. London: Allen & Unwin, 1953.

Vernon, James. "The Ethics of Hunger and the Assembly of Society: The Techno-Politics of the School Meal in Modern Britain." *American Historical Review* 110, no. 3 (2005): 693–725.

Vernon, James. *Hunger: A Modern History*. London: Belknap, 2007.

Vester, Katharina. *A Taste of Power: Food and American Identities*. Berkeley: University of California Press, 2015.

Victora, Cesar G., Saul S. Morris, Fernando C. Barros, Mercedes de Onis, and Ray Yip. "The NCHS Reference and the Growth of Breast- and Bottle-Fed Infants." *Journal of Nutrition* 128, no. 7 (1998): 1134–38.

Vincent, David. *Poor Citizens: The State and the Poor in Twentieth-Century Britain*. London: Longman, 1991.

Walker, J. B. "The Feeding Problem." *London Hospital Gazette* 48 (1945): 150–51.

Walker, Paul. "Institutional Audience and Architectural Style." In *Colonial Modernities: Building, Dwelling, and Architecture in British India and Ceylon*, edited by Peter Scriver and Vikramaditya Prakash, 127–52. London: Routledge, 2007.

Walker, Peter, and Susan Purdin. "Birthing Sphere." *Disasters* 28, no. 2 (2004): 100–11.

Wall, Wendy. *Recipes for Thought: Knowledge and Taste in the Early Modern English Kitchen*. Philadelphia: University of Pennsylvania Press, 2016.

Wallerstein, Mitchel. *Food for War, Food for Peace: United States Food Aid in a Global Context*. Cambridge: MIT Press, 1980.

Wallerstein, M. B., and E. R Pariser. "Fish Protein Concentrate: A Technological Approach That Failed." *Food and Nutrition Quarterly* 4, no. 1–2 (1978): 8–14.

Walters, F. P. *A History of the League of Nations*. London: Oxford University Press, 1960.

Warnock, John. *The Politics of Hunger: The Global Food System*. London: Methuen, 1987.

Waterlow, John Conrad. *Fatty Liver Disease in Infants in the British West Indies*. London: HMSO, 1948.

Waterlow, John Conrad. *Protein-Energy Malnutrition*. London: Edward Arnold, 1992.

Waterlow, John Conrad, and Philip Payne. "The Protein Gap." *Nature* 258, no. 5531 (1975): 113–17.

Watson, Chalmers. *Food and Feeding in Health and Disease: A Manual of Practical Dietetics*. London: Oliver and Boyd, 1910.

Way, Wendy. *A New Idea Each Morning: How Food and Agriculture Came Together in One International Organisation*. Canberra: ANU Press, 2013.

Wear, Andrew. *Knowledge and Practice in English Medicine, 1550–1680*. Cambridge: Cambridge University Press, 2000.

Weatherall, Mark. "Bread and Newspapers: The Making of 'a Revolution in the Science of Food.'" In *The Science and Culture of Nutrition, 1840–1940*, edited by Harmke Kamminga and Andrew Cunningham, 179–212. Amsterdam: Rodopi, 1995.

Webb, Patrick, Beatrice Rogers, Irwin Rosenberg, and Nina Schlossman. *Improving the Nutritional Quality of U.S. Food Aid: Recommendations for Changes to Products and Programs*. Boston: Tufts University, 2011.

Webb, Samantha. "Wordsworth, Count Rumford, and Poverty Relief." *The Wordsworth Circle* 43, no. 1 (2012): 29–35.

Weindling, Paul. "'Belsenitis': Liberating Belsen, Its Hospitals, UNRRA, and Selection for Re-Emigration, 1945–1948." *Science in Context* 19, no. 3 (2006): 401–18.

Weindling, Paul. "Health and Medicine in Interwar Europe." In *Medicine in the Twentieth Century*, edited by Roger Cooter and John Pickstone, 39–50. Amsterdam: Harwood Academic, 2000.

Weindling, Paul. "Introduction: Constructing International Health between the Wars." In *International Health Organisations and Movements, 1918–1939*, edited by Paul Weindling, 1–16. Cambridge: Cambridge University Press, 1995.

Weindling, Paul. "Julian Huxley and the Continuity of Eugenics in Twentieth-Century Britain." *Journal of Modern European History* 10, no. 4 (2012): 480–99.

Weindling, Paul. "Medicine and Modernization: The Social History of German Health and Medicine." *History of Science* 24, no. 3 (1986): 277–301.

Weindling, Paul. "From Moral Exhortation to the New Public Health, 1918–45." In *The Politics of the Healthy Life: An International Perspective*, edited by Esteban Rodríguez Ocaña, 113–30. Sheffield: EAHMH, 2002.

Weindling, Paul. "The Role of International Organizations in Setting Nutritional Standards in the 1920s and 1930s." In *The Science and Culture of Nutrition, 1840–1940*, edited by Harmke Kamminga and Andrew Cunningham, 319–33. Amsterdam: Rodopi, 1995.

Weindling, Paul. "From Sentiment to Science: Children's Relief Organisations and the Problem of Malnutrition in Inter-War Europe." *Disasters* 18, no. 3 (1994): 203–12.

Weindling, Paul. "Social Medicine at the League of Nations Health Organisation and the International Labour Office Compared." In *International Health Organisations and Movements, 1918–1939*, edited by Paul Weindling, 134–53. Cambridge: Cambridge University Press, 1995.

Weinreb, Alice. "'For the Hungry Have No Past, Nor Do They Belong to a Political Party': Debates over German Hunger after World War II." *Central European History* 45, no. 1 (2012): 50–78.

Weiss, Allen. *Feast and Folly: Cuisine, Intoxication, and the Poetics of the Sublime.* Albany: SUNY Press, 2002.

Wells, Roger. *Wretched Faces: Famine in Wartime England, 1793–1801.* Gloucester: Alan Sutton, 1988.

Wessell, Adele. "Between Alimentary Products and the Art of Cooking: The Industrialization of Eating at the World Fairs, 1888–1893." In *Consuming Culture in the Long Nineteenth Century: Narratives of Consumption, 1700–1900*, edited by Tamara Wagner and Narin Hassan, 107–24. Plymouth: Lexington Books, 2007.

Wieters, Heike. *The NGO CARE and Food Aid from America 1945–80.* Manchester: Manchester University Press, 2017.

Wilk, Richard, ed. *Fast Food/Slow Food: The Cultural Economy of the Global Food System*, Plymouth: Altamira, 2006.

Williams, Alison Susan. "Relief and Research: The Nutrition Work of the National Birthday Trust Fund, 1935–39." In *Nutrition in Britain: Science, Scientists and Politics in the Twentieth Century*, edited by David Smith, 99–122. London: Routledge, 1997.

Williams, Cicely. "Kwashiorkor: A Nutritional Disease of Children Associated with a Maize Diet." *The Lancet* 226, no. 5855 (1935): 1151–52.

Williams, Cicely. "Milk and Murder." In *Primary Health Care Pioneer: The Selected Works of Dr. Cicely Williams*, edited by Naomi Baumslag, 66–75. Geneva: World Federation of Public Health Associations, 1986.

Williams, Cicely. "A Nutritional Disease of Childhood Associated with a Maize Diet." *Archives of Disease in Childhood* 8, no. 48 (1933): 423–33.

Williams, Cicely. "On That Fiasco." *The Lancet* 305, no. 7910 (1975): 793–94.

Williams, Cicely. "The Story of Kwashiorkor." *Nutrition Reviews* 31, no. 11 (1973): 334–40.

Wilson, Bee. "Count Rumford's Soup." In *Nurture: Proceedings of the Oxford Symposium on Food and Cookery 2003*, edited by Richard Hosking, 287–99. Bristol: Footwork Press, 2004.

Wilson, Francesca. *Advice to Relief Workers, Based on Personal Experience in the Field.* London: Friends Relief Service, 1945.

Wilson, Francesca. *Aftermath: France, Germany, Austria, Yugoslavia, 1945 and 1946*. London: Penguin, 1947.

Wilson, Francesca. *In the Margins of Chaos: Recollections of Relief Work in and between Three Wars*. London: John Murray, 1944.

Wilson, Geoff. "From Productivism to Post-Productivism… and Back Again? Exploring the (Un)Changed Natural and Mental Landscapes of European Agriculture." *Transactions of the Institute of British Geographers* 26, no. 1 (2001): 77–102.

Winick, Myron, ed. *Hunger Disease: Studies by the Jewish Physicians in the Warsaw Ghetto*. Current Concepts in Nutrition. Vol. 7. New York: Wiley, 1979.

Winick, Myron. "Preface." In *Hunger Disease: Studies by the Jewish Physicians in the Warsaw Ghetto*, edited by Myron Winick, vii–xi. New York: Wiley, 1979.

Wolcot, John. *The Works of Peter Pindar, Esq, to Which Are Prefixed Memoirs of the Author's Life*. 5 vols. London: Printed for J. Walker, G. Wilkie and J. Robinson, 1812.

Woodham-Smith, Cecil. *The Great Hunger: Ireland, 1845–49*. London: Readers Union, Hamish Hamilton, 1964.

Worboys, Michael. "The Discovery of Colonial Malnutrition between the Wars." In *Imperial Medicine and Indigenous Societies*, edited by David Arnold, 208–25. Manchester: Manchester University Press, 1988.

World Bank. *Learning from World Bank History: Agriculture and Food-Based Approaches for Addressing Malnutrition*. Report Number 88740-GLB. Washington, DC: World Bank, 2014.

World Food Program. *Food and Nutrition Handbook*. Rome: WFP, 2001.

World Health Organization. *Guiding Principles for Feeding Infants and Young Children During Emergencies*. Geneva: WHO, 2004.

World Health Organization. *The Management of Nutrition in Major Emergencies*. Geneva: WHO, 2000.

Wrench, Guy Theodore. *The Wheel of Health*. London: Daniel, 1938.

Wylie, Diana. "Disease, Diet and Gender: Late Twentieth-Century Perspectives on Empire." In *The Oxford History of the British Empire, Volume V: Historiography*, edited by Robin Winks, 277–89. Oxford: Oxford University Press, 1998.

Wylie, Diana. *Starving on a Full Stomach: Hunger and the Triumph of Cultural Racism in Modern South Africa*. London: University Press of Virginia, 2001.

Wynter, Andrew. *Our Social Bees, or, Pictures of Town and Country Life And Other Papers*. London: Robert Hardwicke, 1861.

Zack, Naomi. *Philosophy of Science and Race*. London: Routledge, 2002.

Zerfas, Alfred. "The Insertion Tape: A New Circumference Tape for Use in Nutritional Assessment." *American Journal of Clinical Nutrition* 28, no. 7 (1975): 782–87.

Zlotkin, Stanley, Paul Arthur, Kojo Yeboah Antwi, and George Yeung. "Treatment of Anemia with Microencapsulated Ferrous Fumarate Plus Ascorbic Acid Supplied as Sprinkles to Complementary (Weaning) Foods." *American Journal of Clinical Nutrition* 74, no. 6 (2001): 791–95.

Index

Page numbers followed by letter *f* refer to figures.

10-in-1 ration, 95

admission to aid programs: in industrial era, 23–24; labor and, 18, 19, 20–21; patronage and, 4, 21–22; physical measurements and, 5, 8–9, 138–39

Africa: dietary determinism in, 67–69; field trials of Plumpy'nut in, 164, 217n57; high-protein foods produced in, 140, 143–44, 145; kwashiorkor in, 109–11, 172; medicalization of hunger in, 110–13. *See also specific countries*

agribusiness, 147–48

agricultural surpluses: and humanitarian nutrition, 13, 139, 142, 146, 177, 186n27; Marshall plan as outlet for, 147

aid agencies: failure to address social problems, 177–78; military practices embraced by, 94–95; move toward direct operations, 140, 143, 145. *See also* humanitarianism; *specific agencies*

aid workers: Biafra and new cadre of, 138; breadth of reach vs. depth of engagement of, 175–76; humanitarian handbooks and, xv, 6; standardized procedures followed by, xi–xii; training of, military characteristics of, 94–95

Aladdin Oven, 55, 56

alchemy, 3, 34

Aldershot Oven, 95

algae-based foods, 126–27, 135

Algeria, 132, 133

Allenbury's malted food, 100

Amama (high-protein food), 140

American Relief Administration (ARA), 80, 84

Amigen (protein hydrolysate), 139

amino acids, manufacture of, 129

anthropometry, use in relief work, 6–9, 10, 84, 155–56; advantages of, 85; Biafra crisis and, 138–39; criticism of, 155; vs. patronage, 5; sociopolitical systems and, 174. *See also* MUAC

Arlac (high-protein food), 140

army rations: classic, 102; techniques behind, 101; use in refugee camps after World War II, 91, 92, 93*f*, 95–96, 172

Asher, Richard, 111

Astor, Waldorf (Lord), 76–78, 80, 86–87

Atkinson, Edward, 55, 56

Atwater, Wilbur O., 48–49, 51–53, 80, 134, 171; on calorie, 47; and dietary advice, 52, 53, 57

Austin, Jane, 188n45

autopsy: Foucault on, 116–17; starvation studies of 1930s–1940s and, 112–13, 117

Aykroyd, Wallace, 119, 196n36, 200n46; and Burnet-Aykroyd report, 76, 198n9

The Baby Killer (report), 153

Baily, Guy, 111

Bal-Ahar (technical food), 132–33

Bantu societies, Richards on, 73–74

Barona, Josep, 78

beef tea, 38

Beeton, Mrs., 36–37

Bemax ("tonic food"), 97

Bengal famine, 97; starvation treatments during, 97, 104, 105

Bengalis, diet of, 61–62, 65, 69

Benger's Food, 100

Berg, Alan, 158, 159, 215n20

Bergen-Belsen concentration camp, Germany: emergency relief in, 92, 103–5, 172; images from, 103

beriberi, 62

Berman, Marshall, 174–75

bertillonage, 214n7

Berzelius, Jöns Jacob, 35

Biafra: declaration of independence, 137; humanitarian relief in, 137–38, 146, 156; humanitarian techniques developed in, 138–39, 173, 216n43

Bigwood, E. J., 84, 214n4

Bihar famine, 133, 146

biochemistry: and contemporary food relief, 6; founder of, 33, 170, 171; and measurement of malnutrition, 84–85, 155–56; rise of, 33,